Middle Eastern Muslim Women Speak

A Veiled Girl

Pet onion!
    in your layers of veil and gown;
all beauty in one mirror, or
a turnip in a sack?
No matter where I look:
                 up or down,
you're not my pet or sweet
or even a human bean—
wrapped in that black and purple skin
you are an aubergine.

Translated by Omar S. Pound from the Persian of Iraj (1874–1924).
Copyright © 1976 by Omar S. Pound.

The Dan Danciger Publication Series

Middle Eastern Muslim Women Speak

النساء المسلمات فى الشرق الاوسط يتحدثن

زنان مسلمان خاورميانه سخن ميگويند

Edited by Elizabeth Warnock Fernea and Basima Qattan Bezirgan

University of Texas Press/Austin

Fifth Paperback Printing, 1990

Requests for permission to reproduce material from
this work should be sent to Permissions, University
of Texas Press, Box 7819, Austin, Texas 78713-7819.

♾The paper used in this publication meets the
minimum requirements of American National
Standard for Information Sciences—Permanence
of Paper for Printed Library Materials, ANSI
Z39.48-1984.

Library of Congress Cataloging-in-Publication Data
Main entry under title:
Middle Eastern Muslim women speak.
1. Women—Near East—Addresses, essays,
lectures.
2. Women, Muslim—Addresses, essays, lectures.
I. Fernea, Elizabeth Warnock.   II. Bezirgan, Basima
Qattan, 1933–
HQ1170.M53   301.41'2'0956   76-16845
ISBN 0-292-75033-1 (cloth); 0-292-75041-2 (paper)

To our children,

Basma, David, Laila, Laura Ann, Najdet, and Yasir,

who patiently bore our many hours and evenings of mutual work on this manuscript, we dedicate the book with affection.

Contents

The editors of the present anthology have made a valiant effort to unveil an important dimension of Middle Eastern history and society, a dimension that has been, for the most part, hidden from view because of the false notion that the world of Islam is a world created by men for men rather than the joint creation of men and women. Modern scholars have occasionally recorded the role of some Middle Eastern Muslim women in religious, literary, and political life, but only when these women succeeded in breaking into public life as mystics, poets, or queens and performed public functions that were thought to be reserved for men. For the rest, Middle Eastern women have been the object of the most malicious campaign of defamation in human history, a campaign that was initiated in early anti-Muslim theological tracts, continued in the anti-clerical sex literature of modern times, and survives today in many cheap novels. The persistent theme of this campaign is that Islam is a religion that serves men's cupidity as well as a religion that exploits that cupidity for its own ends, using women as its chief instrument.

One may hope that the present collection of documents will provide educated western readers with a somewhat clearer view of the conditions, aspirations, struggles, and achievements of Middle Eastern Muslim women. It will surely enable them to understand the diversity of the physical and social environment in which Middle Eastern Muslim women live and the diversity of the perspectives through which they pursue their roles in societies that are fairly complex and suffer tensions created by the survival of older traditions and the impact of modern ideas. The biographical, autobiographical, and anthropological form of many of these documents, and the fact that the editors are themselves women, should in principle assure the readers of a direct view of the world of Middle Eastern Muslim women as seen by these women themselves.

Yet the fact is that today most of these women, especially the educated and "modernized" among them, aspire to the same roles as those of men in modern society—to men's presumed power, rights, and achievements. This fact is noticeable in many of the documents in this volume, where Middle Eastern Muslim women appear to join, or wish to join, a world-wide movement that aims to assure women the same rights as those of men. But one may wonder whether the polarization created by this movement for equality and justice is not a necessary step to something that in a way transcends the current struggle, which is a greater awareness of the fact that *man* and *woman* are relative terms. For even though "man" and "woman" appear to perform separate functions, each is created male-and-female and female-and-male; that is, to varying degrees they are already polarized within themselves. Relations between men and women cannot be explained without taking into account this inner polarity within each of the two and without seeing human life as the sum total of this double polarity. There is no such thing as a "man's world" or a "woman's world"; each is already impregnated with the other. How to penetrate this complex man-and-woman world in studying the history and societies of the Islamic Middle East is a question that needs the help of modern psychology, not the psychological approach that transforms complex situations into psychological complexes, but one that is equally capable of penetrating into the elements that make up the wholeness of human life and sees their proper interrelations. One of the virtues of the present volume is that it suggests the need for a fresh view of Middle Eastern Muslim men as well.

Muhsin Mahdi

James Richard Jewett Professor of Arabic and director of the Center for Middle Eastern Studies, Harvard University

Acknowledgments

We would like to acknowledge the contributions of many persons, without whose encouragement and aid this volume would never have been possible. Among those who helped particularly were Michael Albin, director of the Middle East Collection, University of Texas at Austin; Mounah Khouri, professor of Arabic, University of California at Berkeley; Robert Fernea, professor of anthropology, University of Texas at Austin; and Halim Barakat, professor of sociology, Lebanese National University. We would also like to thank Sharon Bastüg, Karen Haynes, Kristin Koptiuch, and James Malarkey for varied assistance. The Center for Middle Eastern Studies, University of Texas at Austin, under its director, Paul W. English, gave us very real and continuing aid, and we are grateful especially to William D. Smallwood and also to Beverly Bowman, Ruperto Garcia, Patti Haardt, Jean Hester, Dorcas Navarro, Pam Pape, Carla Richardson, Laurie Stevenson, Melissa Weaver, and Pam Westfall who typed drafts of the manuscript.

Finally, our thanks go to our families, who bore with us through the various stages of the book's development.

Note on Transliteration

Arabic words and names used in this book have been transliterated according to the Library of Congress system, but the diacritical marks have been omitted for greater ease in reading.

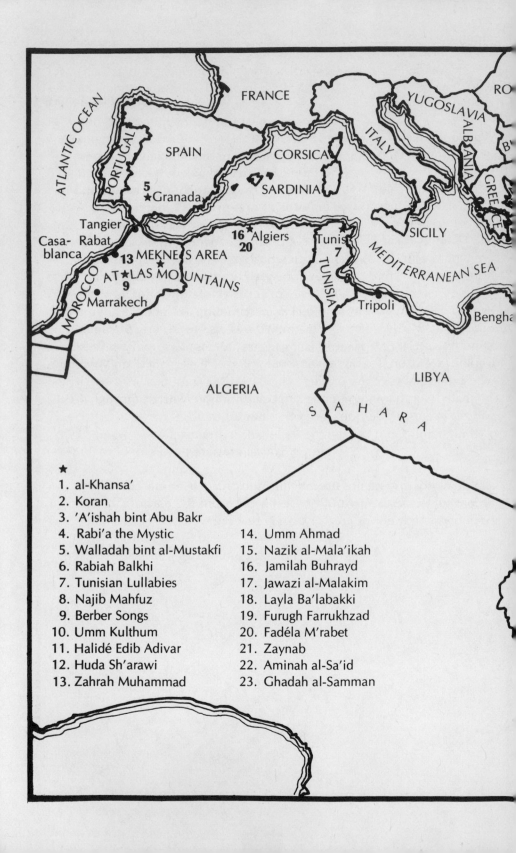

★
1. al-Khansa'
2. Koran
3. 'A'ishah bint Abu Bakr
4. Rabi'a the Mystic
5. Walladah bint al-Mustakfi
6. Rabiah Balkhi
7. Tunisian Lullabies
8. Najib Mahfuz
9. Berber Songs
10. Umm Kulthum
11. Halidé Edib Adivar
12. Huda Sh'arawi
13. Zahrah Muhammad
14. Umm Ahmad
15. Nazik al-Mala'ikah
16. Jamilah Buhrayd
17. Jawazi al-Malakim
18. Layla Ba'labakki
19. Furugh Farrukhzad
20. Fadéla M'rabet
21. Zaynab
22. Aminah al-Sa'id
23. Ghadah al-Samman

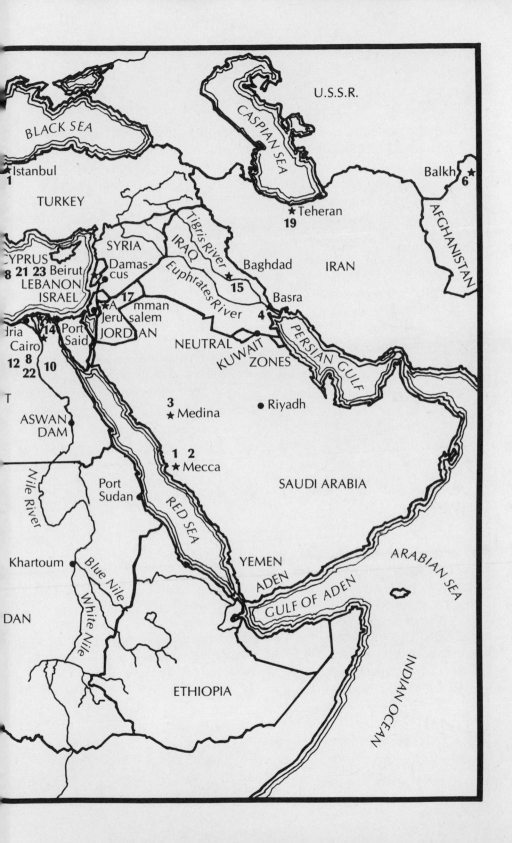

BLACK SEA

★ Istanbul
1

TURKEY

U.S.S.R.

CASPIAN SEA

Balkh ★
6

AFGHANISTAN

CYPRUS
8 21 23 Beirut
LEBANON
ISRAEL

SYRIA

Damas-
cus

Tigris River

IRAQ

Euphrates River

★ Teheran
19

Baghdad
★
15

IRAN

Basra
4

PERSIAN GULF

★ A.
17
mman
Jeru salem
JORDAN

NEUTRAL

KUWAIT

ZONES

ria
14 Port
Cairo Said

12 8
22 10

ASWAN
DAM

Nile River

T

3
★ Medina

● Riyadh

1 2
★ Mecca

SAUDI ARABIA

Port
Sudan

RED SEA

Khartoum ●

Blue Nile

White Nile

DAN

YEMEN

ADEN

GULF OF ADEN

ARABIAN SEA

INDIAN OCEAN

ETHIOPIA

Middle Eastern society has posed continual conundrums for westerners. The folk tales and legends of early centuries were soon replaced by the views of the medieval church theologians, whose translations and commentaries on Middle East documents remained a principal source for western scholars until the last century. The scholars of the church saw Islam through eyes clouded by faith. Their views of the infidel Saracen, against whom the entire economic, moral, and military might of the Christian world had been expended during the Crusades, could hardly be expected to be sympathetic. Yet it is through their pious eyes that we see our earliest images of Middle Eastern society; later images emerged from the culturally astigmatic writings of nineteenth-century colonial missionaries, travelers, and scholars.

The church theologians and the colonial travelers were largely men and, since they usually translated and observed the works of other men, their analyses tended to be one-sided. Many articles and books even in this century have been written as though the female half of the Middle East did not exist or, if so, lived in a kind of semi-world of passivity and seclusion, removed from the actual life of their own society.

In such a situation, the Middle Eastern woman might well agree with Marcel Proust, who wrote more than half a century ago that "the image that other people form of our actions and behavior is no more like that which we form of them ourselves than an original drawing is like a spoiled copy, in which, at one point, for a black line, we find an empty gap, and for a blank space, an unaccountable contour."[1] Proust was speaking of perceptions misunderstood between one individual and another, within the same culture. How much greater, then, the refraction or even distortion when persons from different cultures view each other through the prism of their own cultural values?

In the last decades some movements to correct these refracted views of Middle Eastern women have become apparent. The scholarly efforts have come primarily from two sources: Orientalists and ethnographers or anthropologists. For a number of reasons, the new work has resulted in a reshuffling or recycling of old attitudes and stereotypes. The Orientalists have taken a new look at the old documents, with a view toward correcting the distortions of the church theologians and the Victorian visitors and interpreting the materials more objectively and more sympathetically. Their work is based on a study of historical materials, the origins of Islam, rather than on observations and analyses in modern Middle Eastern communities. The ethnographer, on the other hand, without the training of an Orientalist, looks at the life of Middle Eastern women in a variety of community settings and tends to give more weight to the evidence of family and tribal custom as it is practiced in the individual communities.

Thus, different points of view and different materials have led to different conclusions. Reuben Levy, the late distinguished British Orientalist, tells us that "in so fundamental a matter as the position held by women and children in his community, Muhammad was able to introduce profound changes."[2] And the *Shorter Encyclopedia of Islam* states that "Islam reformed the old marriage laws in far reaching fashion; here, as in other fields of social legislation, the chief aim of the Ku'ran was the improvement of the woman's position."[3] But Germaine Tillion, a French ethnographer of good reputation who has worked in North African communities, says: "The feminine veil has become a symbol; that of the slavery of one portion of humanity. . . . the Mediterranean woman is one of the serfs of the modern world . . . [Her position] diminishes the national potential and consequently weakens the state . . . it paralyzes all collective and individual development, masculine as well as feminine . . . and consequently slows or hinders progress, in that it produces in the child, and thus in the future, many irreparable prejudices. . . . as for the man, supposed beneficiary of this oppression, he is at all ages of his life, as father, husband, and child, the direct victim."[4]

Which of these two opposing points of view is correct? Both are true —and false. For it is quite correct to say that the Koran was in many ways a radical document in its time, and not the least in its provisions for the legal position of women. And it is also quite correct to say that the Middle Eastern woman has historically appeared to be in a state of bondage from which she has had no recourse and no escape. The continuing confusion in western views of Middle Eastern women arises from the assumption that the real truth lies in one or the other of these apparently contradictory positions; all Middle Eastern society is then viewed through the lens of one or the other position. Just as visitors to an amusement park will, in looking into the distorted mirrors, see themselves bulbously round from one vantage point and hopelessly thin from another point only a few feet away, so scholars, looking into the same mirror of Middle Eastern society, have found different images greeting them, depending on their position before the mirror.

The truth obviously lies somewhere between the two contrasting poles. This central paradox of Middle Eastern society may best be understood if one thinks of a straight line as representing that society. At one extreme end of the line stands the Koran, the codification of the word of God and the ideal touchstone to which all actions of life are to be conformed and related. At the other extreme end of the line lie the forces of tribal and family custom (the word of men).

individual solutions

Koran   ◄—├┼┼┼┼┼┼┼┼┼┼┤—►   tribal and family custom
the word of God   *the word of men*

communal practice

Throughout the ages, we suggest, the women of Islam, like the men, have resolved the contradiction within the communal practice found in their own communities. The substance of individual and community solution may lie closer or farther from the Koranic ideal, closer or farther from tribal custom, depending on the social and economic position of the individual involved, the environment, the composition of the family group to which he or she belongs, and the individual position within the family group.

If one concedes the basic contradiction implied in the paradox, then it can be seen to include many other apparent contradictions. For example, the superiority of men over women is a basic premise of Islam; this was found in the tribal society preceding Muhammad and was reiterated in the Koran. "Men are in charge of women, because Allah hath made one of them to excel the other," says Surah IV, verse 34.

In this society, then, women and men are not equal: women and men are different, their strengths and weaknesses are dissimilar, they behave in different ways, and they are treated differently. Yet, obviously, the proposition of male superiority versus female inferiority cannot be absolute in all matters, and many forces mediate between the two opposing poles. Within the unit of the family, male-female relationships work out differently, depending on the character and personality of the individuals involved. Women have great latitude and authority within their own households and in the rearing of children, particularly daughters. Men's authority is greater outside the household. Labor is divided but not always on the basis of the male-female, superiority-inferiority proposition.

So, too, must resolution be found for the social equality of all peoples enunciated in the Koran and the obvious differences of class and wealth within society. Another basic contradiction involves sexuality and sexual behavior. The Koran's acceptance of human sexuality as a good to be enjoyed by both men and women, on earth and in paradise, is opposed by a male view that female sexual drives are dangerous and in need of curbing. The Koran stipulates that sexual enjoyment must have legal bounds (marriage); tribal and family custom expresses its fear and anxiety in the concepts of shame and honor: the chastity of the woman represents the honor of the family, and any violation must be punished. The ultimate sanction is death, at the hand of a male member of the family, but in a few areas (notably Egypt and the Sudan) precautionary measures are taken in the form of female circumcision. No such measures are enunciated in the Koran. Here the word of men (tribal and family custom) overrules the word of God.

Citing the paradox is useful only as a metaphor within which one may examine the often diverse and contradictory materials evident in Middle Eastern society. These fragments or elements of the society have all been present for many years, as the multicolored shapes are always present in the kaleidoscope; observers have turned the instrument so that one pattern of colors or the other appears paramount and this, then, seems to the viewer a truer pattern than others. Our premise and suggestion here is that all the individual patterns may be true in practice within the basic metaphor we have posed.

The only way to get a fresh view through the kaleidoscope of Middle Eastern society and to combat the stereotyped thinking of the past is to go back to the primary sources, the multicolored shapes within the instrument, and let Middle Eastern women speak for themselves. The book which follows is an attempt to do precisely that, to present autobiographical and biographical statements by and about Middle Eastern women, some still living and working in the area. The documents have been chosen from different historical periods and regions of the Middle East, as well as from different social and economic groups.

In one brief volume it is impossible to do more than suggest the range of women's experience in the Middle East, extending as it does from Morocco on the Atlantic Ocean, across the Mediterranean basin (Algeria, Tunisia, Libya, Egypt, Lebanon, and Turkey), south into the desert and oasis country of Jordan, Syria, and Iraq to the Persian Gulf (Saudi Arabia, Kuwait, and the Trucial States), and across the Indian Ocean to the mountains of Persia, Afghanistan, and Pakistan. (Substantial Muslim communities also exist in Indonesia, India, and the Philippines and in many parts of Africa, most notably the Sudan, Kenya, Nigeria, Tanzania, and Senegal.) From this vast area, we have chosen a sample of women from twelve countries. Despite their different backgrounds and experiences, the women represented will all be seen to have worked out their own solutions within the context of local practice established between the two contradictory poles of Koranic injunction and family and tribal custom. (Rabi'ah al-'Adawiyah, the Sufic saint, is, for example, far closer to the Koranic end of the spectrum than the poetess Walladah bint al-Mustakfi, a woman of the world rather than the spirit.)

As we hope to demonstrate, Middle Eastern women have been shaped by a culture and a religious tradition very different from, though certainly influenced by, the west. They have developed their own cultural values, their own definitions of status and prestige, whether the settings have been urban, rural, or nomadic. Further, their solutions to the problems of life within that tradition undergo changes as their life cycle progresses. What is allowable for a female child changes with the onset of puberty, again at marriage and at the time of childbearing, and once more as the woman approaches old age.

Present-day activity designed to change laws relating to women may seem on the surface to have little to do with the paradox, but, closely observed, it will be seen to be a quite different phenomenon than the seemingly parallel activities of women's movements in the west. The difference is partly the result of long centuries of struggle between Islamic orthodoxy and tribal and family custom.

Thus, before examining the personal statements of the women themselves, it may be well to provide a brief historical framework as well as a summary of the general social situation in the area. This may help the reader to visualize the setting within which the central paradox emerged and in which communal solutions continue to be sought.

We begin with the Koran, because everything which follows historically in the Middle East is somehow related to it. Ernest Gellner wrote recently that "the unity of Middle Eastern civilization is notoriously a religious one";[5] few serious scholars of the area would disagree. Islam has shaped, in one fashion or another, all the societies of the Middle East and continues to do so, if only as a force with which modern movements must reconcile their aims and methods.

The Koran, basis of Islam, is an anomaly in itself. Considered the word of God, literally, it is also considered legally binding on its adherents. Surely this is a unique situation, not now to be found in the other major religions of the world: Christianity, Judaism, Hinduism, or Buddhism.

The Koran itself was a solution to the paradoxes of its time, a time when urban centers, based on commercialism, were developing in a primarily nomadic and tribal society. The clash of values had been evident for some years. "[Muhammad's] years of poverty must have made him fully aware of the spiritual malaise affecting Mecca as a result of its material prosperity. He is said to have been in the habit of meditating on such matters. About 610 in the course of his meditations he had some strange experiences and came to the conclusion that he was receiving messages from God to communicate to the people of Mecca."[6]

By the time of Muhammad, in the seventh century, pre-Islamic Arabia was already a legend. The tales of a matriarchy in this society have been revived in recent literature of the women's movement, and, hence, it may be well to examine what scattered evidence is available. The poetry of the Jahiliyah, or pre-Islamic period, shows that some women enjoyed great prestige and were on occasion celebrated for their bravery in battle. Robertson Smith argues for an ancient custom of polyandry (plural husbands) at this time, along with matrilineal inheritance and descent. This would have been a complete reversal of contemporary Middle Eastern practice with its strong patrilineal emphasis and custom of polygamy (plural wives). If Robertson Smith's arguments are to be accepted, property would have passed to a man from his maternal uncle, and households would have been formed of a group of sisters and their mother, who were visited by one or more men.

Under such conditions, one may speculate that women may have had a stronger voice in community affairs and on occasion assumed positions of leadership. However, that the society was completely governed by women seems unlikely, given our present state of evidence. Does one assume, for example, that Britain, India, or, recently, Israel are matriarchies because their heads of state are female? The problem is far more complex, as Robertson Smith himself states. But Smith's study does suggest a social standing for women in earlier times which had shifted by the time of Muhammad.

The city of Mecca in the seventh century was indeed the center of the changes developing within the society. Although the evidence is again fragmentary, it appears that a variety of influences from Byzantium, from Turkish law, had undermined, among the Arabs, the old shared convictions in regard to the position of women. Nothing any longer prevented women from being totally subjugated to their male kinsmen, who had ultimate authority over them. Thus, fathers could dispose of unwanted daughters through exposure at birth; they could marry daughters to husbands who might take additional wives and divorce all or any of the women as they wished; and brothers could divide their inheritance without provision for their sisters.

The case of Khadijah, the first wife of Muhammad, is often cited to show that such lowly conditions of women were not universal. Khadijah was a wealthy merchant with her own caravan; Muhammad began his career in her employment. How, in a situation of male dominance, did Khadijah manage to be so wealthy and independent? The answer is simple; she had outlived all the male kin who might have had authority over her, and she had inherited the estate of her late husband. Thus, she stood outside the system and was an exception to the general rule.

In a time of conflict and confusion of values, in which women's positions varied from that of Khadijah to that of chattel and slave, the

Koran's pronouncements on the subject of all women can be recognized as revolutionary. Infanticide was prohibited; the number of legal wives which a man could take at one time was reduced to four; legal machinery was set up by which women could protest injustice and ill treatment, institute divorce in certain situations, and sue if their share of inheritance (half a man's share) was denied them. The Koran gave women the right to inherit property for the first time and also granted them inalienable rights to their own inherited wealth, to their personal jewelry, and to their own earnings. (Even in the poorest tribal communities, a man who takes his wife's jewelry, for example, is highly frowned upon; it is considered scandalous and unmanly behavior.)

Thus, in the area of women's rights as in other areas of life, the Koran served to resolve many conflicting ideas and tendencies within the society of its time. A synthesis of social and moral values, the Koran also synthesized centuries of Arabic oral tradition; the language itself is considered a miracle, which was to set a pattern and a standard for the Arabic language which has seldom, if ever, been approached. Art, religion, and social need combined to form this unique document, from which we have extracted most of the verses and surahs relating to women so that they may be seen in their entirety. This is the group of revelations which changed the society of the time and vastly improved the lot of women.

The Koran was also an important element in the development of al-shari'ah, or the canon law of Islam, which still governs personal status cases, that is, those cases involving marriage, divorce, the support of minor children, and inheritance in many Middle Eastern countries. Some nations, notably Syria, Lebanon, Algeria, Tunisia, and Egypt, have replaced areas of the al-shari'ah law with modern personal status codes based on civil rather than religious law, yet even these codes rely somewhat on Koranic precedent, and the Koran is still cited in legal opinions of all sorts across the face of the Islamic world.

In juxtaposition with the Koranic verses, we have placed some of the traditions or sayings usually attributed to 'A'ishah, the Prophet's favorite wife of his later years. The comparison of the two documents sheds light on the type of male-female dialogue in progress in the seventh century and shows that 'A'ishah's opinions may possibly have influenced the Prophet.

Despite the reforms which the Koran effected in the status of women, the basic premise remained that "men are in charge of women." It was not long before the pull of old tribal and family custom began to assert itself, and the early doctors of the faith used this surah to justify quite different practices with regard to women than the Prophet had had in mind. "Even after the Prophet's time all Muslims without regard to sex were treated alike by authority . . . later, in spite of the clearly expressed intentions of the Koran, its interpreters . . . frequently men of Persian or Turkish origin . . . who had been brought up in an environment in which men avowedly ruled, imposed their own views and traditions upon the Muhammadan world. It is thus that in most of the standard collections of 'traditions,' a hadith is to be found to the effect that most of the inhabitants of Hell are women, and that 'because of their unbelief.' "[7]

Thus, while the formal provisions of the Koran specified certain rights for women and theoretically limited male authority over them, practice remained in or reverted to the hands of men who could easily forestall any female demands for justice which might be a negative reflection on the family honor. The same consideration which obligated the woman's male kinsmen to support her in widowhood or after divorce required them to kill her should she jeopardize their honor through sexual misconduct.

Local "interpretations" have therefore usually affected women negatively. In most tribal societies, even today, women do not commonly inherit productive property; many marriages are still between cousins; and, since the property is in the family, the woman's share is not considered separately. Only when a woman marries outside the family group will her husband sometimes institute a legal case to regain her share.

According to the Koran, also, a woman married to an abusive husband has the right to claim damages before the *qadi*, or judge of the religious court; a woman deserted by her husband has the right to institute divorce proceedings. Yet even an educated woman would be unlikely to undertake either of these actions without the support and encouragement of the male members of her natal family, which is not always forthcoming. In Marrakech in 1972, for example, the family of a deserted wife was unwilling to take legal steps against the missing husband because he was a first cousin, and such public proceedings as a law case were seen as bad for the reputation of the entire family. This (the reputation of the group) was a more important consideration than was the plight of a single member of the group, in this case the deserted wife. The woman's father and mother, however, continued to support her and her three-year-old daughter.

Local practice separates men and women even more than the Koran might have intended, particularly in the customs of social segregation between the sexes which are found in the Middle East. Sexual segregation is not unique to the area; many societies operate in sexually segregated ways, either directly or indirectly, but in the Middle East the segregation has been made explicit, underscored, and dramatized by the customs of veiling and seclusion.

Veiling and seclusion did not exist in early Arabia, but the Prophet admonished women to cover themselves modestly, and his own wives were veiled in public. The Prophet's wives set the example, and gradually the veil became a sign of prestige. One hundred and fifty years after the death of the Prophet "the system [of seclusion of women] was fully established . . . in which, among the richer classes, the women were shut off from the rest of the household under the charge of eunuchs."[8] Levy suggests that this, too, was a result of influence of the early interpreters of the Koran, who had originated in Persia where women had long been secluded.

The veil is a symbol with multiple meanings, depending on the situation in which it is found. In the memoirs of Halidé Edib Adivar, which are excerpted in the reader, Mme Adivar used the veil as a disguise in her flight from Turkey; Egyptian feminist Huda Sh'arawi used it to dramatize her fight for women's rights. Early historical chronicles indicate that, in the time of the Prophet, a veil was the sign of a respectable woman; but in later years, in Iraq, for instance, as the veil has been discarded by respectable women, prostitutes have adopted it, mainly to conceal their identity from male kin, who might take vengeance upon them to "clear" the family honor. Among the Tuareg of the southern Sahara, it is the *men*, not the women, who are veiled, yet this is not viewed as a sign of repression; quite the contrary.

The local practices of veiling, seclusion, and general social segregation of the sexes have helped to maintain two quite different societies: the world of men and the world of women. The world of women has developed separately from the world of men, and much is yet to be learned about these separate worlds, their expression in verbal, emotional, and social terms, their interactions and juxtapositions in all aspects of life. The separate-but-equal concept is mediated by many factors, such as differences in attitude toward various ages in the life cycle of both men and women, and the personality and character of the individuals involved. Only in the past few years have some women social scientists begun to look at the world of Middle Eastern women from the women's own point of view and perceive the complex network of relationships and power bases that emanate from it.[9]

Polygamy is another issue which stresses the unequal relationship between men and women, but here, in the conflict between the Koran and local custom and tradition, the solution seems to be closer to the Koranic end of the spectrum. The Koranic injunction allowing a man to legally take four wives at one time was a great improvement over the situation before the time of Muhammad, a situation which seems to have bordered on license. Even so, the Prophet placed obstacles in the way of a man inclined to polygamy; the surah states clearly that four wives were possible only if the husband could provide for all of them equally. Consequently, polygamy has not been common and is found most frequently among the rich, but it exists, even today. The ideological implication is clear: a man may take four wives, but a woman is allowed only one husband at a time. Aside from the legal implications, the existence of the institution of polygamy has been a source of worry and insecurity for women, as the personal documents in our collection will testify: for example, Halidé Edib's description of the unhappiness brought into the household of her childhood with her father's third marriage.

Women's economic position was strengthened by the Koran, but local custom has weakened that position in its insistence that women must work within the private sector of the world: the home, or at least in some sphere related to the home. Thus, to the outside observer, the Islamic woman's economic activities have been disguised throughout the centuries by the customs of seclusion and social segregation. Dr. Nadia Youssef, an Egyptian sociologist now teaching in the United States, states in a recent article on labor-force participation by women of Middle Eastern and Latin American countries that the "Middle East reports systematically the lowest female activity rates on record" for labor.[10] This certainly gives the impression that Middle Eastern women have little or no economic role, until one notes that the statistics are based on *nonagricultural labor outside the home.*

Such statistics do not account for the thousands of women in the Middle East who have adapted themselves to the communal practice of not working in the public sector and have still managed to earn income and often to support whole families: who weave or sew or embroider for other families; take consignments of piece work from factories or shops to finish at home; cook and sell the products of their kitchen; care for children or work as servants; function as *mullah*(s) (religious specialists), *shaykhah*(s), or *muqaddamahs*(s); operate as midwives, pediatricians, fortune tellers, and sorcerers; raise chickens, sheep, goats, or vegetables; sell raw milk and yogurt from door to door. (The colloquial Arabic title Umm Leban, used to refer to a peasant woman, obviously originated in this latter activity.) As Dr. Youssef points out, women in the Middle East are only now breaking with traditional practice, which confines them to the home and associates work in public places with promiscuity and threats to the family honor. But as the old preindustrial society begins to break up, it seems obvious that, for economic reasons, communal practice may change in order to accommodate the greater needs of the family. The biography of Umm Kulthum, one of our documents, demonstrates the change in the father-daughter relationship which took place as Umm Kulthum's earnings rose. Presumably this may happen more frequently in the future.

Women's role in the religious rituals of Islam is another area of confusion and controversy. From the Koran it is clear that men and women are considered equal in the sight of God and are both expected to carry out the religious duties of all believers: profession of faith, prayer, fasting, the giving of alms to the poor, and the making of pilgrimage to the holy places. Women prayed in the mosques in Muhammad's time, but soon, again, the local traditions and customs interfered. The learned doctors of the faith could not reconcile public appearances with the communal practice of secluding women to assure the maintenance of the family honor. Attendance of the women at the mosques gradually declined and they were encouraged to pray at home. Today the incidence of women's public prayer is not consistent from country to country. Communal practice varies, particularly for women of childbearing age.

But in some areas of women's life the Koran has seemed to prevail over the word of men by providing a socially permissible outlet for a woman: religious vocations. A long-standing tradition of women saints and religious functionaries is present in Islam, particularly in some of the mystic orders. Rabi'ah al-'Adawiyah, the most famous, is credited with much of the early development of Sufic doctrine; we have included some excerpts from her biography to suggest the spiritual life of a woman in early Islam. Rabi'ah has been a strong legend and remains so today; school children memorize her poems, and several biographies have recently appeared in Egypt.

Rabi'ah is not alone. Scores of women are recorded in official lists of saints; the shrines of some of the more famous women—such as Sayyidah Zaynab in Cairo, Lalla Imma Tifellut in Algeria, and Mai Supran in the Punjab—are still visited by the faithful each year. Convents for Muslim nuns existed from very early times, and rich and pious women were also noted for their bounty in establishing monasteries for men![11] Today women continue to belong to mystic orders, particularly in North Africa and Turkey, where their membership numbers in the thousands. In some orders they act as *muqaddamah*(s), or functionaries in the rituals. Usually women are members of the women's group of the order, but men and women members join in prayer on special feast days, such as *mawsim*(s) in North Africa.

Education is another area not proscribed by the Koran and in which communal practice has been more flexible. In early periods of Islam, few persons, male or female, could afford or would need advanced education. To be literate meant to be able to read the Koran; writing was an art acquired and practiced by scribes, primarily men. However, exceptions exist: individual women who have managed to reconcile the oppositions inherent in our paradox, whether from economic need, religious conviction, or the absence of supervisory male kinsmen. Thus, it is recorded that the scribe Fatimah, famous for her beautiful calligraphy, was employed to copy the twelfth-century treaty between the Islamic state and the court of Byzantium.

The learned women of the early period and the golden age were saints or religious leaders as well, just as western scholars, until the Renaissance, tended to be theologians or church officials. Shuhdah bint al-Ibari is mentioned by many early biographers of the saints as Fakhr al-Nisa' (the glory of womankind) and al-Katibah (the woman scribe). She was famed for her learning, particularly in hadiths, or traditions of the Prophet, and is supposed to have given "instructions to large numbers of students. . . . thus she formed a link between the traditionists of the rising generation and those of the past."[12] Ignaz Goldziher notes that women often were reckoned as links in the chains of authorities cited to guarantee the validity of various traditions of the Prophet. Such women scholars were called musnida(s). Levy states that "their evidence is often of prime importance . . . they continued to appear as authorities until the tenth century of the hejra,"[13] that is, until the seventeenth century. Shuhdah was a religious teacher, like other women licensed to teach religion, particularly the traditions, during the eleventh, twelfth, and early thirteenth centuries. Women who had acquired knowledge in the explanation of the Koran were known as shaykha(s).

The participation of women in the great tradition of Arabic poetry has never been proscribed by either Koranic injunction or local practice, especially since it could take place in the privacy of the home. Given the long hours of toil required of the majority of Middle Eastern women, however, one would not expect a high percentage of female representation in the ranks of the poets. But this point of view neglects the strong oral tradition in the Islamic world, among women as well as men; a favorite pastime for women, after daily tasks are completed and children are in bed, is composing and reciting poetry aloud. With poetry an ingredient of daily life in all milieus of society, it is logical that some women would emerge, with men, in the first ranks of written poetry.

In this volume we have chosen two very different poets from early periods, Rabiah Balkhi of Afghanistan and Walladah bint al-Mustakfi of Granada. Walladah represents one extreme of our paradox. The daughter of a Christian slave woman and the Muslim caliph who died while ruling the Andalusian court, Walladah was an independent and self-willed woman who never wore the veil and who conducted a salon where she entertained the scholarly, artistic, and famous men and women of her day. After the death of her father, Walladah became even more independent. Rabiah, by falling in love with Baktash, a slave in her father's household, violated the Koranic code as well as tribal and family custom and died at her own brother's hand, the ultimate sanction for such behavior.

The golden age of Islam came to an end toward the fourteenth century, as the Ottoman Empire overran most of the smaller Middle Eastern and European states. A general decline can be observed in the economy, in letters, in the position of all subject peoples; the status of women was also affected. This time, from the fourteenth through the eighteenth centuries, has been called the Dark Ages of Islam, although there were periods of magnificence within the Ottoman court.

The rapid changes in the Middle East in the twentieth century began to emerge as the Ottoman Empire weakened and the nineteenth century came to a close. As representative of the women of this period, we have chosen two characters in the novel *Bayna al-Qasrayn* (Between two palaces), by the Egyptian novelist Najib Mahfuz. Both women are middle class, unable to read and write, devoted to their families; yet their behavior is quite different. Mahfuz has delineated here the human consequences of a crisis in the resolution of a conflict within our central paradox between the word of God and the word of men.

The excerpt from Mahfuz marks another transition point: the opening of the Middle East to outside influences, particularly from the west. By the end of the nineteenth century, the period depicted in the novel, Napoleon had come to Egypt and departed, leaving traces which would never be erased. Western missionaries had established colleges and schools in Syria, Lebanon, Turkey, Egypt, Iran. Colonialism appeared: the French were in Algeria, the British in Jordan and Iraq; the Germans in Turkey—all looking for markets for European goods and outposts where natural resources could be developed. After centuries as an Ottoman fiefdom, the Middle East was suddenly opened to the outside world. Western ideas and technology accompanied the colonial administrators and the missionary schoolteachers.

By the turn of the century the first revolt of the fellaheen against their landlords had taken place in the Egyptian Delta: Sa'ad Zaghlul and Muhammad Abduh were gathering about them young Egyptian nationalists. Turkish youth formed illegal groups to discuss ways of disentangling the Turks from repressive religion, conservatism, and foreign domination. Thousands of young men and women were being educated in the new colonial and missionary schools; some were sent abroad for further education and returned to their homelands from Europe and America, full of idealism or despondent with disillusion but transformed. Some were even questioning the tenets of Islam and the traditions of the past. Tension between the two poles of the paradox tightened, pulled by influences that had never been present in the Middle East.

The memoirs of Turkish novelist and revolutionary Halidé Edib Adivar give us a clear picture of what was happening to the young people in Turkey. The little girl who was carried to the sultan's palace in the middle of the night so that she might say good night to her father (the sultan's secretary) was, ten years later, enrolled in an American school in Istanbul. She learned French and English and began to write in Turkish. She lectured on the necessity for women's education; she became involved in politics. Yet she was also crushed by her husband's marrying another woman and was only able to get a divorce with some difficulty. Personal ties and old community practices were harder to discard than languages and political views. Halidé Edib's personal solution may be viewed as one within a local practice transcended temporarily by war and revolution; yet the word of God was still used to strengthen her position: her great nationalistic speech was given before the great mosque of Sultan Ahmed.

The same ferment apparent in Turkey emerged in Egypt. Women who had been educated in the foreign schools began to organize; they wanted to force a change in the old customs and practices (the word of men) as they pertained to women's role, and for the first time they agitated publicly to this end. Huda Sh'arawi, daughter of a rich and prominent Egyptian pasha, marched with her friends through the streets of Cairo in the 1920's, tearing off her veil in symbolic protest against what she conceived her status to be.

By the 1950's, when Gamal Abdel Nasser was nationalizing the Suez Canal and the overthrow of colonial regimes was taking place in Morocco, Algeria, and Iraq, the winds of change were also beginning to affect that center of Islamic culture: Arabic poetry. A woman was one of the pioneers in the development of a new style. Nazik al-Mala'ikah, descendant of a long line of poets in a traditional Baghdadi family, carried on the family art in a slightly different tone. In the introduction to her first volume of poetry, she called for rejection of the rigid rules of meter and versification which had dominated Arabic poetry for centuries. Her call for a newer, freer verse (see excerpt) was severely criticized, but soon young poets began to adopt her recommendations. Free verse became a great fad. But in Nazik's case, the pull of tradition and custom was too strong. In 1954 she rebuffed the movement she had begun.

Less than a decade later, the new Arabic prose movement was further revised in the direction of freedom and outspokenness, again by a woman. Layla Ba'labakki's short story, "A Space Ship of Tenderness to the Moon," treated sex in such a concrete way that she was indicted and prosecuted in her native Lebanon on an obscenity charge. Her own defense (see excerpt) aided in her final acquittal. Layla Ba'labakki had challenged the traditional practice at the far end of the paradox, but, with her education and, still more importantly, the support of her family, she won.

Movements for nationalism, greater freedom in literature, and a new definition of women's role were accompanied by drives for social and economic reform. Nationalist leaders attacked the traditional policies of land tenure, in which large amounts of land were in the possession of a small minority while the majority of farmers worked as tenants, bound by unbreakable cycles of debt and drought. Illiteracy, health, maternal and child welfare, bad conditions in village and rural areas—these were all to be improved in the new independent states. Great steps have been made in this direction, but, even so, many Middle Eastern countries are still subject to the double bind of overpopulation and limited natural resources, with the result that thousands of their citizens live on the edge of poverty. Women in such circumstances have no levers to manipulate the paradox; they are unable to influence communal practice and must make whatever adjustments are possible, dependent upon their family situations. This kind of life is exemplified in the autobiography of Umm Kulthum, a life forever limited unless, as in the case of Umm Kulthum, great talent provides a means to overcome obstacles. Still, Umm Kulthum began her career rather close to the Koranic end of the spectrum; her talent was first recognized in the singing of religious songs and chants. Comparing the childhood memories of Halidé Edib and Umm Kulthum is instructive because of the distance between them; yet, for both, their relationships with their male kin (fathers) were key factors in helping them to clear the early barriers which tradition places on a girl's life.

To give some picture of the lives of peasant and village women who are unable to read and write, we have asked women anthropologists who have worked in the area to share some life histories gathered in interviews and conversations with the women themselves. Included are samples from Morocco, Egypt, Lebanon, and Jordan.

Here, too, the contrasts are great, not only between life styles but also in the kinds of solutions that the women have found: Umm Ahmad, wife of a small shopkeeper in an Egyptian Delta town, used the resources available to her—her bride wealth, the good will of her sons and daughters—to manipulate the paradox and ensure a reasonable future for her children and herself. Zahrah Muhammad had no mediating influences in her struggle to survive, and her story is not an uncommon one. Her relative content in middle age seems due to her luck in finding a good husband. Jawazi al-Malakim represents the women's classic participation in the economic activities of the family, at least during the nomadic period of her life. However, a settled, sedentary existence is rather different, and how Jawazi's daughters and sons will resolve the paradox between the word of God and the word of men remains a question.

Zaynab, an urban working-class woman from Lebanon, represents thousands of women in the rapidly changing society of the Middle East who, cut off from the traditional ties of kin, turn to neighbors for support. This new residence pattern, a growing phenomenon, may very well shatter traditional ties and jar the poles of our paradox.

Politics and the struggle for independence from foreign rule provided a situation in which ordinary traditional practices were suspended temporarily. Thus, women have taken an active part in the political movements of their societies, for example, in Turkey, Iraq, Morocco, and Algeria. Jamilah Buhrayd is one of many Algerian women who suffered arrest, torture, and long imprisonment for her assistance to the FLN movement (Fronte de Liberation Nationale) against French domination. Jamilah's ordeal, and that of other women who took part in the underground movement, alerted the French public to what was happening in Algeria and helped change the tide of public opinion in favor of the Algerian cause. "Jamilah" became a kind of code word in the Middle East during this time, a word signaling admiration, respect, and desire for freedom, as Nizar Qabbani's poem indicates.

When the wars were over, local custom and tradition (the word of men) reasserted themselves. But Algerian women had had a taste of independence and were determined not to return to old ways. Among the most active was the Algerian journalist Fadéla M'rabet. Ms. M'rabet conducted a weekly newspaper column for women and received countless letters from women of all ages who considered her their friend and champion. These letters were used by Fadéla M'rabet as important evidence that the promises of the revolution, particularly to women, were not being kept. A Marxist, she has also focused her energies toward implementing the new personal status code which has replaced *shari'ah* law, officially at least, in contemporary Algeria. With the support of her male kin, her father and her husband, she has managed to maintain a rather individualistic solution to the paradox, although her current residence in France may indicate disillusion with the issue.

Like Fadéla M'rabet, Aminah al-Sa'id of Egypt has used the power of the press, in magazines, books, and articles, to promote the cause of greater freedom for women. But she has worked within the existing institutions to improve conditions and change laws, attempting to balance the poles of traditional practice and Koranic ideal. On the other hand, Ghadah al-Samman, Lebanese novelist, speaks personally and urgently as an individual and not a member of a group, another new development.

From the diverse colored shapes of the Middle Eastern kaleidoscope provided by the documents of women's experiences, is it possible to form one pattern, which might be termed a characteristic Middle Eastern woman? We do not think so, except in one instance: all the individual shapes have been molded by the same crucial paradox between the word of God and the word of men as it has operated in Islamic society since the seventh century. In that sense, the shapes do form a pattern. The remarkable stability of Islamic society, apart from the conditions of preindustrialism which have remained constant in the area until this century, may be attributed also to the flexibility allowed to the followers of Islam in resolving the paradox.

Except where Islam and local custom have not proscribed activities—such as in the case of religious vocation, working within the home, gaining an education—the woman has been bound by the conditions of the society of which she is a part. Further, she has been unable, except indirectly or with the consent of her male kin, to take part in modifying the forms of local custom and tradition. This, too, is a consistent pattern.

But the pattern is shifting, due to economic forces which are transforming the agricultural preindustrial society of the Middle East and due to educational forces which have now penetrated the majority of most rural areas.

Halidé Edib, Huda Sh'arawi, Fadéla M'rabet, Umm Kulthum, Layla Ba'labakki, Aminah al-Sa'id, and Nazik al-Mala'ikah have played an important role in changing the supposedly static conditions of the society into which they were born. They have been more active publicly than their ancestors in mediating conflicts of values within their own communities. In one way or another, they have been instruments of change.

Today, where women are working outside the home and contributing to the family income, their voices must become increasingly important in domestic councils. Where women have been educated to know their legal rights according to the Koran, they have begun to act accordingly.

Yet, within the Koranic injunction, several problem areas remain for women, which activists are now attempting to reform: divorce, marriage, and inheritance laws, in particular. After a period of war and revolution, when men and women have transcended traditional boundaries, it becomes more difficult to return to the old practices.

But change brings disruption in private as well as in public life and fresh dilemmas for which new solutions have yet to be found. Young women workers interviewed in Algiers complained that their lives were more proscribed than before, since their male relatives watched every move they made in public. A father who educates his daughter in a public university may find it more difficult to arrange a marriage for her; marriages which are not arranged in the traditional manner create insecurities and tensions in both men and women, who find difficult male-female relationships which are not based on the old, familiar tribal and family custom and expectation. As one Iraqi woman stated, "I find to my dismay that I am full of conflict. I am pulled more strongly by the strings of tradition and Islam than I would have believed. I thought I was a modern woman, but what is that exactly? I am an Islamic woman first."

The Middle East today is in the throes of political upheaval, but it is also torn by conflicts between ideologies and values. Not for many centuries, perhaps not since the time of Muhammad, has the base of shared conviction been so uneven. Turkey has proclaimed a policy of strict secularism in all its attitudes, while, nearby, Colonel Muammar al-Qaddafi, prime minister of Libya, declares that Middle Eastern salvation lies in a return to conservative Islam: women in the home and covered by the veil. In Egypt a commission including the head of al-Azhar, the conservative Islamic university, has submitted a draft proposal for more equitable divorce laws to the Ministry of Justice;[14] in Saudi Arabia the issue is scarcely even discussed!

Women who outlive their male kinsmen and thus their supervision or women who embrace religious vocations—these women have always stood outside the rigid poles of our paradox. The difference today is that for the first time, as education becomes widespread and the preindustrial society slowly disappears under a new kind of economic pressure, all women are gaining more power to actively modify the communal practice within which they live, and this may eventually weaken the forces of tradition. The fragments within the kaleidoscope are shifting. The instrument is turning in new directions which have yet to be defined.

The Koran, though unchangeable, has shown itself to be flexible in its social applications. How the future will be shaped in terms of our paradox, whether the fragments present in the kaleidoscope will actually form a new pattern or remain fixed in the old paradox, depends on the woman's and the man's ability and willingness to adapt together the word of God to a new word of men.

Notes

1. Marcel Proust, *Remembrance of Things Past,* 1:911.
2. Reuben Levy, *The Social Structure of Islam,* p. 91.
3. H. A. Gibb and J. H. Kramers, eds., *Shorter Encyclopedia of Islam,* p. 471.
4. Germaine Tillion, *Le Harem et Les Cousins,* p. 209.
5. Ernest Gellner, Introduction to *The Desert and the Sown,* ed. Cynthia Nelson, p. 8.
6. Richard Bell, *Bell's Introduction to the Qur'an,* p. 10.
7. Levy, *Social Structure of Islam,* p. 130.
8. Ibid., p. 127.
9. See Susan Schaefer Davis, "A Separate Reality: Moroccan Village Women," delivered at the MESA meeting, Milwaukee, 1973; Cynthia Nelson, "Public and Private Politics: Women in the Middle Eastern World," *American Ethnologist* 1, no. 3 (Fall 1974): 551–564; and Elizabeth Warnock Fernea, *Guests of the Sheik.*
10. Nadia Youssef, "Differential Labor Force Participation of Women in Latin American and Middle Eastern Countries: The Influence of Family Characteristics," *Social Forces* 51 (December 1972): 135.
11. Margaret Smith, *Rabi'a the Mystic and Her Fellow-Saints in Islam,* p. 175.
12. Ibid., p. 153. Also Ignaz Goldziher, *Muslim Studies,* 2:361–368.
13. Levy, *Social Structure of Islam,* p. 133.
14. *New York Times,* March 7, 1976.

References

Bell, Richard. *Bell's Introduction to the Qur'an.* Revised and enlarged by W. Montgomery Watt. Edinburgh: University of Edinburgh Press, 1970.

Davis, Susan Schaefer. "A Separate Reality: Moroccan Village Women." Paper delivered at annual meeting of the Middle Eastern Studies Association, Milwaukee, 1973.

Fernea, Elizabeth Warnock. *Guests of the Sheik.* New York: Doubleday, 1965.

Gellner, Ernest. Introduction to *The Desert and the Sown,* edited by Cynthia Nelson. Berkeley: University of California Press, 1973.

Gibb, H. A., and J. H. Kramers, eds. *Shorter Encyclopedia of Islam.* Ithaca: Cornell University Press, 1953.

Goldziher, Ignaz. *Muslim Studies.* Translated by S. M. Stern and C. R. Barber. London: Allen and Unwin, 1970.

Levy, Reuben. *The Social Structure of Islam.* Cambridge: At the University Press, 1957.

Nelson, Cynthia. "Public and Private Politics: Women in the Middle Eastern World." *American Ethnologist* 1, no. 3 (Fall 1974): 551–564.

New York Times, March 7, 1976.

Proust, Marcel. *Remembrance of Things Past.* Translated by C. K. Scott Moncrieff. New York: Random House, 1934.

Smith, Margaret. *Rabi'a the Mystic and Her Fellow-Saints in Islam.* Cambridge: At the University Press, 1928.

Smith, W. Robertson. *Kinship and Marriage in Early Arabia.* London: A & C Black, 1903. [Re-issued by Beacon Press, Boston, n.d.]

Tillion, Germaine. *Le Harem et Les Cousins.* Paris: Editions du Seuil, 1966.

Youssef, Nadia. "Differential Labor Force Participation of Women in Latin American and Middle Eastern Countries: The Influence of Family Characteristics." *Social Forces* 51 (December 1972): 135–153.

Part **1** **Tradition**

1

al-Khansa'

الخنساء

Poet of Early Islam

A.D. 600–670

One of the great poets of the period just before and during the emergence of Islam was al-Khansa' (Tumadir bint 'Amru al-Harith bin
al-Sharid). Her life spans a time of unrest in the history of Arabia, the
years before the rise of the Prophet Muhammad and the acceptance of
his message. Tribesmen and townsmen competed for dominance, tribal
battles were frequent, and the followers of Muhammad at first found
great resistance to the new religion.

Al-Khansa' was born into a noble, nomadic tribe, the Madar, which
was well known not only for its courage and heroism in battle, but also
for its eloquence of language and talent in the composition and recita-
tion of poetry.

Al-Khansa''s life began well. She was considered talented and beautiful despite the slightly turned nose which gave her the nickname of
al-Khansa'. She refused to marry until she found the husband of her
own choice. Later tragedy overcame her. Her two brothers, Mu'awiyah
and Sakhar, to whom she was devoted, were killed in tribal skirmishes.
After the death of her brothers, she was converted to Islam, and this
added to her sorrow: her brothers had died before professing the faith.

Photos: The Empty Quarter, Arabian Peninsula

Married three times, al-Khansa' outlived all her husbands. Four of her sons were killed in the Battle of Qadasiyah,[1] but on hearing the news, she is reported to have said, "I consider it an honor that they died for the sake of Islam. I ask only that God allow me to meet them in Paradise."

Her poetry, from the time of her brothers' deaths, assumed a dark and somber quality, but the most severe critics, past and present, attest to its magnificence.[2] Muhammad himself is said to have been very fond of her poetry and often asked her to recite for him when she was in his company.

Al-Khansa' regularly took part in the poetry contests of the time: several poets would gather and recite their work before a judge and an interested audience. On one such occasion, after two men poets had recited, the judgment angered the losing competitor. The judge is supposed to have turned to al-Khansa' and said, "What do you think? Recite some of your poetry for us." She replied with a line still considered classic, which has achieved the status of a proverb in Arabic.

Among desert guides, Sakhar was peerless
Like a beacon on the peak of a high mountain.

After hearing the line, the annoyed competitor is alleged to have said, "We've never seen a better woman poet than you." To this al-Khansa' replied, "Don't you want to say that I am the *best* poet, male *or* female?"

Al-Khansa' outlived most of her contemporary kinsmen. She died in A.D. 670 during the time of the Omayyad Caliph Mu'awiyah. She was seventy years old. According to legend, she died in the desert. Her work is still cited as a great example of early Arabic poetry.

Lament for a Brother/al-Khansa'

What have we done to you, death
that you treat us so,
with always another catch
one day a warrior
the next a head of state;
charmed by the loyal
you choose the best.
Iniquitous, unequalling death
I would not complain
if you were just
but you take the worthy
leaving fools for us.

Fifty years among us
upholding rights
annulling wrongs,
impatient death
could you not wait a little longer
He still would be here
and mine, a brother
without a flaw. Peace
be upon him and Spring
rains water his tomb but
could you not wait
        a little longer
        a little longer,
you came too soon.

[Previously published in Omar S. Pound, *Arabic and Persian Poems*. Copyright
© 1970 by Omar S. Pound. Reprinted by permission of New Directions Publishing Company and Omar S. Pound.]

Notes

1.   One of the decisive battles of early Islamic history: In the winter of A.D. 637, the Arabs triumphed over the Persian army at Qadasiyah on the Euphrates; a year later the Arabs had wrested control of the entire Tigris and Euphrates area from the Persians.
2.   R. A. Nicholson, *A Literary History of the Arabs*, p. 126.

References

Husayn, Qadriyah. *Shahirat Nisa'fi al-'Alam al-Islami*. Beirut: Dar al-Katib al-'Arabi, n.d.
Nicholson, Reynold Alleyne. *A Literary History of the Arabs*. Cambridge: At the University Press, 1956.

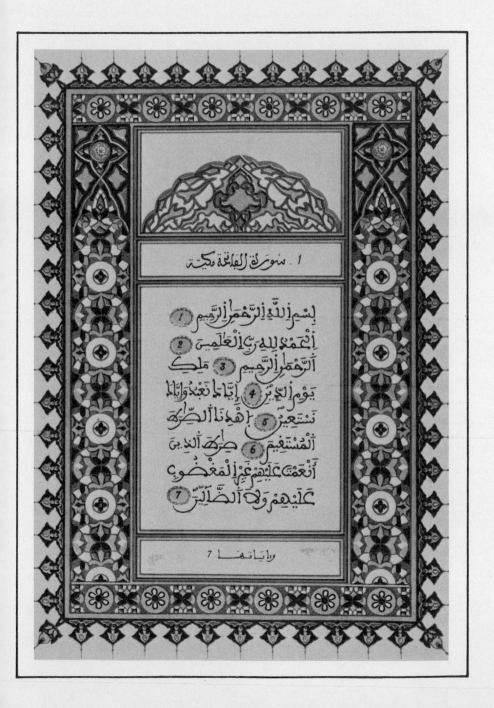

١ ـ سورة الفاتحة مكية

بِسْمِ اللَّهِ الرَّحْمَٰنِ الرَّحِيمِ ﴿١﴾ الْحَمْدُ لِلَّهِ رَبِّ الْعَالَمِينَ ﴿٢﴾ الرَّحْمَٰنِ الرَّحِيمِ ﴿٣﴾ مَالِكِ يَوْمِ الدِّينِ ﴿٤﴾ إِيَّاكَ نَعْبُدُ وَإِيَّاكَ نَسْتَعِينُ ﴿٥﴾ اهْدِنَا الصِّرَاطَ الْمُسْتَقِيمَ ﴿٦﴾ صِرَاطَ الَّذِينَ أَنْعَمْتَ عَلَيْهِمْ غَيْرِ الْمَغْضُوبِ عَلَيْهِمْ وَلَا الضَّالِّينَ ﴿٧﴾

وآياتها 7

2

The Koran
on the Subject of Women

القرآن

Selections by the Editors

The Koran, sacred book of Islam, consists of a series of more than a hundred chapters, or surahs, outlining and recommending behavior for men and women in all aspects of life. Muslims believe that the surahs are literally the word of God and were revealed by Gabriel to the Prophet Muhammad over a period of years ranging from A.D. 620 to about 640. The revelations took place in the city of Mecca and in the city of Medina, in what is today the country of Saudi Arabia.

The Koran has been called untranslatable, and a good deal of controversy still exists among scholars about which of many English translations is the best attempt to reproduce the spirit as well as the letter of this remarkable document. The order in which the surahs were revealed is also the subject of dispute. Here we have used the translation by Mohammed Marmaduke Pickthall because, first, it is a translation recognized and approved by Islamic theologians and, second, it is conveniently organized and indexed for general use. However, some minor discrepancies are found which change the intended meaning slightly, such as the use of the word *orphan* when what is actually meant is "orphan girls of marriageable age." Also, Pickthall uses the English word

---

Photo: The Koran, Surah al-Fatihah

scourge as a translation for *dharaba*. Although technically *dharaba* may mean scourge, the actual severity of the blow varies according to the context in which *dharaba* is used. We have examined translations by R. Bell, A. J. Arberry, and N. J. Dawood and plan to note the following translation where such small errors occur.

Most of the chapters and verses relating to women are reproduced on the following pages. Selected from different surahs of the Koran, they are gathered here in their entirety.

The Koran on Women

Surah II. The Cow

221.   Wed not idolatresses till they believe; for lo! a believing bond-woman is better than an idolatress though she please you; and give not your daughters in marriage to idolaters till they believe, for lo! a believing slave is better than an idolater though he please you. These invite unto the Fire, and Allah inviteth unto the Garden, and unto forgiveness by His grace, and expoundeth thus His revelations to mankind that haply they may remember.

222.   They question thee (O Muhammad) concerning menstruation. Say: It is an illness, so let women alone at such times and go not in unto them till they are cleansed. And when they have purified themselves, then go in unto them as Allah hath enjoined upon you. Truly Allah loveth those who turn unto Him, and loveth those who have a care for cleanness.

223.   Your women are a tilth for you (to cultivate) so go to your tilth as ye will, and send (good deeds) before you for your souls, and fear Allah, and know that ye will (one day) meet Him. Give glad tidings to believers, (O Muhammad).

226.   Those who forswear their wives must wait four months; then, if they change their mind, lo! Allah is Forgiving, Merciful.

227.   And if they decide upon divorce (let them remember that) Allah is Hearer, Knower.

228.   Women who are divorced shall wait, keeping themselves apart, three (monthly) courses. And it is not lawful for them that they should conceal that which Allah hath created in their wombs if they are believers in Allah and the Last Day. And their husbands would do better to take them back in that case if they desire a reconciliation. And they (women) have rights similar to those (of men) over them in kindness, and men are a degree above them. Allah is Mighty, Wise.

[Selections from Mohammed Marmaduke Pickthall, *The Meaning of the Glorious Koran* (New York: New American Library, Mentor Books, 1953). Reprinted by permission of George Allen & Unwin Ltd.]

229. Divorce must be pronounced twice and then (a woman) must be retained in honour or released in kindness. And it is not lawful for you that ye take from women aught of that which ye have given them; except (in the case) when both fear that they may not be able to keep within the limits (imposed by) Allah. And if ye fear that they may not be able to keep the limits of Allah, in that case it is no sin for either of them if the woman ransom herself. These are the limits (imposed by) Allah. Transgress them not. For whoso transgresseth Allah's limits: such are wrongdoers.

230. And if he hath divorced her (the third time), then she is not lawful unto him thereafter until she hath wedded another husband. Then if he (the other husband) divorce her it is no sin for both of them that they come together again if they consider that they are able to observe the limits of Allah. These are the limits of Allah. He manifesteth them for people who have knowledge.

231. When ye have divorced women, and they have reached their term, then retain them in kindness or release them in kindness. Retain them not to their hurt so that ye transgress (the limits). He who doeth that hath wronged his soul. Make not the revelations of Allah a laughing-stock (by your behaviour), but remember Allah's grace upon you and that which He hath revealed unto you of the Scripture and of wisdom, whereby He doth exhort you. Observe your duty to Allah and know that Allah is Aware of all things.

232. And when ye have divorced women and they reach their term, place not difficulties in the way of their marrying their husbands if it is agreed between them in kindness. This is an admonition for him among you who believeth in Allah and the Last Day. That is more virtuous for you, and cleaner. Allah knoweth: ye know not.

233. Mothers shall suckle their children for two whole years; (that is) for those who wish to complete the suckling. The duty of feeding and clothing nursing mothers in a seemly manner is upon the father of the child. No one should be charged beyond his capacity. A mother should not be made to suffer because of her child, nor should he to whom the child is born (be made to suffer) because of his child. And on the (father's) heir is incumbent the like of that (which was incumbent on the father). If they desire to wean the child by mutual consent and (after) consultation, it is no sin for them; and if ye wish to give your children out to nurse, it is no sin for you, provided that ye pay what is due from you in kindness. Observe your duty to Allah, and know that Allah is Seer of what ye do.

234.   Such of you as die and leave behind them wives, they (the wives) shall wait, keeping themselves apart, four months and ten days. And when they reach the term (prescribed for them) then there is no sin for you in aught that they may do with themselves in decency. Allah is Informed of what ye do.

235.   There is no sin for you in that which ye proclaim or hide in your minds concerning your troth with women. Allah knoweth that ye will remember them. But plight not your troth with women except by uttering a recognised form or words. And do not consummate the marriage until (the term) prescribed is run. Know that Allah knoweth what is in your minds, so beware of Him; and know that Allah is Forgiving, Clement.

236.   It is no sin for you if ye divorce women while yet ye have not touched them, nor appointed unto them a portion. Provide for them, the rich according to his means, and the straitened according to his means, a fair provision. (This is) a bounden duty for those who do good.

237.   If ye divorce them before ye have touched them and ye have appointed unto them a portion, then (pay the) half of that which ye appointed, unless they (the women) agree to forgo it, or he agreeth to forgo it in whose hand the marriage tie. To forgo is nearer to piety. And forget not kindness among yourselves. Allah is Seer of what ye do.

240.   (In the case of) those of you who are about to die and leave behind them wives, they should bequeath unto their wives a provision for the year without turning them out, but if they go out (of their own accord) there is no sin for you in that which they do of themselves within their rights. Allah is Mighty, Wise.

241.   For divorced women a provision in kindness: a duty for those who ward off (evil).

Surah LXV. Divorce

At-Talaq, "Divorce," is so called from 1–7, which contain an amendment to the laws of divorce set forth in Surah II. . . .

The date of revelation is the sixth year of the Hijrah or a little earlier.

In the name of Allah, the Beneficent, the Merciful.

1.   O Prophet! When ye (men) put away women, put them away for their (legal) period and reckon the period, and keep your duty to Allah, your Lord. Expel them not from their houses nor let them go forth unless they commit open immorality. Such are the limits (imposed by) Allah; and whoso transgresseth Allah's limits, he verily wrongeth his soul. Thou knowest not; it may be that Allah will afterward bring some new thing to pass.

2.   Then, when they have reached their term, take them back in kindness or part from them in kindness, and call to witness two just men among you, and keep your testimony upright for Allah. Whoso believeth in Allah and the Last Day is exhorted to act thus. And whosoever keepeth his duty to Allah, Allah will appoint a way out for him.

3.   And will provide for him from (a quarter) whence he hath no expectation. And whosoever putteth his trust in Allah, He will suffice him. Lo! Allah bringeth His command to pass. Allah hath set a measure for all things.

4.   And for such of your women as despair of menstruation, if ye doubt, their period (of waiting) shall be three months, along with those who have it not. And for those with child, their period shall be till they bring forth their burden. And whosoever keepeth his duty to Allah, He maketh his course easy for him.

5.   That is the commandment of Allah which He revealeth unto you. And whoso keepeth his duty to Allah, He will remit from him his evil deeds and magnify reward for him.

6.   Lodge them where ye dwell, according to your wealth, and harass them not so as to straiten life for them. And if they are with child, then spend for them till they bring forth their burden. Then, if they give suck for you, give them their due payment and consult together in kindness; but if ye make difficulties for one another, then let some other woman give suck for him (the father of the child).

Surah IV. Women

An-Nisa, "Women," is so-called because it deals largely with women's rights. The period of revelation is the months following the battle of Uhud, or, as [Th.] Noldeke, a careful critic, puts it, "between the end of the third year and the end of the fifth year" of the Prophet's reign at Al-Madinah. As the Surah contains no reference to the siege of Al-Madinah ("The War of the Trench") by the allied tribes, which took place in the fifth year, I should rather say, between the end of the third year and the beginning of the fifth year.

Many Muslims were killed at the battle of Uhud, hence the concern for orphans and widows in the opening verses which lead on to a declaration of some rights of women of which they were deprived among the pagan Arabs.

The period of revelation is the fourth year of the Hijrah.

In the name of Allah, the Beneficent, the Merciful.

1.   O mankind! Be careful of your duty to your Lord Who created you from a single soul and from it created its mate and from them twain hath spread abroad a multitude of men and women. Be careful of your duty toward Allah in Whom ye claim (your rights) of one another, and toward the wombs (that bare you). Lo! Allah hath been a Watcher over you.

2.   Give unto orphans their wealth. Exchange not the good for the bad (in your management thereof) nor absorb their wealth into your own wealth. Lo! That would be a great sin.

3.   And if ye fear that ye will not deal fairly by the orphans, marry of the women, who seem good to you, two or three or four; and if ye fear that ye cannot do justice (to so many) then one (only) or (the captives) that your right hands possess. Thus it is more likely that ye will not do injustice.

4.   And give unto the women, (whom ye marry) free gift of their marriage portions; but if they of their own accord remit unto you a part thereof, then ye are welcome to absorb it (in your wealth).

5.   Give not unto the foolish (what is in) your (keeping of their) wealth, which Allah hath given you to maintain; but feed and clothe them from it, and speak kindly unto them.

6.   Prove orphans till they reach the marriageable age; then, if ye find them of sound judgement, deliver over unto them their fortune; and devour it not by squandering and in haste lest they should grow up. Whoso (of the guardians) is rich, let him abstain generously (from taking of the property of orphans); and whoso is poor let him take thereof in reason (for his guardianship). And when ye deliver up their fortune unto orphans, have (the transaction) witnessed in their presence. Allah sufficeth as a Reckoner.

7.   Unto the men (of a family) belongeth a share of that which parents and near kindred leave, and unto the women a share of that which parents and near kindred leave, whether it be little or much—a legal share.

8.   And when kinsfolk and orphans and the needy are present at the division (of the heritage), bestow on them therefrom and speak kindly unto them.

9.   And let those fear (in their behaviour toward orphans) who if they left behind them weak offspring would be afraid for them. So let them mind their duty to Allah, and speak justly.

10.   Lo! Those who devour the wealth of orphans wrongfully, they do but swallow fire into their bellies, and they will be exposed to burning flame.

11.   Allah chargeth you concerning (the provision for) your children; to the male the equivalent of the portion of two females, and if there be women more than two, then theirs is two-thirds of the inheritance, and if there be one (only) then the half. And to his parents a sixth of the inheritance, if he have a son; and if have no son and his parents are his heirs, then to his mother appertaineth the third; and if he have brethren, then to his mother appertaineth the sixth, after any legacy he may have bequeathed, or debt (hath been paid). Your parents or your children: Ye know not which of them is nearer unto you in usefulness. It is an injunction from Allah. Lo! Allah is Knower, Wise.

12.   And unto you belongeth a half of that which your wives leave, if they have no child; but if they have a child then unto you the fourth of that which they leave, after any legacy they may have bequeathed, or debt (they may have contracted, hath been paid). And unto them belongeth the fourth of that which ye leave if ye have no child, but if ye have a child then the eighth of that which ye leave, after any legacy ye may have bequeathed, or debt (ye may have contracted, hath been paid). And if a man or a woman have a distant heir (having left neither parent nor child), and he (or she) have a brother or a sister (only on the mother's side) then to each of them twain (the brother and the sister) the sixth, and if they be more than two, then they shall be sharers in the third, after any legacy that may have been bequeathed or debt (contracted) not injuring (the heirs by willing away more than a third of the heritage) hath been paid. A commandment from Allah. Allah is Knower, Indulgent.

13.   These are the limits (imposed by) Allah. Whoso obeyeth Allah and His messenger, He will make him enter Gardens underneath which rivers flow, where such will dwell for ever. That will be the great success.

14.   And whoso disobeyeth Allah and His messenger and transgresseth His limits, He will make him enter Fire, where such will dwell for ever; his will be a shameful doom.

15.   As for those of your women who are guilty of lewdness, call to witness four of you against them. And if they testify (to the truth of the allegation) then confine them to the houses until death take them or (until) Allah appoint for them a way (through new legislation).

16.   And as for the two of you who are guilty thereof, punish them both. And if they repent and improve, then let them be. Lo! Allah is Relenting, Merciful.

17.   Forgiveness is only incumbent on Allah toward those who do evil in ignorance (and) then turn quickly (in repentance) to Allah. These are they toward whom Allah relenteth. Allah is ever Knower, Wise.

18. The forgiveness is not for those who do ill deeds until, when death attendeth upon one of them, he saith: Lo! I repent now; nor yet for those who die while they are disbelievers. For such We have prepared a painful doom.

19. O ye who believe! It is not lawful for you to forcibly (to inherit) the women (of your deceased kinsmen), nor (that) ye should put constraint upon them that ye may take away a part of that which ye have given them, unless they be guilty of flagrant lewdness. But consort with them in kindness, for if ye hate them it may happen that ye hate a thing wherein Allah hath placed much good.

20. And if ye wish to exchange one wife for another and ye have given unto one of them a sum of money (however great), take nothing from it. Would ye take it by the way of calumny and open wrong?

21. How can ye take it (back) after one of you hath gone in unto the other, and they have taken a strong pledge from you?

22. And marry not those women whom your fathers married, except what hath already happened (of that nature) in the past. Lo! It was ever lewdness and abomination, and an evil way.

23. Forbidden unto you are your mothers, and your daughters, and your sisters, and your father's sisters, and your mother's sisters, and your brother's daughters, and your sister's daughters, and your foster-mothers, and your foster-sisters, and your mothers-in-law, and your step-daughters who are under your protection (born) of your women unto whom ye have gone in—but if ye have not gone in unto them, then it is no sin for you (to marry their daughters)—and the wives of your sons who (spring) from your own loins. And (it Is forbidden unto you) that ye should have two sisters together, except what hath already happened (of that nature) in the past. Lo! Allah is ever Forgiving, Merciful.

24. And all married women (are forbidden unto you) save those (captives) whom your right hands possess. It is a decree of Allah for you. Lawful unto you are all beyond those mentioned, so that ye seek them with your wealth in honest wedlock, not debauchery. And those of whom ye seek content (by marrying them), give unto them their portions as a duty. And there is no sin for you in what ye do by mutual agreement after the duty (hath been done). Lo! Allah is ever Knower, Wise.

25.   And whoso is not able to afford to marry free, believing women, let them marry from the believing maids whom your right hands possess. Allah knoweth best (concerning) your faith. Ye (proceed) one from another; so wed them by permission of their folk, and give unto them their portions in kindness, they being honest, not debauched nor of loose conduct. And if when they are honourably married they commit lewdness they shall incur the half of the punishment (prescribed) for free women (in that case). This is for him among you who feareth to commit sin. But to have patience would be better for you. Allah is Forgiving, Merciful.

26.   Allah would explain to you and guide you by the examples of those who were before you, and would turn to you in mercy. Allah is Knower, Wise.

27.   And Allah would turn to you in mercy; but those who follow vain desires would have you go tremendously astray.

28.   Allah would make the burden light for you, for man was created weak.

29.   O ye who believe! Squander not your wealth among yourselves in vanity, except it be a trade by mutual consent, and kill not one another. Lo! Allah is ever Merciful unto you.

30.   Whoso doeth that through aggression and injustice, We shall cast him into Fire, and that is ever easy for Allah.

32.   And covet not the thing in which Allah hath made some of you excel others. Unto men a fortune from that which they have earned, and unto women a fortune from that which they have earned. (Envy not one another) but ask Allah of His bounty. Lo! Allah is ever Knower of all things.

34.   Men are in charge of women, because Allah hath made the one of them to excel the other, and because they spend of their property (for the support of women). So good women are the obedient, guarding in secret that which Allah hath guarded. As for those from whom ye fear rebellion, admonish them and banish them to beds apart, and scourge them. Then if they obey you, seek not a way against them. Lo! Allah is ever High Exalted, Great.

35.   And if ye fear a breach between them twain (the man and wife) appoint an arbiter from his folk and an arbiter from her folk. If they desire amendment, Allah will make them of one mind. Lo! Allah is ever Knower, Aware.

43. O ye who believe! Draw not near unto prayer when ye are drunken, till ye know that which ye utter, nor when ye are polluted, save when journeying upon the road, till ye have bathed. And if ye be ill, or on a journey, or one of you cometh from the closet, or ye have touched women, and ye find not water, then go to high clean soil and rub your faces and your hands (therewith). Lo! Allah is Benign, Forgiving.

124. And whoso doeth good works, whether of male or female, and he (or she) is a believer, such will enter paradise and they will not be wronged the dint in a date-stone.

127. They consult thee concerning women. Say: Allah giveth you decree concerning them, and the Scripture which hath been recited unto you (giveth decree), concerning female orphans unto whom ye give not that which is ordained for them though ye desire to marry them, and (concerning) the weak among children, and that ye should deal justly with orphans. Whatever good ye do, lo! Allah is ever Aware of it.

128. If a woman feareth ill-treatment from her husband, or desertion, it is no sin for them twain if they make terms of peace between themselves. Peace is better. But greed hath been made present in the minds (of men). If ye do good and keep from evil, lo! Allah is ever Informed of what ye do.

129. Ye will not be able to deal equally between (your) wives, however much ye wish (to do so). But turn not altogether away (from one), leaving her as in suspense. If ye do good and keep from evil, lo! Allah is ever Forgiving, Merciful.

130. But if they separate, Allah will compensate each out of His abundance. Allah is ever All-Embracing, All-Knowing.

177. They ask thee for a pronouncement. Say: Allah hath pronounced for you concerning distant kindred. If a man die childless and he have a sister, hers is half the heritage, and he would have inherited from her had she died childless. And if there be two sisters, then theirs are two-thirds of the heritage, and if they be brethren, men and women, unto the male is the equivalent of the share of two females. Allah expoundeth unto you, so that ye err not. Allah is Knower of all things.

Surah V. The Table

In the name of Allah, the Beneficent, the Merciful.

5.   This day are (all) good things made lawful for you. The food of those who have received the Scripture is lawful for you, and your food is lawful for them. And so are the virtuous women of the believers and the virtuous women of those who received the Scripture before you (lawful for you) when ye give them their marriage portions and live with them in honour, not in fornication, nor taking them as secret concubines. Whoso denieth the faith, his work is vain and he will be among the losers in the Hereafter.

6.   O ye who believe! When ye rise up for prayer, wash your faces, and your hands up to the elbows, and lightly rub your heads and (wash) your feet up to the ankles. And if ye are unclean, purify yourselves. And if ye are sick or on a journey, or one of you cometh from the closet, or ye have had contact with women, and ye find not water, then go to clean, high ground and rub your faces and your hands with some of it. Allah would not place a burden on you, but He would purify you and would perfect His grace upon you, that ye may give thanks.

Surah XXIV. Light

An-Nur, "Light," takes its name from vv. 35–40, descriptive of the Light of God as it should shine in the homes of believers, the greater part of the Surah being legislation for the purifying of home life. All its verses were revealed at Al-Madinah. Tradition says that vv. 11–20 relate to the slanderers of Ayeshah [the Prophet's wife] in connection with an incident which occurred in the fifth year of the Hijrah when the Prophet was returning from the campaign against the Bani'l-Mustaliq, Ayeshah, having been left behind on a march, and found and brought back by a young soldier who let her mount his camel and himself led the camel. A weaker tradition places the revelation of vv. 1–10 as late as the ninth year of the Hijrah.

The period of revelation is the fifth and sixth years of the Hijrah.

In the name of Allah, the Beneficent, the Merciful.

2.   The adulterer and the adulteress, scourge ye each one of them (with) a hundred stripes. And let not pity for the twain withhold you from obedience to Allah, if ye believe in Allah and the Last Day. And let a party of believers witness their punishment.

3.   The adulterer shall not marry save an adulteress or an idolater. All that is forbidden unto believers.

4.	And those who accuse honourable women but bring not four witnesses, scourge them (with) eighty stripes and never (afterward) accept their testimony—They indeed are evildoers.

5.	Save those who afterward repent and make amends. (For such) lo! Allah is Forgiving, Merciful.

6.	As for those who accuse their wives but have no witnesses except themselves; let the testimony of one of them be four testimonies, (swearing) by Allah that he is of those who speak the truth;

7.	And yet a fifth, invoking the curse of Allah on him if he is of those who lie.

8.	And it shall avert the punishment from her if she bear witness before Allah four times that the thing he saith is indeed false,

9.	And a fifth (time) that the wrath of Allah be upon her if he speaketh truth.

10.	And had it not been for the grace of Allah and His mercy unto you, and that Allah is Clement, Wise, (ye had been undone).

11.	Lo! they who spread the slander are a gang among you. Deem it not a bad thing for you; nay, it is good for you. Unto every man of them (will be paid) that which he hath earned of the sin; and as for him among them who had the greater share therein, his will be an awful doom.

12.	Why did not the believers, men and women, when ye heard it, think good of their own folk, and say: It is a manifest untruth?

13.	Why did they not produce four witnesses? Since they produce not witnesses, they verily are liars in the sight of Allah.

14.	Had it not been for the grace of Allah and His mercy unto you in the world and the Hereafter an awful doom had overtaken you for that whereof you murmured.

15.	When ye welcomed it with your tongues, and uttered with your mouths that whereof ye had no knowledge, ye counted it a trifle. In the sight of Allah it is very great.

16.	Wherefor, when ye heard it, said ye not: It is not for us to speak of this. Glory be to Thee (O Allah); This is awful calumny.

17.	Allah admonisheth you that ye repeat not the like thereof ever, if ye are (in truth) believers.

19.	Lo! those who love that slander should be spread concerning those who believe, theirs will be a painful punishment in the world and the Hereafter. Allah knoweth. Ye know not.

23.	Lo! as for those who traduce virtuous, believing women (who are) careless, cursed are they in the world and the Hereafter. Theirs will be an awful doom.

24.	On the day when their tongues and their hands and their feet testify against them as to what they used to do,

25.   On that day Allah will pay them their just due, and they will know that Allah, He is the Manifest Truth.

26.   Vile women are for vile men, and vile men for vile women. Good women are for good men, and good men for good women; such are innocent of that which people say: For them is pardon and a bountiful provision.

27.   O ye who believe! Enter not houses other than your own without first announcing your presence and invoking peace upon the folk thereof. That is better for you, that ye may be heedful.

30.   Tell the believing men to lower their gaze and be modest. That is purer for them. Lo! Allah is Aware of what they do.

31.   And tell the believing women to lower their gaze and be modest, and to display of their adornment only that which is apparent, and to draw their veils over their bosoms, and not to reveal their adornment save to their own husbands or fathers or husbands' fathers, or their sons or their husbands' sons, or their brothers or their brothers' sons or sisters' sons, or their women, or their slaves, or male attendants who lack vigour, or children who know naught of women's nakedness. And let them not stamp their feet so as to reveal what they hide of their adornment. And turn unto Allah together, O believers, in order that ye may succeed.

32.   And marry such of you as are solitary and the pious of your slaves and maid-servants. If they be poor, Allah will enrich them of His bounty. Allah is of ample means, Aware.

33.   And let those who cannot find a match keep chaste till Allah give them independence by His grace. And such of your slaves as seek a writing (of emancipation), write it for them if ye are aware of aught of good in them, and bestow upon them of the wealth of Allah which He hath bestowed upon you. Force not your slave-girls to whoredom that ye may seek enjoyment of the life of the world, if they would preserve their chastity. And if one force them, then (unto them), after their compulsion, Lo! Allah will be Forgiving, Merciful.

58.   O ye who believe! Let your slaves, and those of you who have not come to puberty, ask leave of you at three times (before they come into your presence): Before the prayer of dawn, and when ye lay aside your raiment for the heat of noon, and after the prayer of night.[1] Three times of privacy for you. It is no sin for them or for you at other times, when some of you go round attendant upon others (if they come into your presence without leave). Thus Allah maketh clear the revelations for you. Allah is Knower, Wise.

59.   And when the children among you come to puberty then let them ask leave even as those before them used to ask it. Thus Allah maketh clear His revelations for you. Allah is Knower, Wise.

60.   As for women past child-bearing, who have no hope of marriage, it is no sin for them if they discard their (outer) clothing in such a way as not to show adornment. But to refrain is better for them. Allah is Hearer, Knower.

61.   No blame is there upon the blind nor any blame upon the lame nor any blame upon the sick nor on yourselves if ye eat from your houses, or the houses of your fathers, or the houses of your mothers, or the houses of your brothers, or the houses of your sisters, or the houses of your fathers' brothers, or the houses of your fathers' sisters, or the houses of your mothers' brothers, or the houses of your mothers' sisters, or (from that) whereof ye hold the keys, or (from the house) of a friend. No sin shall it be for you whether ye eat together or apart. But when ye enter houses, salute one another with a greeting from Allah, blessed and sweet. Thus Allah maketh clear His revelations for you, that haply ye may understand.

Surah XXXIII. The Clans

In v. 37 the reference is to the unhappy marriage of Zeyd, the Prophet's freedman and adopted son, with Zeynab, the Prophet's cousin, a proud lady of Qureysh. The Prophet had arranged the marriage with the idea of breaking down the old barrier of pride of caste, and had shown but little consideration for Zeynab's feelings. Tradition says that both she and her brother were averse to the match, and that she had always wished to marry the Prophet. For Zeyd, the marriage was nothing but a cause of embarrassment and humiliation. When the Prophet's attention was first called to their unhappiness, he urged Zeyd to keep his wife and not divorce her, being apprehensive of the talk that would arise if it became known that a marriage arranged by him had proved unhappy. At last, Zeyd did actually divorce Zeynab, and the Prophet was commanded to marry her in order, by his example, to disown the superstitious custom of the pagan Arabs, in such matters, of treating their adopted sons as their real sons, which was against the laws of God (i.e. the laws of nature); whereas in arranging a marriage, the woman's inclinations ought to be considered. Unhappy marriage was no part of Allah's ordinance, and was not to be held sacred in Islam.

The Surah contains further references to the wives of the Prophet in connection with which it may be mentioned that from the age of twenty-five till the age of fifty he had only one wife, Khadijah, fifteen years his senior, to whom he was devotedly attached and whose memory he cherished till his dying day. With the exception of Ayeshah, the daughter of his closest friend, Abu Bakr, whom he married at her father's request when she was still a child, all his later marriages were with widows whose state was pitiable for one reason or another. Some of them were widows of men killed in war. One was a captive, when he made the marriage the excuse for emancipating all the conquered tribe and restoring their property. Two were daughters of his enemies, and his alliance with them was a cause of peace. It is noteworthy that the period of these marriages was also the period of his greatest activity, when he had little rest from campaigning, and was always busy with the problems of a growing empire.

The period of revelation is between the end of the fifth and the end of the seventh years of the Hijrah.

In the name of Allah, the Beneficent, the Merciful.

4.   Allah hath not assigned unto any man two hearts within his body, nor hath he made your wives whom ye declare (to be your mothers) your mothers, nor hath he made those whom ye claim (to be your sons) your sons. This is but a saying of your mouths. But Allah sayeth the truth and He showeth the way.

5.   Proclaim their real parentage. That will be more equitable in the sight of Allah. And if ye know not their fathers, then (they are) your brethren in the faith, and your clients. And there is no sin for you in the mistakes that ye make unintentionally, but what your hearts purpose (that will be a sin for you). Allah is Forgiving, Merciful.

6.   The Prophet is closer to the believers than their selves, and his wives are (as) their mothers. And the owners of kinship are closer one to another in the ordinance of Allah than (other) believers, and the fugitives (who fled from Mecca), except that ye should do kindness to your friends. This is written in the Book (of nature).

28.   O Prophet! Say unto thy wives: If ye desire the world's life and its adornment, come! I will content you and will release you with a fair release.

29.   But if ye desire Allah and His messenger and the abode of the Hereafter, then lo! Allah hath prepared for the good among you an immense reward.

30.   O ye wives of the Prophet! Whosoever of you committeth manifest lewdness, the punishment for her will be doubled, and that is easy for Allah.

31. And whosoever of you is submissive unto Allah and His messenger and doeth right, We shall give her reward twice over, and We
have prepared for her a rich provision.

32. O ye wives of the Prophet! Ye are not like any other women.
If ye keep your duty (to Allah), then be not soft of speech, lest he in
whose heart is a disease aspire (to you), but utter customary speech.

33. And stay in your houses. Bedizen not yourselves with the
bedizenment of the Time of Ignorance. Be regular in prayer, and pay the
poor-due, and obey Allah and His messenger, Allah's wish is but to
remove uncleanliness far from you, O Folk of the Household, and
cleanse you with a thorough cleansing.

34. And bear in mind that which is recited in your houses of the
revelations of Allah and wisdom. Lo! Allah is Subtile, Aware.

35. Lo! Men who surrender unto Allah, and women who surrender,
and men who believe and women who believe, and men who obey and
women who obey, and men who speak the truth and women who speak
the truth, and men who persevere (in righteousness) and women who
persevere, and men who are humble and women who are humble, and
men who give alms and women who give alms, and men who fast and
women who fast, and men who guard their modesty and women who
guard (their modesty), and men who remember Allah much and women
who remember—Allah hath prepared for them forgiveness and a vast
reward.

36. And it becometh not a believing man or a believing woman,
when Allah and His messenger have decided an affair (for them), that
they should (after that) claim any say in their affair; and whoso is
rebellious to Allah and His messenger, he verily goeth astray in error
manifest.

37. And when thou saidst unto him on whom Allah hath conferred
favour and thou hast conferred favour: Keep thy wife to thyself, and fear
Allah. And thou didst hide in thy mind that which Allah was to bring to
light, and thou didst fear mankind whereas Allah had a better right that
thou shouldst fear Him. So when Zeyd had performed the necessary
formality (of divorce) from her, We gave her unto thee in marriage, so
that (henceforth) there may be no sin for believers in respect of wives of
their adopted sons, when the latter have performed the necessary formality (of release) from them. The commandment of Allah must be
fulfilled.

49. O ye who believe! If ye wed believing women and divorce them
before ye have touched them, then there is no period that ye should
reckon. But content them and release them handsomely.

50.   O Prophet! Lo! We have made lawful unto thee thy wives unto whom thou hast paid their dowries, and those whom thy right hand possesseth of those whom Allah hath given thee as spoils of war, and the daughters of thine uncle on the father's side and the daughters of thine aunts on the father's side, and the daughters of thine uncles on the mother's side and the daughters of thine aunts on the mother's side who emigrated with thee, and a believing woman if she give herself unto the Prophet and the Prophet desire to ask her in marriage—a privilege for thee only, not for the (rest of) believers—We are aware of that which We enjoined upon them concerning their wives and those whom their right hands possess—that thou mayst be free from blame, for Allah is Forgiving, Merciful.

51.   Thou canst defer whom thou wilt of them and receive unto thee whom thou wilt, and whomsoever thou desirest of those whom thou hast set aside (temporarily), it is no sin for thee (to receive her again); that is better; that they may be comforted and not grieve, and may all be pleased with what thou givest them. Allah knoweth what is in your hearts (O men) and Allah is Forgiving, Clement.

52.   It is not allowed thee to take (other) women henceforth, nor that thou shouldst change them for other wives even though their beauty pleased thee, save those whom thy right hand possesseth. And Allah is Watcher over all things.

53.   O ye who believe! Enter not the dwellings of the Prophet for a meal without waiting for the proper time, unless permission be granted you. But if ye are invited, enter, and, when your meal is ended, then disperse. Linger not for conversation. Lo! that would cause annoyance to the Prophet, and he would be shy of (asking) you (to go); but Allah is not shy of the truth. And when ye ask of them (the wives of the Prophet) anything, ask it of them from behind a curtain. That is purer for your hearts and for their hearts. And it is not for you to cause annoyance to the messenger of Allah, nor that ye should ever marry his wives after him. Lo! that in Allah's sight would be an enormity.

54.   Whether ye divulge a thing or keep it hidden, lo! Allah is ever Knower of all things.

55.   It is no sin for them (thy wives) (to converse freely) with their fathers, or their sons, or their brothers, or their brothers' sons, or the sons of their sisters or of their own women, or their slaves. O women! Keep your duty to Allah. Lo! Allah is Witness over all things.

58.   And those who malign believing men and believing women undeservedly, they bear the guilt of slander and manifest sin.

59.   O Prophet! Tell thy wives and thy daughters and the women of the believers to draw their cloaks close around them (when they go abroad). That will be better, that so they may be recognised and not annoyed. Allah is ever Forgiving, Merciful.

73.   So Allah punisheth hypocritical men and hypocritical women, and idolatrous men and idolatrous women. But Allah pardoneth believing men and believing women, and Allah is ever Forgiving, Merciful.

Surah LX. She Who Is to be Examined

Al-Mumtahanah, "She who is to be Examined," takes its name from v. 10, where the believers are told to examine women who come to them as fugitives from the idolators and, if they find them sincere converts to Al-Islam, not to return them to the idolators. This marked a modification in the terms of the Truce of Hudeybiyah, by which the Prophet had engaged to return all fugitives, male and female, while the idolators were not obliged to give up renegades from Al-Islam. The more terrible prosecution which women had to undergo, if extradited, and their helpless social condition were the causes of the change. Instead of giving up women refugees who were sincere and not fugitives on account of crime or some family quarrel, the Muslims were to pay an indemnity for them; while as for Muslim husbands whose wives might flee to Qureysh, no indemnity was to be paid by the latter but, when some turn of fortune brought wealth to the Islamic State, they were to be repaid by the State what their wives had taken of their property. In v. 12 is the pledge which was to be taken from the women refugees after their examination.

The date of revelation is the eighth year of the Hijrah.

In the name of Allah, the Beneficent, the Merciful.

10.   O ye who believe! When believing women come unto you as fugitives, examine them. Allah is best aware of their faith. Then, if ye know them for true believers, send them not back unto the disbelievers. They are not lawful for the disbelievers, nor are the disbelievers lawful for them. And give the disbelievers that which they have spent (upon them). And it is no sin for you to marry such women when ye have given them their dues. And hold not to the ties of disbelieving women; and ask for (the return of) that which ye have spent; and let the disbelievers ask for that which they have spent. That is the judgement of Allah. He judgeth between you. Allah is Knower, Wise.

11. And if any of your wives have gone from you unto the disbelievers and afterward ye have your turn (of triumph), then give unto those whose wives have gone the like of that which they have spent, and, keep your duty to Allah in whom ye are believers.

12. O Prophet! If believing women come unto thee, taking oath of allegiance unto thee that they will ascribe nothing as partner unto Allah, and will neither steal nor commit adultery nor kill their children, nor produce any lie that they have devised between their hands and feet, nor disobey thee in what is right,[2] then accept their allegiance and ask Allah to forgive them. Lo! Allah is Forgiving, Merciful.

Notes

1. The prayer to be offered when the night has fully come.
2. This is called the woman's oath of allegiance. It was the oath extracted from men also until the second pact of Al-Aqabah when the duty of defense was added to the men's oath.

References

Arberry, Arthur J. *The Koran Interpreted*. Paperback. New York: Macmillan, 1964.

Bell, Richard. *Introduction to the Qur'an*. Rev. ed. New York: Aldine, 1958.

Dawood, N. J. *The Koran*. Classic series. Paperback. London: Penguin, n.d.

3

'A'ish

Wife c

ca. A.D. 613–678

Biographical Sketch by the Editors
Hadith Translated and Notes Prepared by Susan Spectorsky

'A'ishah bint Abi Bakr is well known as the favorite wife of the Prophet Muhammad's later years, and the important role she played in his life made her an influential figure in the early development of the Islamic community.

Muhammad's first wife, Khadijah, was a wealthy widow of Mecca who had married him when he was an orphaned and relatively unknown young man. She was the first to believe in his message and his prophethood and, during her lifetime, he took no other wives. She died in 619 or 620, by which time Muhammad had converted a number of followers to the new religion of Islam and had established himself as its prophet. However, her death left him lonely and disconsolate, and he sought advice about remarrying from Khawlah bint Hakim, the wife of 'Uthman, one of his most prominent followers. She counseled him to marry Sawdah bint Zam'ah, who was recently widowed, or 'A'ishah, the daughter of his close friend and supporter Abu Bakr.

Muhammad married Sawdah and also asked for 'A'ishah's hand, but her father, Abu Bakr, had some misgivings about the marriage: as was customary at the time, 'A'ishah, though only a child of seven, had

Photo: Pilgrims around the Kaaba in Mecca

...nised in marriage to her cousin Jubair, and the Prophet
...ged man. However, Abu Bakr's misgivings were over-
...the Prophet was betrothed to the child 'A'ishah, who
...d to live with her parents.

...this point in his career, Muhammad had been so successful in
...ining adherents to Islam that many of the leading Meccans felt he was
a threat to their authority. Their hostility became so great that Muhammad decided to immigrate, with a small band of followers, to the city of
Medina. This "Hijrah" or flight, took place in A.D. 622.[1]

'A'ishah had traveled with her parents on the Hijrah and remained
with them in Medina. But in 623, when she was about ten, her marriage
to Muhammad was consummated, and she took her toys with her to her
new home. She lived in one of the small private apartments built for
members of Muhammad's family, apartments which adjoined the new
Mosque of the Prophet. Sawdah lived in one apartment, the youthful
'A'ishah in another, and soon a third wife, Hafsah bint Umar ibn-al-
Khattab, who had lost her husband in a recent battle, joined the household. A year later Muhammad married Zaynab bint Khuzaimah, also
widowed, but she died several months after the marriage. Then came
Hind, Umm Salamah, as the Prophet's fourth living wife.

Muhammad divided his days and nights equally among his wives, but
'A'ishah seems to have emerged gradually, as she matured, as his
favorite. Several of the traditions, or sayings of the Prophet and his
followers, indicate this, as well as the fact that 'A'ishah's special place in
Muhammad's heart was recognized by his other wives.[2]

'A'ishah said, "When Muhammad wanted to travel, he would draw
lots among his wives and take the winner with him." Further, he
would parcel out his time among his wives equally, spending a day
and night with each of them except Sawdah; for she had given her
turn to 'A'ishah, hoping thereby to please Muhammad.[3]

Umm Salamah said, "My companion wives asked me to speak to
Muhammad so that he would order the believers to give him their
gifts wherever he happened to be, rather than arrange to give him
gifts on 'A'ishah's 'day,'[4] for we are just as worthy as she is. I said
all this to Muhammad who was silent and didn't answer. I reported
this to my companion wives who urged me to try again. I did
several times, and finally Muhammad said, 'Don't trouble me about
'A'ishah. She is the only one of my wives in whose house I receive
revelations.' "[5]

She said, "I seek refuge from Allah for vexing you about 'A'ishah."[6]

Like any good wife, 'A'ishah was sensitive to her husband's moods and did not hesitate to tell him what she thought; he responded in the same fashion:

'A'ishah said that Muhammad said, "I can tell when you are angry and when you are pleased."
She said, "How do you know that, O Messenger of Allah?"
He said, "When you are angry, you say, 'O Muhammad,' and when you are pleased you say, 'O Messenger of Allah.' "[7]

However, 'A'ishah was not always perfect in her behavior, either, as the following tradition testifies:

A prisoner was brought to Muhammad, but I paid no attention to him and he escaped. When Muhammad came in he said, "What happened to the prisoner?"
I said, "I was preoccupied with the women and he escaped."
"What is the matter with you?" exclaimed Muhammad. "May Allah cut off your hand!" Then he went out and gave orders that the prisoner should be sought after and returned. After the prisoner was brought back, Muhammad came in and found me examining my hands. He said, "What is the matter with you? Have you gone mad?"
I said, "You cursed me, so I am examining my hands, wondering which one of them will be cut off."
Then he praised and extolled Allah and raised his hands high, saying, "O Allah, I am only human. I get angry like any other human. Let me atone for any believer I may have cursed."[8]

By about the fifth year of the Hijrah, Muhammad's position as both leader and prophet seems to have been assured. An increasing number of visitors, of all classes and types, came to the mosque to see him and often spoke to the wives when they could not find the Prophet himself. In this rather informal atmosphere, some of the less enthusiastic adherents to Muhammad's cause, those known as the *munafiqun* or "hypocrites," were alleged to have insulted Muhammad's wives. When they were chided for their rudeness, they excused themselves by saying that they had mistaken Muhammad's women for slaves. As a result of such goings on, the Prophet was urged by many to seclude his women.

Many reasons are given for the *hijab,* or seclusion, of the Prophet's wives behind a curtain, but, as Nabia Abbott tells us, "As prophet-king it was not surprising, that [Muhammad] . . . adopted some measure of personal and family exclusiveness in the rough-and-tumble democracy of his day."[9] Seclusion and some form of veiling were not unknown among the upper classes before the time of Muhammad, and perhaps the followers of the Prophet felt his women should now be placed in an honored category, which would indicate their difference from others. For whatever reasons, the *hijab* was instituted, and "Muhammad's wives found themselves, on the one hand, deprived of personal liberty and, on the other hand, raised to a position of honor and dignity."[10]

The custom was legitimized for all time in the Koran (Surah XXXIII, verse 59): "O Prophet! Tell thy wives and thy daughters and the women of the believers to draw their cloaks close around them (when they go abroad). That will be better, so that they may be recognized and not annoyed. Allah is ever Forgiving, Merciful . . ."[11]

It is in this setting that we must view one of the great crises of 'A'ishah's life, the incident known as the "affair of the slander." Traveling in a closed litter placed on camelback, 'A'ishah had accompanied Muhammad on an expedition against the tribe of the Banu al-Mustaliq. Early one morning, when the group stopped on its way back to Medina, 'A'ishah walked away from the camp to perform her ablutions. When she returned, she found that she had lost her necklace of Yemeni beads and went back to look for it. But she had left the curtains of the litter closed, and Muhammad, thinking her inside and ready to go, gave the signal to depart. When 'A'ishah came back, she found that she had been left behind and sat down on the ground to wait until her absence was noticed and someone sent back for her. Meanwhile, a young man, Safwan ibn al-Mu'ttal, came by on his own way to Medina. Seeing 'A'ishah alone, he offered her his camel, and she accepted; the young man led the camel. The sight of 'A'ishah, favorite wife of the Prophet, arriving in the city in the company of a handsome young man gave rise to much gossip and ultimately a great many accusations.

Some of the Prophet's enemies and rivals accused 'A'ishah of improper behavior and some even whispered that, since Safwan was young and handsome, 'A'ishah preferred his attentions to those of the aging Prophet.

This period seems not to have been a good one for Muhammad in any sense. He was personally upset because he had not received any revelations for some time, he had many enemies, and the community of Muslims at Medina was not as peaceful and unified as he had wished.

Obviously the "affair of the slander" was being used to discredit not only 'A'ishah but also the Prophet himself. The Prophet consulted several people to see what should be done. His son-in-law, 'Ali, urged him to repudiate 'A'ishah; Samat, son of the Prophet's own adopted son, praised 'A'ishah and tried to convince Muhammad of her innocence. 'A'ishah herself was terribly upset, as she records:

I despaired and became ill, so I asked Muhammad to send me to my father's house. He sent a slave with me. When I entered I found Umm Ruman ['A'ishah's mother], who asked what had happened. I told her and she said, "Calm yourself. Seldom is a beautiful woman who is beloved by her husband not envied by her fellow wives and not spoken ill of by them!" I asked if my father knew. She said he did and that Muhammad knew too. Then I wept copiously.

Abu Bakr who was upstairs reading heard my voice and came down to ask my mother what the matter with me was. She said, "She has heard what is being said about her." Then his eyes filled and he said, "I urge you to return to your house."

So I returned and he and my mother came with me and remained with me until Muhammad came in after the afternoon prayer. He bore witness that there was no God but Allah and praised and extolled Him. Then he said to me, " 'A'ishah, if you have been tempted to evil or done wrong, repent; for Allah accepts repentance from his servants."

Meanwhile, a woman of the Ansar had come and seated herself in the doorway and I said, "Aren't you shy of speaking of the matter in front of this woman?" Then I said to my father, "Answer," but he said, "What shall I say?" I appealed to my mother, but she too was at a loss.

Then I bore witness that there was no God but Allah and praised and extolled Him and said: "If I said that I had done nothing and Allah knows that I would be telling the truth, you would not believe me for you already think me guilty. If I said I were guilty and Allah knows I am not, you would say I had confessed. Thus, all I can do is cite Joseph's father: 'My course must be fitting patience, and Allah's help is to be sought for the problem you describe.' "

Then Muhammad received a revelation after which I perceived joy on his face. He wiped his forehead and said, "Rejoice 'A'ishah, Allah has revealed your innocence."

I became as angry as possible. My parents said I should get up and go to Muhammad, but I said, "I shall neither go to him nor praise him nor you who believed what you heard about me and did not deny it. I shall praise Allah who revealed my innocence."

Before this [i.e., the revelation], Muhammad had come to my house and asked a slavegirl about me. She said, ". . . By Allah, I know of her purity the way the goldsmith knows of the purity of nuggets."[12]

The revelation which Muhammad received at the time of 'A'ishah's crisis is contained in the Koran; in effect, it established the religious law which is used to this day in dealing with accusations of adultery. "And those who accuse honourable women but bring not four witnesses, scourge them (with) eighty stripes and never (afterward) accept their testimony—They are indeed evildoers" (Surah XXIV, verse 4).[13] Muhammad implemented this verse immediately by flogging publicly three of the men who had been active in spreading gossip during the "affair of the slander."

As the years passed, 'A'ishah bore no children, a source of great sadness to her. Women who were barren often fostered children, taking them into their homes, educating or supporting them; some of these children were identified with their foster mothers, and their foster mothers with them. For women, as they matured and bore children, were known then, as they are now in Islamic countries, not only by their name given at birth but also by their *kunyah,* or mother designation, Umm So-and-so (Mother of so-and-so). 'A'ishah complained to Muhammad one day about this and asked him to designate a foster child for her.

'A'ishah said to Muhammad, "Each of your wives has a *kunyah* except me."

He said, "Take the *kunyah* of Umm Abd Allah."[14]

Then she was called Umm Abd Allah until she died. She never had any children of her own.[15]

Despite the fact that Muhammad had many wives during this period, he never tired of praising his first wife, Khadijah. This was a source of annoyance to 'A'ishah.

Whenever Muhammad mentioned Khadijah, he used to heap praises upon her. Once I became jealous and said, "How often you mention that old woman! Allah has replaced her with better!"

Muhammad said, "Indeed, He has not replaced her with better.

She had faith in me and believed in me when no one else did, and she shared her worldly goods with me when everyone else scorned me, and Allah has granted me her offspring and no other woman's."[16]

Muhammad seems always to have been a kind and considerate husband, solicitous for all of his wives' comfort; but jealousies did exist and incidents between the women at one point were so numerous and unpleasant they became almost too much for him. He retired to be alone, to contemplate and meditate. Rumors spread that Muhammad was about to divorce all his wives, which filled the whole community of believers, and especially the women of his household, with great alarm. However, at the end of the period of meditation, Muhammad reappeared, and the first "day" was that of 'A'ishah. He is supposed to have then repeated to her what has become known as the "Verse of the Choice."[17]

Muhammad said, " 'A'ishah, I want to present a matter to you that I don't want you to act upon without consulting your parents, Abu Bakr and Umm Ruman." [In the original of this tradition, the first is quoted several times to impress upon 'A'ishah the gravity of the situation.]
    'A'ishah said, "What is it?"
    "Allah has said to me, 'O Prophet, say to your wives, "If you desire the life of the world and its embellishments, then come and I will compensate you and release you honorably, but if you desire Allah and his Prophet and the life of the hereafter, then Allah will prepare for the chaste among you a great reward." ' "
    She said, "I want Allah and His messenger and the hereafter. I don't need to consult my parents."
    She said that Muhammad laughed and went to his other wives and told them what 'A'ishah had answered. They all agreed with her.[18]

At the end of his life, shortly before his death, the Prophet's preference and fondness for 'A'ishah reasserted itself.

When the Prophet became seriously ill, he said, "Where should I be tomorrow?"
    They said, "With so and so [whichever wife's turn it was]."
    He said, "And the day after tomorrow?"

They said, "With so and so."

Then his wives knew that he wanted 'A'ishah, so they said, "O messenger of Allah, we give our days to our sister 'A'ishah."[19]

'A'ishah said, "When Muhammad became seriously ill and his pain worsened, he asked permission from his wives that he be nursed in my house. They granted him that . . ."[20]

He died in 'A'ishah's arms in June, A.D. 632. After some controversy over where he was to be buried, Abu Bakr, 'A'ishah's father, recalled that Muhammad had said a prophet is buried where he expires.[21] He was accordingly buried beneath 'A'ishah's house.

'A'ishah was eighteen when Muhammad died. She lived on to become a powerful force in the emerging political situation following the death of the Prophet, who left no male heir. How is it that she alone managed to maintain a position of power, even after the Prophet's death, when this was not true of his other wives? Of course, her father, Abu Bakr, became the first orthodox caliph of Islam and reigned for two years, from A.D. 632 to 634, and this helped to continue his daughter's position. Another reason often given for 'A'ishah's influence on the affairs of the Islamic state, in addition to her obvious personal magnetism and her reputation as the Prophet's favorite wife, is her learning and intelligence.[22] Since it was known that the Prophet received revelations in her presence, she was often called upon for advice even while the Prophet was alive. After his death, people would consult her in matters regarding the Prophet, asking her to interpret traditions and sayings which she had recorded. Gradually, she became an authority on traditions, and this gave her an intellectual position in the new community of Islam which few women could rival.

She was important behind the scenes but also publicly, as in her active role in the "Battle of the Camel." This ill-fated excursion took place between two opposing groups: the forces of the Prophet's son-in-law, 'Ali, who had been elected caliph following the death of Abu Bakr and 'Uthman ('Ali is supposed to have arranged 'Uthman's murder) and the forces of Talhah and al-Zubayr, who, with 'A'ishah, had supported the now deceased 'Uthman. 'Ali's army triumphed, but it was not a lasting victory. 'A'ishah continued to be a rallying point for the opposing group, who emerged as the sect known as Sunni Muslims. 'Ali's forces eventually became the Shi'ite sect of Islam. Many believe that 'A'ishah's opposition to 'Ali, and the subsequent split in Islam, may be traced back to the "affair of the slander"; it is said that 'A'ishah never forgave 'Ali for advising the Prophet to repudiate her.

At any rate, 'A'ishah's place in Islamic history is secure. She was nearly sixty-five when she died. She lives on in the accounts of Muhammad's life and the later political developments in the community, as well as in the traditions of Islam.

Notes

1.   The date of Hijrah is used as the beginning of the Islamic calendar, for it marks one of the most decisive events in Islam. The Hijrah dates throughout the manuscript are based on the tables prepared by Heinrich Ferdinand Wüstenfeld (1808–1899) which appear in *Mahler'sche Vergleichungs—Tabellen zur Muslimischen und Iranischen Zeitrechnung. Ansar* is the name given to the early Muslims of Medina who welcomed Muhammad and his followers after the Hijrah from Mecca and who helped them settle in Medina.

2.   The traditions of Islam are individually and collectively referred to as *hadith,* in Arabic. The hadith form a body of material second in importance only to the Koran. Each individual hadith consists of a story about something the Prophet or one of his followers said or did, related by a reliable chain of transmitters. The major collections of hadith were compiled in the ninth century, A.D., and are the main source of information about the early Islamic period. The hadith quoted in this selection are from two of the better known collections.

3.   Ahmad b. Muhammad Ibn Hanbal, *Musnad al-Imam Ahmad ibn Hanbal,* 6:117.

4.   It was customary for Muhammad's followers, usually referred to as believers, to bring him gifts, often of food or livestock. Because it was widely known that 'A'ishah was his favorite, the believers seemed to feel he would prefer receiving gifts on her "day."

5.   Ibn Hanbal, *Musnad,* 6:293.

6.   Ibid., 6:293; Nabia Abbott, *Aishah, the Beloved of Mohammed,* p. 46.

7.   Ibn Hanbal, *Musnad,* 6:30.

8.   Ibid., 6:52.

9.   Abbott, *Aishah,* p. 25.

10.   Ibid., p. 26.

11.   Mohammed Marmaduke Pickthall, *The Meaning of the Glorious Koran,* p. 306.

12.   Ibn Hanbal, *Musnad,* 6:60; Abbott, *Aishah,* pp. 30–35.

13.   Pickthall, *Glorious Koran,* pp. 253–254.

14.   Abd Allah was the son of 'A'ishah's own sister, Asma, and her

husband, Zubayr ibn al-'Awwam; 'A'ishah developed a very close relationship with her foster child, a motherly affection noted by many
historians and recorded in many traditions.
15.   Ibn Hanbal, *Musnad*, 6:151.
16.   Ibid., 6:117. Muhammad's children by Khadijah were four
daughters, Fatimah, Ruqayyah, Umm Kulthum, and Zaynab. He also had
two sons by Khadijah who died early. His only other son, Ibrahim, by
the Coptic slave Maryam, died early as well.
17.   Abbott, *Aishah*, pp. 55–56.
18.   Ibn Hanbal, *Musnad*, 6:212.
19.   Muhammad Ibn Sa'd, *Kitab al-Tabaqat al Kubra*, 2:233.
20.   Ibid., 2:232.
21.   Abbott, *Aishah*, p. 69.
22.   Ibid., p. 205.

References

Abbott, Nabia. *Aishah, the Beloved of Mohammed*. Chicago:
University of Chicago Press, 1942.

Gibb, H. A., and J. H. Kramers, eds. *Shorter Encyclopedia of Islam*.
Ithaca: Cornell University Press, 1953.

Ibn Hanbal, Ahmad b. Muhammed. *Musnad al-Imam Ahmad ibn
Hanbal*. Beirut: al-Maktab al-Islami lil-Tiba'ah wa-al-Nashr, 1969.

Ibn Sa'd, Muhammad. *Kitab al-Tabaqat al-Kubra*. Beirut: Dar
al-Sadir, 1957–1968.

Pickthall, Mohammed Marmaduke, trans. *The Meaning of the
Glorious Koran*. New York: New American Library, Mentor Books, 1953.

Wüstenfeld, Heinrich Ferdinand. *Mahler'sche Vergleichungs—
Tabellen zur Muslimischen und Iranischen Zeitrechnung*. Wiesbaden:
Deutsche Morgenländische Gesellschaft, 1961.

سَقَتْنِي حُمَيَّا الْحُبِّ رَاحَةُ مُقْلَتِي   وكَأْسِي مُحَيَّا مَنْ عَنِ الْحُسْنِ جَلَّتِ ١

فَأَوْهَمْتُ صَحْبِي أَنَّ شُرْبَ شَرَابِهِم   بِهِ سِرَّ سِرِّي فِي انْتِشَائِي بِنَظْرَتِي

وبِالْحَدَقِ اسْتَغْنَيْتُ عَنْ قَدَحِي ومِنْ   شَمَائِلِهَا لَا مِنْ شُمُولِي نَشْوَتِي

فَفِي حَانِ سُكْرِي حَانَ شُكْرِي لِفِتْيَةٍ   بِهِمْ تَمَّ لِي كِتْمُ الْهَوَى مَعَ شُهْرَتِي

ولَمَّا انْقَضَى صَحْوِي تَقَاضَيْتُ وَصْلَهَا   ولَمْ يَغْشَنِي فِي بَسْطِهَا قَبْضُ خَشْيَتِي ٥

4 Rabi'a the Mystic

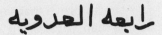

A.D. 712–801

Excerpts from *Rabi'a the Mystic and Her Fellow-Saints in Islam*
by Margaret Smith

Part One / Chapter I / Rabi'a al-'Adawiyya: Her Birth and Early Years

In the history of Islam, the woman saint made her appearance at a very
early period, and in the evolution of the cult of saints by Muslims, the
dignity of saintship was conferred on women as much as on men. As far
as rank among the "friends of God" was concerned, there was complete
equality between the sexes.

It was the development of mysticism (Sufism) within Islam, which gave
women their great opportunity to attain the rank of sainthood. The goal
of the Sufi's quest was union with the Divine, and the Sufi seeker after
God, having renounced this world and its attractions, being purged of
Self and its desires, inflamed with a passion of love to God, journeyed
ever onward, looking towards his final purpose, through the life of
illumination, with its ecstasies and raptures, and the higher life of contemplation, until at last he achieved the heavenly gnosis and attained to
the Vision of God, in which the lover might become one with the
Beloved, and abide in Him for ever.

Such a conception of the relations between the saint and his Lord left

Photo: Sufi poetry

no room for the distinction of sex. In the spiritual life there could be "neither male nor female." All whom God had called to be saints could attain, by following the Path, to union with Himself, and all who attained, would have their royal rank, as spiritual beings, in the world to come.

'Attar, to prove that saintship may be found in a woman as naturally as in a man, says:

The holy prophets have laid it down that "God does not look upon your outward forms." It is not the outward form that matters, but the inner purpose of the heart, as the Prophet said, "The people are assembled (on the Day of Judgment) according to the purposes of their hearts." . . . So also 'Abbas of Tus said that when on the Day of Resurrection the summons goes forth, "O men," the first person to set foot in that class of men (i.e. those who are to enter Paradise) will be Mary, upon whom be peace. . . . The true explanation of this fact (that women count for as much as men among the saints) is that wherever these people, the Sufis, are, they have no separate existence in the Unity of God. In the Unity, what remains of the existence of "I" or "thou"? So how can "man" or "woman" continue to be? So too, Abu 'Ali Farmadhi said, "Prophecy is the essence, the very being, of power and sublimity. Superiority and inferiority do not exist in it. Undoubtedly saintship is of the same type."

So the title of saint was bestowed upon women equally with men, and since Islam has no order of priesthood and no priestly caste, there was nothing to prevent a woman from reaching the highest religious rank in the hierarchy of Muslim saints. Some theologians even name the Lady Fatima, daughter of the Prophet, as the first *Qutb* or spiritual head of the Sufi fellowship. Below the *Qutb* were four *'Awtad'*, from whose ranks his successor was chosen, and below them, in the next rank of the hierarchy, were forty *'Abdal'* or Substitutes, who are described as being the pivot of the world and the foundation and support of the affairs of men. Jami relates how someone was asked, "How many are the 'Abdal'?" and he answered, "Forty souls," and when asked why he did not say "Forty men," his reply was, "There have been women among them." The biographies of the Muslim saints, such as those compiled by Abu Nu'aym, Farid al-Din 'Attar, Ibn al-Jawzi, Jami and Ibn Khallikan and many others, are full of the mention of women Sufis, their saintly lives, their good deeds, and their miracles. The influence which these women saints exercised both during their lives and after their deaths, is perhaps best proved by the fact that Muslim theologians, opposed to the Sufi movement, denounce also these women saints and the worship known to be given to them.

The high position attained by the women Sufis is attested further by the fact that the Sufis themselves give to a woman the first place among the earliest Muhammadan mystics and have chosen her to be the representative of the first development of mysticism in Islam.

This was the saintly Rabi'a, a freedwoman of the Al-'Atik, a tribe of Qays b. 'Adi, from which she was known as al-'Adawiyya or al-Qaysiyya, and also as al-Basriyya, from her birth-place: of whom a modern writer says, "Rabi'a is the saint par excellence of the Sunnite hagiography." Her biographer 'Attar speaks of her as

That one set apart in the seclusion of holiness, that woman veiled with the veil of religious sincerity, that one on fire with love and longing, that one enamoured of the desire to approach her Lord and be consumed in His glory, that woman who lost herself in union with the Divine, that one accepted by men as a second spotless Mary—Rabi'a al-'Adawiyya, may God have mercy upon her. If anyone were to say, "Why have you made mention of her in the class of men?" I should say . . . "God does not look upon the outward forms. . . . If it is allowable to accept two thirds of our faith from 'A'isha the Trustworthy, it is also allowable to accept religious benefit from one of her handmaids [i.e. Rabi'a]. When a woman walks in the way of God like a man, she cannot be called a woman."

A later biographer, al-Munawi, says of her:

Rabi'a al-'Adawiyya al-Qaysiyya of Basra, was at the head of the women disciples and the chief of the women ascetics, of those who observed the sacred law, who were God-fearing and zealous . . . and she was one of those who were pre-eminent and experienced in grace and goodness.

He gives the names of several well-known women saints and goes on to say, "She was the most famous among them, of great devotion and conspicuous in worship, and of perfect purity and asceticism."

Unfortunately there is no writer very near her own time to give us her biography, and for an account of her early life we can find material only in the *Memoir of the Saints* of 'Attar, already mentioned, who lived more than four hundred years after Rabi'a. Much of what he tells of her must be regarded as purely legendary. Yet though the legends which surround Rabi'a's name may not, and in many cases certainly do not, correspond to historic facts, at least they give some idea of her personality and shew the estimation in which she was held by those who lived after her and had heard of her fame.

She was born probably about A.H. 95 or 99 (= A.D. 717) in Basra, where she spent the greater part of her life.

Born into the poorest of homes, according to 'Attar (though a modern writer says she belonged to one of the noble families of Basra), miraculous events were reputed to have taken place even at the time of her birth. 'Attar tells us that on the night of her birth there was no oil in the house, no lamp nor swaddling clothes in which to wrap the new-born child. Her father already had three daughters, and so she was called Rabi'a (= the fourth). The mother asked her husband to go and ask for oil for the lamp from a neighbour, but he had made a vow that he would never ask anything of a creature (i.e. as a true Sufi he would depend only upon God to supply his needs), and so he came back without it. Having fallen asleep in great distress at the lack of provision for the child, he dreamt that the Prophet Muhammad appeared to him in his sleep and said, "Do not be sorrowful, for this daughter who is born is a great saint, whose intercession will be desired by seventy thousand of my community." The Prophet said further:

Tomorrow send a letter to 'Isa Zadhan, Amir of Basra, reminding him that every night he is wont to pray one hundred prayers to me and on Friday night four hundred, but this Friday night he has neglected me, and as a penance (tell him) that he must give you four hundred *dinars*, lawfully acquired.

Rabi'a's father awoke, weeping; he rose up, wrote the letter as directed and sent it to the Amir through the latter's chamberlain. The Amir, when he had read the letter said:

Give two thousand *dinars* to the poor as a thank-offering, because the prophet had me in mind, and four hundred *dinars* to that Shaykh and say to him that I desire that he should come before me that I may see him, but it is not fitting that such a person as he is should come to me, but I will come and rub my beard on his threshold.

But in spite of this event of good augury, 'Attar relates that misfortunes fell upon the family, and when Rabi'a was a little older, her mother and father died and she was left an orphan. A famine occurred in Basra and the sisters were scattered. One day, when Rabi'a was walking abroad, an evil-minded man saw her and seized upon her and sold her as a slave for six *dirhams* and the man who bought her made her work hard. One day a stranger (one who might not look at her unveiled) approached her. Rabi'a fled to avoid him and slipped on the road and dislocated her wrist. She bowed her face in the dust, and said, "O Lord, I am a stranger and without mother or father, an orphan and a slave and I have fallen into bondage and my wrist is injured, (yet) I am not grieved by this, only (I desire) to satisfy Thee. I would fain know if Thou art satisfied (with me) or not." She heard a voice saying, "Be not sorrowful, for on the day of Resurrection thy rank shall be such that those who are nearest to God in Heaven shall envy thee."

After this Rabi'a returned to her master's house and continually fasted in the daytime and carried out her appointed tasks and in the service of God she was standing on her feet till the day. One night her master awoke from sleep and looked down through a window of the house and saw Rabi'a, whose head was bowed in worship, and she was saying, "O my Lord, Thou knowest that the desire of my heart is to obey Thee, and that the light of my eye is in the service of Thy court. If the matter rested with me, I should not cease for one hour from Thy service, but Thou hast made me subject to a creature." While she was still praying, he saw a lamp above her head, suspended without a chain, and the whole house was illuminated by the rays from that light. This enveloping radiance or *sakina* (derived from the Hebrew Shekina = the cloud of glory indicating the presence of God) of the Muslim saint, corresponding to the halo of the Christian saint, is frequently mentioned in the biographies of the Sufis.

Rabi'a's master, when he saw that strange sight, was afraid and rose up and returned to his own place and sat pondering until day came. When the day dawned, he called Rabi'a and spoke kindly to her and set her free. Rabi'a asked for leave to go away; so he gave her leave, and she left that place and journeyed into the desert. Afterwards she left the desert and obtained for herself a cell and for a time was engaged in devotional worship there. According to one account, Rabi'a at first followed the calling of a flute player, which would be consistent with a state of slavery. Then she became converted and built a place of retreat, where she occupied herself with works of piety.

Among other stories related of this period of her life, is one telling how she purposed performing the pilgrimage to Mecca and set her face towards the desert; she had an ass with her to carry her baggage, and in the heart of the desert the ass died. Some people (in the caravan) said to her, "Let us carry thy baggage." She said, "Go on your way, for I am not dependent upon you (for help)," *i.e.* she placed her trust in God and not in His creatures.

So the people went on and Rabi'a remained alone, and bowing her head, she said, "O my God, do kings deal thus with a woman, a stranger and weak? Thou art calling me to Thine own house (the Ka'ba), but in the midst of the way Thou hast suffered mine ass to die and Thou hast left me alone in the desert."

She had hardly completed her prayer, when the ass stirred and got up. Rabi'a put her baggage on it and went on her way. The narrator of this story said that some time afterwards he saw that same little ass being sold in the bazaar.

Another story tells us how she went into the desert for a few days and prayed, "O my Lord, my heart is perplexed, whither shall I go? I am but a clod of earth and that house (the Ka'ba) is only a stone to me. Shew Thyself (to me) in this very place." So she prayed until God Most High, without any medium, spoke directly within her heart, saying, "O Rabi'a . . . when Moses desired to see My Face, I cast a few particles of My Glory upon the mountain (Sinai) and it was rent into forty pieces. Be content here with My Name."

It is told how another time she was on her way to Mecca, and when half-way there she saw the Ka'ba coming to meet her and she said, "It is the Lord of the house whom I need, what have I to do with the house? I need to meet with Him Who said, 'Whoso approaches Me by a span's length I will approach him by the length of a cubit.' The Ka'ba which I see has no power over me; what joy does the beauty of the Ka'ba bring to me?"

In connection with this legend, which indicates how highly favoured by God Rabi'a was, in the eyes of her biographers, it is related that Ibrahim b. Adham spent fourteen years making his way to the Ka'ba, because in every place of prayer he performed two *raka's*, and at last when he arrived at the Ka'ba, he did not see it.

He said, "Alas, what has happened? It may be that some injury has overtaken my eyes." An unseen voice said, "No harm has befallen your eyes, but the Ka'ba has gone to meet a woman, who is approaching this place." Ibrahim was seized with jealousy, and said, "O indeed, who is this?" He ran and saw Rabi'a arriving and the Ka'ba was back in its own place. When Ibrahim saw that, he said, "O Rabi'a, what is this disturbance and trouble and burden which thou hast brought into the world?" She said ,"I have not brought disturbance into the world, it is you who have disturbed the world, because you delayed fourteen years in arriving at the Ka'ba." He said, "Yes I have spent fourteen years in crossing the desert (because I was engaged) in prayer." Rabi'a said, "You traversed it in ritual prayer (*namaz*) but I with personal supplication (*niyaz*)." Then, having performed the pilgrimage, she returned to Basra and occupied herself with works of devotion.

For these early years only legends are available, but they give us a clear idea of a woman renouncing the world and its attractions and giving up her life to the service of God, the first step on the mystic Way to be trodden by the Sufi saint.

Chapter II / Rabi'a's Choice of Celibacy: Her Associates

Rabi'a al-'Adawiyya received many offers of marriage, but rejected them all, feeling that in the celibate life only could she pursue her quest unhindered. Among those who sought her hand in marriage was 'Abd al-Wahid b. Zayd, who was renowned for his asceticism and the sanctity of his life, a theologian and a preacher and an advocate of solitude for those who sought the way to God; the reputed writer of verses declaring that

The Ways are various, the Way to the Truth is one,
Those who travel on the way of Truth must keep themselves apart.

He was the founder of one of the first monastic communities near Basra, and died in A.D. 793. Rabi'a did not welcome his offer but shunned him with the greatest loathing, and said to him, "O sensual one, seek another sensual like thyself. Hast thou seen any sign of desire in me?"

Another who sought her hand was Muhammad b. Sulayman al-Hashimi, the 'Abbasid Amir of Basra from A.H. 145, who died in A.H. 172. He offered a dowry of a hundred thousand *dinars* and wrote to Rabi'a that he had an income of ten thousand *dinars* a month and that he would bestow it all on her, but she wrote back, "It does not please me that you should be my slave and that all you possess should be mine, or that you should distract me from God for a single moment."

Another account of this offer says that the governor wrote to the people of Basra asking them to find him a wife, and they agreed upon Rabi'a, and when he wrote to her expressing his wishes, her reply was as follows:

Renunciation of this world means peace, while desire for it brings sorrow. Curb your desires and control yourself and do not let others control you, but let them share your inheritance and the anxiety of the age. As for yourself, give your mind to the day of death; but as for me, God can give me all you offer and even double it. It does not please me to be distracted from Him for a single moment. So farewell.

Another story tells how Hasan of Basra, with whom the legends persistently associate her (though he died more than seventy years before her death), and others are also said to have come to Rabi'a, urging her to take a husband, and to choose from among the Sufis of Basra whom she would. She replied, "Yes, willingly. Who is the most learned of you, that I may marry him?" They said, "Hasan of Basra," so she said to him, "If you can give me the answer to four questions, I will be your wife." He said, "Ask, and if God permit, I will answer you."

She said then, "What will the Judge of the world say when I die? That I have come out of the world a Muslim or an unbeliever?"

Hasan answered, "This is among the hidden things, which are known only to God Most High."

Then she said, "When I am put in the grave and Munkar and Nakir question me, shall I be able to answer them (satisfactorily) or not?" He replied, "This also is hidden."

She said next, "When the people are assembled at the Resurrection and the books are distributed, and some are given their book in the right hand and some in the left, shall I be given mine in my right hand or my left?" He could only say, "This also is among the hidden things."

Finally she asked, "When mankind is summoned (on the Day of Judgment), some to Paradise and some to Hell, in which of the two groups shall I be?" He answered as before, "This, too, is hidden, and none knows what is hidden save God, His is the glory and majesty."

Then she said to him, "Since this is so, and I have these four questions with which to concern myself, how should I need a husband, with whom to be occupied?"

She is said to have emphasized her refusal with the following beautiful lines, but they cannot be attributed to her with any certainty:

My peace, O my brothers, is in solitude,
And my Beloved is with me alway,
For His love I can find no substitute,
And His love is the test for me among mortal beings,
When-e'er His Beauty I may contemplate,
He is my "mihrab," towards Him is my "qibla"
If I die of love, before completing satisfaction,
Alas, for my anxiety in the world, alas for my distress,
O Healer (of souls) the heart feeds upon its desire,
The striving after union with Thee has healed my soul,
O my Joy and my Life abidingly,
Thou wast the source of my life and from Thee also came
    my ecstasy.
I have separated myself from all created beings,
My hope is for union with Thee, for that is the goal of my desire.

This story is given in more than one account, and though chronologically it is almost impossible that Hasan of Basra should be the suitor in the case, it is possible that it refers to some other offer of marriage.

Another legend also gives an account of an offer said to have been made by Hasan of Basra, in which the same feeling is evident in Rabi'a's answer. Hasan is reputed to have said, "I desire that we should marry and be betrothed." Her reply was:

The contract of marriage is for those who have a phenomenal existence (*i.e.* who are concerned with the affairs of this material world). Here (*i.e.* in my case) existence has ceased, since I have ceased to exist and have passed out of Self. My existence is in Him, and I am altogether His. I am in the shadow of His command. The marriage contract must be asked for from Him, not from me.

So, like her Christian sisters in the life of sanctity, Rabi'a espoused a heavenly Bridegroom and turned her back on earthly marriage even with one of her own intimates and companions on the Way.

Rabi'a had many disciples and associates, who resorted to her house day and night to seek her counsel or her prayers or to listen to her teaching. As already stated, her biographers constantly associate her with Hasan of Basra, whom they portray as her disciple and follower, though he must have been so much her senior. Either her name has been introduced into anecdotes relating to Hasan, or else Hasan's name has been substituted for that of one of her own contemporaries in anecdotes which relate to her. Hasan of Basra was one of the earliest

Sufis, a saint who took the gloomiest view of life, both in this world and the next, and whose faith was overshadowed by the fear of Hell to such an extent that he even envied the man who would be saved after a thousand years in Hell, and said, "Would that I were like this man." Hasan was a learned man, eloquent and a great preacher of sermons. He was strict in ritual observances and constantly under the influence of godly sorrow. He was the author of a number of works of a theological nature, and his opinions on Sufi doctrine carried great weight with those who came after him. He died in A.D. 728.

'Attar states that if Rabi'a were not present in Hasan's assembly, he left the assembly at once.

The same writer relates that Hasan of Basra said about his relationship with Rabi'a, "I passed one whole night and day with Rabi'a speaking of the Way and the Truth, and it never passed through my mind that I was a man nor did it occur to her that she was a woman, and at the end when I looked at her, I saw myself a bankrupt [i.e. spiritually worth nothing], and Rabi'a as truly sincere."

Again, he tells a story of how once Rabi'a was passing Hasan's house and Hasan had his head out of the window and was weeping; and his tears fell on to Rabi'a's garment. She looked up, thinking it was not rain, and when she was certain that it was Hasan's tears, she at once came to him, and said, "O teacher, this weeping is from pride of self; rather weep tears (as a result) of looking into your heart, that within thee they may become a river such that within that river you will not by searching find your heart again unless you find it in the Lord of Might." Hasan, who had a sufficient opinion of himself, found that a hard saying and was silent.

Another ascetic with whom she is associated, and in this case with great probability, since he was both her contemporary and also of the same school of thought, is Rabah al-Qays of Basra, who died in A.D. 810. A modern writer, associating him with Rabi'a, says, "With these two ascetics, both of the school of Basra, the quest of the ascetic life leads to mystic states already differentiated and brings up delicate problems of casuistry and dogma." He introduced ideas of the glorious light of God (*tajalli*), of the divine friendship (*Khulla*) and of the superiority of the saint over the prophet. In the moral life, he advocated chastity, repentance and acts of piety.

Abu Nu'aym gives an anecdote which shews how her associates depended upon Rabi'a's help when faced with a difficult problem. He says that Rabah relates it thus:

I came to Abrad b. Dirar of the Bani Sa'd and he said to me, "Are

the days and nights long to you?" and I said, "Why?" He said,
"Because of your desire to meet God." Rabah said, "I was silent
and said nothing until I came to Rabi'a and said, 'Veil yourself with
your garment, for al-Abrad has asked me a question and I could say
nothing in answer to it.' " She said, "What did he ask you?" I said
to her, "He said to me, 'Are the days and nights long to you from
your desire to meet God?' " Rabi'a said to me, "And what did you
say?" I said, "I did not say 'Yes,' lest I should tell a lie, and I did not
say 'No,' lest I should debase his soul."

I heard the rending of her chemise under her cloak as she said,
"My answer is 'Yes.' "

Abu Nu'aym is also the source of a story related by Abu Bakr al-Sarraj
about Rabah and Rabi'a:

Abu Ma'mur 'Abdallah b. 'Amr said: "I saw Rabi'a with Rabah
al-Qays and he was kissing a boy belonging to his family and
embracing him and she said, 'Do you love him, O Rabah?' He said,
'Yes,' and she said, 'I did not suppose there was room in your heart
for loving any but God.' Rabah cried out and fell in a swoon; when
he recovered, he wiped the sweat from his brow and said,
'Compassion is from God Most High and He has put it into the
hearts of his servants towards little children.' "

Sufyan al-Thawri appears in all the biographies of Rabi'a as a very
intimate friend and a constant visitor at her house, and much of the
teaching attributed to her was the result of his questions or of conversation with him. He was born at Kufa in A.H. 95 (= A.D. 713–14) and
died in A.D. 778; he was therefore contemporary with Rabi'a and it is
reasonable to suppose that he would come into contact with her. He
was a great authority on the Traditions, and Rabi'a appears to have taken
him to task more than once for his devotion to them. Abu Talib relates
in this connection that Rabi'a al-'Adawiyya used to say of al-Thawri,
"Yes, Sufyan would be a (good) man, if he did not love the Traditions,"
and she used to say, "The seductive power of the Traditions is stronger
than the enticement of property and children" (i.e. the study of the
Traditions distracted him from the life with God even more than worldly
possessions would have done), and she said once, "If only Sufyan did
not love this world, that is to say the gathering of people round him for
(discourse on) the Traditions, what a good thing it would be."

The same writer relates how one day Sufyan al-Thawri said in Rabi'a's
presence, "O God, mayst Thou be satisfied with us!" and she said, "Are

you not ashamed before God to ask Him to be satisfied when you are not satisfied with Him?" and he said, "I ask forgiveness from God."

Again Sufyan, who seems to have been somewhat of a *poseur*, or at least anxious to provoke Rabi'a to retaliation, said to her, "Alas, for my sorrow! (for my sins)," but she rejoined, "Do not lie, but say rather, 'Alas, for my lack of sorrow,' and if you were truly sorrowful, life would have no delight for you."

That her intercession was valued even in her lifetime by her disciples, is proved by an account of a man who said to Rabi'a, "Pray for me," and she said, "Who am I? Obey your Lord and pray to Him, for He will answer the suppliant when he prays."

More than one episode, of doubtful authenticity, connects Rabi'a with the great Egyptian Sufi Dhu al-Nun al-Misri, one of the chief exponents of the Sufi doctrine and especially the doctrine of the heavenly gnosis (*ma'rifa*) derived from spiritual experience, not from acquired learning. He elaborates the Sufi conception of Unification (= *tawhid*) and employs for the love of God to the saint and the saint's love to Him, the term which Rabi'a also used (*hubb*). He died in A.D. 856 and therefore survived Rabi'a for nearly half a century. It is quite possible, however, that he may have met her in his early years.

There is a story connecting the two which has a good deal of interest, related by Sa'd b. 'Uthman, who says,

I was with Dhu al-Nun the Egyptian . . . and behold, someone arrived and I said, "O teacher, someone has come," and he said to me, "See who it is, for no one sets foot in this place, except my friends," and I looked and lo, it was a woman, and I said, "It is a woman," and he said "She is a friend, by the Lord of the Ka'ba," then he ran up to her and greeted her . . . and said, "I am your brother Dhu al-Nun and there is no one present (*i.e.* no strangers)," and she said, "May God welcome your soul in peace." Then he said, "What led you to enter this place?" and she said, "A verse from the book of God. . . . His most exalted Word says, 'Is not God's earth wide? Therefore wander about in it.' " Then he said to her: "Expound Love to me," and she said, "Praise be to God, for you speak with the tongue of knowledge and (yet) you ask me about it." He said to her, "The asker has a right to an answer."

Then she is said to have recited her famous verses on the two types of love to God.

Another of her contemporaries and acquaintances was 'Abd al-'Aziz b. Sulayman Abu al-Rasibi of Basra, who died in A.H. 150 (= A.D. 767), an ascetic and devotee whom Rabi'a called "The Chief of the Devotees" (Sayyid al-'Abadin).

Others mentioned as visitors to her house who came to discuss problems with her, were Salih b. 'Abd al-'Aziz and Kilab b. Hari, the latter a Sufi Shi'ite. More than one story associates Rabi'a with Malik b. Dinar, a very well known ascetic, who was one of the disciples of Hasan al-Basri. As he died in A.H. 128 (= A.D. 745) Rabi'a can have known him only in her youth.

It was chiefly among men that Rabi'a found her disciples and friends, we hear less of her association with women. Among her companions who were evidently of her own kinsfolk we hear of Mu'adha al-'Adawiyya, a famous woman ascetic, and Layla al-Qaysiyya. Rabi'a's name is often connected with that of Umm al-Darda, but the latter must have been considerably older than Rabi'a. We are given the names of two of her servants, who were themselves pious and devout women. One of these was Mariam of Basra, a devotee and ascetic who loved Rabi'a greatly and became her servant, and survived her for some time. She used to listen to and take part in discussions on Love and was so deeply moved thereby that she would at times lose consciousness. On one occasion she was in the assembly (of the Sufis) when they were speaking of Love, and the effect on her was so great that she yielded up her soul, there in the assembly. Among her sayings was this, "I have not concerned myself with my daily bread, nor wearied myself in seeking it since I heard this verse from the Word of God, 'In Heaven is your provision and what has been promised to you.' " The other was 'Abda bint Shuwal, who is described as herself one of the virtuous handmaids of God Most High, of whom several stories are told in connection with her service to Rabi'a and who was with Rabi'a at the time of the latter's death.

The anecdotes related in this chapter show that Rabi'a al-'Adawiyya associated on equal terms with the Sufi leaders of her day, and her biographers, in despite of the Oriental preference for the male sex and belief in its essential superiority, are prepared to grant to Rabi'a a position of equality with, even of pre-eminence above her contemporaries, including those who were accepted as leaders of thought and revered teachers of the Sufi doctrine.

Chapter III / Rabi'a's Asceticism: Her Prayer-Life

To the Sufi, as to the Christian saint, the life of Purgation was the first stage towards the attainment of the mystic's goal, and asceticism was enjoined on all who entered the novitiate. Only when the novice had purged himself of the carnal Self and its desires, could he hope to enter on the way which would lead to Union with the Divine. Ascetic (*zahid*) was the most common appellation of the Sufi, and even those who had attained to sainthood, with few exceptions, practised asceticism to the end of their lives. As a Sufi writer expresses it: "If you ask, Who is the traveller on the road (the mystic Way)? It is one who is aware of his own origin. . . . He is the traveller who passes on speedily; he has become pure from Self as flame from smoke."

Rabi'a al-'Adawiyya was an ascetic who followed the path of poverty and self-denial with unwavering steps to the end. Again and again her friends would have given her of their substance to alleviate her poverty and discomfort, but she would have none of their proffered gifts and looked only to the Lord she served, to provide for the needs of His servant.

For some time after her release from slavery, according to 'Attar, she retired to the desert and there lived the life of a recluse in a cell, and even after her return to Basra she lived apart from the world, so far as the constant visits of her disciples and other visitors made it possible.

Al-Jahiz, our oldest authority, says that some of her friends said to Rabi'a al-Qaysiyya, "If we were to speak to the men of your kinsfolk, they would purchase a servant for you, who would look after the needs of your house," but she said, "Verily, I should be ashamed to ask for worldly things from Him to Whom the world belongs, and how should I ask for them from those to whom it does not belong?"

A similar story is told of a man who brought her forty *dinars* and said to her, "Spend them on something you need," and she wept and lifted up her head and said, "God knows that I am ashamed to ask Him for this world, though He rules it, and how shall I take it from one who does not rule it?"

'Attar relates that some people came to see her and she was tearing a piece of meat with her teeth, and they said to her, "Have you no knife with which to cut it?" She said, "From fear of cutting off (separation from God) I have never had a knife in my house, so I have none."

He also tells a story of how Rabi'a learnt the lesson of giving up all worldly desires in order that she might serve God without distraction.

Once for seven days and nights she had been fasting and had eaten nothing, and during the night she had not slept at all, but had spent every night in prayer. When she was in extremity from hunger, someone came into the house and brought her a cup of food. Rabi'a took it and went to fetch a lamp. When she returned, a cat had upset the cup. She said, "I will go and fetch a jug and break my fast (on water)." When she brought the jug, the lamp had gone out. She intended to drink the water in the darkness, but the jug fell from her hands and was smashed to pieces. Rabi'a broke into lamentations and heaved such a sigh that it almost seemed as if the house would catch fire.

She said, "O my Lord, what is this which Thou art doing to wretched me?" She heard a voice saying,

Have a care, if you desire it, I will endow you with all the pleasures of this world, but I shall take concern for Me out of your heart, for such concern and the pleasures of this world cannot dwell together in one heart. O Rabi'a, you have a desire and I have a desire, I cannot combine my desire and your desire in one heart.

She said,

When I heard this warning, then I separated my heart from worldly things and so cut off my worldly hopes that for thirty years every prayer which I have performed, I have prayed as if it were my last, and I have cut myself off from the creatures so that when day broke, from fear lest anyone should distract me from Him, I have said, "O Lord, make me occupied with myself, lest they should distract me from Thee."

The austerity of her views is shewn by a little anecdote which tells how Rabi'a went out on a feast-day, and when she returned she was asked, "What did you think of the feast?" She said, "I saw how you went out (nominally) to make the Sunna a living force and to put a stop to heresy, but you displayed a love of luxury and soft living and thereby you brought humiliation upon the Muslims."

Illness and suffering Rabi'a accepted as her Lord's will for her, enduring them with fortitude, and she even shewed herself oblivious to pain; more than one story tells how she was unaware of injury until others reminded her of it. It is related that one day her head was struck by some boughs and began to bleed, but she paid no attention to it, and when someone said to her, "Do you not feel the pain?" she said, "My concern is to accommodate myself to His will; He has made me occupied with something other than the tangible things which you see."

Another story to the same effect tells how one night she was making supplication and the result was that she fell asleep from the extremity of her absorption and a blood-vessel in her eye broke, but when she awoke, she was quite unaware of it. The capacity of these ascetics for enduring physical pain and rising above it is exemplified by the story of another woman, of Rabi'a's time, named Batja, who followed the sect of

Qadirivya al-Hururiyya. Zayd, Amir of Basra, when he heard of this, took her and cut off her hands and feet. The people came to visit her in her illness and [when] they said to her, "How do you feel, O Batja?" she answered, "Awe of the future has distracted me from the cold of your iron."

On one occasion Rabi'a fell ill, and her sickness was serious. Her friends came and asked her what was the cause of her illness, and she said, "I looked towards Paradise and the Lord has chastened me. At daybreak my heart looked in the direction of Paradise (*i.e.* I longed for its joys) and my Friend has reproached me. This illness is a reproach from Him."

Her unwillingness to depend on any save God is shown in another account by the same writer, who tells how Hasan of Basra once came to visit her when she was ill and said that on his way he saw one of the merchants of Basra at the door of Rabi'a's cell, with a purse of gold, weeping. Said Hasan, "O merchant, why are you weeping?" He said, "On account of this ascetic of our time [Rabi'a], for if her blessings upon mankind were to cease, mankind would perish," and he added, "I have brought somewhat as a recommendation to her, but I fear that she may refuse it. Do thou intercede for me, that she may accept it."

Hasan went in and spoke about it to Rabi'a, who looked at him out of the corner of her eye and said:

Shall not He who provides for those who revile Him, provide for those who love Him? He does not refuse sustenance to one who speaks unworthily of Him, how then should He refuse sustenance to one whose soul is overflowing with love to Him? Ever since I have known Him, I have turned my back upon mankind. How should I take the wealth of someone of whom I do not know whether he acquired it lawfully or not? . . . Make my excuses to that merchant, that my heart may not be in bondage (to a creature).

Rabi'a made clear her attitude on the subject of resignation and the renunciation of desire to certain visitors who came to see her during one of her illnesses. These were 'Abd al-Wahid 'Amr, and her constant visitor Sufyan. The former relates:

I and Sufyan Thawri visited Rabi'a when she was sick, and from awe I was not able to begin to speak, and I said to Sufyan, "Say something." He said (to Rabi'a), "If you would utter a prayer, (God) would relieve your suffering." She turned her face to him and said, "O Sufyan, do you not know Who it is that wills this suffering for me, is it not God Who wills it?" He said, "Yes." She said, "When you know this, why do you bid me ask for what is contrary to His will? It is not well to oppose one's Beloved."

Sufyan said then, "O Rabi'a, what is your desire?" She replied, "O Sufyan, you are a learned man, how can you ask me such a question as 'What do I desire'? I swear by the glory of God that for twelve years I have desired fresh dates, and you know that in Basra dates are plentiful, and I have not yet tasted them. I am a servant and what has a servant to do with desire? If I will (a thing) and my Lord does not will it, this would be unbelief. That should be willed which He wills, that you may be His true servant. If He Himself gives anything, that would be a different matter." Sufyan was silenced and offered no more on the subject.

One of her acquaintances, Muhammad b. 'Amr, says:

I went in to Rabi'a, and she was a very old woman of eighty years, as if she were a worn-out skin almost falling down, and I saw in her house a reed-mat and a clothes-stand of Persian reed, of the height of two cubits from the ground and upon it were her shrouds and the curtain of the house was made of palm-leaves, and perhaps there was a mat and an earthen jug and a bed of felt, which was also her prayer-carpet.

Another friend of hers, Malik Dinar, once found her lying on an old rush mat, with a brick under her head to serve as a pillow and drinking and making her ablutions from a cracked jar and his heart was pained at the sight and he said, "I have rich friends and if you wish, I will take something from them for you." She said, "O Malik, you have made a great mistake. Is it not the same One Who gives daily bread to me and to them?" Malik said, "It is." She said, "Will He forget the poor because of their poverty or remember the rich because of their riches?" He said, "No." Then she said, "Since He knows my state, what have I to remind Him of? What He wills, we should also will."

Rabi'a's devotion to the life of prayer is evident in all the accounts given of her life, and her biographers speak frequently of her custom of spending her nights in prayer. As a modern authority on Sufism has written, "In Mohammedan mysticism it is Prayer that supplies the best evidence of personality—not the ritual prayer (salat) but the free prayer (du'a') and in particular the loving converse with God (munajat) when the mystic speaks out of the depths of his heart," and Rabi'a's prayers reveal her personality more clearly perhaps than anything else.

It is told of her that at one time she was laid aside by sickness and, in the weakness which followed it, she gave up her night-prayers and slept instead and for some days she recited her portion when the day had risen, although it was the portion appointed for the night-prayer. Then God restored her to health, but for a time, through the languor produced by sickness, she went on reciting the portion by day and neglected rising at night. Then she says:

One night, while I was sleeping, it seemed to me in my sleep as if I were lifted up to a green park containing palaces and beautiful plants. While I was wandering about in it, astonished at its beauty, I saw a green bird and a maiden pursuing it as if she wished to take it, and her beauty distracted me from its beauty, and I said, "What do you want with it? Leave it alone, for truly I have never seen a bird more beautiful than that." Then she said, "Shall I show you something more beautiful than that?" I said, "Yes, surely." Then she took my hand and led me round that garden until she brought me to the gate of a palace and she sought to open it and it opened to her and from the door were cast rays from a candlestick the light of which shone before me and behind me, and she said to me, "Enter," and I entered the house, in which the sight was dazzled by the beauty of it, I know nothing in the world like it and while we were going round it, there appeared to us a door opening from it on to a garden and she hastened towards it and I with her and there met us a band of servants, with faces like pearls, and in their hands aloeswood, and she said to them, "What do you seek?" and they said, "We seek such a one, who was drowned in the sea, as a martyr." She said, "Will you not perfume this woman?" They said, "She had her portion in that, and she left it." Then (Rabi'a said) she withdrew her hand from mine, and approached me and said:

"Your prayers were light and your worship rest,
Your sleep was ever a foe to prayer,
Your life was an opportunity which you neglected,
     and a preparation
It passes on and vanishes slowly and perishes."

Then she vanished from before my eyes and I awoke as the dawn appeared and verily I remembered it, and thought of it only as confusion of my mind and a phantom of my soul.

When Rabi'a had related her dream she fell unconscious and her servant said that after this vision she never slept at night, until her death.

It is related of her that at night she used to go up on to her roof and pray thus:

O my Lord, the stars are shining and the eyes of men are closed, and kings have shut their doors and every lover is alone with his beloved, and here I am alone with Thee,

and then she began her prayers. When she saw the dawn appearing, she would pray:

O God, the night has passed and the day has dawned. How I long to know if Thou hast accepted (my prayers) or if Thou hast rejected them. Therefore console me for it is Thine to console this state of mine. Thou hast given me life and cared for me and Thine is the glory. If Thou wert to drive me from Thy door, yet would I not forsake it, for the love that I bear in my heart towards Thee.

Then she is said to have recited these verses:

O my Joy and my Desire and my Refuge,
My Friend and my Sustainer and my Goal,
Thou art my Intimate, and longing for Thee sustains me,
Were it not for Thee, O my Life and my Friend,
How I should have been distraught over the spaces of the earth,
How many favours have been bestowed, and how much hast Thou
    given me.
Of gifts and grace and assistance,
Thy love is not my desire and my bliss,
And has been revealed to the eye of my heart that was athirst,
I have none beside Thee, Who dost make the desert blossom,
Thou art my joy, firmly established within me,
If Thou art satisfied with me, then
O Desire of my heart, my happiness has appeared.

'Abda bint Shuwal, already mentioned in the last chapter, says of her:

Rabi'a used to pray all night, and when the day dawned she allowed herself a light sleep in her place of prayer, until the dawn tinged the sky with gold, and I used to hear her say, when she sprang up in fear from that sleep, "O soul how long wilt thou sleep and how often wilt thou wake? Soon wilt thou sleep a sleep from

which thou shalt not wake again until the trumpet call of the Day
of Resurrection."

A story is related of how Rabi'a visited Hayyuna, an ascetic who practised the greatest austerity and who used to pray, "O God, I would that
the day were night that I might enjoy Thy proximity." In the middle of
the night sleep overcame Rabi'a, and Hayyuna rose and came to her and
kicked her with her foot, and said, "Rise up, the Bridegroom of the truly
guided ones has come. The adornments of the brides of night are revealed by the light of the night-prayers." This anecdote is remarkable in
that it is the only passage I have met with which makes a reference to
the Spiritual Marriage of lover and Beloved, in these terms, applied to
Sufis, and it appears also as if there might be a reference to the parable
of the Ten Virgins.

One of the biographers tells how she used to pray a thousand *raka's*
in the day and night, and someone said to her, "What are you seeking
(to gain) by this?" and she replied, "I do not desire God's forgiveness
(by this), I do it only that the Apostle of God on the Day of Resurrection
may be able to say to the rest of the Prophets, 'Behold this woman of
my community, this is her work.' "

Her friend, Sufyan al-Thawri, relates:

I approached Rabi'a, and she was in the mihrab, where she was
praying till day, while I, in another corner, was praying until the
time of dawn and I said, "How shall we give thanks for His grace
given to us, whereby we spent the whole night in prayer?" She
said, "By fasting to-morrow."

Rabi'a for the most part was filled with a radiant faith and joy in the
service of God, which left little room for the gloomy fears by which
Hasan of Basra was so constantly obsessed, but an old writer tells us
how once, overcome by a dread of judgment, she prayed, "O my God,
wilt Thou burn in Hell a heart that loves Thee?" and she heard an unseen voice speaking to her inner consciousness, "O Rabi'a, We shall not
do this. Do not think of Us an Evil thought."

Among the prayers recorded by her biographer 'Attar are several
beautiful examples, shewing how prayer to her in truth was "loving
converse" with her Lord, not supplication on her own behalf or on behalf of others but simply communion with the Divine Friend, and perfect
satisfaction in His presence. Among those quoted are the following:

O my Lord, whatever share of this world Thou dost bestow on me,

bestow it on Thine enemies, and whatever share of the next world
Thou dost give me, give it to Thy friends. Thou art enough for me.

One night Rabi'a said, "My God, when I make my prayer, take from
my heart all Satanic suggestions, or through Thy generosity, accept my
prayer with these suggestions."
Again she used to pray,

O my Lord, if I worship Thee from fear of Hell, burn me in Hell,
and if I worship Thee from hope of Paradise, exclude me thence,
but if I worship Thee for Thine own sake then withhold not from
me Thine Eternal Beauty.

Yet another prayer was this:

O my God, my concern and my desire in this world, is that I should
remember Thee above all the things of this world, and in the next,
that out of all who are in that world, I should meet with Thee
alone. This is what I would say, "Thy will be done."

In the last sentence is fittingly summed up Rabi'a's attitude to this life
and to the Lord of life.
We are given yet another prayer with which this chapter may close:

O my God, the best of Thy gifts within my heart is the hope of
Thee and the sweetest word upon my tongue is Thy praise, and the
hours which I love best are those in which I meet with Thee. O my
God, I cannot endure without the remembrance of Thee in this
world and how shall I be able to endure without the vision of Thee
in the next world? O my Lord, my plaint to Thee is that I am but a
stranger in Thy country, and lonely among Thy worshippers.

Chapter IV/The Miracles of Muslim Saints: Rabi'a's Miracles

The saints of Islam, like the saints of Catholic Christendom, were expected to work miracles, as part of their claim to canonization, and their
biographers were not slow to attribute to them the power of performing
these *karamat* (lit. favours from God). It is hardly necessary to say that
most of these miracles rest on no historic foundation and yet, like other
legends of the saints, they have their value in throwing light upon the
personality of the one to whom these wonderful powers are ascribed
and still more perhaps, in shewing the high estimation in which such a
saint was held.

The Sufis themselves set little value upon the exercise of such miraculous powers. We are told that Abu Yazid al-Bistami said:

The saints do not rejoice at the answers to prayers which are the essence of miracles, such as walking on water, and moving in the air and traversing the earth and riding on the heavens, since the prayers of unbelievers receive an answer and the earth contains both Satans and men, and the air is the abode of the birds, and the water of the fish. Let not anyone who is perplexed by such things, put any faith in this trickery.

Of Abu Yazid it is also related that a man came to him and said, "I heard that you could pass through the air (fly)." He said, "And what is there wonderful in this? A bird which eats the dead passes through the air, and the believer is more honourable than a bird."

There is no lack of stories of miracles ascribed to Rabi'a of Basra, and in any account of her life these must find a place. Most of them tend to shew God's care for His servant and her needs and to justify her complete dependence upon Him. 'Attar has collected a number of these legendary stories, some of which are also to be found in other writers.

He tells how one night a thief came into Rabi'a's cell when she was asleep and took possession of her veil (in another account it is said that he tried to steal all her clothes). Then he attempted to get away with his booty, but could not find the way to the door. He put down the veil, and found the way again, so he seized the veil once more, but again failed to find the way out. He repeated this seven times, then from a corner of the cell came an unseen voice, saying, "O man, do not trouble thyself since for all these years she has entrusted herself to Us and Satan has not had the courage to go round about her and shall a thief have courage to go round about her veil? Concern not thyself with her, O pickpocket, if one friend is asleep, another friend is awake and keeping watch." And al-Munawi in his version of the story adds, "This is true and certain, as God Most High has said: 'There shall be angels in front of him (i.e. God's servant), and behind him.' "

There is an anecdote given of provision for her bodily needs, to indicate her faith in God's promises, which is much more entertaining to the reader than her biographer can have intended it to be.

He tells how two religious leaders came to visit Rabi'a. Both of them were hungry and said to one another, "Perhaps she will give us something to eat, because her food is always obtained from a lawful source." When they sat down, a cloth containing two loaves was set before them and they were pleased. Before they had time to begin eating, a beggar came in and Rabi'a gave him both loaves. The two shaykhs felt annoyed but said nothing. After a time a slave-girl came in bearing a quantity of hot bread and said, "My mistress has sent this," Rabi'a counted the loaves and found that there were eighteen and said, "I think she has not sent me these," and whatever the slave-girl said was of no use. The slave-girl had brought all except two loaves, which she had taken out for herself; going away, she put the two loaves back in their place and then returned. Rabi'a counted the loaves again and found there were twenty. She said, "This is what you were ordered to bring," and she set the loaves before her guests and they ate. They were astonished at the number of them and said, "What is the secret of this? We were wishing for your bread, before you took it up and gave it to the beggar. Then of that bread (which was sent you) you said that there were eighteen loaves and that they did not belong to you. When they became twenty, you took them." She said:

When you came in I knew you were hungry and I said, "How can I set two loaves before two honourable persons?" When the beggar came in, I gave them to him and I prayed to God Almighty, "O my Lord, Thou hast said that Thou wilt give ten for one, and I am sure of this. Now I have given two loaves for the sake of pleasing Thee in order that Thou mayest give me back ten for each of them." When the eighteen loaves came, I knew that either there was a deficiency due to misappropriation or that they were not meant for me.

Another story, told quite naively by 'Attar, is equally entertaining to the modern reader.

He relates how on one occasion Rabi'a's servant was going to prepare wild onions, because for some days they had not prepared any food, and she needed an onion, so the servant said, "I will go and ask for one from a neighbour," but Rabi'a said, "Forty years ago I made an oath with God that I would not ask for anything except from Him. I can do without the onion." Immediately after she had spoken a bird flying in the air dropped an onion—ready skinned—into Rabi'a's frying pan. But she was still doubtful and said, "I am not safe from a trick" (*i.e.* perhaps Satan had sent the onion), so she left the fried onion alone and ate bread without any seasoning.

A much simpler and more probable account of this event is given by an earlier writer, who tells us that 'Abd Allah b. 'Isa said, "Rabi'a was boiling some food in a cooking pot and she needed an onion but had none, and there appeared a bird with a wild onion in its beak and threw it down to her."

There is an attractive story told of Rabi'a containing an element of the miraculous, which seems as if it might be drawn from Buddhist sources, and reminds us of stories told of Prince Gautama. 'Attar tells how one day Rabi'a had gone to the mountains and there a band of wild creatures gathered round her, deer and gazelle and mountain goats and wild asses, who came and looked at her and drew close to her. Suddenly Hasan al-Basri appeared, and when he saw Rabi'a he approached her, and those wild creatures, when they saw Hasan, all fled away forthwith and Rabi'a was left alone. Hasan was vexed when he saw that, he looked at Rabi'a and said, "Why did they flee in terror from me, while they were friendly with you?" Rabi'a said, "What have you eaten to-day?" He said, "Some onions (fried) in fat." She said, "You eat of their fat, how should they not flee from you?"

Al-Munawi says that among Rabi'a's *karamat* it was related that she had sown corn and the locusts fell upon it, and she prayed, "O my Lord, this is my provision, upon which I have spent money, and if Thou willest, I will give it as food to Thine enemies or Thy friends." Then the locusts flew away as if they had never existed.

The same writer relates a miracle which is perhaps a variant of a story told previously of how Rabi'a went on pilgrimage, on a camel, and it died before she reached her destination, and she asked God to restore it to life. It recovered and she rode it until she reached the door of her own house.

An amusing legend is told of how Hasan of Basra tried to exploit Rabi'a's power of working miracles for his own glory but only succeeded in reaping a rebuke for his vanity.

One day he saw Rabi'a near the river-side, Hasan cast his prayer-mat on to the surface of the water and said, "O Rabi'a, come and let us pray two *raka's* together," evidently counting on her powers to keep the carpet from sinking. Rabi'a said, "O Hasan, was it necessary to offer yourself in the bazaar of this world to the people of the next? (*i.e.* was it needful to seek to win worldly reputation by a spiritual gift?) This is necessary for people of your kind, because of your weakness." Then Rabi'a threw her prayer-mat into the air and flew up on to it and said, "O Hasan, come up here that people may see us." But that station was not for Hasan and he was silent. Rabi'a, wishing to gain his heart (to comfort him), said, "O Hasan, that which you did, a fish can do just the same, and that which I did, a fly can do. The real work (for the saints of

God) lies beyond both of these and it is necessary to occupy ourselves with the real work."

Another story tells of a miracle which has perhaps a mystical significance. One night Hasan and two or three friends are said to have come to Rabi'a and she had no lamp and she desired for them an illuminated heart. Rabi'a blew upon the tips of her fingers, and throughout that night, until daylight came, her fingers gave forth light like a lamp, and they sat until morning in that illumination. Her biographer adds by way of comment:

If anyone were to say, "How was this?" I should say it was like the hand of Moses, and if it should be observed that he was a prophet, I should say, "Whoever obeys a prophet may obtain as his reward a share in the gift of prophecy." So the Prophet has said, "He who restores a small part of what was obtained unlawfully, has obtained one degree of prophecy."

Yet another legend, proving that God provided for Rabi'a's needs when she herself was occupied in His service, tells how Hasan went one day to Rabi'a at the time of the second prayer of the day, when she was preparing to cook some meat in a pan and was putting water into it. He goes on to say:

When she came to speak to me she said, "This discourse is better than anything cooked in a pan," so she went on talking till we performed the evening prayer. She brought a piece of dry bread and a jug of water that we might break our fast. Rabi'a then went to take off the pan and burnt her hand; we looked and there was the pan boiling and bubbling over, by the power of God Most High. She brought it and we ate of that meat and the food composed of that meat was the pleasantest we had ever tasted. Rabi'a said, "The food from that pan would have been suitable for an invalid just convalescent."

Rabi'a herself disclaimed these miraculous powers and was anxious to avoid a reputation for working miracles. We are told of an interesting conversation between her and Zulfa bint 'Abd al-Wahid, who addresses Rabi'a as her aunt, while Rabi'a calls her her brother's daughter. If this represents a genuine relationship and not merely a term of affection, it is of great interest, as Zulfa is the only one of Rabi'a's own family who is mentioned by name by any of her biographers, nor have we any mention elsewhere of a brother of Rabi'a. But the terms "aunt" and "niece" are still used in the East as terms of endearment without any real relationship between the parties concerned.

Zulfa is reported to have said:

I said to Rabi'a, "O my aunt, why do you not allow people to visit you?" Rabi'a replied, "I fear lest when I am dead, people will relate of me what I did not say or do, what if I had seen, I should have feared or mistrusted. I am told that they say that I find money under my place of prayer, and that I cook (food) in the pot without a fire." I said to her, "They relate of you that you find food and drink in your house," and she said, "O daughter of my brother, if I had found such things in my house I would not have touched them, or laid hands upon them, but I tell you that I buy my things and am blessed in them."

These anecdotes of Rabi'a are trivial in themselves, but they shew that her biographers believed that she had the power to work miracles, attributed to all true saints of Islam, and moreover, that miracles were wrought on her behalf, that God might justify his servant in the eyes both of friends and enemies, and as 'Attar's own comment shews, these miracles, wrought by, or for her, indicated to all who heard of them that the grace of God was with her.

Chapter V / Rabi'a's Declining Years: Her Illness and Death

Rabi'a, like so many of the saints, lived to a ripe old age, and must have been nearly ninety when she died. Some of the authorities quoted by her biographers apparently knew her only in her old age, when she was feeble in body and yet so clear in mind that she was still the guide and spiritual director of the many souls who came to seek counsel of her.

The author of the "Siyar al-Salihat" says that when she heard others speak of death she shivered and her fingers trembled, and others say that if she heard the mention of fire, or even the crackling of it, she became unconscious.

An overwhelming dread of judgment after death and the constant fear of Hell was characteristic of the early Sufis, as we have already noted, and especially of the school of Hasan al-Basri. The most that he felt could be hoped for was an alleviation of the punishment for the believer, in that the period of torment in Hell would be shortened, and here seems to be in embryo the doctrine of purgatory for those who were true Muslims, and yet had fallen short and sinned. It is plain that the early Sufis had a strong sense of the moral turpitude of sin and the idea that it might mean separation from God—for the Sufi the greatest of all deprivations—in the next world. The Christian doctrine that sincere repentance cannot fail to win forgiveness, together with the Christian doctrines of Atonement and Redemption, had not entered into the Sufi conception of the relation between God and His servant. We are told of Sha'wana the ascetic that she said at the time of her death, "I cannot bear to meet with God," and when asked why, she said, "Because of the multitude of my sins." The same feeling led to a different result with 'Ubayda bint Abi Kilab, who is said to have spent forty years in weeping, until her sight was lost. She was asked, "What do you desire?" She said, "Death," and when those with her asked "Why?" she replied, "Because every new day that dawns I fear lest I should commit some sin which would mean my loss on the Day of Resurrection."

Yet to some of the Sufis the longing to be with their Lord was stronger than their fear of judgment. Al-Junayd was told that the Sufi Abu Sa'id al-Kharraz was in great ecstasy at the time of his death. "Is it to be wondered at?" said al-Junayd, "his soul has taken flight full of longing (to see God)." Fatima, sister of the Sufi Abu 'Ali al-Rudhabari, said that when her brother was at the point of death he opened his eyes and said, "Here are the gates of heaven opened and here is Paradise adorned and here is one saying, 'O Abu 'Ali, thou hast reached the highest rank.' "

As we shall see from the account of her teaching, it is hardly conceivable that Rabi'a was amongst those who were afraid of death, which to her represented Union with her Beloved, above and beyond the temporary experience of union which was all that could be attained in this life. Her faith soared to heights above those to which Hasan attained or al-Fudayl, of whom it was said that "sadness left the world when al-Fudayl left it"; hers was a confident and radiant faith founded on her intimate knowledge of—and communion with—her Lord. She would have said with 'Abd al-'Aziz, "Death is a bridge whereby the lover is joined to the Beloved."

As regards the effect upon her of the mention of fire, this element seems to have been chiefly associated with Hell and with evil in the minds of the early Sufis, and a later Sufi, Rumi, contrasts Fire with Light, as evil with good, the defiled with the pure, that which perishes with that which is immortal. Al-Hujwiri also contrasts the "fire of wrath" and the "light of mercy." On the other hand the Persian writers constantly speak of the "fire" of love and its consuming power. 'Attar speaks of Rabi'a as "that woman on fire with love," and in this sense fire is regarded as a pure and holy element, causing suffering yet purging of dross. Al-Kalabadhi, using the term in such a sense, says, "He is burnt who feels the fire, but he who is fire, how shall he be burnt?" *i.e.* he who is still under bondage to self and his sins, must feel the wrath of God, but he who is on fire with love to God, what fear has he of judgment? Again al-Ghazali says of the longing of the mystic that it is "the fire of God which He has kindled in the hearts of His saints, that thereby may be burned away what exists in them of vain fancies and desires and purposes and needs." This is the sense in which the Spanish mystic, St John of the Cross, says, "Love has set the soul on fire and transmuted it into love, has annihilated it and destroyed it as to all that is not love."

Rabi'a, consumed by love and desire for God, might be compared with St Catherine of Genoa, who felt the consuming fire of her love to God so hot within her that she was dried up by it and her body was burning to the touch, and fire for her had a significance equal to that felt by Rabi'a, who swooned from her strong emotion at its mention. Yet this emotion was more probably ecstasy than fear, to Rabi'a her Lord was "the One God Who is the Fire of Pain and the Light of Joy to souls, according as they resist Him or will Him, either here or hereafter." In Rabi'a "the fire of her all-conquering love" demanded "eternal union with an eternal flame," and the mention of Death made her tremble, not with apprehension, but with infinite joy.

In one respect, certainly, Rabi'a was like her great successor, in that her health was frail, perhaps as the result of her ceaseless asceticisms, perhaps because of the hardships of her youth. We hear constantly of her illnesses and her sufferings from weakness. As with St Catherine, too, her illness sometimes had its source in spiritual rather than physical disturbance. We are told how one day she was suffering and lamenting and her friends said to her, "O venerable one of this world, we see no visible cause of illness and yet you are in pain and crying out." She said:

My sickness is from within my breast, so that all the physicians in the world are powerless to cure it, and the plaster for my wound is union with my Friend; (only so) shall I be soothed. Not to-morrow (*i.e.* not yet) shall I attain my purpose. But since pain is not affecting me, I appear to be in pain, I cannot do less than this.

(*I.e.* the outward signs of my spiritual sickness should not be less than the outward signs of physical illness.) So also the Christian mystic:

The soul that loves God lives more in the next life than in this, because it lives rather where it loves than where it dwells, and therefore esteeming but lightly its present bodily life cries out: "Behold, the malady of love is incurable, except in Thy presence and before Thy face." The reason why the malady of love admits of no other remedy than the presence and countenance of the Beloved is that the malady of love differs from every other sickness, and therefore requires a different remedy . . . love is not cured but by that which is in harmony with itself. . . . There is no remedy for this pain except in the presence and vision of the Beloved.

In what appears to have been her last illness, Rabi'a was said to have been visited by three of her friends, Hasan of Basra, Malik Dinar and Shaqiq Balkhi, and they, like the friends of Job, endeavoured to teach her the duty of resignation.

Hasan said, "He is not sincere in his claim (to be a true servant of God), who is not patient under the chastisement of his Lord." Rabi'a said, "I smell egotism in this speech." So Shaqiq took up the thread and said, "He is not sincere in his claim who is not thankful for the chastisement of his Lord." Rabi'a said, "Something better than this is needed." Then Malik Dinar tried, "He is not sincere in his claim who does not delight in the chastisement of his Lord." Rabi'a said, "Even this is not good enough." They said, "Do thou speak," and she shewed her idea of the true resignation in her reply, "He is not sincere in his claim who does not forget the chastisement in the contemplation of his Lord."

And 'Attar commends her answer, saying, "It would not be surprising, since the women of Egypt in their contemplation of a creature were oblivious to the pain of their wounds; and therefore if anyone in the contemplation of the Creator were in this state, it would not be strange."

One writer says that her shroud was always before her, in her place of worship. When the time of her departure from this world drew near, she called her servant, 'Abda bint Abi Shuwal, and said to her, "O 'Abda, do not inform anyone of my (approaching) death, but shroud me in this gown of mine, of hair." So when she died, she was shrouded in that gown and in a woollen scarf which she used to wear. 'Abda relates further how she saw Rabi'a in a dream, a year or so after her death, and she was wearing a robe of green silk embroidered with gold and a scarf of fine green silk brocade and never had 'Abda seen anything in this world more beautiful, and she cried out, "O Rabi'a, what have you done with the shroud in which you were buried and the woollen scarf?" and Rabi'a answered her, "They were taken from me and I was clothed with what you see upon me and what I wore as a shroud was folded up and sealed and carried up to the angels, so that my garments might be complete on the Day of Resurrection." 'Abda said to her, "Were you working for this, in your earthly days?" She said, "What is this in comparison with the grace of God to His saints?"

Her Persian biographer gives the following account of her death. He says:

At her last moments many pious folk were sitting around her and she bade them, "Rise and go out; for a moment leave the way free for the messengers of God Most High." All rose and went out and when they had closed the door, they heard the voice of Rabi'a making her profession of faith and they heard a voice saying, "O soul at rest, return to thy Lord, satisfied with Him, giving satisfaction to Him. So enter among My servants and enter into My Paradise."

There was no further sound heard, they returned and found that her soul had departed. As soon as she had rendered up her last breath, the doctors who were assembled had her body washed, recited over it the prayers for the dead and placed it in its last abode.

The religious leaders said of her that Rabi'a came into this world and departed into the next and never was she wanting in reverence to her Lord, and never did she desire anything or say "Give me this or do this for me," much less did she desire anything from any of His creatures.

After her death, she was seen in a dream and the dreamer said to her, "Tell us of your state and how you escaped from Munkar and Nakir." She said, "Those beings came and said, 'Who is your Lord?' I said, 'Return and tell your Lord, Notwithstanding the thousands and thousands of Thy creatures, Thou has not forgotten a weak old woman. I, who have only Thee in all the world, have never forgotten Thee, that Thou shouldest ask, Who is thy lord?' "

Rabi'a al-'Adawiyya died in A.H. 185 (= A.D. 801) and was buried at Basra.

It is said that Muhammad b. Aslam al-Tusi and Na'mi Tartusi both visited Rabi'a's grave, and said, "O thou who didst boast that thou wouldst not bow thy head for the two worlds, hast thou reached that exalted state?" and they heard a voice in reply, "I have reached that which I saw."

She had attained the goal of her quest, she was united at last and for ever, with her Friend, she beheld the Everlasting Beauty, and so we leave her, with the closing words of her faithful biographer, "May God have mercy upon her."

[Excerpts from Margaret Smith, *Rabi'a the Mystic and Her Fellow-Saints in Islam* (Cambridge: Cambridge University Press, 1928). Reprinted by permission of the publisher. Notes in the original text are not included in the excerpts.]

5

Walladah bint al-Mustakfi

ولادة بنت المستكفى

Andalusian Poet

ca. A.D. 1001–1080

Biographical Sketch by the Editors

Walladah bint al-Mustakfi lived in the Andalusian kingdom of Cordova in the eleventh century and is a legendary figure in the literary history of the Arab world. From a time when women were supposedly hidden from public view, Walladah emerges as an independent and individualistic woman, the focus of an important literary circle, a poet in her own right, and the idol of many great men—and women—of the era.

Biographical data about Walladah is unfortunately extremely scanty; references by contemporaries are few and generally related to her liaison with the poet Ibn Zaydun. Later material is often contradictory. However, a few facts do exist which give us the general outlines of this famous woman's life and indicate her complexity.

Walladah's father was the caliph, or ruler, of Cordova from A.D. 1023 or 1024 to 1031 or 1032.[1] A direct descendant of Abd al-Rahman al-Nasir, one of the most famous Omayyad caliphs in Andalusia, Walladah's father was known as al-Mustakfi bi-Allah.[2] The identity of Walladah's mother is not entirely certain, though most historians believe she was an Ethiopian Christian slave, Bint Sakra al-Mawruriyah, whom the caliph married after she had borne him a son.[3]

Photos: The Alhambra, Granada

Little is known of Walladah's early life. The historians are unanimous in noting her father's fondness for the pleasures of this world, which, combined with a none-too-nimble wit, managed to reduce him to temporary poverty. Historian-philosopher Ibn Hayyan states, "I knew him in the days of despair and poverty that came upon him and his family at the time of the dynasty of Hamudiyah . . . He had no pride whatsoever and he went to the peasants of the area at the time of the harvest and asked them personally to give him alms."[4]

Despite his "pure descent" from the early Omayyads, al-Mustakfi seems generally to have been a bad lot. "When he was elected caliph, in 1023 or 1024, he assassinated his cousin . . . and from then on gave way totally to his lusts and desires. His main concerns were his gastronomic and sexual needs; he thought of nothing else."[5] Eventually the people denounced him and began plotting to put down the house of Nasir. Soon the people of Cordova rebelled, and al-Mustakfi fled, hiding between two women. And when he reached the city of Iflij, one of his own officers poisoned him and he died.[6]

When her father died and her family fell from power in 1031 or 1032, Walladah was about thirty. At this point she seems to have liberated herself from the traditions by which women were encouraged to cover themselves modestly with a veil, stay at home caring for husband and children, and not mix socially with men who were strangers. Walladah did none of these things. First, she did not marry. She inherited a large enough fortune to make her economically independent and she proceeded to open her house to people of letters, both men and women. Her salon became a center for brilliant soirées, to which poets and artists flocked. Poetry readings and discussions and musical evenings were regular features of Walladah's circle.

Ibn Bassam records that Walladah took off her veil and had two of her own verses embroidered on the sleeves of her robe.[7] The one on the right sleeve read:

I am, by God, fit for high positions,
And am going my way, with pride!

And the one on the left sleeve read:

Forsooth, I allow my lover to touch my cheek,
And bestow my kiss on him who craves it.[8]

A. R. Nykl explains, "This novelty, which may have appeared very daring in Cordova, was not her original idea; she merely copied the customs of women in Harun al-Rashid's harem. Despite this notoriety, Ibn Bassam believes that her behavior was pure."[9]

The majority of historians and biographers record that Walladah was virtuous and that, although many men sought to become her lover, she seems to have resisted all but three: Ibn Zaydun the poet; Abu 'A'mir Ibn 'Abdus, a rich man of Cordova; and Abu 'Abd al-Allah Ibn al-Qalas. (The latter is supposed to have given up in despair before ever winning Walladah's heart.)

According to al-Maqqari,[10] "Her father was stupid, illiterate, and disreputable, but the daughter represented the utmost in cultivation, good manners, and wit."[11] She was widely read and well informed on a number of subjects. Badr al-din al-Sadiqi, a man of letters of the seventeenth century, goes so far as to assert that Walladah had earned a license to be a teacher and to give formal opinions and interpretations of the traditions of the Prophet. Since al-Sadiqi does not give a source for this information and he is the only biographer to mention it, the fact seems somewhat doubtful.[12] Whatever the case, there is no question that Walladah was well educated; in addition to her knowledge and her poetic gifts, she was well known for her singing.[13]

Ibn Khaqan describes her as follows: "She bewitched both the hearts and minds of those around her. Her presence encouraged the old to behave like the young."[14]

Walladah described herself and behavior by saying, "When people look at me and my beauty, I am like the deer of Mecca, whose hunting is forbidden." She added that she realized her free and flirtatious talk with men might be considered improper, even a vice, but explained that "what keeps me from adultery is Islam."[15]

Walladah was the great love of Ibn Zaydun, generally considered one of the outstanding poets of the Andalusian period.[16] Born in Cordova in A.D. 1003 or 1004, Ibn Zaydun was the son of a distinguished *faqih* (or religious notable) who was a littérateur and a member of Cordova's city government. Despite the civil disorders in Cordova at the time, Ibn Zaydun acquired a thorough classical literary education, and before he was twenty he had attracted public attention with his poetic talent.

Ibn Zaydun visited Walladah's literary salon and fell madly in love with her, and she with him. His "fatal attachment to Walladah," according to Nykl, "was the source of inspiration for his greatest masterpieces."[17] Their love was celebrated by many poems, including Walladah's own lines, inviting her admirer:

Be ready to visit me as darkness gathers.
For I believe that night keeps all secrets best;
The love I feel for you—did the sun feel it thus—
It would not shine, moon would not rise, stars would cease
    traveling! [18]

For some months it appears they enjoyed a mutual attraction, although their relationship was clandestine and beset by gossip, slander, and even political intrigue. Ibn Zaydun, it is said, may have had political aspirations and was constantly watched.

During this early period, Walladah wrote some of her best-known lines to Ibn Zaydun:

1.   I wonder; is there no way for us to meet again
       After this separation, and tell again each other of our love?

2.   Before, when you visited me during the wintry season
       I spurned the brazier, so great was my fire of passion!

3.   How can I bear this being cut off from you, alone?
       Yes, Fate did hasten what I had been afraid of!

4.   Time passes, yet I see no end to your long absence,
       Nor does patience free me from the bondage of yearning!

5.   May God pour rain on the land where you're dwelling
       From every cloud, in mighty streams, to refresh it! [19]

But, despite such declarations of true love, Walladah and Ibn Zaydun seemed to be very jealous people. Walladah, for example, had a black maid who was a fine singer. Stories vary, but one states that Ibn Zaydun asked the maid to sing a song in Walladah's presence without asking her mistress's permission. Supposedly, Walladah noticed Ibn Zaydun's attraction to the maid and she wrote him a poem, chiding him for his fickleness:

1.   If you were just in keeping our pact of love,
        You would not love my slave-maid, preferring her,

2.   Leaving aside the bough that produced beauty's fruit,
        Inclining toward a bough that no such fruit does show;

3.   You know full well that I'm the heaven's full moon,
        Yet to my grief, you let *al-mustari* [Jupiter] beguile you![20]

From this period, Walladah seems to have tired of Ibn Zaydun, but his obsession with her remained. He wrote her passionate verses, which she did not answer, and then a series of reproaches, including the following lines:

25.   . . . being beguiled by Walladah's promises
        Is like a fleeting mirage or a lightning's flash!

26.   She is like water, difficult to hold in hand:
        Its seething foam prevents getting it easily![21]

Walladah seems not to have been impressed, and she continued her flirtation with a new suitor, Ibn 'Abdus. Ibn Zaydun, almost beside himself with jealousy, finally wrote a long scathing letter ridiculing Ibn 'Abdus, which later became famous in the literature. The letter, he said, was for Walladah to give to Ibn 'Abdus, as she spurned his advances. This act by Ibn Zaydun backfired. Walladah wrote him a venomous letter in return, and Ibn 'Abdus, outraged and humiliated, took revenge by accusing Ibn Zaydun (falsely) of having illegally taken over the estate of one of his own freedmen. For this offense, the poet was thrown into jail for more than a year. He finally escaped from prison, still in love with Walladah. He is supposed to have roamed through the city, hoping to get a glimpse of his beloved, and he actually wrote her a long poem asking her to go away with him. Walladah did not reply. After various wanderings, followed by many efforts on his behalf by his friends, Ibn Zaydun was restored to favor in Cordova, where he became court poet.

By this time Walladah seems to have shifted her affections to Muhjah bint al-Tayani al-Qurtubiyah, who, we are told, was "one of the most beautiful young women and lively spirits of the time."[22] Walladah is said to have fallen in love with Muhjah and undertook the girl's education. Muhjah became a poet herself and wrote satires of Walladah's own verse. Muhjah, like Walladah, did not wear the veil. Her satirical poetry is reputed to have been very obscene, so obscene that a contemporary, Ibn Bassam, excused himself from quoting two lines of Walladah's verse, written in response to Muhjah, on the grounds that they were unprintable.[23] But a sample of Muhjah's work is quoted by 'Ali Abd al-Azim, and we have translated it below. One of Muhjah's lovers gave her a peach and she replied by writing:

As for he who brings his lover a peach,
Well, he's welcome as a piece of ice!
A peach may be beautiful, the same shape as the breast,
But their uses are different![24]

Beautiful, rich, and intelligent, Walladah was as much a figure of controversy in her own time in Andalusian society as she continues to be for biographers and historians. Her contemporaries tell us that people were divided into two camps in their attitudes toward Walladah. She had many admirers and supporters, but others criticized her for flaunting the conventions of the time, customs, it is said, which were designed to protect Arab women and keep them from being taken advantage of by men. As a caliph's daughter, Walladah was supposed to set a traditional example. She did not. Ibn Makki still praises her but adds, "Her behavior did not match her noble descent."[25]

Ibn Bassam suggests that she was not careful and therefore gave people cause to criticize her for speaking up frankly about her worldly desires and for disdaining the traditions of her forefathers.[26]

As the years passed, Walladah was also criticized for her relationship with Muhjah and for writing obscene satirical verse instead of traditional poetry. Said one critic, "This kind of verse was not accepted from a man, so what would one expect of such lines written by a woman, and a woman from the best of homes, with good family background and an outstanding position in society."[27] Even Ibn Bassam, one of her greatest supporters, refuses to quote any of her verse from this period.

Not surprisingly, critics are also divided in their estimate of her overall poetic achievement. Al-Dabbi says she was "well versed in poetry . . . excelled many male poets, was able to take part in discussions with men of letters. She is with those at the top of the field."[28] Others place her much lower on the scale of poetic excellence and point out that she was competing with the best, for Andalusian poets are known for the delicacy and elegance of their love poetry. Yet all agree that Walladah's love poetry has, in spite of some exaggeration in expression, "much truth in feeling."[29] For us, this is a difficult issue to judge, since of all the poetry Walladah is supposed to have written, scarcely more than twenty authenticated lines remain, lines which have been quoted here in context.

Walladah never married. In her later years, she gave up her salon, lost her fortune, and went to live in the house of her old suitor, Abn 'Abdus, who supported her until she died.[30] Some say she lived to be nearly one hundred, others that she died in her eighties. Ibn Zaydun married and had a family, but is said to have remained in love with Walladah all his life. He died in Seville in 1070 or 1071, while on a mediation mission for the new conqueror and ruler of Cordova, Al Mu'tamid.

What are we to make of Walladah? Depending on whether one reads Islamic or western sources, her character emerges rather differently. According to Nuzhat al-Absar w-al-asma, quoted by 'Ali Abd al-Azim, "she was of a dominant personality, beautiful, pure of descent, and of noble character. She did not allow anyone to misbehave in her presence."[31] Al-Maqqari states that, among her contemporaries, there was no one like her; "she was unique in her beauty, her gentleness, and her culture."[32] Nykl, in his work *Hispano-Arabic Poetry* admits that without Walladah's influence, on Ibn Zaydun, "Arabic poetry would have remained without some of its most precious gems." Yet, Nykl goes on, "her behavior is marked by strong passion, mixed with extreme coarseness and materialistic realism reminding one of George Sand." And further, "Ibn Bassam's portrait of Walladah, though outwardly favorable, gives us several details which allow us to catch a few glimpses of her peculiar moods and whims, not unlike those of certain college women, movie stars, and actresses of our day."[33] Finally, Nykl says that Walladah's "soul was thoroughly corrupt."[34] Why? Because she spurned the great Ibn Zaydun, attached herself instead to a "mediocre man" (Ibn 'Abdus) "whom she could dominate," and "had a close relationship with the poetess Muhjah."[35] Yet her contemporary Abd Allah ibn Makki praises her virtue, wit, intelligence, and eloquence.[36] The two portraits which emerge, that of the western biographer and that of the biographers of her own Islamic culture, are rather different.

Was Walladah atypical for her time? Or was she representative of a group of women like herself, freed of custom and tradition who lived somewhat differently than historians would have us believe was the case for women of the period? Does her life suggest that not all Muslim women were subjugated, veiled, and sequestered? Or was her character and her economic position unusual enough so that she was able to live outside and above the traditions and conventions of her day? The evidence, screened through a succession of (male) biographers and historians, is inconclusive.

But as we look back at Walladah, through a mist of nearly nine hundred years of fact, legend, opinion, and contradictory statements, one cannot but agree with Ibn Zaydun, her great love, who characterized her thus:

She is like water, difficult to hold in hand:
Its seething foam prevents getting it easily!

Notes

1.   Other rumors about her parentage exist, but, according to several contemporary sources of the period, this point is generally accepted. The dates used are from the Wüstenfeld conversion tables, which transpose dates from the Islamic calendar (Hijrah, dating from the time of the Prophet Muhammad's flight to Medina) into dates corresponding to those on the Christian calendar.
2.   His full name was Muhammad Ibn Abd al-Rahman Ibn 'Ubayd Allah al-Nasir. See 'Ali Abd al-Azim, *Ibn Zaydun 'Asrahu wa-Hayatahu wa-Adabahu.*
3.   Ibid., p. 141.
4.   Ibid., p. 140.
5.   Ibid., p. 141.
6.   Ibid.
7.   Ibn Bassam al Dakhinah, Abu al-Hasan 'Ali, was an Arabic grammarian who lived just after Walladah. He died in A.D. 1147.
8.   Alois Richard Nykl, *Hispano-Arabic Poetry and Its Relations with the Old Provencal Troubadours,* p. 107.
9.   Ibid.
10.   Al-Maqqari, Ahmad Ibn Muhammad, a seventeenth-century man of letters and author of books on logic and on the hadith, who lived in Fez and Cairo. He died in 1631.
11.   al-Azim, *Ibn Zaydun,* p. 143.
12.   Ibid., p. 146.
13.   Ibid.
14.   Ibid. Ibn Khaqan, al-Fath, who died in 1140, wrote a collection of biographies of Andalusian poets.
15.   Ibid., p. 147.
16.   Most of the biographical material about Ibn Zaydun is summarized from details in Nykl, *Hispano-Arabic Poetry;* Reynold Alleyne Nicholson, *A Literary History of the Arabs;* and Reinhart Dozy, *Spanish Islam;* as well as the material in al-Azim, *Ibn Zaydun.*
17.   Nykl, *Hispano-Arabic Poetry,* p. 107.

18.   Ibid., p. 108.
19.   Ibid., p. 110.
20.   Ibid.
21.   Ibid., p. 113.
22.   al-Azim, *Ibn Zaydun*, p. 148.
23.   Ibid.
24.   Ibid.
25.   Ibid., p. 147.
26.   Ibid.
27.   Ibid., p. 153.
28.   Ibid., p. 144.
29.   Ibid., p. 152.
30.   Ibid., p. 148.
31.   Ibid., p. 142.
32.   Ibid., pp. 144–145.
33.   Nykl, *Hispano-Arabic Poetry*, p. 107.
34.   Ibid., p. 111.
35.   Ibid., p. 112.
36.   al-Azim, *Ibn Zaydun*, p. 144.

References

al-Azim, 'Ali Abd. *Ibn Zaydun 'Asrahu wa-Hayatahu wa-Adabahu.* Cairo: Maktabat al-Anjlu Misriyah, 1955.

Dozy, Reinhart. *Spanish Islam.* Translated by Francis Griffin Stokes. London: Chatto and Windus, 1913.

Nicholson, Reynold Alleyne. *A Literary History of the Arabs.* Cambridge: At the University Press, 1956.

Nykl, Alois Richard. *Hispano-Arabic Poetry and Its Relations with the Old Provencal Troubadours.* Baltimore: J. H. Furst, 1946.

6

Rabiah Balkhi

رابعه بلخی

Medieval Afghani Poet

ca. A.D. 1100–?

Biographical Sketch by Mohammed H. Razi

Rabiah Balkhi was the pioneer of mystic poetry in the Persian language (Dari) and one of the most outstanding Afghan poets.[1] Her greatest literary contributions were made as the Samanid supremacy (890–939) was ending and the Ghaznavid era was beginning (989–1149)—the fourth century of the Solar calendar.[2] The Ghaznavid era was a golden era of accomplishment for Afghanistan both as an empire and as a center of learning and culture. The story of Rabiah's life during this time has been told down through the generations.

Over one thousand years ago in the city of Balkh, often called the "Mother of Cities," a beautiful princess was born in the palace of Kab Quzdari Balkhi—the king of Balkh. From the time of her birth, this little girl was so gentle of manner and so beautiful that her family knew she would be a special joy and pride to them. They named her Rabiah. Many of the people of the kingdom feared that God would claim Rabiah while she was very young because she was reputed to be too beautiful and gentle to live among mortals.

Rabiah had one brother—Haris, who was a handsome youngster but not of gentle nature. He was very impressed with his own importance as

---

Photo: Persian garden, fifteenth-century miniature

a prince and was rude and unkind to people. In addition, he was intensely jealous of Rabiah because of the attention and love bestowed on her by everyone.

Kab Quzdari Balkhi was a righteous and good king. He encouraged artists, musicians, writers, and athletes to perform in his court. Balkh became a center of learning and culture. Rabiah and her brother often watched these performances. When the performers were finished, the king presented each with a gift for their contribution—and sometimes Rabiah was asked by her father to make these presentations—which thrilled her and pleased the recipients.

When Rabiah was about ten years old, her mother died—and this led to a closer bond between father and daughter. Raenah, her childhood nurse, now became her constant companion and closest confidant. Rabiah and Raenah spent long hours in the mosque praying and listening to readings from the holy Koran.[3]

As she grew, Rabiah became more beautiful and articulate and developed skills in archery, horsemanship, hunting, and swimming. To celebrate her flowering into womanhood, the king built a suite of rooms especially for her and Raenah. Rabiah began to spend a part of each day writing love poetry—mostly to God. A very religious young woman, she chose this manner to express her love for God and all that He created. Most of these writings were placed in a locked chest.

Haris continued to be jealous of Rabiah's abilities. He insisted that she should be more retiring as a woman and that it was demeaning for a princess to occupy herself writing and reciting poetry.[4]

Among the talented people who appeared at the court were many athletes. One of the greatest was a young slave owned by Haris, named Baktash, who consistently won over all his adversaries. Rabiah often watched these feats of strength and grew to admire the young slave's talents.[5] But she was aware of her position and the responsibilities demanded of her, and she told no one of her admiration for Baktash—not even Raenah. But she thought constantly of Baktash and would write down her thoughts in poem form, then lock the poems in her writing chest.[6]

King Kab Quzdari Balkhi, aged and worn with years of the responsibility of ruling, took to his bed in illness. Haris, impatient to assume the kingship, conspired to hurry his father's death by poisoning him. He decreed that the king was much too ill to see anyone. But Rabiah learned of her brother's plan. She went to her father's bedchamber to warn him. Before she could speak, Haris entered. She and her father bade each other a tearful farewell. The king then turned to his son and informed him that he would be a guest in this palace for only a short

time. He admonished Haris to assume the responsibilities of the kingdom and his subjects with honor and righteousness. He gave Rabiah's
welfare and happiness into the hands of his son and then quietly slipped
away on the arm of death.

With Haris's ascension to the throne, many things in the kingdom
changed. Haris was not the wise and righteous ruler that his father had
been. Rabiah was more confined to her quarters and allowed less and
less to participate in the activities that made her happy. She became ill
and restless and spent more of her time writing poetry. Haris was
secretly very pleased that Rabiah was ill and hired Sarbatah, a herbal
doctor, to mix a concoction of herbs and roots that would cause Rabiah's
death. But when Sarbatah came to Rabiah's quarters, she refused the
medication, explaining that no medicine could cure her illness. Raenah
had become most concerned for Rabiah's health and finally persuaded
her to confide in her. Rabiah confessed to Raenah her love for Baktash
and the impossibility of ever telling him of this admiration—for she was
a princess and he a slave.[7] Raenah was very sad but told Rabiah that if
she should need any help in the matter she would do whatever Rabiah
wished.

After a time, Rabiah decided to write a poem directly to Baktash.
Raenah delivered the poem and Baktash was overwhelmed with the idea
that anyone so lovely and gentle as Rabiah should admire him. On his
way to see Rabiah, the guards of her suite attempted to stop him, but he
overpowered them. After this first meeting, they met several more times
and Baktash told Rabiah of his own admiration of her beauty and
gentleness.

One day Rabiah's writing chest was stolen—apparently by someone
who thought that it contained her jewels. But when the chest was
opened and the poems read, there was the name of Baktash, the slave.
The chest and its contents were taken to Haris, who immediately
assigned Baktash to a post far from the city of Balkh.

Haris's reputation as an unfit king spread far and wide and finally
reached the ears of one of his oldest and strongest enemies, who sent
word that he was on his way to Balkh to challenge Haris in a feat of
strength. Haris was not athletic and knew that he would be no match for
his arch enemy. In a desperate move, he sent word to Baktash that, if he
would return to the city of Balkh and defend the honor of its king and
the city, he would be rewarded with an influential position and with
riches. Baktash returned.

On the day of the contest, Rabiah heard that her brother had ordered
the guards to kill Baktash if he should be successful in defeating his
adversary. Baktash defended his king well. While the spectators in the

arena were still cheering Baktash's victory, Rabiah rode a swift steed onto the field of combat, assisted Baktash into the saddle, and rode away—thus saving his life.[8]

To the north of Balkh lay the kingdom of Bokhara (now in Russia). Haris received an invitation to attend a great festival in this city where all the finest artists, writers, musicians, and athletes would gather to compete. Among those present was one of the greatest writers of the times, Rudaki. Rudaki had challenged Rabiah in poetic debate and admired her talent and wisdom. He mentioned her name at the public festival, bemoaning the fact that, despite her poetic talent, gentle ways, and fine upbringing, her heart belonged to Baktash—one of Haris's slaves. Haris became angry; he felt that his own prestige and that of his kingdom had been sorely damaged by the insinuations of Rudaki. He chose to hide his anger in the presence of those at the festival, but as soon as possible he made great haste to return to Balkh. The closer he came to his palace, the more his anger welled within him, and he decided that the only possible solution to the intolerable situation was to kill Baktash and Rabiah.

He had Rabiah taken to a public bath where her veins were slashed, and she was left to bleed to death. But Raenah helped Baktash escape from the pit and gave him a dagger. Baktash set out for the palace and killed the wicked Haris. He then rushed to the public bath to save the life of his beloved Rabiah—only to find that the warmth of her body was already gone.[9]

Before she died, Rabiah had dipped her finger in her life's blood and written on the walls of the bath the name of Baktash, a poem, and a statement which told how wrong were her brother's evil thoughts about her love for Baktash. Baktash was so despondent over finding Rabiah dead that he too dipped his finger in her blood, wrote her name beside his own, and then fell upon his dagger in death.

Thus ended the life and rule of Haris, which historians have recorded with dishonor—and thus ended the lives of two beautiful, honorable, and talented young lovers. The predictions made by the astrologer Atrush did indeed come true: Rabiah was as shining as the light of a star to the world, and she met with a tragic death.

Rabiah Balkhi wrote her poetry in both Arabic and Persian (Dari), and sometimes she used both languages in a single writing.[10] Her style of writing is known as the *ghazal*.[11] This is a type of stanza in which each line contains a complete thought; the thoughts are not necessarily related and do not depend on each other for explanation or clarity.

Of the many poems which Rabiah supposedly wrote, only a limited number of excerpts have been preserved.

The following excerpt was written as a protest toward the uncaring attitude shown by her lover:

My prayer to God is this:
that you be bound in love with someone
Unmoving as stick and stone,

For only having suffered love's agony
of pain and separation
Shall you come to feel and value
my love for you.[12]

This excerpt is one in which she expresses her wonderment at the beauty and perfection of spring:

The fresh roses are such a lovely
company, in beauty and splendor,
They surpass the celebrated
paintings of the inimitable Mani.

The roses have put on the fairest
colours from Leila's face;
For not otherwise would the eyes
of Majnoon behold them from the clouds.
Night has so filled the tulips with
her wine, that in the dawn
Flush they sway like ruby chalices.

The narcissus blooms carry the
tint of silver and gold,
Each of them looking like a crown
fit to adorn a princely head.

The frail violets appareled in
their delicate hues,
Look like a company of nuns
receiving their ordination from nature.[13]

The last excerpt is probably one of her best known, for it is the poem which she supposedly wrote upon the wall of the public bath with her own life's blood. Addressed to her brother, Haris, it reads:

You judged my love a sin, you have been my undoing;
With what heart shall you face up to God,
in the hour of questioning?

The glories of this world and more,
without him are as little;
But Hell, if he were with me,
I should willingly embrace.

The wiseman's saying comes true.
Sooner or later, pride has its fall.[14]

The Afghan nation continues to honor the memory of Rabiah Balkhi,
even today. A newly established high school for young girls bears her
name, and the Republic of Afghanistan has recently decided to produce
a movie based on the life and work of Rabiah Balkhi as part of a renewal
of national interest in preserving the historical and cultural heritage of
the Afghan people.

A thousand years of legend and story have only added to the luster
associated with the name of Rabiah Balkhi.

Notes

1.   Mohammed H. Zhobal, *Tarikh-i Adabyat-i Dari dar Afghanistan*,
p. 82.
2.   Jan Rypka, *History of Iranian Literature*, p. 144.
3.   G. H. Nawabi, *Rabia-i Balkhi*, p. vii.
4.   Ibid.
5.   Zhobal, *Tarikh-i Adabyat-i Dari dar Afghanistan*, pp. 82–83.
6.   Ibid.
7.   Nawabi, *Rabia-i Balkhi*, p. xix.
8.   Ibid., p. ix.
9.   Zhobal, *Tarikh-i Adabyat-i Dari dar Afghanistan*, pp. 82–83.
10.   Rypka, *History of Iranian Literature*, p. 144.
11.   Hussain Farviar, *Tarikh-i Adabyat-i Iran wa Tarikh-i-Shu'ara*,
p. 96.
12.   Zabih Allah Safa, *Tarikh-i Adabyat dar Iran*, p. 451.
13.   Ibid.
14.   Ibid.

References

Farviar, Hussain. *Tarikh-i Adabyat-i Iran wa Tarikh-i-Shu'ara*.
Teheran, 1962.

Nawabi, G. H. *Rabia-i Balkhi*. Kabul: Government Printing House,
1965.

Rypka, Jan. *History of Iranian Literature*. Dordrecht: D. Reidel, 1968.

Safa, Zabih Allah. *Tarikh-i Adabyat dar Iran*. Teheran, 1967.

Zhobal, Mohammed H. *Tarikh-i Adabyat-i Dari dar Afghanistan*.
Kabul: Ministry of Education Printing House, 1956.

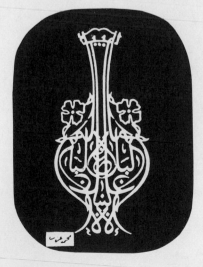

Part **2** **Transition**

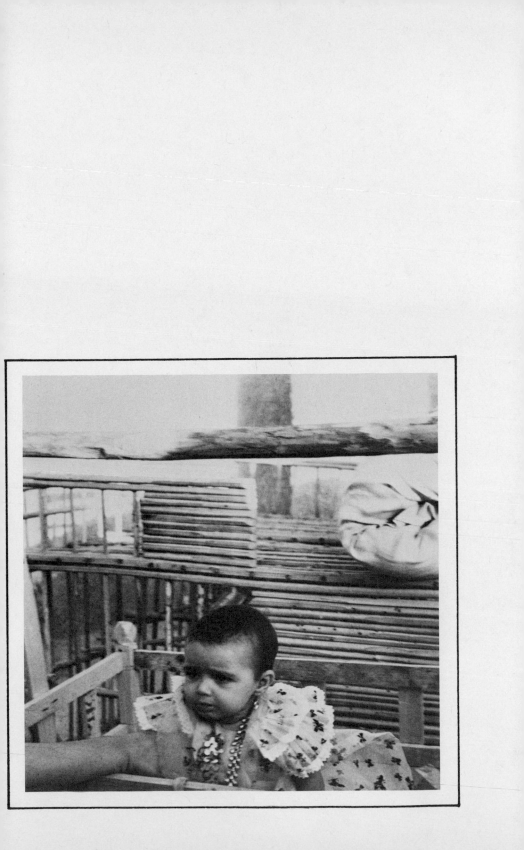

7 Tunisian Lullabies

اغانى لهدهدة الطفل

Collected and Translated by Sabra Webber

Variants of the following lullabies are found in many areas of Tunisia.[1] The melodic accompaniment to the words will range from an almost spoken chant to a simple tune, depending on the individual woman's taste, age, and the part of the country in which she lives. The rhythm, too, is flexible and can be peaceful and repetitive or so lively and irregular that it would seem unlikely to induce sleep! The child is bounced and patted on the back in rhythm with the song.

Since lullabies are in the nature of work songs (the work being the lulling of a baby), it is not surprising that many of them are actually daydreams or fantasies of the mother about what the child will do for *her* in the future. In a sense, she is anticipating her reward for the work. The mother will even sometimes choose a song which she will call a lullaby but which may have nothing at all to do with the child or the mother-child relationship; such songs may be, rather, a popular song of the day or a traditional song about a woman and her lover. The examples presented here are basically mother-child oriented.

A Tunisian woman of about forty described an alternative function for these lullabies quite different from that of inducing sleep. She stated

---

Photo: Village child in crib

that she remembers, from her childhood, young mothers using these songs in verbal duels. One example she gave was that of two mothers, living in homes with adjacent courtyards, one with a boy baby and the other with a girl, "debating" in a series of these lullabies whether it is better to be the mother of sons or daughters. As can be seen from the texts, the debates can become quite rough and might end, as she recalled, with one or the other of the young mothers running into the house in tears.

From these lullaby texts we can see that daughters are viewed differently than sons. A son, when he grows up, may provide money or fine things for his mother, but the daughter is with her mother from a very early age—cleaning, cooking, receiving guests, and in general sharing her mother's life and work. In an urban area, there is not much work for a son to do for his mother or for his father. But a girl is always necessary to the household, whether it be rural or urban, and, in families where there are no girls, one is often adopted at a very young age. These adopted children are fed and clothed and often schooled and married off by their new families.

The texts of the lullabies thus not only express the mothers' attitudes toward sons and daughters, but also reveal that daughters fulfill different needs for the mother than do sons.

I

A girl child is better than ten thousand boys;
If she's far away she asks after her mother;
If she's near she brings me her love
And gives me part of her food.
So don't be too happy, mother of a son!
My daughter will grow up and take him.
She'll build her house on a hill far from you;
He'll earn the living, but she'll spend it!

Jood Joowad, Jood Joowad.
Gift! A Gift! Gift! A Gift!
A girl is better than a thousand boys,
For if my daughter lives in town,
She'll come each morning to see me;
She'll comfort me when I'm ill,
And if I should die
She'd mourn for a long time.

Gift! A Gift! Gift! A Gift!
I say my son is better.
He brings me wheat and barley;
He brings me a granddaughter and a grandson,
Who stay in my house and play together,
My son wears burnooses woven with silver,
Only black-eyed women are good enough for him!

III

She who gives birth to a girl

And her husband not to sleep
    with her anymore.
She deserves to be tied up

But she who gives birth to a boy

Deserves a basket of henna,
A sheep slaughtered for her,
A big barbecue,

She who brings good news of a
    son
A house facing east toward
    Mecca,
A good foreign slave,

And she who bears a girl
Deserves to stay home

Ah, but don't be too happy,
    O mother of a son
We'll eat up the stores of her
    house.
And you'll keep on nagging

Deserves to be hit with a
    pottery mug,
She deserves his anger.

And hung from a vine tree.

Deserves the [minaret] and
    the village,
Jingling anklets,
Great celebration,
And the fat tail of the sheep.[2]

Deserves a camelload of
    good things,
Servants and slaves,

A handsome man-servant.

Deserves a blow with a mug,
To be hidden away.

My daughter will grow up
    and take him.
I'll use her oil to shine my
    hair
Just like a yapping dog!

She is my good fortune, she is my good fortune.
Sing for her and keep the Evil Eye from her.
Suitors already are coming to court her,
But we won't let her go.
All Tunis should be hers.
All the oil of the coast should gloss her braided hair
And the wheat of Africa fill all the corners of her house.

My daughter, your suitors stand in line,
Their heads humbly bowed.
Your father asks for thousands,
But your mother says it's not enough.

We won't give you up, my daughter,
Not till the son of the bey comes,
Who has ruled since his youth,
Who wears a robe of silk.
He'll bring you anklets
That will jingle and move when you move.
He will offer 130 camels,
But in the eyes of a mother
That's not enough for a beloved daughter.

Notes

1.   These lullabies were collected between July 1968 and March 1969 from Tunisian Muslim women aged forty to sixty.
2.   This piece is traditionally considered the most succulent part of the animal.

8 Najib Mahfuz

نجيب محفوظ (الخطأ)

"The Mistake"
An Excerpt from *Bayna al-Qasrayn* (Between two palaces)

Bayna al-Qasrayn (Between two palaces), from which the following excerpt is taken, is the first of the three novels which make up *al-Thulathiyyah*, Najib Mahfuz's famous trilogy, chronicling the lives of a middle-class Egyptian family from 1918 to 1944. The second novel, *Qasr al-Shawq*, was followed by *Sukariyah*. For this monumental work, unprecedented in Arab letters, Mahfuz received the State Prize for Literature in Egypt.

In the three volumes of *al-Thulathiyyah*, Mahfuz covers a vital period of change in Egyptian political, social, and economic life. The influence of the west was felt; colonialism and nationalism clashed; old ways slowly gave way to new. Mahfuz records these traumatic events in Egyptian history through their impact on the lives of a single family, that of 'Abd al-Jawad. The daughters marry. The second-oldest son, Fahmi, becomes involved in politics and is killed in a nationalist demonstration. Kamal, the youngest son, is the central figure of *Qasr al-Shawq*; he grows up, goes to teachers' college, reads Darwin, and quarrels with his father about Islamic belief. The third novel, *Sukariyah*, deals with the third generation of the family, specifically two grandsons who also

Photo: Bayna al-Qasrayn street, Cairo

become enmeshed in political struggles. A social realist, Mahfuz is esteemed throughout the Arab world for his insight into character, his sense of history, and his literary style.

The excerpt from *Bayna al-Qasrayn* which follows introduces two women of strongly contrasting character and behavior, one no less representative than the other. Both types may still be found in Egypt today, though the spectrum of behavior has been broadened by modern education and increased economic opportunities. They are more typical, however, of middle-class women in Egypt at the turn of the century, before the current period of revolutionary change.

One spring morning, Sayyid Ahmad, the father of the family, departed on a business trip to Port Said. In the father's sudden and unexpected absence a strange atmosphere of release and relaxation enveloped the household, a feeling which had nothing to do with the spring. For spring, the end of the long, bare winter months and the beginning of the flowering and blooming which offered new hope and warmth, brought Sayyid Ahmad's family no liberty which winter might have prevented. On this particular day, however, the father's departure from Cairo happened to coincide with the natural desire for change which the spring encouraged. Further, the day was Friday, a holiday for everyone in the family. Each member began to think about how he or she might be able to spend this wonderful day, a day of freedom from the ever-present, ever-watchful eyes of the father, the constant monitor of every activity of each member of the household.

Kamal, the youngest son, thought he might spend the whole time playing, inside the house or outside the door of the house, whichever he pleased. The two sisters, 'A'ishah and Khadijah, wondered whether they might be able to slip away and spend the evening at the house of Maryam, their neighbor and close friend.

But the mother, Aminah, vetoed these plans. The family, she said, should continue its usual pattern of life, despite the fact that the father was away. Even though she did not always agree with the limits he had placed on their activities, she felt the limits should be maintained, whether he was there or not. She always supported his decisions, out of fear of him and also out of some belief in his judgment and authority.

This time, however, Yasin, the eldest son, spoke up. "Oh, Mother, don't forbid such simple pleasures. Our family lives the kind of life nobody else would dream of. And something else. Why don't you enjoy yourself a little for a change?" And he turned to the rest of the family. "What do you think about that?"

Everyone stared at Yasin in amazement, but no one said a word. His mother looked at him in a reproachful way, but he went on talking.

"What are you staring at me for? After all, I didn't make a mistake in al-Bukhari.[1] It's only a little outing I'm suggesting, Mother, not a crime, for heaven's sake. And, my mother, when you've come back, you'll have

[An excerpt from Najib Mahfuz, Bayna al-Qasrayn (Cairo: Matbu'at Maktabat Misr, 1960). Printed with the permission of the American University in Cairo Press, which holds exclusive world English translation and publication rights to Bayna al-Qasrayn. Translated by the Editors.]

seen a bit of the quarter and the street where you've lived for fourteen years without visiting any of it!"

The mother sighed and murmured, "May God forgive you!"

Yasin laughed. "Why should God forgive me? What have I done? What sin have I committed? My God, Mother, if I were you, I'd go right now and pay a visit to the shrine of Sayyidna al-Husayn. Sayyidna al-Husayn! Do you hear what I'm saying? The saint for whom you have such a great devotion! The saint to whom you've always prayed so piously! The saint who is so near and dear to you! Go! He's calling you!"

The mother's heart began to beat faster. The sudden emotion was reflected on her flushed face, and she lowered her head, ashamed, trying to hide the effect which Yasin's suggestion had produced. Her whole being was attracted by his suggestion. Something within herself had exploded. The violence of her reaction surprised her as well as the other members of the family who stood around her now, watching her. The effect was as if an earthquake had erupted unexpectedly in a part of the world which had never known earthquakes. Aminah was confused; she could not explain how and why her heart had responded so quickly to the idea of a visit to Sayyidna al-Husayn. How was it that her eyes could look so easily beyond forbidden boundaries? How could such an outing take place? How? The whole idea was diabolical, tempting, overwhelming. Soon she began to feel that a visit to Sayyidna al-Husayn was a perfectly good excuse for overstepping boundaries. Were there not religious justifications for such a venture? Aminah was not the first human being in whom such transformations have taken place, within whom justifications have been manufactured for obeying deep inner instincts, for releasing long-pent-up emotions, just as the instinct for battle and for conflict, for example, is justified by the defense of freedom or the desire for peace.

The mother did not know exactly how to express her dangerous acceptance of the plan. She looked up at Yasin and said, rather hesitantly, "A visit to Sayyidna al-Husayn has always been one of the great desires of my life. But . . . what about your father?"

Yasin laughed. "Father's on his way to Port Said and he won't be back before tomorrow noon. But if you're still concerned, why don't you borrow the servant's *milayah*? [2] Then if somebody sees you leaving or returning to the house, they'll just think it is a visitor."

The mothers' eyes wandered from one to the other of her children, rather timidly, a bit embarrassed before them. 'A'ishah and Khadijah reassured her, expressing their enthusiasm for the visit, almost as though they were reacting to their own wishes, something they longed to do. For they realized that now, after this great and unexpected turn of

events, their visit to Maryam was assured. Kamal was so overcome that
he cried, "I'll come with you, Mother, and show you the way!"

Fahmi, the second-oldest son, was much moved by the look on his
mother's face, the innocent happy look of a child with a new toy. "Oh,
Mother," he said, "go on and have a look at the world. Don't worry
about anything. The only thing I worry about is that one day you'll forget
how to walk because you've stayed so long in the house."

Khadijah ran to get the *milayah* from Umm Hifni, the servant. Kamal
ran to put on his suit and his tarboosh. Sounds of laughter and happy
talk filled the house. The day had become a gay feast, a feast which no
one had experienced before. No one realized how their own long-
suppressed feelings of rebellion were welling up now against the strong
will of their absent father.

The mother wrapped herself in the borrowed *milayah*, pulled the veil
down over her face, and looked in the mirror. She couldn't help laughing at the strange image, and she laughed until her whole body shook.

"Come on, Mother!" Kamal ran to the entrance hall of the house, but
the mother did not follow him. She stood still, and a strong premonition
of disaster passed through her, as sometimes happens in moments of
crisis and decision. She looked at Fahmi, standing near and said, "Tell
me what you really think. Should I go or not?"

Yasin stood firm. "Go ahead, Mother, and may God go with you!"

Khadijah took her by the arm, pushed her gently, and said, "Say the
fatihah,[3] Mother, and then you'll be safe." She held her mother's hand
until the older woman was down the steps. Then the mother went
through the house alone, the family following her. At the door Umm
Hifni waited, eyeing the newly-donned *milayah* critically. She came
forward, rearranged the robe around her mistress's body, and showed
her how to hold the edge of it in the proper position. Aminah obeyed,
following the instructions carefully, for she was wearing the *milayah* for
nearly the first time in her life. As she wound it about her, the shape of
her body was outlined through the robe, a shape which her full
jallabiyah[4] had hidden for many years. Khadijah looked at her mother
admiringly, winked at 'A'ishah, and the girls both giggled.

As the mother crossed the doorstep and stepped out onto the street,
she experienced a moment of panic. Her throat became dry and her
great happiness was diminished by feelings of guilt and worry. She
moved forward slowly, holding nervously to Kamal's hand. She walked
unsteadily, like a child taking its first steps, out of shyness and uncer-
tainty, as she moved among people whom she knew only from observ-
ing them through the *mushrabiyah*[5] windows of her own house.

"There is 'Amm Hasanayn, the barber," she thought, "and Darwish, the fool peddler, and the milk seller, and Bayumi al-Sharbatli, who brings around the sweet drinks, and Abu Sair', the owner of the fry shop."

She felt, even though she was veiled, that these people must see her and recognize her as she recognized them. But then she thought, "How can they know me, they've never laid an eye on me!" As this realization filled her, they came to Darb Qirmiz, the shortest route to the shrine of Sayyidna al-Husayn. Darb Qirmiz has few shops, and few people would be on the streets, unlike the Nahasin road, where Sayyid Ahmad's own shop was located. Still, the mother hesitated for a moment before stepping into the *darb*.[6] She looked back toward her own house and saw there the two shadows of her daughters behind one shutter, and at the other shutter, open wide, she saw Yasin's and Fahmi's smiling faces. That familiar sight gave her strength and she stepped forward, moving easily with Kamal along the almost deserted alley. The feeling of guilt and worry did not leave her completely but receded before her enthusiasm at discovering the new world about her, one of many alleys, many squares, a strange building, a group of people. In sharing with this small group of humanity its movement along the street, something she had never done before, she experienced a naïve pleasure, a release. Hers was the sudden happiness of one who had been in prison for a quarter of a century, closed between four walls except for a carefully counted number of annual visits to her mother, who lived in the district of al-Khuranfash. These visits always happened in the same way: Sayyid Ahmad took his wife in a carriage, and on these occasions she sat beside him meekly, not having the courage to even glance outside at the street around her.

But, today, she began asking Kamal about everything, the places they were passing, the buildings, and the boy replied eagerly, proud of his role as guide.

"This, Mother," he said, "is the tomb of Qirmiz, it's well known. One should recite the *fatihah* before entering it in order to protect oneself from the evil spirits that haunt it. And there, that's the Maydan Bayt al Qadi. See the tall, elegant trees!" Kamal himself used to call the place the square of the pasha's beard or give it the name of the flowers which bloomed at the top of the flame trees bordering the square. And some-times he would call it the square of Shinjarelli, after the Turkish peddler who sat there, selling chocolate. "And this big building, Mother, that's the Jamaliyah police station." Although the little boy could not find any-thing noteworthy to point out about this building, except the sword hanging from the waist of the guard, the mother looked at the police station with interest. Here was the place where a man worked who had asked for her daughter's hand in marriage; somehow, seeing the building where her daughter's suitor worked gave the man more importance in the mother's mind.

Soon they reached the kindergarten of Khan Ja'far, where Kamal had spent a year before entering the Khalil Agha primary school. "There, Mother," said Kamal. "There's the balcony where Shaykh Mahdi would make us face the wall for the least thing and then he'd kick us with his shoes five or six or even ten times, as many times as he wanted." Below the balcony was a little shop, and Kamal said, in a tone which his mother understood, "That's 'Amm Saddiq's place. He sells candy." Kamal did not move until he had received a piaster and had bought a piece of red chewing gum.

At the school, the mother and her son turned into Khan Ja'far road, from which part of the shrine of Sayyidna al-Husayn was visible in the distance. The parapets of the wall of the shrine, decorated with cut out stone, reminded Kamal of the points of spears. They could see a great window cut into the side of the shrine, very old, decorated with fine arabesque script. As the shrine came into view, a strong feeling of joy welled up in Aminah's heart, and she began to walk faster than she had since she left home.

"Yes, Mother, that's it," nodded Kamal, and Aminah smiled to herself and rejoiced, "Ah!" she murmured. "At last! Sayyidna al-Husayn."

Now she began in her mind to compare the two images of Sayyidna al-Husayn: the real mosque, which she had been approaching since she had left her house, and the image of the shrine, which she had created in her mind over the years, using details and bits of the mosques which she could see from her own windows, the Barquq mosque and the Qala'un mosque. She discovered that the real shrine was very different from the imaginary shrine she had created. In her mind, as the years passed, she had lengthened and widened the walls of the shrine; she had embellished it with more and more beautiful decoration, in order to give it a splendor suitable to the saint buried there. For to Aminah, Sayyidna al-Husayn deserved a very high place indeed and, therefore, she had built him an imaginary shrine proportionate to his importance, enriching her design with the glory and magnificence she felt were equal to the saint's importance to herself.

Yet, though the reality was different from the picture she had constructed in her imagination, it did not diminish her pleasure, her joy in seeing the shrine at last. She felt her whole body suffuse with the unexpected emotion of the experience.

Kamal and his mother walked around the mosque to the green door, where they entered with a crowd of women. When Aminah put her foot on the ground of the shrine, her emotion increased: she felt as though her earthly body were melting away in a passion of love for the great saint; she felt as if she were becoming a spirit, fluttering its wings high in the sky above, faraway, near the great places of prophecy and revelation. Her eyes filled with tears, tears which helped her release the turmoil of love and faith and happiness, of gratitude to God which filled her to overflowing. She looked about eagerly, noting the details of the shrine, its ceilings, its carpets, the pillars, the chandeliers, the mimbar, and the two mihrabs.

Kamal, also, was looking at these things which his mother found so wonderful, but he was seeing them in a different way. He wondered about the shrine, which, during the day and on into the first part of the evening, is filled with visitors and pilgrims. But then, when everybody leaves and the shrine is empty, what happens then? Kamal thought of the shrine as a home for the martyr, the Sayyid Husayn. Did the martyr then, Kamal wondered, roam around his house as an occupant would in any house, praying in the mihrab, using the furniture, looking through the windows to see the streets outside? Oh, how Kamal wished they would forget about him and leave him in the mosque after the doors were locked. Then he would have a chance to see al-Husayn face to face and stay in his presence a whole night. Kamal thought about what he would do during such a time, the manner of loving submission which might be appropriate, whether he should ask something from the martyr, from his store of love and grace. He imagined himself approaching the martyr, his head bowed, and the martyr asking him gently, "And who are you?" And Kamal visualized himself replying, after kissing the martyr's hand, "Kamal Ahmad 'Abd al-Jawad."

Probably the martyr would ask him his profession, and Kamal thought he would reply that he was a student, and he would not forget to mention his outstanding record in Khalil Agha primary school. Then no doubt the martyr would wonder what had brought the boy to the shrine at such a late hour. And he, Kamal, would reply that he had come because of his love for Al al-Bayt—the family of the Prophet and of 'Ali— and for the love of the martyr Husayn in particular. At that point, Kamal thought, the martyr would smile warmly and ask the boy to accompany him on his nightly rounds of the shrine. Then Kamal planned to tell the martyr of his hopes and ask him a favor. "Please sir," he would say, "would you guarantee that I can play inside or outside the house whenever I want and that 'A'ishah and Khadijah stay home forever? And would you please change my father's temper and give my mother eternal life? And, finally, would you please guarantee that I can take as much as I need from my spending money and that all of our family goes to heaven, without judgment for our sins?"

These different thoughts filled the minds of Aminah and her son Kamal as they moved slowly, with the current of pilgrims which was bringing them gradually to the tomb of the martyr, the tomb which Aminah had yearned to see for so long, yearning toward a dream which she had not expected to be realized on earth. One can see her there, standing between the pillars of the supporting walls, in the room where the tomb is placed; no, now she is standing beside the tomb itself, and she can see it through her tears. She wishes she could prolong this moment, to savor the taste of her happiness, but the crowd of pilgrims is pushing her along. She stretched out her arm to touch the wooden frame around the tomb; Kamal did the same and they recited the *fatihah*. The mother stroked the wall of *mushrabiyah* which surrounded the tomb, she kissed it, and she continued to praise and plead with the martyr. She wanted to stay longer, to stand or to sit in a corner and meditate before going around the tomb once more. But the servant of the shrine was watching; he did not let anyone pause too long, and he urged forward the women who lagged behind, warning them with his long stick to keep moving and finish the turn of the shrine so that their pilgrimages might be completed before the Friday noon prayers.

When Aminah found herself at the exit of the *masjid*, or mosque, she pulled herself away unwillingly. She had drunk from this fountain of holiness, yet it had not quenched her thirst. The pilgrimage had aroused her longing and now nothing would quench that thirst. She dragged herself away with a feeling of sorrow, saying a final goodbye but leaving her heart behind her. Still, since it had always been her nature to be contented with what was given to her, she left with some pleasure also. The bit of happiness she had been granted helped to overcome the sadness she felt in leaving the place of pilgrimage.

Kamal wanted to show her his school, so they walked to the end of Shari' Sayyidna al-Husayn and stopped for a moment to look.

"Now let's go back," said Aminah and, at her words, Kamal felt as though a warning had been sounded. The end of this beautiful excursion with his mother was near, an excursion he would not have dreamed possible. He tried to prolong the occasion by suggesting they walk through the new road to al-Ghuriyah. To overcome his mother's opposition, which he could see in the frowning kind of smile barely visible behind her veil, he called out, "By the grace of Sayyidna al-Husayn, let's go." She surrendered and let him lead her along by the hand, through the crowds of people coming from all directions, hundreds of people compared to the few she had passed in the quieter streets. In the crowds the mother began to feel uneasy, she was afraid she was losing control of herself, and she told Kamal of her discomfort. But Kamal's burning desire to prolong the excursion made him shut his ears to her complaining. He encouraged her to keep going, and he tried to distract her by pointing out the shops, the carriages, the people.

At the turning to al-Ghuriyah stood a pastry shop, and the boy began to think of ways in which he could persuade his mother to enter the shop and buy some cakes. He was so preoccupied that he dropped his mother's hand and moved toward the shop. When he turned back, he saw his mother falling forward and heard her moaning cry. His eyes widened in fear, and he saw, at the same time, out of the corner of his eye, a car stopping suddenly, leaving a great trail of smoke and dust, its brakes screaming to a halt. The car had been about to run over that form lying on the ground, the form that was his own mother, if it had not swerved a hand's breadth and managed to avoid her. Kamal ran and knelt beside his mother. He held her hand and called to her, but she did not answer. A crowd had gathered quickly around the spot, just as children will run when they hear the whistle of the magician calling them to a performance. They formed a dense circle around his mother, lying on the ground, and Kamal looked up at the faces around him and began to cry bitterly. Some of the people in the crowd tried to comfort him with meaningless words; others bent toward his mother, some to see how she was, some to see whether her death had come—death appearing once more, knocking this time at some stranger's door, taking a soul which was not their own. They looked at the woman lying on the street as though they were rehearsing for a performance with which all of us are destined to end our stay on earth.

"The left door of the car hit her in the back," shouted one.

The driver insisted, "She swerved off the sidewalk suddenly! I couldn't avoid hitting her. I stopped suddenly. The blow was very light, but if it hadn't been for God's blessing, I could easily have run over her."

"She's still breathing. She only fainted," someone else said.

The policeman with his sword broke through the crowd, and the driver said, "It's only a slight accident, officer. It didn't hurt her at all. She's all right. Really she is."

At this point Aminah sat up, and the person nearest to her called out, "Move away! Give her room to breathe. She's opened her eyes. Thank God, she'll be all right." The stranger spoke as though he alone were responsible for restoring her to life. And he turned to Kamal and said, "Don't worry my son. Your mother's all right. Come help me lift her up." Kamal could not stop crying, but he saw his mother moving, and he put his left arm under her elbow and the man helped raise her up until, with great effort, they managed to make her stand. Her *milayah* had fallen away, and now many hands came forward to cover her once more. The owner of the pastry shop offered her a chair, and they brought her a glass of water. The mother sipped the water, half dripping it onto her neck and chest and she wiped it off with her hand.

Then she sighed and began to pant, almost, and, looking at the crowd of faces surrounding her, she asked in bewilderment, "What's the matter? What happened? Why are you crying, Kamal?"

"Are you hurt, Mama? Can you walk to the police station?"

The words *police station* reached her and she replied fearfully, "Why should I go to the police station? No, I'll not go. No, never!"

"But you've been hit by a car, and you fell," insisted the policeman. "If you're hurt, you should come with me and the driver to the station and report the accident."

"Oh, no," said Aminah, panting once more. "I'm fine. There's no need."

"Are you sure?" asked the policeman. "Stand up and let's see whether you're hurt."

The mother stood up immediately, forced out of her bewilderment by the ominous sound of the words *police station*. Pulling herself together, she took Kamal by the hand and began to brush the dust from her *milayah*.

"I'm fine," she said to the policeman, hoping to put an end to the questioning. "Let the driver go. There's nothing wrong with me."

She did not feel weak but stood upright, facing the crowd and the policeman. However, she could feel herself beginning to tremble, from the effects of the accident and the curious gazes of the people around her and the concern of the policeman, and she tried to strengthen herself with a sense of pride, disdain even, and the long years of concealing and veiling herself helped give her the strength to walk along. But an image of her husband came to her as she walked, the two cold, stony eyes of Sayyid Ahmad which she saw as a warning of disaster; she could not bear the image and felt she might fall. But she clasped Kamal's hand tightly and walked away.

No one stopped her, and, as soon as they had turned away from the pastry shop, she sighed and said to Kamal in a strange voice, as though she were talking to herself.

"God, what happened? What did you see, Kamal? It was like a horrible dream. I felt as though I were falling from a high cliff and the earth was moving beneath my feet. I felt as though I were in another, dark world, and then I opened my eyes to see all those people. Oh, God! Did he really want to take me to the police station? Oh, merciful God, who grants me safety each day; oh, preserving God, help me! When are we going to get home? Kamal, you cried too much; oh, dear, I hope your eyes don't hurt; here, wipe your face with this handkerchief until we get home and then you must wash your face. Oh, God!"

She stopped walking toward the end of the gold market and leaned on Kamal, her face twisted with pain.

The boy looked at her and asked uneasily, "What's the matter, Mother?"

"I'm tired, very tired. My legs won't hold me. Call the first carriage you see, Kamal."

Kamal looked about, but he could see only horse-drawn carts, standing by the entrance to the Qala'un hospital. He called one and the cart driver brought the cart to his mother. With Kamal's help and the driver's, she managed to get up onto the floor of the wagon, where she sat cross-legged, sighing from exhaustion. Kamal sat beside her. The donkey began walking slowly and the wagon bumped along, swaying back and forth behind the donkey.

"Oh," murmured Aminah to herself, "oh, what a great pain in my shoulder!"

Kamal stared at her, fear in his eyes, while the wagon passed along the Nahasin road, passing the shop of his father, Sayyid Ahmad. But the boy was so worried he did not even notice the shop. He looked ahead to the *mushrabiyah* balconies of their house, and found he could no longer remember the pleasant beginnings of the day's excursion, but only its miserable ending.

Umm Hifni opened the door. She was taken aback to see her mistress sitting cross-legged on a wagon. For a moment she thought it might have occurred to Aminah to end her outing by hiring a wagon to take a pleasant turn around, but then she saw Kamal's red eyes and her mistress drooping with fatigue and pain. She rushed to the cart, saying, "Sitti,[7] God forbid, what's the matter?"

"She's only tired, *inshallah* [God willing]. Help me get her down," said the driver.

Umm Hifni did so and took her mistress inside, Kamal also supporting her.

Khadijah and 'A'ishah had hurried out of the kitchen to wait in the foyer, both trying to think of a welcoming greeting. But when they saw Umm Hifni practically carrying their mother, they both screamed and ran forward.

"Mother! Mother! What's the matter with you?" they cried, helping to carry her, while Khadijah kept asking Kamal, "What happened? What happened?"

The boy muttered fearfully, "A car! It was a car!"

The two girls repeated, "A car? What car?"

The word seemed to have a frightening effect on them. Khadijah began to cry, "Oh, what bad luck! Poor Mother! May God prevent any evil arising from this!"

'A'ishah was speechless. She burst into tears.

The mother was not unaware of her surroundings and, despite her fatigue, she whispered in a weak voice, trying to comfort them all, "I'm fine, don't worry. There's nothing wrong with me. I'm just very tired."

The noise and confusion below finally reached Yasin and Fahmi, who looked over the railing of the balcony and hurried down the stairs.

"What happened?" they asked. "What's the matter?"

Khadijah could not resist pointing to Kamal, to let him answer, thus saving herself from repeating the dreadful word, *car*. The two young men turned to the little boy, who again murmured in a choked voice, "Car! It was a car," and began to cry all over again.

The young men carried their mother to the girls' room, where they put her on the sofa.

"Oh, Mother," cried out Fahmi, "tell us what's the matter with you. Please tell us."

But the mother lay back on the sofa and did not answer. By this time Umm Hifni, Kamal, Khadijah, and 'A'ishah's weeping had grown so loud that Fahmi lost his temper. "Shut up, all of you!" he yelled. "Be quiet!" And he pulled Kamal to one side and said, "Now, Kamal, tell me, how did the accident happen? What did they do to the driver? Did they take you to the police station? How did Mother react to all this?"

Kamal stopped crying and began to answer his older brother's questions at length, and in detail. The mother seemed to follow the conversation in spite of her weakness, for when the little boy finished she added, "I'm fine, Fahmi. Don't worry yourself so much. They wanted us to go to the police station, but I refused. I walked to the end of the gold market and there my strength gave out. Don't worry. I'll be all right after I've rested a bit."

Yasin, meanwhile, was suffering a great deal, for he had first suggested his mother's outing and therefore felt responsible for the entire ill-fated excursion. Through Yasin that outing had taken place, and long afterward, whenever the family referred to that day, they spoke of it as "the ill-fated excursion." Now he said suddenly, "I'm going to call a doctor," and left without waiting for other opinions.

At the mention of the doctor, the mother began to tremble with fear, in the same way she had trembled when the police station had been mentioned earlier. She begged Fahmi to go after Yasin and stop him.

"There's nothing wrong with me," she said. "I don't want a doctor."

But Fahmi refused, trying to explain that the doctor was needed.

'A'ishah and Khadijah helped their mother off with her *milayah* and Umm Hifni brought water. They stood around her, looking at her pale face, and asking her over and over again, "How do you feel?" "Are you all right?"

She tried her best to be calm and to convince them she was fine by saying, even when overcome by twinges of pain, "It's only a little hurt in my right shoulder. There's no need to call the doctor."

The truth was that the prospect of seeing a doctor filled her with uneasiness. On the one hand, she had never seen a doctor, not only because she had been healthy but also because she had generally been successful in treating her slight ailments with her own methods. She did not really believe in professional doctors, and in her mind she connected the calling of a doctor with a major disaster. On the other hand, she felt that calling a doctor would magnify the importance of the accident, something she did not want at all, for she hoped to be able to cover the whole thing up before her husband's return. She explained all this to her children, but they paid no attention, being more concerned for her well-being.

Yasin was back in a quarter of an hour, bringing the doctor from his office in nearby Maydan Bayt al Qadi. The doctor came in to see the mother, and the room where she lay was emptied except for Yasin and Fahmi.

"What bothers you?" the doctor asked the mother, and Aminah pointed to her right shoulder and said, reluctantly, "I feel pain here."

The doctor's examination seemed to take a long time, at least to the two young men waiting inside and to those who waited outside, listening anxiously.

Finally, the doctor turned to Yasin and said, "The collarbone is broken, that's all."

Everyone was surprised that the doctor would say, "that's all," as if that were all they needed now, all they could take, a broken bone. But then they realized that the doctor's tone was somewhat reassuring. Fahmi asked anxiously, "Is it dangerous?"

"Oh, no, not at all," answered the doctor. "I'll set the bone and bandage the shoulder, but she must sleep sitting up for several nights, reclining against a pillow, for she won't be able to sleep either on her back or on her side. The broken bone should be back to normal in two or, at most, three weeks. There's nothing to worry about! Now leave me alone and let me do my job!"

After this announcement, those inside and outside the mother's room breathed easier. Khadijah murmured, "Let the blessing of Sayyidna al-Husayn come upon her, for she left the house only to visit him."

Khadijah's words seemed to remind Kamal of an important matter he had forgotten, for he said in a confused way, "But how on earth could this thing happen to my mother after she'd just had the blessing of Sayyidna al-Husayn?"

Umm Hifni said simply, "Who knows what would have happened, God forbid, if she had not had the blessing Sayyidna al-Husayn had just given her. It might have been worse!"

"Oh, God," burst out 'A'ishah. "When will it all end and everything go back the way it was before?"

At that, Kamal was seized with fear and guilt, and his personal responsibility for the affair became clear; it was his dreadful crime, he saw it all now, but he tried to evade the blame he feared might be placed upon him and said quickly, "Well, she wanted to have a walk in the street, Mother did. I tried to discourage her, but it made no difference."

Khadijah looked at him sharply, in an accusing way, and was about to scold him when she stopped. The child's face was pale and fearful, and she said instead, "Well, never mind, what's happened has happened, and let's worry about the situation we're in now."

The door of the room opened, and the doctor came out, saying to the two young men who followed him, "I'll have to visit her several times until the bone knits together. But, as I say, there's no need to worry, no need at all."

The children rushed into the room, to see their mother sitting up in bed, leaning against pillows. Nothing about her appearance had changed, except that a large lump was visible on the right shoulder of her dress, where the heavy bandage had been placed. They all went toward her, saying, "Oh, Mother! Thank God you're all right!"

The mother looked at her children. How painful it had been when the doctor was resetting the broken shoulder! She had moaned and moaned, but, if she had not been such a shy and retiring person, she would probably have screamed aloud, it had hurt her so much. But now the pain was no longer with her, or that was how it seemed to be, and she felt relatively comfortable and at peace. As the pain diminished, her mind began to clear and she began to think of different aspects of the situation.

"Oh," she said fearfully. "What am I going to say to your father when he gets back?"

Just as rocks standing in the sea will impede the calm passage of a ship to shore, so did this question by Aminah disturb the gentle waves of peace that had descended on the family, now that they could see their mother was to be all right. Still, this was not an unexpected disturbance in their minds. Perhaps the question had lain deep in the subconscious of each member of the family as soon as he heard the sad news of the accident, but they had all postponed considering it. Now there was no escape from it. The question of their father posed worse problems than the actual accident, from which, after all, their mother had escaped with only minor injuries. Aminah felt the danger, too, from the complete silence which greeted her question. For a moment she felt like the guilty one in a group whose colleagues have left alone when the guilt is finally exposed.

"I suppose," she said quietly, "he'll learn about the accident, and, worse than that, then he'll find out about my leaving the house, which caused the accident in the first place."

Umm Hifni was aware of the gravity of the situation. She was no less worried than the other members of the family, but she felt that, as an old and trusted family servant, she should not keep silent in this moment of crisis, for fear the family would think she cared nothing for their troubles. So, knowing that the comforting words she was about to utter had no relation to reality at all, she still said, "If my master hears what happened to you, he can do nothing except forgive you your little mistake and thank God for your safety."

This remark was received with the indifference it deserved, but Kamal believed it and said enthusiastically, as though continuing Umm Hifni's sentence, "Yes, and especially if we were to tell him we went to visit Sayyidna al-Husayn."

The mother looked from Yasin to Fahmi and said again, "What am I going to tell him?"

Yasin, plagued by his own sense of responsibility in the situation, answered, "Oh, mother, what devil could have misled you when I urged you to go out? The words just came out of my mouth and I wish they never had. But perhaps this is what fate decreed, that all of us be placed in such a miserable plight. Don't worry, though, we'll find something to tell him, and don't think about what's going to happen. Leave that to God. You've suffered enough today."

Yasin spoke with passion. Though his words made no difference in the situation, speaking them aloud made him feel better and relieved him somewhat of the feelings of guilt and embarrassment that had become like a tightness in his chest. At the same time his speech conveyed to the other members of the family that he knew what was going through their minds; he would save them the trouble of accusing him by exposing himself first. Experience had taught Yasin that sometimes the best defense is to attack oneself; such a confession of guilt encourages others to forgive just as self-defense sometimes encourages them to attack. His greatest fear was that Khadijah would take it upon herself to announce that he, Yasin, alone was responsible for advising his mother to go out, which had led to what it had led. His doubts were not unjustified, but after Yasin's speech Khadijah was reluctant to attack him. She nagged her brother a good deal, Khadijah, but she did not hate him. The speech improved slightly the feelings between the members of the family, but the over-all situation remained as hopeless as before. Then Khadijah said, "Why don't we say she fell down the stairs?"

The mother looked quickly at her daughter, like one searching for any crumb of comfort, and then she looked at Fahmi and Yasin to see how they responded to the suggestion. But Fahmi shook his head. "What about the doctor, who'll be coming to visit her every day? Surely he'll run into our father during one of those visits."

Yasin held back. He did not want to close the door on this vague possibility of hope and freedom, which might release him from his inner torment. He said, "We could all agree with the doctor on what should be said."

Looks were exchanged. Was this is a real possibility, a real way out of the difficulty? A sense of relief passed over the faces of the members of the family, and the atmosphere in the room suddenly became less tense, less ominous, and seemed to become clearer, lighter, just as a patch of blue sky appears unexpectedly in a bank of dense, threatening clouds, and in a few moments the dark sky is completely cleared and the sun comes out.

With a deep sigh, Yasin said, "I think we're safe, thank God!"

"Oh, yes," answered Khadijah regaining her usual sharpness in the general clearing of the air, "but it is *you* who are saved, O great adviser!"

Yasin laughed until his huge body began to shake, and he said, "Yes, Khadijah, I'm saved from your scorpion's tongue. For a moment there, I thought I was about to get stung."

In their happiness at the sudden release, the family nearly forgot that their mother lay in bed with a broken collarbone. But she had also been about to forget it. . . .

[After a night of sleep, during which 'A'ishah and Khadijah stayed with her, Aminah woke to find it nearly noon. The girls were convinced, she could see, that all was well, but the mother was not happy at the thought of lying to her husband.]

"Can this secret be kept forever?" Aminah asked herself. "Isn't it likely to reach the man some day?" She feared lying almost as much as she feared the truth. She found she was not sure which choice awaited her.

At that moment Umm Hifni came in, whispering as though afraid she might be heard outside the room. "My master is here, Sitti."

The two girls jumped out of bed at once and stood beside their mother.

"Don't say a word," warned the mother. "He might take out his anger on you. Leave the matter to me and God will help."

A total, tense silence filled the room, like the fearful silence which overcomes children when they hear footsteps in the dark and think that devils are walking close by. Outside, the footsteps of the father, Sayyid Ahmad, could be heard, climbing the stairs, coming closer and closer. With great effort, the mother broke the nightmarish silence by saying, "If we let him go to his room, he won't find anybody there." And to Umm Hifni, she said, "Tell him I'm here, sick, but nothing more."

The girls went out quickly, leaving their mother alone. Suddenly she realized she was totally alone, alone as though she were the only person in the world. Deep inside her, something told her that, with all the tension and pain and confusion, her own self-confidence was shattered. She tried to gather her thoughts together and remember what she should say. But at the same time she resigned herself to whatever would happen, with a kind of negative courage that seemed to her one way of dealing with what was to come.

In a moment the tap of a walking stick sounded on the floor of the room. The Sayyid had arrived.

She murmured, half to herself, "God help me and have mercy on me."

Then she looked toward the door and saw her husband's huge body, tall and heavy, framed in the doorway. She watched him approach, gazing at her with a sort of intentness in his big eyes, until he stopped in the middle of the room and she realized he was questioning her, in a quiet voice unusual for him.

"What's the matter?"

Lowering her head, she said, "Thank God for your safe arrival, my master. I am well as long as you are well."

"But Umm Hifni told me that you are sick."

She pointed to her right shoulder and said, "My shoulder is hurt; may God not wreak the same misfortune upon you, my master."

The man looked at her shoulder, and she could see concern in his eyes. "What has happened to it?"

The moment has come, she told herself, the decisive moment. Nothing remained except to tell the lie that might save her, resolve the crisis peacefully, and gain her some compassion for her injury.

She raised her head and looked directly into his eyes. She felt her heart begin to beat quickly, painfully. At that moment her plan to lie simply evaporated. Whatever determination she had mustered vanished. She gave him a look, as of someone in misery, and did not say a word. The Sayyid was astonished at his wife's behavior, and he began to urge her to say something, to explain. "What happened, Aminah? What happened?"

She did not know what to say. She felt there was nothing to say. She found herself unable to tell the planned lie. The chance had slipped past her, she could not say how. If she had had an opportunity to try the lie once more, she felt it would ring false, incomplete somehow. If she had been called upon to act in this manner while in her normal frame of mind, she would not have been able to do it, but at this time she was like someone hypnotized. The moment passed, and she retreated further into a kind of confusion and despair, which was very apparent to the Sayyid.

"Aminah, why don't you say something?" he shouted.

His normal tone of voice was returning, which marked the usual end of his patience. Anger would soon follow. "Oh, God," she thought, "how much am I in need of your help! What devil tempted me to take that ill-fated excursion?"

"Strange!" he said. "Don't you want to talk?"

Silence suddenly was no longer possible. She had to speak. Forced by despair, she got out, "I made a grave mistake, my master. A car hit me."

The Sayyid's eyes widened with astonishment, and with annoyance which he tried to conceal. He looked as though he were about to pass judgment on her sanity. The woman could no longer bear the hesitance, the silence. Nothing remained except to tell the truth and all the truth, no matter what the consequences might be, just as a person might gamble with his life by submitting to dangerous surgery to relieve a pain too great to bear. As her feelings of guilt increased, the dangers involved in confession loomed larger, and her eyes began to water involuntarily. She began to speak in a choked, sobbing voice, and she was not able to tell herself whether the crying was a natural reaction or whether she was using it as a last resort to gain her husband's sympathy.

"I thought Sayyidna al-Husayn called me to visit him. I answered the call and went. On the way back there was an accident. It was God's judgment. I got up from my fall without anyone's help."

She spoke the last sentence in a clear voice. The sobs were receding.

"In the beginning I felt that nothing was the matter. There was no pain. I thought everything was all right and so I walked home. Then the pain started. They brought the doctor and he said my collarbone is broken and he will visit me every day until the bone is healed. I made a mistake, a big mistake, my master. I know it. I have been punished as I deserved and God is forgiving and merciful."

The Sayyid listened to her in frozen silence. Her eyes did not move from his face, a face blank of any expression which might have indicated his inner mood. Then she lowered her head in a gesture of humility, as someone awaits a sentence. The Sayyid still did not speak. Aminah could not tell what this silence meant, what it indicated about the fate which might await her. As the silence grew, her feeling of fear and punishment increased. The Sayyid said, after some moments, in a very strange and calm way, "And what did the doctor say? Is the break serious?"

Aminah raised her head. She had expected anything except this gentleness. If the situation had not been so grave, she would have asked him to repeat his words, to make sure she had heard him correctly. Once more her eyes began to water and she pressed her lips tightly together to prevent sobbing. She said, "The doctor tells me there is no need to worry at all; may God save you from all evil, my master."

The man stood there a moment, fighting back a strong desire to ask more questions. But he overcame this urge and turned to the woman, as he left the room, saying, "You'd better stay in bed until God bestows his mercy upon you." ...

[Three weeks passed. Aminah stayed in bed, recovering.]

On the first morning after her convalescence had ended, the mother rose before dawn, with the lightness and energy of a young girl. She was full of happiness, like a king returning to his throne after banishment. Down to the kitchen she went, to resume the household routine from which she had been cut off for the past three weeks.

"Umm Hifni!" she called.

The woman sprang up quickly from her bed, put her arms around her mistress, and uttered a prayer for her safety. The two women began their morning duties with light hearts.

At the first rays of the sun, the mother went up to the first floor, where four of her children received her with embraces and good wishes. Afterward she went to Kamal's room. The boy opened his eyes and saw his mother beside him. He leaped up and hugged her joyfully. He showered her with kisses and began to laugh and tease her. "Okay, Mama," he said, "when are we going the next time?"

"Now, Kamal," she answered, slightly reproachful but still smiling, "when God leads you to the straight path, we will go, not when you try to force me to take a path where I almost lost my life!"

Kamal realized she was referring to his stubbornness at the pastry shop, which was the real cause of what had happened. He laughed, with the whole-hearted laughter which the guilty one laughs after he has been released from his sentence. Kamal had been afraid that his brother's investigation of the circumstances of the accident would lead eventually to him, the real cause, especially because both Khadijah and Yasin seemed to be suspicious already. If his mother had not kept silent and defended him, he would have borne the whole burden on his own shoulders. And when the investigation passed into the hands of his father, Kamal's fears increased. He expected to be summoned into his father's presence at any moment. That, combined with the torture of having his mother in bed for three weeks, in pain, unable to get up or lie down—now that was all over, and with it the investigation and the possible punishment. His mother was well and had come to wake him up in the morning. She would put him to bed in the evening. Everything had returned to normal. Peace had descended on the household. He had a right to laugh, he thought, and he reassured his conscience that all was well.

The mother left Kamal's room and climbed to the next level of the house. As she approached the door the the Sayyid's room, she heard his voice raised in the early morning prayer, "Praise be to thee, O God, the most glorious!"

She stood before the door, hesitating. Should she go in and say good morning? Or should she first get breakfast ready? Her hesitation was, she realized, a way of evading an encounter with fear or humiliation or perhaps both. Aminah's position was like that of a man who creates new and more difficult situations in order to escape the real difficulty which must be faced eventually. She decided to go down into the dining room and she began to prepare breakfast with special care. She found that her sense of worry had increased. She began to wonder how she could possibly have been afraid to enter her own room, as though she were entering it for the first time. After all, the Sayyid had visited her each day while she lay in bed. But now, with the return of health, the protection of illness had been taken from her. She did feel as though she were going to meet him, by herself, for the first time since she had confessed her mistake.

When the children came, one after the other, into the dining room, her feeling of isolation lessened somewhat. Then the Sayyid entered, impressive in his flowing *jallabiyah*. He glanced at Aminah, but his face registered no emotion whatsoever. In a calm voice he said, "You've come?" and, turning to his place at the table, he said to his children, "Sit down," and they obeyed and began to eat their breakfast. She stood nearby in her accustomed place. Although some tension had communicated itself to her the moment he entered, she gradually began to relax, as the meal progressed normally. The first meeting since her illness had taken place and had passed in peace. Soon she began to feel she would have no difficulty in facing him alone.

Breakfast was over and the Sayyid went to his room. In a few minutes she followed, carrying the coffee tray which she had prepared. She set the tray on the table and waited to one side until he had finished drinking his coffee. Then, as usual, she would help him put on his clothes.

The Sayyid sipped his coffee in silence. It was not a comfortable silence, or a natural silence of relief after great fatigue, or a silence of someone who simply had nothing to say. It was a dead silence, full of intent. Still the woman did not give up hope that he might say a gentle word to her or at least start speaking about household matters, as he used to discuss them with her in these early morning hours.

The silence grew. Aminah began to ask herself, "Is there still something yet to come?" Worry descended again, like needles pricking into her heart. The dead, ugly silence continued. The man was thinking rapidly and intensely, and he did not enjoy his thoughts; they were not the kind of thoughts which come on the spur of the moment; they were the other, stubborn feelings which had not left him during all the previous days. The struggle of the past three weeks had come to a climax; now was the moment for it to be resolved. Without lifting his head from his empty coffee cup, he asked, "Have you recovered?"

Aminah answered, in a low voice, "Yes, thanks be to God, my master."

The man burst out bitterly, "I am amazed! My amazement simply has no end! How did you dare do what you did?"

A feeling of immense sorrow overcame Aminah. She had never been able to bear his anger while fighting on someone else's behalf. How could she possibly do it when she was the guilty one?

"Have I been deceived by you all these long years," continued the Sayyid in the same bitter tone, "deceived and didn't know or realize it?"

Aminah spread her hands in supplication and pain and whispered, "God forbid, my master. I know my mistake is indeed grave, but I do not deserve such an accusation."

The man paid no attention to her but went on speaking in a bitter, calm tone. The words would have been easier for Aminah to bear if he had been shouting. "How did you dare commit such a mistake? Just because I left home for one day?"

"I made a mistake, my lord," answered Aminah, in a voice that was almost a sob; she was trembling all over. "You have the power to forgive me. My soul wished to visit Sayyidna al-Husayn and I thought such a blessed visit would justify my going out, at least this once."

He shook his head. "There's no point in arguing." Then he raised an angry face to her and said in a tone that allowed no contradiction, "I have only one thing to say. Leave my house immediately!"

The judgment fell upon her like a fatal stroke. A moment passed. She could not move or utter a word. During the hardest time of her difficulty, while she was awaiting his return from Port Said, various kinds of fearful possibilities had occurred to her: he might scream out his rage, he might curse her, shout, even beat her; any of these things she would have expected. But to throw her out of the house—that had never occurred to her. She had lived with him for twenty-five years and she could not imagine that a simple thing like leaving the house once without permission could banish her forever from the home of which she had become a part, with which she felt inseparable.

As for the Sayyid, his last words resolved the conflict that had raged in his mind during the past three weeks, the struggle that had begun the moment she confessed her mistake, crying, while she lay in bed. At first he had not been able to believe his ears. After a little, he recovered himself and began to consider the ugly reality of the incident, which challenged both his pride and his authority. He had postponed giving vent to his anger and had waited to see how her shoulder would mend. Or, and perhaps this was the real truth, he could not bear to face the fact that his pride had been challenged by the woman in whom he had put all his faith and trust, the woman he had known so long and of whose character and behavior he had always been proud. And, on this occasion, he found, to his terror, that instead of feeling anger he felt pity for the woman. He had prayed to God to save her. His anger was held in check by his concern for her health. And his pity and concern, he felt, were eroding his anger and tyranny, were wakening the real passion for her which he had suppressed for years and hidden somewhere deep in his soul.

The first day he had gone to his room full of sorrow and despair, although what was going through his mind did not show on his face. His wife and children had no idea what he was feeling. But, as he watched Aminah improving rapidly day after day, his pity and sorrow receded, and his ordinary calm returned. Gradually he began to consider the incident as a whole, its causes and possible results. He began to look at the situation from another point of view, that is, from the old tyrannical view with which he had always looked at his family and his household. For Aminah, it was unfortunate that he should have returned to his old point of view while alone. Gradually he came to believe that, if he forgave his wife, he would have capitulated to his passion for her, something he desired, somewhere deep inside him. But, if that were to happen, he would lose his dignity, his status in society, his traditional pride and position. Everything would be out of his control, and the family, like a necklace of precious beads, would scatter and be lost. The family, he felt, had to be treated with firmness and severity. On the whole, he concluded, he would not be himself if he forgave her, he would not be Ahmad Abd al-Jawad. He would be somebody else and he could not accept that other person.

Had he had an opportunity to vent his anger at the time Aminah was confessing her mistake, the Sayyid might have gotten it off his chest and the whole incident would have passed over without serious consequences. But seeing her there, in pain, he found himself incapable of being angry. Later when she had recovered, and particularly after the peace which had lasted for three weeks, he did not find it appropriate to express his anger. He felt then that anger would be closer to scorn and disdain and not real anger. He was still furious, but, when his natural emotions did not find their outlet at the time they occurred, he tended to wait and express them at a planned moment. And he had had the opportunity to think and brood; he had figured out how he could keep his own identity and pride in a manner which suited the gravity of the woman's guilt. The danger that threatened her life had allowed her temporary escape from his anger, but the postponement and his own fear of loss of pride had worked against her and resulted in a totally unexpected and severe punishment.

Frowning, the Sayyid stood up, turned his back on the woman, picked up his clothes from the couch, and said roughly, "I'll put my clothes on myself."

The woman stood rooted to the same place, dazed, unaware of her surroundings. But the sound of his voice roused her, and she realized he was ordering her to leave. She shuffled out. Before she reached the door, she heard him say, "I don't want to see you here when I return at noon." . . .

[Banished, Aminah returned to her mother's house in the district of al-Khuranfash. Meanwhile, the distraught children decided that the situation could not continue, and they met to plan what might be done to get their mother back. First, they appealed to the neighbors. Several came, including Umm Maryam, to try to talk to their father, but it did not help. The Sayyid suspected the children were involved, and this only increased his anger.]

But one day Khadijah knocked on her father's door. "Teizé is here," she announced. "The widow of the late Shawkat. She wants to see you."

"What does she want?" asked the Sayyid. He looked angrily at Khadijah, as if to say, "We have scarcely finished with one mediator yesterday and already you're bringing me another. How dare you all plot against me like this?"

"By God, I swear I don't know anything about the widow Shawkat," insisted Khadijah, her face paling as she spoke.

The Sayyid shook his head as if to say, "But you do know and I know that you know. These tricks of yours won't succeed. They'll only lead to worse consequences." But aloud, he shouted, "Well, then, let her come in! I can't even drink my coffee in peace these days! My room, my whole house has become a court of law, full of witnesses. May God curse you all!"

But he spoke the last words to the air, for Khadijah had quickly disappeared before he finished, tripping over her slipper as she went out. For a moment the Sayyid was more furious than ever, and then into his mind came the image of Khadijah, scuttling away, tripping over her slipper, and banging into the door. A smile passed over his face and a feeling of tenderness replaced the anger in his heart. "Poor children," he thought. "They cannot forget their mother, even for a moment."

He looked toward the door, rearranging his face and feelings so as to receive the visitor with a calm, untroubled face, as though the idea that he had been outraged at the very idea of her visit had never crossed his mind. In the privacy of his home, the Sayyid had always had difficulty controlling his fury for minor reasons or even for no reason at all. But in this case it was necessary, for the widow Shawkat was a rather special person. None of the women who occasionally visited the house could equal her in status.

The Shawkat family and the Sayyid's family had a long history of friendship, going back to the time of their grandfathers. The late Shawkat had been like a father to the Sayyid, and he had always held the old man in great respect; Shawkat's wife had enjoyed the same position as a mother. For it was the widow Shawkat who had served as the matchmaker for him and had asked for Aminah in marriage. When his children had been delivered by the midwife, the widow Shawkat had held them in her own hands the first time they had looked upon the world. Further, to be friendly with the Shawkat family was an honor in itself, not only because of their Turkish descent but also because of their social status and economic position. They owned many estates and much land between al-Hamzawi and the district of Bayna al-Qasrayn. If the Sayyid's family was considered middle class, the Al Shawkat were at the very top of that class.

Perhaps the maternal relationship between the Sayyid and the widow made him receive her efforts at mediation with a mixture of appre-hension and embarrassment. He knew she would not speak to him with much respect. Nor was she the kind of person to beg his kindness or ask favors of him. Because of her age and position, she did not need to behave in such ways, and she was furthermore well known for her frank-ness and openness, even it it hurt the other person.

All these thoughts passing through the Sayyid's mind were interrupted by the sound of footsteps. He rose.

"*Ahlan wa-sahlan* [You are welcome]," he said. "The Prophet himself has visited us."

The old lady approached him slowly, using her umbrella as a cane. Her sheer white veil did not hide her face, her clear, fair complexion seamed with a myriad of wrinkles. She returned his greeting with a smile that exposed her gold teeth, and she took a seat beside him without any further formalities.

"Well," she began, "live and learn, I always say. What's this I'm hear-ing? That even with you, the best of men, and even in this house, the best of houses, things that are not pleasant to speak of are really hap-pening. By the God of the great Sayyidna al-Husayn, you must be getting old, Sayyid, or else you're losing your good sense and becoming senile."

She went on talking in this way for some moments, like a horse who begins to gallop and is given free rein, not allowing the Sayyid a chance to interrupt or comment. She told him that she had come to visit and had discovered that his wife was not at home.

"At first I thought she'd gone to visit somebody, and I beat my chest hard with my own hand, and I said to myself, 'God, what is happening in this world? How can the Sayyid let her out of the house, breaking all religious laws, all human laws, and the Ottoman rules, too!' " She took a breath but did not drop her heavily sarcastic tone. "Then I realized what had happened and I said to myself, 'Well, thank God, the world is in good shape after all; that's the kind of thing the Sayyid would do, banish his wife, the good Sayyid, yes, that's him, all right, that's the least we can expect of him.' " She went on, reviling the man for his severity and re-peating again and again that his excellent wife, Aminah, was the last woman in the world to deserve any kind of punishment whatsoever. Whenever he tried to break in, she would shout angrily, "Hush! Not a word from you! Not a single word! Don't try and get around me with talk —that won't work. I want good deeds from you, not honeyed words." And she continued, "Sayyid, you are completely overdoing your responsibilities to your family. And you're doing it in a way that goes beyond all bounds of normal behavior. Your family needs more love, more consideration, a peaceful atmosphere from you, not this kind of nonsense."

The Sayyid listened to her politely for a long time and, when she finally allowed him to speak, he explained his own position. Neither her strong denunciation of him nor her status nor the respect in which he held her prevented the Sayyid from explaining that his policy toward his family was one of firmness. He would not, he said, change a decision, once made. Finally, he promised her, as he had promised Umm Maryam the day before, that things would be all right in the household eventually, and he added that he felt it was time to end the session.

The widow Shawkat paid no attention. She made no motion to leave and began to speak all over again. "The absence of Aminah Hanim is an unhappy surprise for me," she said, "not only because I wanted to talk to her about something important, but also because my health makes it harder and harder these days for me to go out. Now I'm not sure whether it's wise for me to talk to you or whether I should wait until Aminah comes home."

"We are all at your service," answered the Sayyid, with a polite smile.

"Well," went on the widow, "I wish your wife were here, so she could be the first one to hear what I have to say and to hear it from me directly. I know perfectly well you won't allow her any role in the matter I've come to discuss; my only consolation is that I'm preparing a happy reason for her to return home."

This conversation completely baffled the Sayyid. He could not guess what the widow Shawkat was after. "What's behind all this?" he asked.

The old lady tapped the carpet with the point of her umbrella and replied, "I won't make it long and tedious. I've decided to ask 'A'ishah to become the wife of my son Khalil."

The Sayyid's surprise at the widow's announcement was soon replaced by annoyance. Long ago he had decided not to marry his younger daughter until after the older one was married. Now his wish was being thwarted and he saw that he would be unable to fulfill this promise to himself. He knew also that the old lady beside him was aware of his plan, and yet she had still come and asked for the youngest. The widow Shawkat was challenging his authority! She would not accept his decision in this matter; she had already decided to override his judgment.

"Well, what's the matter with you?" asked the old woman. "Why are you silent? Are you pretending you didn't hear what I said?"

The Sayyid smiled, rather shyly and uneasily, and said quickly, to mask what was going on in his mind, "This is indeed a great honor for us!"

The old woman looked at him as if she were saying clearly, "You'd better find other ways to answer than that kind of pretty talk," and then she said aloud, in a tone of attack, "I don't want or need smiles and empty words. I'll accept only complete agreement from you. Khalil has asked me to choose a wife for him. To me, 'A'ishah is the best he could find and he is pleased with my choice. He did not say a word about not wanting to be related to your family by marriage."

As the Sayyid still did not speak, the widow said, "Come, come, Sayyid. Has the time really arrived when you would receive a request like this from me, myself, the widow Shawkat, with such silences and evasions! God! God! What is happening to the world?"

"The matter is not as simple as you think," said the Sayyid. Privately, he was wondering how he could manage this complicated situation without hurting one of his daughters. He looked at the old woman, as though he were begging her to be kind and understanding. "Your request brings us great honor and is much appreciated, but . . ."

"Ah, there's always a *but* . . . ," broke in the widow. "Don't say that you've decided not to marry the youngest until the oldest is married. Who are you to set yourself up to decide this and that? Leave things to God. God is most merciful and compassionate. I can give you hundreds of examples of younger sisters who married before their older sisters and this did not stand in the way of good marriages for the older ones. Khadijah is a very capable girl and won't be denied the good husband she deserves when it is God's will that she marry. Why do you want to stand in the way of 'A'ishah and her good fortune? Isn't she worthy of your love and consideration too?"

The Sayyid thought to himself, "If Khadijah is as capable as you say, why don't you choose her?" and for a moment he was tempted to say the words aloud, to embarrass the old lady as she had embarrassed him. But he held back, for he was afraid she might reply in a way that might hurt, both himself and, in the end, Khadijah, as well. Instead, he said, gravely, "It isn't that, but I am sorry about Khadijah."

The widow Shawkat answered him fiercely, as though she, not he, were the one of whom the request had been made, "Matters like this happen every day without people hesitating and becoming upset like you. God does not like to see pride and stubbornness in his servants.

Approve of my request and leave the rest to God. Don't refuse, for I
have not asked anyone such a favor before."

"As I said a few minutes ago, this is a great honor, Widow Shawkat."
The Sayyid tried to cover his emotions with a smile. "All I ask is for you
to give me a little time to discuss the matter with myself. I'm sure my
decision will be in your favor, if God wills it so."

The old lady nodded and stood up. "I shouldn't take more of your
time. And it's true that the more I say yes, the more you say no. I don't
think you are in a mood to receive my request with the proper attitude,
and, as you know, I'm a person who, when I want something, am impatient to have an immediate 'yes,' without any 'maybes' and 'buts.'
Well, I won't add anything to what I've said except one sentence: Khalil
is my son and yours and 'A'ishah is your daughter and mine."

[In a few days, the Sayyid sent his sons to the house of Aminah to
bring their mother home.]

Notes

1.   *Bukhari* is a traditional collection of sayings of the Prophet
Muhammad.
2.   The *milayah* is the all-enveloping black cloak worn by Egyptian
women when outside the home. When wrapped about the body, it may
be somewhat revealing of the body contours as well.
3.   The *fatihah* is the first surah of the Koran and quoted on important occasions, such as marriages, funerals, moving to new houses,
before entering shrines, and in moments of personal crisis.
4.   The *jallabiyah* is the traditional full floor-length garment worn by
both men and women in Egypt.
5.   *Mushrabiyah* means literally carved wooden screening. Windows
in traditional Egyptian houses were covered with such decorative
screens, which allowed people of the house to view the street without
being seen.
6.   A *darb* is a covered street or a street somewhat larger than the
usual residential lanes of old Cairo. It may also refer to an area.
7.   *Sitti* is a polite term of address for a woman, meaning literally,
"my lady" or "ma'am."

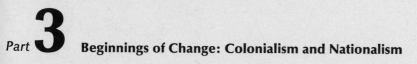

Part **3**   **Beginnings of Change: Colonialism and Nationalism**

[The following songs were recorded from an oral recital by Mririda N'ait Attik in the Tachelhait dialect by René Euloge in *Les Chants de la Tassaout* (Casablanca: Maroc Editions, 1972). Translated by Elizabeth Warnock Fernea.]

9

Women's Songs
from the Berber Mountains

أغنيات نسائية

of Morocco

Translated by Elizabeth Warnock Fernea

I
Improvised Song

I'm in love with the son of Sidi Daud.
Why won't he look at me?
    She's in love with the son of Sidi Daud.
    Who wants to guess why he won't look at her?
    ——Because his father was with him!
    ——Because your breast popped out of your blouse!
    ——Because he's worried about money!
    ——Because a wasp stung his nose!
    ——Because he came to haul dung!
    ——Because the shaykh signed him up for forced labor!
    ——Because his friend got a girl in trouble!
    ——Because the tea gave him a stomach ache!
    ——Because you're so beautiful. He's afraid to look at you!
    ——Because he loves you, and your look burns him to the
          heart!
    Tell him you'll meet him tonight in the village square
    And tomorrow it's you who won't dare look at him!

Photo: Berber women singers

My sister, don't scold me.
It's true, I shouldn't have slept in the shepherd's hut.
For you know, my sister, what happens in a shepherd's hut,
On a spring evening, with a young man.
Am I the only girl who ever spent the night
In a young man's arms, my sister?
You're telling me, my sister, that such lovely nights
Are not worth the morning after.
Well, at least keep the secret, my sister.
Old Tamoucha knows all about those plants,
The plants which will soon deliver me from my trouble.
Nothing shows yet, you know.
Tamoucha has already bought the alum and resin
To make me a new virginity.
She's even promised to promote a marriage for me.
Do you believe it? To our dear cousin.
Tell me, my sister, will he make a good husband?
Oh, how would we survive against men
If we didn't have these tricks and smiles?

Women—deceivers—Oh, my cousin!

III
The Second Wife

The stranger has come; she has her place in the house.
Her tattoos are not like ours,
But she's young, she's beautiful, just what my husband wanted;
The nights aren't long enough for their play,
But we'll soon see if she's as good for work.
Now she's dolled up in silks and scarves
In colors brighter than *bagzoua* feathers,
But soon her skin will have to get used to rough wool,
To carry the firewood, milk the cows, and cook.
People are criticizing my husband,
Not for taking a second wife,
But for bringing a stranger to our land,
A stranger we don't know much about.
Some say her parents were of Ait Tarkebout;
She can't be a daughter of the Ait Takbout.
She claims she's of the Ait Bou Ou Guemmez;
I think she's probably from Ait Bou Demmez.
Since she's come, the house is not the same,
As though the doorsills and the walls were sulking;
Perhaps I'm the only one who notices it,
Like a mule before his empty manger.
But I must accept my new lot,
For my husband is happy with his new wife.
    Once I, too, was beautiful, but my time is past.

The father and the mother said:
"She will never be your wife!"
And the grandfather clenched his two fists
And beat upon his head with heavy blows.
The father and the mother said:
"He will never be your husband!"
And the grandfather clenched his two fists
And beat upon his head with heavy blows.
People of the valley, have you thought of uniting these two?
This boy—to this girl—oh, no, that can never be.
They were enemies before birth; there is blood between the
    families,
Mourning and hatred for generations,
Like a wall of stone higher than the Taissa mountains.
But love's despair is deaf to reason,
And since the lovers could not live together
They chose to die together.
They left home without a word. Night fell
At the hour when the pot is on the fire,
Like a black horseman on a red horse,
Who fights his rider and kicks in place.
The lovers stopped on the floor of the valley
While up above, on the mountain, their fists clenched,
The two grandfathers beat upon their heads with heavy blows.
Thunder rumbled. Lightning clawed across the sky.
"O Moulay Souliman, King of Spirits,
Lord of the woods and the waters,
We invoke you with all our hearts.
We no longer wish to live.
We want to leave this world, clasped in each other's arms,
So we will be together forever in death.
O God, in your pity and infinite mercy, receive us!"
Moulay Souliman heard their prayer.
He called Iggig, the god of thunder; he called the fire in the sky
To grant the wish of the desperate lovers.

    And ever and forever you will be together.
You will become the laurel tree
And she the faithful honeysuckle.

You will support her with all your strength,
And she will twine her arms around you lovingly,
As she did in your last embrace.
You will protect her from the wind and the cold.
In the summer, you will shelter her in your shade.
She will grow as high as your forehead,
And her head will rest on your shoulder.
The wasp will tell you when summer is here,
The pigeon will come in autumn, the crow in winter,
And the turtle-doves, drunk with love,
Will sing to you in spring.

When he came in with my mother
And sat down in the shade,
I knew what his coming meant.
But so what? Many others besides me,
Many others have been divorced!
The men say, "Women are bad."
And the women say there are hardly any good husbands.
Mine was so naïve, he let himself be plucked
Like a young partridge from the nest.
That other, she knew how to seduce him and I'm sorry for him,
But also for myself, for I bear his child,
A child he doesn't care much about.
He talked and talked—what good are his fine words
When I feel like swords are plunging in my womb,
And sharp knives are cutting at my heart?
Well, I fought my two sicknesses,
The one in my heart and the one in my body.
I swallowed my grief, all my grief.
I didn't have to swallow my tears,
For I pressed my lips together tight before they fell.
I pasted a wide, a very wide smile
Across my weary and some would say dishonored face,
And that smile, which made me ill, told him
Of my contempt, but also my forgiveness and my pity.
He left, hardly turning his head,
And my mother began to cry.

VI
Poor Naïve Young Man

Poor naïve young man, stop hassling me!
I came to the village to visit my parents,
Not to look for a husband—God preserve me from that!
And soon I'll go back to Azilal, if God so wishes it.
You say you want me to be your wife
After just one night of my love making.
Well, I know how long your desire would last!
And what can you offer that's sweeter than freedom?
Come on now, don't give me that look
To try to shame me in my profession,
My profession, thanks to which you enjoyed yourself so last night!
What other life could make me happier?
And you, who beg me to be yours alone,
What can you give me, tell me that, naïve young man?
Days without meat, without sugar, and without songs,
The sweat and dirt of hard work,
The dung of the stable, stinking clothes,
And that awful smoke in the dark kitchen,
While you're off on the mountain, dancing the dance of the rifles?
And you'll keep after me, all the time
To bear boys, boys, and more boys!
Can't you see I'm not made for all that?
No, let me go back to the market in Azilal.
You're wasting your time, this pleading is making me tired.
Why should I work here, for you,
When there they load me with presents and silver?
I'm like a flower with a seductive scent
That only blossoms for a pleasant reason,
To receive, when it chooses, each night and each day,
The freshness of the dawn, the caress of the sun.

O wind of Tizoula! O wind of Amsoud!
Blow over the plains and above the sea,
Carry, oh, carry my thoughts
To him who is so far, so far,
And who has left me without a little child.
O wind! Remind him I have no child.

O wind of Tizoula! O wind of Amsoud!
Blow away that desire for riches
That sends our young men away
And makes them forget the girls they've married, their mothers,
And the old ones left in the village.
O wind! Remind him I have no child.

O my husband, so far, so far away,
If we are healthy and have few needs,
Do we need so much money
To enjoy the time which is passing?
And to be happy together, by the grace of God,
With a little child, by the grace of God.

O wind! O wind! Blow my sorrow to him,
To soften his faraway heart.
My life is as bitter as the laurel tree,
For a woman can't live without a man,
Without a vigorous man, the honey of life—
And he left me without a little child.

Wind! O wind! Bring his song to me,
A song that will soar up the valley
As soon as he's near our village;
When I hear his voice, I'll run, my heart beating,
Down the path where the vines and green hedges,
The virgin's bower, and all the wild roses
Are covering themselves with blossoms to welcome him!

10
Umm Kulthum

أم كلثوم

Famed Egyptian Singer

A.D. 1910–1975

Umm Kulthum, the youngest daughter of a religious shaykh, was born about 1910 in a small village in the Egyptian Delta. She grew up on poverty and simplicity, in a traditional family, and was given a classical religious education in the *kuttab,* or Koranic school. Her great talent, a voice of tremendous power and range, was recognized early by her father, and from the time she was very young she accompanied her father to religious celebrations and sang with him. The memoirs which follow are an account of her early years and her struggle to achieve recognition in the capital of Egypt and the cultural center of the Middle East. After she achieved success, she lived in a modest villa in Cairo with her husband, Dr. Hasan Hifnawi. They had no children. She gave her last concert in Cairo in the spring of 1973. In early February 1975, Umm Kulthum died after a year's illness, and Cairo Radio chanted the Koran, following the news, an honor usually reserved for heads of state. Her funeral drew dignitaries from all the Arab countries and millions of citizens mourned her passing. Following her death, many periodicals and newspapers throughout the Arab world devoted entire issues to her life

Photos: Umm Kulthum as a young girl and in concert

—a fitting tribute to one of the greatest artists and most-beloved figures the Middle East has produced in modern times. Today her villa in Cairo is a national museum.

The Umm Kulthum Nobody Knows

The village of Tammay lies in the district of Sinbalawin, in the central Delta of Egypt. It is a small village and the houses are small, two or three rooms of sun-dried mud bricks built around an inner courtyard. In one of these houses lived Shaykh Ibrahim and his wife, Fatimah.

It was 1910. Fatimah lay on a mat in one of the rooms of her house. All night she had been in labor, suffering and in pain, attended by the village midwife. As the new day broke, the child started from the womb and looked out upon the world.

"Thank God, Fatimah is delivered safely!"

The midwife came out to Shaykh Ibrahim, who sat in the courtyard, reading aloud a story about the family of the Prophet Muhammad. But she did not announce the sex of the child, for fear of disappointing the father.

At that moment Shaykh Ibrahim was reading the names of Muhammad's daughters. "We will call our daughter Umm Kulthum!" he shouted.

He had known from the midwife's tone that the new baby was a girl, but he was happy, for he was a pious man and believed sincerely that, whether the child was a boy or a girl, it had been sent by God and was a matter for rejoicing.

The name of Umm Kulthum was not a common one in those days in the village of Tammay or in any of the neighboring villages. Fatimah did not object to the name, but relatives and friends found it strange, and, accordingly, they tried to persuade Shaykh Ibrahim to choose another name for the baby, something more familiar and lively, like Sitt al-Dar or Badawiyah or Khudrah.

"No," said Shaykh Ibrahim. "I don't care for such ordinary names. I want my new child to have the same name as one of the Prophet's daughters. Is not that an honorable name?"

The relatives and friends dropped the subject, but my mother must have shared some of their feelings, for as long as I can remember she called me Sumah.

My mother couldn't read or write, but she knew well how to perform her duties toward her husband and her children. And she never argued with my father in front of us. She never spoke ill of other people. Perhaps it is because of her wisdom and simplicity that my father never

[Excerpts from *Umm Kulthum Allati la Ya'rifuba Ahad*, as told to Mahmud 'Awad. Kitab al-Yawm series (Cairo: Akhbar al-Yawm, 1969). Translated by the Editors.]

took another wife. This was not common then in the Rif [countryside]; not even in our family itself, for I had three uncles and each of them had married two or three times. But my father respected my mother and I think he loved and valued her.

My father was the imam of the village mosque. For calling the daily prayers and leading the weekly services on Fridays, he was paid a small salary by the Ministry of Waqfs branch in Sinbalawin district.[1] But since this was not enough to support his family, he took on extra work, reading the Koran and singing at *mawlids* and on other religious occasions.[2] Together the two jobs did not yield a total income of more than twenty piasters a month,[3] which had to support all of us, my father, my mother, my sister, my brother, my grandmother, and myself.

It is difficult for me to imagine how we managed to live on such a small income, but, to be honest, my earliest memories of my childhood are not all of the problems of poverty. True, I remember the heavy tea, the cheap goat cheese, the bones that were our meat, the wealth which the smallest coin represented. And I do remember that once my father did not have enough money to buy a sack of grain. This was a crisis, and my mother collected her jewelry, what little bits and pieces she had, and gave it to my father so we would have something to eat. Her jewelry was barely enough to exchange for that sack of grain.

But my childhood did not differ from most of those of the children of my time in my village. Childhood is always linked with play, a passion, a happiness from a small thing. I remember clearly the rag doll which my grandmother, Sitti Nasrah, made for me. I see a picture of her in my mind still: a thin, dark lady, my father's mother, wearing black garments, and a *tarhah*, or head scarf, sitting on the mat and cutting and sewing a doll from scraps of cloth. When she had finished sewing the doll, she stuffed its limbs and body with cotton, and then upon its face she painted eyes, eyebrows, a nose, and lips. Afterward she cut some of her own hair and pasted it onto the doll's head while I watched in admiration. How could she do it?

My mother had very simple ways of bringing up children. We were mischievous and often broke things. She did not punish us severely. She would say, "Be careful," or, "If you break something and admit it to me, I will give you a piece of candy." But she felt strongly about some things. "He who steals anything," she used to say, "will be cursed by God, and his face will be changed into that of a donkey."

Once I tried to steal from my mother. She wasn't home, and a peddler came by selling cotton candy. The children of the rich people in the village were hurrying out of their doors to buy the cotton candy. My eyes were fastened on that beautiful pink candy. I longed so much to have a piece. I went inside the house, put my hand into the pocket of one of my mother's dresses, and found half a piaster! I took the coin and went rushing out to the peddler. But suddenly I stopped. I began to feel my face anxiously. Was God going to change it into that of a donkey? I ran home and put the half-piaster back in my mother's pocket. Then I went out onto the street, but all the other children were eating that delicious cotton candy and the sight was too much for me. I ran back home, only to find that my mother had returned. I burst out with what I had done. Mother listened to my confession in silence.

"Thank God!" she said, as though she had really saved my face from being changed into that of a donkey! And then she gave me the half-piaster to buy the cotton candy.

My other clear memory of this time is of my brother, Khalid, carrying his book and going off each morning to the *kuttab*, the village religious school. I wanted desperately to go with him. I loved my mother and my grandmother and I loved my rag doll, but I wanted to go to the *kuttab* as my brother did. I cried and cried and begged my mother to let me go.

"No, my dear," she answered. "You're still young."

I went to my father and cried and begged until finally he yielded and promised he would try to send me to the *kuttab*.

So off I went, and every morning I would sit in the class conducted by Shaykh 'Abd al-Aziz, and I was happy, for now I was doing everything my brother did. What I did not realize was that he was learning, while I was merely sitting there and not learning a thing.

One day I heard my father and mother whispering together after the morning prayer.

"I can't let her continue in the *kuttab*," said my father, "for you know I have only one extra *kursh* and that must go for my son's education."

My mother began to plead, quietly but persistently, asking my father to find an extra coin "so the child will not be heartbroken."

How or where my father found that extra coin every week, I will never know, but I did not have to leave the *kuttab*. Now, however, my happiness was less than perfect, for I was required to take part in the lesson; I was not allowed to simply sit in class any longer. Once the teacher, Shaykh 'Abd al-Aziz, treated me unjustly, I felt, in some incident with a girl named Azizah, who sat on the low wooden stool next to mine. To gain revenge, I went early to the *kuttab* one morning and, opening the drawer where Azizah kept her slate, I took it out. Just as I was getting ready to break it, an inspector from the Ministry of Education appeared unexpectedly, and I jumped away and saluted him.

"Where is your teacher, child?" asked the inspector, who apparently had not noticed what I was doing.

"He hasn't come yet," I answered.

Some time went by, while the inspector's irritation grew. When Shaykh 'Abd al-Aziz finally did arrive, the inspector said unpleasantly, "Well, well, this little girl comes to school well before time, but your majesty, the teacher, manages to be half an hour late!"

Naturally, Shaykh 'Abd al-Aziz did not like such a reprimand. I seemed to be the principal cause of his disgrace, and, from then on, he lost no opportunity to ask me difficult questions or humiliate me in front of the class. When no one else could answer a question, he would turn to me and say, "Well, smarty, and what's the answer to that?"

And all the pupils would laugh and after class they would taunt me, shouting, "Smarty, smarty, smarty!"

I began to dread those hours at the *kuttab*. I hated school, I hated Shaykh 'Abd al-Aziz, and I began to hate the world.

But one day, o wonder of wonders, heaven smiled upon me. Shaykh 'Abd al-Aziz died! At first I could not believe it. I went to the *kuttab*, and everyone said, "Yes, our master is dead." I went to his house, saw the tears of his wife, his mother, and his daughters, but I still could not believe it. The funeral procession passed our house, and I still doubted it. Only when I saw them take the body out of the coffin and put him in the ground and cover him with earth—only then was I convinced. I suppose I had always thought Shaykh 'Abd al-Aziz was one of those people who could not die. And even after the funeral was over, I would occasionally have the feeling that soon he would creep out of his grave and shout at me, "Well, smarty, and what's the answer to that?"

For awhile I thought that teaching and school were buried in the grave with the body of Shaykh 'Abd al-Aziz, that he was the one who had created the idea of learning and, since he was dead, that was the end of school. I was wrong. The door of Shaykh 'Abd al-Aziz's *kuttab* was closed, but others were open, and my father enrolled Khalid and me in a *kuttab* about three miles away. With my cousin, we walked those three miles each morning and the three miles home, but, in reality, we walked much longer distances, for we played a game on the way, taking turns carrying each other from one electric pole to the next. Sometimes we would argue, and then all of us would go back to the first pole and start all over again. We must have walked seven or eight miles a day. But the new shaykh was not as unpleasant as Shaykh 'Abd al-Aziz, and he never ridiculed us, even if we did not know the lesson. Gradually, I began to love learning once more.

About this time, my father began to teach Khalid the chants and songs which he sang at the *mawlids,* for he wanted Khalid to help him in his work and perhaps become an imam himself. I listened to the chanting,[4] and I sang the songs to my doll, over and over again, until I had learned them, too. My father must have overheard me, for one day he said, "Umm Kulthum, sing to me, just as you were singing now."

I sang to him. I remember that he watched me very carefully, and from then on included me in the chanting sessions. One day he asked me to come with him to a *mawlid* being held by the *shaykh al-balad*, the chief of a tribe in our village.

I shook my head. "I don't want to go."

My father offered me candy, but I still refused. When he offered me a plate of *mahalabiyah*, or milk pudding, however, which I dearly love, my stubbornness melted and I agreed to go along.

About fifteen people were present at the party, which seemed a great number to me. My father asked me to sit beside him on the wooden bench and sing, as was the custom then for singers when performing. But I said no, and I stood up instead, on top of the bench. I wasn't afraid. I stood there and sang the way I always sang to the doll which Grandma Sitti Nasrah had made for me. Today, I fear my audiences. I worry about them, for they know me. I have a debt to them, somehow, a responsibility to fulfill. But then at that *mawlid* long ago, I was five or six years old and I had more self-confidence than I have today. When I finished, I heard applause for the first time in my life, but I do not remember that it touched me. The only thing I remember was turning to my father and saying, "Where is the plate of *mahalabiyah*?"

In the audience that day were some important members of the provincial government and, when the evening was over, they asked my father to bring me to sing at their *mawlids*. That, then, is how I began to sing.

When I think back now, I do not remember hearing from either my father or my mother any complaints about their poverty. They tried to hide it, the monthly struggle to make ends meet, and never spoke about it in front of their children. The only way I remember it was from overhearing their whispers after the morning prayers, when they thought we were still asleep. One morning I remember clearly.

"Oh, Shaykh Ibrahim, what's the matter, why couldn't you sleep last night?"

"You know the feast of 'Id al-Fitr[5] is coming, and we can't afford to buy new clothes for the children."

I felt my parents' pain. Later in the day, I went to my mother and said, "I don't need a new dress for the feast, for my old one is still pretty and I'm so fond of it; please, mother, let me wear it this year."

My mother burst into tears and threw her arms around me and kissed me. At that moment I felt as though I were wearing the prettiest dress in the world.

But it wasn't often I could solve any of my parents' problems. Those sorrowful, despairing whispers at dawn remained with me and rang in my mind, even more so because I could see no real way in which I could help them out of their difficulties. The only thing I could think of was to open my arms to heaven and cry out, "O God, help my mother!" It never occurred to me that one day I might be able to earn a penny to ease my parents' worries. But one night this began to change.

The second or third *mawlid* at which I sang was held in a house more than three kilometers from our village. I carried my little cat. I always told her my troubles and hopes and she always listened to me with great attention.

On this night, when we arrived at the house where the *mawlid* was to be held, the cat ran under one of the couches to hide, and I crawled in after her. We must have sat there together for quite awhile, for I heard my father calling and calling me, and then the cat and I came out. The crowd that night was bigger, but again I did not think about the audience, only about the plate of *mahalabiyah* which would be my treat when I had finished singing.

That night the host gave me a coin, a silver piece of ten piasters, almost half my father's total monthly income. I closed my fingers on that silver coin, very tightly and very carefully, for at that moment it seemed to me that I held the fortune of Qarun in my hand,[6] that the silver coin would solve all my parents' financial problems. Since then I have held thousands of pounds in my hands, but none has moved me as much as did that small silver coin.

When the *mawlid* was over, I was nearly asleep, for it was very late. One of the *shaykhs* in our group carried me on his shoulder back to the village. When I saw my mother, I opened my tightly closed fingers and gave her the fortune of Qarun. I felt her arms surrounding me and holding me tightly and with tenderness, and I felt myself falling into a deep, marvelous sweet sleep.

Now, although my father did not stop teaching my brother Khalid to sing, he began to teach me in earnest. Stories of the little girl who sang were spreading to villages near Tammay and even to villages outside our district. The distances we had to walk to perform were growing longer and longer. Our income rose to the point that we began to be able to travel third class by train to some of our jobs. I still remember the excitement of taking a train for the first time in my life, the train between Sinbalawin and Abu Shaquq. I stood on the seat looking out the open window, while my father held onto the back of my dress so I would not fall out. I remember being struck by something very strange: although the train was going forward in one direction, the palm trees and the telegraph poles went by in the opposite direction. I was so entranced that, when the train stopped at the Abu Shaquq station, I did not want to get off. My father promised that we would go home on the train tomorrow, the same train, but I would not believe him until he swore to me that in the name of God he was telling the truth. I finally got off the train.

This particular performance was limited to the well-to-do people of Abu Shaquq, since each ticket cost one piaster. The concert began with a great deal of fighting and confusion among the members of the audience, which took almost an hour to die down. Then I began to sing the religious songs which we always sang, the *tawashih al-nabawiyah*. Then the fighting and the shouting and the hullabaloo began again and lasted almost another hour. Of the four hours of the concert, three and a half hours at least were taken up in fighting and arguing between the members of the audience, and our singing lasted only about half an hour.

Such arguments and quarrels were part of every public concert or party held in the countryside at that time, and we never expected to sing for more than a single half-hour. But once, at the village of Mit Rumi, in the northern Delta, something happened we had not counted on. The audience was completely silent from the beginning. We began to sing, and no one interrupted us. There were no shouts, no fighting. We sang everything we had prepared in half an hour, and the party was scheduled to last until dawn. My father seemed bewildered. He kept looking at his watch, as though he thought it had stopped. The other singers with us were also confused. What were we to do? My father decided we would sing again the same songs which the audience had already heard. They did not object, and so we went on, repeating, three, four, five, six times. No one seemed to mind, but, after this incident, my father began to teach us many more songs, so that we could sing for longer periods of time.

Once we went to sing in a village close to Qarshiyah near the city of Tanta. Before the party began, the host guided us to a big tent, where we were to perform, and showed us a small kerosene lantern.

"When this lantern breaks," said the host, "you must come into this little side room so no harm will come to you."

"What?" said my father, surprised.

"Well, you see," said the host, "I'm not holding this party for the wedding of my son or my daughter. I brought you here only so that the people of our neighboring village will come, and then we can beat them up."

That night, I sang to the lantern. I sang, "Glory to the God that sent you, full of mercy for all those who hear and who see." And all the time I was singing my eyes, my ears, my mind, all my senses were concentrated on that lantern, for I knew that when it broke I would have to run quickly to the little room, in order to protect myself. Finally the lantern broke. The shouting and the fighting started. We ran to our hiding place, and, when things had quieted down, we came out of our shelter, only to find that not the guests but the host and his fellow villagers were the ones who had lost the battle and been beaten up themselves!

Fighting in the audience was not our only difficulty. Sometimes we had to deal with problems which were due to nothing more than the simplemindedness of the villagers. Once we were invited to a wedding quite far away. We walked several miles from Tammay to the center of Sinbalawin where we took the train to al-Mansurah. Then we took a boat across the Nile to Talkha, then the Delta train to Nabrawah, where we were to perform. But the host was not waiting for us at the station, as was usually the case. My father said that probably the people were so busy preparing for the party they had forgotten to come and meet us. So we hired donkeys and rode on to the small village where the wedding was to be. We asked for the house of the man who had hired us, and when he came to the door my father said, "Well, did you forget us or what?"

The host stared at us in surprise but said nothing.

"What's the matter?" asked my father. "You were supposed to send donkeys to the station."

The host still did not answer, but he looked as though he did not know what my father was talking about.

"Come on now," said my father. "Isn't this Tuesday? Isn't this the day of the party you hired us for?"

The host finally spoke. "But we've cancelled it!" he said.

"Cancelled it?" said my father.

"Yes, we've cancelled the party."

My father drew a deep breath. "All right," he said, "but why didn't you send someone to tell us so we wouldn't have come all this way for nothing?"

The host looked quite astonished. "But the whole village knows that we have postponed the party," he said, and, turning to some of the children who had gathered round to listen, he shouted, "Hey, Khalil, hey, Hassan, didn't we cancel the party? Sayyid, didn't your father know we had cancelled the party?" And when the children nodded yes, he turned back to my father and said, "See, everybody knows."

What could my father do? We went back the way we came, riding the donkeys to the Nabrawah station, the train to Talkha, the boat to al-Mansurah, the train to Sinbalawin, and finally we walked the last miles to Tammay.

Our fame was spreading and our fee went up. The six of us, my father, myself, Khalid, and the three other Shaykhs now received 100 piasters per concert. Soon it went up to 150 piasters. By the standards of the little village of Tammay, we were rich! So my father decided we should try to behave like rich people. Rich people had photographs taken of their children, so why shouldn't he, Shaykh Ibrahim, have a picture taken of his children?

We went to a photographer in Zaqaziq, which seemed a big city to us. We were supposed to be quiet and serious, but, when Khalid and I saw the man standing behind the camera with the big black cloth over his head, we were convulsed with laughter. The photographer was annoyed and spoke sharply to my father. Did he not know that children in a picture were supposed to be solemn, serious, and above all motionless as statues? After many attempts, we finally calmed down and the exasperated photographer was able to take what he called "a proper picture."

Father also began reading about the behavior of other singers, and he spent a good deal of time explaining to me how they acted, apparently so that I, too, would behave like them and create the impression that I, too, was an important singer, even though I was still only a child. For example, Father was told that Shaykh Hassan Jabir, one of the well-known singers of the time, was offered a bottle of soda water at the parties where he sang. So Father added a new condition to our contract, that is, that the party of the first part (the host) was to offer the party of the second (me!) a bottle of soda water!

Our fortunes were improving, my family's poverty was eased, and life seemed to me full and wonderful. People sent donkeys for us to ride to their concerts, I was given a plate of *mahalabiyah* each time, and now, in addition to all that, a whole bottle of soda water. What more could one ask?

But though life seemed good to me, I could tell that my father was uneasy. The idea that his daughter should be a singer was a difficult thing for him to accept. His son, yes, but a daughter, ah, that was something else, and besides I was growing up. So he began to dress me in boys' clothes, a *zibun*, or long vest, over the *jallabiyah* (or full-length garment) and on my head the *'iqal* and the *kuffiyah*.[7] I sang in this garb for several years. I realize now that my father wanted to deceive himself, to postpone in his mind what he was doing, letting his daughter sing in public. And he also wanted to deceive the audience and convince them that the singer was not a young girl but a young boy.

I had walked the entire countryside of the Delta before I ever put a foot in Cairo. By this time our contracts stipulated that donkeys were to be provided, both coming and going to the concerts. The host always fulfilled the first condition, but, when the party was finished, the donkeys always seemed to have disappeared. Thus, we usually walked home, often long distances; from two to five kilometers a night was about average. We did not mind the walking so much, but we often had to wait hours and hours for the trains. The trains passed the small stations only twice a day, once at 6 A.M. and once at 6 P.M. If we missed the morning train, we had to wait twelve hours for the evening train. There was nothing else to do. Sometimes we would hurry to the station when we had finished a concert, only to find that we had missed the train by a few minutes. Alas, in those days the trains always seemed to be very punctual, particularly on the days we missed them! And sometimes we would have to wait in cold and rain; in my memory it seems to me that the days we missed the trains were always cold and rainy. Eventually my father discovered how to deal with that problem. He discovered that, if I sang a few songs to the stationmaster, the waiting room would be opened so we did not have to wait in the rain. For we were poor villagers, and the stationmaster would never have let us sit in the waiting room under ordinary circumstances. Thus, I sang on hundreds of station platforms, in many, many stations along the Delta railroad line, and in exchange for my singing we found shelter from the weather.

As the months passed, I began to realize that there was a world beyond the Delta railroad line, that there were other cities, even bigger than Zaqaziq. One day we were invited to a big city called Cairo, which I had never heard of before. This is how it happened. A well-known pasha, 'Izz al-Din Yakun, was speaking with the estate manager in our village, telling him about the special festivities planned in his palace at Hilwan, to celebrate the night of Mi'raj (the night when the Angel Gabriel first spoke to Muhammad.)

The estate manager said, "By God, we have a girl right here in Tammay who has a beautiful voice."

"Well," said the landowner, "bring her to sing for us, why not?"

We traveled with the estate manager to Cairo. I don't remember anything about the city, and I have no impression of it at all in my mind, except the Bab al Luq station, where my father bought me a piece of candy better than any I had ever had before. Then we took the train to

Hilwan, to the palace. The pasha, who came out to meet us, looked me up and down several times, in some surprise. "You mean this . . . child . . . is the one who is going to lead the singing at my great *mawlid*?" He shook his head.

So they put us in the basement with the servants.

I don't remember feeling surprised or insulted by this treatment. We sat for hours in that basement while above us the chief singer, Shaykh Isma'il Sukkar, sang to the glittering audience. When he had finished by pleasing the guests and the party was considered a success, the host must have remembered us for he sent one of the servants to get me.

"All right," said the servant. "The pasha wants you to come and sing now. Let's see what you can do."

The main floor of the palace was very large and grand. I stood up on one of the benches, as I usually did, and I sang. The audience asked for encores, again and again. So did the great Shaykh Isma'il.

Finally, one of the servants said, "The lady of the house wants to see you in the *harim*."

We were led to a big salon, full of magnificent shining furniture. A voice said, "Come in!" We looked for the source of the voice but could see no one. We heard the voice again, saying, "Come in, come in!" We looked in every corner of that great room, but we could find no one. Then I saw what was making the noise. It was a bird in a cage, and it said, "Come in! Come in!" I was overcome by a fear I could not understand and I began to cry out, "A crow that talks! A crow that talks!" My brother and I rushed out of the salon and collided with the lady of the house, the wife of 'Izz al-Din Yakun. The lady saw that I was frightened, and she tried to calm me.

"What's the matter, my dear?"

I was shivering and shouting, "That crow talks! That crow talks!"

The lady began to laugh, but in a nice way, and she said, "Don't worry, my dear, it's not a crow, it's a parrot, and all parrots talk."

But of course, I didn't believe that! I went back to my village and told all my friends about Cairo, the city of wonders where crows can talk!

· · · · · · · · · · ·

Some time passed before I realized that, although I knew many songs, I was singing without emotion; I was simply repeating what I had learned from my father, in the same way a small child learns in school to recite the multiplication tables. A record player changed this, the record player that belonged to the *umdah*, or mayor of Tammay. On this machine I first heard the voice of Shaykh Abu al-'Ila, then the leading religious singer in Egypt, the person who was the principal exponent of the classical Islamic tradition of singing, the tradition of maqam.[8] When I first heard the voice of Shaykh Abu al-'Ila, I was greatly moved. I felt he was singing for me alone the songs and poems which celebrate the dreams of religious love and the dreams of secular love. "I will sacrifice myself to him whether or not he honors my love," sang the shaykh, and, after the record player stopped, the voice of Shaykh Abu al-'Ila continued to sound in my heart and in my mind.

In the village my friends sang, too, but they sang the popular songs of the day, about going to the well with their water jars to meet their own true loves. But I found myself singing the songs of Shaykh Abu al-'Ila. I thought that the shaykh was dead, and thus on a day when we were at the train station in Sinbalawin and I heard someone say, "Look! Look! There is Shaykh Abu al-'Ila," I could not believe my ears.

My father rushed forward toward a very tall man and began shaking his hand in a most respectful fashion. I rushed after my father and shook the shaykh's hand and tried to interrupt everyone else and tell the shaykh how much I admired him. The great shaykh did not pay much attention to me and went on talking to my father and the other men. I was determined to talk to the shaykh and I said he must come with us to visit our village. So insistent was I that finally my father, too, urged the shaykh to have lunch with us, and the shaykh agreed.

When we reached our house, I remember going in and saying to my mother, "Oh, mother, the most important man in the world is honoring us by coming to eat in our house. Please, please, let us give him a marvelous meal. Let's kill all our chickens and the neighbors' chickens, too, so that we can honor him properly."

I still could hardly believe that in my own house sat my idol, the great Shaykh Abu al-'Ila. I sat down next to him and asked him to sing for us. By this time my father must have told him that this stubborn daughter of his was also a singer, for the shaykh asked me to sing first. I refused, not daring to sing in front of the great man. He insisted, and finally I did sing for him and he sang for me. At that moment, I think I felt that in my own house in the village had come fulfillment of my greatest dream.

His voice was much more beautiful than it had sounded on the record player. I thought then he was the greatest singer I had ever heard in my life, and I think so still. Not only did he have a great voice, but he also managed to convey, better than any other singer I have known, the meanings of the words he sang. His work has given new vitality and meaning to the old traditions of tawashih and maqam.[9]

Shaykh Abu al-'Ila was very generous, for after lunch he went on singing, and I sang, too, for several hours. At the end of that afternoon, he suggested that we should leave the village of Tammay and go to Cairo.

"Oh, no," protested my father. "We couldn't do that. Tammay is our home, we know her, and she knows us. We cannot leave her. What would we do in Cairo?"

"But Shaykh Ibrahim," said Shaykh Abu al-'Ila to my father, very gently, "the future of your daughter is much greater than the village of Tammay. Other people should hear her, too. It's a shame to imprison the great talent which she has in such a small village."

When my father said no, I found myself speaking up, and, for the first time in my life, I argued with him. He tried to change the subject, but I kept returning to it; I insisted and pleaded, and he tried to change the subject again. I saw that argument at that time was fruitless. I stopped pleading, but I resolved never to give in. And later on, we did go. The call of Cairo was stronger, much stronger than any of us realized.

. . . .

At first only my father, my brother, Khalid, and I went to the city. We took a room in the Jordan House Hotel on Fuad Street, a room with three beds, one for each of us. But the room did not seem small to me; I thought that this humble hotel must be the biggest hotel in Cairo, for there were balconies from which I could look out on Fuad Street, on the high school, and on the Cinema Josy Palace. From the balcony I saw a movie for the first time. I saw people moving on a big white screen. It was very exciting! I saw a young man kissing a young woman. I saw a strange world I had never seen before, not in Tammay, not in Zaqaziq, not even in al-Mansurah.

Shaykh Abu al-'Ila came often to visit us in the Jordan House Hotel, and I would sit beside him, listening to him singing and listening to him talk about the music he sang, the words and the rhythm of the poems, the history of the songs. One evening while we sat on the balcony together, the shaykh turned to me and said, "Now then, Umm Kulthum, I have sung a lot for you tonight, will you sing for me?"

I sang and I sang. After I had finished, the night was very quiet around us, and the shaykh was silent for a long time. I could not understand why he didn't speak, until I leaned forward and saw tears running slowly down his cheeks.

"Ah, my daughter," he said. "I will listen to that voice for as long as I live."

And it did happen this way. From that evening, Shaykh Abu al-'Ila accompanied us to all of our concerts, wherever they were held.

Shaykh Abu al-'Ila had a great influence on me. He taught me a great
deal. He taught me to understand what I was singing. For, until I met
him, I was still a parrot, exactly like the parrot at the house of the Pasha
'Izz al-Din Yakun, repeating words I was hearing without really compre-
hending them at all. Gradually, I found that I could no longer sing
properly the words I could not understand.

One night I had trouble with a line of a song, "Praise to him who
touched your cheek with jasmine and pomegranate blossoms and
selected pearls for your teeth." The word for "pearl" stopped in my
mouth for some reason and refused to come out properly, so I kept
silent at this point in the song and let the rest of the group sing it without me. My father thought I had forgotten the word and did not pay
much attention, but when I missed this part of the line several times, he
asked me what was the trouble.

"Father, I don't know how to say this particular word. I don't understand how it goes. Am I supposed to be happy or sad about that phrase?
Shall I sing it as though I'm smiling or frowning? Please explain, because
it doesn't make sense to me."

That was the first time I had faced my father with what Shaykh Abu
al-'Ila had taught me, which was that I needed to understand the context
and meaning of the lines and words before I could sing them properly.

Through Shaykh Abu al-'Ila, I came to know the poet Ahmad Rami.
Apparently, Ahmad Rami asked the shaykh what he thought about a new
young singer, a girl named Umm Kulthum.

"She gives her whole soul in the one syllable 'Ah!' " Shaykh Abu
al-'Ila is supposed to have replied.

Thus, on the shaykh's recommendation, Ahmad Rami came to one of
my concerts in the Azbakiyah Gardens and during intermission came
backstage and introduced himself as a friend of Shaykh Abu al-'Ila.

Everyone in Cairo at that time knew of Ahmad Rami's work, and I
was so pleased he had come to hear me that I sang that evening his own
famous poem, "The Eyes of the Lover Betray Him." It turned out that
Rami was a lover of singing and I was a lover of poetry.

Whether it was Shaykh Abu al-'Ila's influence or Ahmad Rami's, I do
not know, but those first years in Cairo I felt a great urge to read. I
began to read novels and much poetry. I had enjoyed poetry from the
day when I found a book of my brother's in the house, The Sighs, by
Mustafa Lutfi al-Manfaluti; I read it, liked it so much I could not put it
down, and went on to read all of Manfaluti's work. Often I did not
understand very well what I was reading, and really at that time I
thought poetry was simply a collection of rhymed words that the poets
had put together so they might be sung more easily!

With Ahmad Rami's help, I began to appreciate what poetry really was. He would bring me books and discuss them with me. I learned about meters and rhythms and forms. I read the mystic Ibn al-Farid the Sufi. I read Ibn al-Rumi and al-Bukhari. I read *al-Aghani*[10] and selected from this collection some poems which seemed to me suitable for singing. I read *al-Amali*,[11] I read *al-Hamasah* by al-Mutanabbi, and I read al-Sharif al-Radi, Mihyar al-Daylami. I began to buy anthologies of other poets. In other words, I really began to love poetry. I read these poems with the same joy and enthusiasm which a young girl might bring to her first love story. I might have tried to express my own feelings in poetic form if I had not felt so humbled before the great writers I was reading then, under Rami's direction and with his help. The trouble is that, the more one learns, the more one realizes what remains to be learned. I knew by this time how little I knew, and I would not have dared to attempt to write poetry.

My friendship with my teacher Shaykh Abu al-'Ila continued for many long years. Whenever I sang, I looked for him in the audience, and I sang to him, for I knew that he could judge and appreciate and criticize and help me in my work as no one else could. And whenever we met in our house, I would ask him to sing for me. Nothing meant more to me then than to hear him sing. As the years passed, Shaykh Abu al-'Ila grew old and sick, with a gradual paralysis. He had difficulty pronouncing the words of the songs, but he would continue to sing, and, whenever he found it impossible to say the words, he would turn to me and say, "You know what I want to say, Umm Kulthum." And I would nod and try to keep back my tears, for I realized that he was very ill.

The night that Shaykh Abu al-'Ila died I could not stay in my house. My brother, Khalid, and the violinist Sami Shawa walked with me through the streets of Cairo. My head was full of my teacher's songs, the songs that would never be heard again. I walked through Zamalik, street by street, to Fuad Street, to Queen Nazli Street, back to Zamalik. I thought to myself, "I will wash all the streets of Cairo with my tears," but the tears would not come. Khalid and Sami were urging me to weep, but I could not, I could only repeat over and over again, sometimes aloud, sometimes in my mind, "My master! My teacher!" and I cried without tears for Shaykh Abu al-'Ila, the great man who taught me almost all I know about expressing, in song, thoughts and emotions.

In later years, I met many great musicians, but none ever meant as much to me in the same way as Shaykh Abu al-'Ila, my first teacher after my early training from my father. But I became good friends with Hussni Anwar and with Amin al-Mahdi, one of the best oud players in the early twenties. Amin al-Mahdi and his whole family came to be friends of our family, for now my mother had come to Cairo and we all lived in an apartment in Zamalik.

My first female friend was Ruhiyah, daughter of Amin al-Mahdi. From the moment we met, we both felt great mutual attraction and felt that we had known each other for years. Ruhiyah was a student at the French school, La Mére de Dieu. On Sundays she had no classes so I began to visit the al-Mahdi family every Sunday. I would open my heart to Ruhiyah, and she would open her heart to me.

In those days, Cairo to me consisted of the Azbakiyah Gardens, where I sang in the evenings, and the road from my house in Zamalik to Ruhiyah's house in Maydan Bab al-Khalq. Otherwise, I did not go out except to an occasional party or wedding where I had been engaged to sing. During the first four years of my life in Cairo, I did not go once to a movie house, I did not eat in any restaurant, I did not enter any shops or stores. I stayed home with my mother and read and worked on my music. I went once with my father to the Majestique Theater to see a play in which 'Ali Effendi al-Kassar was acting. But, otherwise, what I knew about Cairo was what I read in the magazines and newspapers and what other people told me when they came to visit us.

But, in spite of this isolation, I began to love Cairo. I felt I was living in the most beautiful city in the world. The response at my first concerts was encouraging. I felt as though my life were beginning to unfold in a glorious way of which I had never dreamed.

One of these days my father came home very disturbed and angry. He did not speak to me but went into his bedroom and called for my mother. When she hurried in, he locked the door behind them. I heard some whispering but did not pay much attention. Suddenly the door opened, and my mother came out, also looking very upset. She was carrying some suitcases, and, without a word to me, she began to pack. I asked what had happened, but she shook her head and said nothing. I asked my father what had happened, and finally he burst out, "It's finished, this business. We're going back to Tammay. We're not going to stay in Cairo any more and we're never coming back!"

I couldn't believe what he was saying. How could we leave Cairo? How could I leave this new life, this beautiful city, all my hopes, my dreams?

"Mother," I said. "My father can't be serious."

She nodded. "He is," she said.

"But why?"

She would not answer. When I asked again, she pointed to a magazine that had fallen on the floor. I picked it up. It was *The Theater*, which was then being published by the drama critic 'Abd al-Majid Hilmi. I flipped through the pages anxiously, searching for the answer to my question. I found nothing. I went through the magazine again, line by line, and then I, too, dropped it on the floor.

For the magazine had published a very strange piece of news about me, something totally false, something designed purposely to destroy my reputation as a respectable person, to blemish my honor as a girl.

At that time, 'Abd al-Majid Hilmi (may God rest his soul in peace) admired another singer, Munirah al-Mahdiyah. Instead of offering her a bouquet of flowers at the end of one of her concerts, he had thrown under her feet the honor and reputation of a new young singer, me!

I was very upset, as upset as my father, but for different reasons. My father knew very well that this article had no truth in it. How could he sacrifice my whole future for such a small thing? Was it right for me, the prey, to pay the price of the butcher's knife? I did not think so. Was running away the best way to fight these false accusations? I could not believe that it was.

I went to friends, seeking help. I asked them to come and try to convince my father to change his mind. They came, all the friends, and they talked to my father. They told him that his daughter had become famous and that one has to pay for fame, and one of the payments is to bear false reports which appear in minor magazines like *The Theater*. My father would not listen. Mother went on packing. Finally, I saw that he would not change his mind, and I went to my room to write a long letter to Ruhiyah, my dearest friend. I told her I was writing to say farewell to her and to my beloved Cairo. I felt as though I were saying good-bye to the whole world.

But, before I could send this letter, Amin al-Mahdi's whole family arrived. They saw all our suitcases, packed and ready, the apartment empty, ready for departure. The al-Mahdi ladies talked first to my father in a rational sort of way, but, when they saw that would not do, they began to talk very emotionally, touching on his one weak point, his love for me.

"It will be the end of her career," they said.

"You are taking that glorious voice and burying it in the soil of Tammay," they said.

My father wavered, I thought, but still he was not convinced.

Finally, Amin al-Mahdi himself spoke. He said, "Let me tell you something, Shaykh Ibrahim. You realize, of course, don't you, that leaving Cairo right after this article appears means only one thing to those of us in the city."

"Yes," said my father. "It means that I will not listen to such stories about my daughter's honor."

"No," said Amin al-Mahdi. "To the people in Cairo, it will mean that the story is true. Here honest people do not run away from false accusations."

My father stared at Amin al-Mahdi. Then he jumped out of his chair, opened one of the suitcases, and began pulling his clothes out of them. "We're staying," he said.

And we did. We settled permanently in Cairo, although we would still spend occasional periods in the village.

Before I go on, my readers might like to know something about Cairo at that time, the kind of a city I came into in the early twenties, a young village girl wearing a long blue coat and a black head scarf and singing the religious songs of the Prophet. For the boys' clothes had now been given up. My father had stopped deceiving himself. I was a girl, I was a singer, and I was making slow progress in the city. But it was not easy for my father, and it was not easy for me.

Cairo, 1926

An egg cost one millieme.
A kilo of meat cost 2 piasters; barbecued, 3 piasters.
A pack of al-Anbarul cigarettes: 2 piasters.
A luxurious sedan car: 360 pounds.
The school text for the government exam was *Zahrab wa-Rustum*.
On the stage 'Ali Effendi al-Kassar was playing the comic role of the
     Nubian in the army.
Yusuf Wahbi was the star of the world of the theater.
The chief of the mixed courts in al-Mansurah was Mr. Sansom.
The population of Egypt was twelve million. Twenty-six percent of the
     population died at birth because of poverty and malnutrition. Those
     who could read and write, over the entire country, totaled 197 per
     thousand. Traveling from Cairo to Alexandria took seven hours on
     the new express trains.

The revolution of 1919 was over, and Egypt fought within itself and with the British army of occupation. Sayyid Darwish summarized the political situation in his satirical operetta, *A Good Relationship* (*al-'Ishrah al-tayyibah*), where the song that brought down the house was "To Rise and Rise and Rise We Have to Bow and Bow and Bow!" Writing and working for reform in Cairo were Taha Husayn, Muhammad Husayn Haykal, Fikri Abadah, Abbas al-Aqqad, and Tawfiq al-Hakim.

During these postwar years, Cairo was full of British soldiers, the army of "occupation," and they thronged the bars and nightclubs which grew

up in the city to accommodate them. Cairenes became worried over the
bad influences on youth and a Committee of Honor was formed to
spread virtue and fight vice and corruption. But the Committee of Honor
had a difficult time with the cabarets and other pleasure palaces which
lined the streets bounded by Maydan al-Opera, Shari Imad al-Din, and
the Fajjalah. Whiskey could be brought anywhere along Shari Imad
al-Din, but if you wanted *araq* [a liquor], you had to go to the Fajjalah.
Drink, dancing, music, entertainment of all kinds was to be found in this
area. Along both sides of Muhammad 'Ali Street stood the little shops,
with musical instruments hanging from their walls and signs, "al-Usta
Hamidah, Oud Player"; or "al-Usta Zubah, belly dancer"; or "Na'imah
al-Misriyah, artiste" (a name which was a general cover term for a female
entertainer, one whose morals were not above reproach). Inside each of
these little shops sat one of the Mutaybatiyah (the good-time makers),
who dealt with customers needing entertainers and who shared the fees.
The Mutaybatiyah, on the nights when their clients were entertaining,
wore gay clothes and rings on their fingers and were responsible for
keeping up the spirit of the audience by continuously applauding.

Entertainers were of different classes and types. If a rich man held a
party, he would engage a singer for the upper-class guests and one for
the ordinary folk. Those who entertained the upper class, such as Shaykh
Hamid Mursi, Shaykh Isma'il Sukkar, and Abd al-Latif al-Banna, wore
suits. The "ordinary folk" entertainers wore *jallabiyah*(s) [long, full-
length traditional garments]; the best known of these at the time were
the Khudari, or green grocers' group; the Qahwaji, or coffee makers'
group; and the Halawani, or sweet sellers' group.

Those who entertained the rich considered this their profession and
they devoted full time to it. But those who entertained the ordinary folk
could not afford such luxury and they usually held several jobs. In addition to the groups who sold vegetables by day and sang by night, one
could see along the streets signs like "Composer of songs, reciter of
religious prayers, and doctor"; or "Undertaker and Koran reciter"; or
"Singer, seller of lottery tickets and cigarettes"; or "Ice cream, the composing of music, and medical assistance."

When I began to sing in Cairo, I still belonged to the category of those
who entertained ordinary folk. For example, Salih Abd al-Hay would
sing on the night of a wedding, and I would be engaged to sing the
night before. I still had a long struggle before me, and the struggle was
even greater if one bears in mind the great disdain in which Egyptian
society held all entertainers, and particularly female entertainers.

Egyptian women had not entered the entertainment field in any
number; their families would not allow them to. Thus, foreign names

were common in the cabarets and among the dancers, and many of the female parts in the theater were taken by male actors. Female actors were often photographed in the clothing of men.

Even Tawfiq al-Hakim, when he began to write for the theater, was criticized. One of his friends described him by saying, "Poor misguided Tawfiq. He is cavorting with actors and artistes, God forbid!"

This attitude of disdain and lack of respect for the entertainer was not limited to the ordinary person but extended throughout the government. Development and encouragement of the arts were then the responsibility of the Ministry of Public Works, and it was considered to have about the same priority as the paving of streets, the cleaning of sewers, and the repairing of bridges.

Still, critics were beginning to be interested in the theater and the arts, and the newspapers were devoting more and more space to the field of amusement. But it was not considered to be quite the right thing to do. Muhammad al-Tabi'i was the theater critic of the newspaper *al-Ahram*, but he signed his articles with a pseudonym, Hundis, because he did not want his name associated with the world of entertainment.

Criticism held other perils. When the performance of al-Sayyidah Mari Mansur was deprecated in the press, al-Sayyidah Mari sent a group of her men friends to give the particular critic a lesson in writing, to prove that the stick is stronger than the pen! Such incidents were common.

Music and, particularly, singing were in a transitional state at the time. The short resurrection of the musical theater, led by Sayyid Darwish, had revived interest in *tawashih*, both religious and secular, but this had declined in popularity, and the new popular songs were light, vulgar, and often obscene. "Draw the Curtains So We Can Enjoy Ourselves; Otherwise the Neighbors Will See Us," was a popular number, as was "Who Among You Is My Mother, Who Among You Is My Father? I Don't Know, and I Have No Way of Knowing." Such songs could be heard in every café and cabaret in the city at the time.

Even Sayyid Darwish was forced by circumstances to write such popular songs in the years before he died.

Artistes were held in low esteem, but the more famous ones had great influence with important government figures. Members of King Fuad's cabinet often gathered at the house of Munirah al-Mahdiyah, "the nightingale of the eastern world," who was the most famous singer in Egypt for years. Sitt Munirah, they say, was able, with a single song, to persuade the prime minister to leave government business for the day and take her to the barrage for a picnic!

Tawfiq al-Hakim has well summarized the attractions of the cabarets of the period: "After the first World War, the blonde entertainers from war-ravaged countries like Austria and Germany flocked to Egypt, which was open to whoever wished to come in. These girls filled the bars and nightclubs and the young playboys of Cairo flocked there to see the girls and make assignations with them for the rest of the evening. The play-boys went not to see the plays or hear the songs, but to look at the beautiful legs of the girls, the artistes."

This was the kind of audience which I faced when I came to Cairo with my father in the twenties, dressed in my long blue coat and *tarhah* and singing the songs of the Prophet Muhammad.

· · · · · · · · · · ·

When we first lived in Cairo, it seemed to us like another planet. Everything was different from what we had known in the village: the houses, the streets, the people, the audiences, the parties, and the business arrangements. In Tammay, if someone wanted us to sing at a wedding, he would come directly to my father to make the agreements. In Cairo, one had to have an agent, and in the beginning we suffered a lot with these agents. My father was a very goodhearted, honest man, naïve in business, and he was not suited for dealing with the agents in Cairo. Perhaps my father's appearance as a villager and mine as a young, simple girl wearing a long coat and a *tarhah* led the agents to believe they could easily cheat us. For example, one of our first agents, Siddiq Ahmad, managed to get our fee reduced in this way: We would agree that I would be paid seven pounds for a performance. But on the evening of the performance, Siddiq would take us to the theater and we would sit behind the curtain waiting for the audience. While we waited, Siddiq would begin complaining. "What a shame!" he would say. "We don't have any audience at all. Look through the curtain! The place is empty."

My father would look through the curtain and indeed the hall was empty. Then Siddiq would say, "Oh, dear, we won't make any money at all," and soon our fee would be reduced from seven pounds to five or even four. "Ya Shaykh Ibrahim, I worked so hard to advertise this concert and now I will lose everything," Siddiq would sigh, and my kind-hearted father would feel so sorry for Siddiq he would agree on a reduced fee.

But, of course, an hour or two later, by the time we had started singing, the house would be filled with people. Our agent had brought us early to the theater on purpose, and when my father, angry at being tricked, would look for Siddiq he had always disappeared very neatly.

Gradually, as we gained more experience in the city, we learned to handle this problem and were not so easily deceived. Then there were problems with the audiences.

At that time, I was still singing religious songs and poems, which were rather out of fashion. The audiences came to hear music, but they wanted really to amuse themselves, and often they came drunk to the concerts. Thus, the light popular songs, often very vulgar and obscene, appealed to them much more than my religious numbers. But I refused to sing these vulgar songs and this created difficulties.

I remember particularly one of the first nights when I sang in the Casino des Sports in Maydan al-Mahattah (called Maydan Bab al-Hadid today). I began that night at ten o'clock with the song "Glory to Him Who Was Sent to Us to Bring Mercy to Whoever Hears and Sees." Soon some members of the audience shouted for me to stop and sing instead, "Draw the Curtains, So We Can Enjoy Ourselves." I shook my head and went on with my religious music. But the voices which objected to the songs of the Prophet got louder and louder and I could hardly sing above the noise. I still carried on, but the matter did not end there. A few members of the audience jumped on the stage and tried to pull the curtains shut on me. At this point, I lost my temper. I felt that whoever came to the Casino that night knew what to expect, for the sign outside the door bore my name and the kind of songs I would sing; there were plenty of places in the Maydan where the kind of popular song they were demanding was being sung. I was so angry I began to shout insults back at the men who came toward me from the audience. I was hardly aware at all of what I was saying until I felt my father slapping me. I burst into tears.

That was the first time my father had ever slapped me at all, let alone in front of an audience! I wept because I knew I was right and my father knew I was right. But he had slapped me in front of the angry audience to please them, to calm me down, for he had then seen the evil on their faces as they approached the stage. He was afraid the men would hurt me, for they were very drunk. So he took the initiative in punishing me instead of letting them do it, to save me further pain, but also, I think, to give me a lesson in good behavior. Whatever the circumstances, he said, the audience was always right. We were performers and could not insult those who came to hear us. After all, hadn't my great teacher, Shaykh Abu al-'Ila, been forced off the stage by an unfriendly audience and had to listen to 'Abd al-Latif al-Banna instead of himself? Had he lost his temper? No. I had to learn, said my father. But it was not easy.

In the first years, hardly a week passed without an incident in which the audience tried to pressure me into singing those popular songs. The temptation was great to simply give in and forget about keeping up a

certain standard, a certain quality in the singing and in the kind of song I was willing to present. I was determined *not* to give in, but the situation was often very difficult and unpleasant.

Even in the countryside, sometimes, we would find drunken audiences like this. Once I was singing in a village close to the town of Mit al-'Amil in the province of Dakhaliyah. The concert was in the reception hall of the *umdah*, or mayor, a very large hall which was full. That night I recognized many faces in the audience, for, during the years I had sung in villages and towns throughout the countryside, people who really wanted to hear *tawashih,* or religious songs, had learned what to expect from me. This was *our* audience, built up over several years. But that night, in addition to our audience, there was a small group reminiscent of the drunk Cairo audiences. These people were in the minority, but they were there.

"Glory to Him . . .," I began. Suddenly a man stood up in the audience screaming, "What's this? Are we in a place of mourning? Has somebody died? We came here to be gay. We want to feel happy!"

"Glory to Him who was sent to us to bring mercy . . .," I continued.

The man started in again. "This is nonsense," he shouted in a louder voice. "We want to feel lighthearted. I want to hear 'Oh, My Love!'"

I continued to sing, and other members of the audience tried to mollify the man.

But in an instant the atmosphere was suddenly charged with electricity, for the drunken man ran out into the middle of the aisle, took a pistol out of his pocket, and began to wave it in the air threateningly.

"All those who don't want to hear 'Oh, My Love,' " he shouted, "get out!"

There was a moment of silence. People began scurrying quickly out of their chairs, and I faced an empty hall. Obviously this man with the gun was someone important, but we had no idea who he was until later, when we discovered he was the son of the *umdah*.

"All right, now you sing what I want you to sing!" he screamed pointing his gun at me.

"I'll sing what I want!" I answered, trying to be polite and calm.

My father, who had moved closer to me, said quickly, "Calm yourself, my son. Don't be upset."

"I'm not upset," said the man in a shrill voice. "But she has to sing 'Oh, My Love,' for me. She has to give me some pleasure. That's what I paid for."

"Yes, yes, my dear son," said my father, "but look. You want to be happy and gay and you are waving a gun around?"

"That's the only way to get what I want with that girl," he said.

I heard my father sigh. "All right, sir, at your service," he answered. "We'll sing everything you want. But first you must calm down. Now, my daughter, sing for him. If we must, we must, and trust the rest to God!"

I refused. My refusal wasn't a sign of courage, it was stubbornness and pride and a strong belief that I was doing the right thing. I don't remember even thinking about the gun.

"Oh, ho, so you're not going to sing for me, the son of the *umdah*, eh?" cried the man in a frenzy. "Well, we'll see about that," and he tried to steady the gun in his shaking, drunken hand.

"She'll sing! She'll sing!" My father's voice was shaking now. "But be patient, for God's sake, be patient."

And God must truly have saved us, for at that moment, someone we knew came quietly into the back of the hall, crept up behind the drunken son of the *umdah*, and seized the loaded gun. Later we discovered that our friend had been simply passing through the village on his way back to Tammay, had seen the sign with my name on it, and had come late to the concert on the chance that it was not yet finished. Thanks to him, to chance, to God's mercy, to who knows what, we survived.

Why didn't my music appeal to those people? This was the question I asked myself over and over. Was something wrong with the audience or with me and my songs? But I had some support, and I believed strongly in the music; I felt it was the kind of music that people would listen to and enjoy if it were sung well enough. So I decided I must work harder, I must sing better, I must improve myself and the music. I wanted to be accepted in Cairo, but I did not want to sacrifice my standards of music and sing songs that I felt were unworthy. It was a taste that needed to be developed in the audience. These were the years in which I benefited from the long years of struggle in the countryside; work was something I expected, why should it not continue? One must work to develop appreciation for the *tawashih*, I felt, and so I continued to work.

My first record was the song "Why Did I Ever Fall in Love with Your Devastating Eyes," set to music by Ahmad Sabri al-Najridi, and recorded by the Sound of Sayyidah Company, a branch of RCA, "His Master's Voice" in Cairo. The company was certain that they would lose on this recording, and so they paid me only eight pounds for the rights, and sold the discs for ten piasters each. To their surprise, they made a great profit, for, although I was a relative unknown in Cairo, I did have an audience in the villages and towns where I had sung as a child and a young girl. Then there were no radio stations in the rural areas, and so a single record of mine was a great present to take back to the village from a trip to Cairo. The company made other records of mine, and my payments rose. Slowly, my supporters in Cairo began to grow, although there was a lot of competition in those years among singers. I knew none of the editors or writers or critics, and so I was constantly being surprised by articles that mentioned me.

In the late twenties, an article was published saying, "There are supporters for the songs of al-Sayyidah Munirah al-Mahdiyah, and supporters for Anisah Umm Kulthum, but who can judge which is best? Well, the record company pays Umm Kulthum fifty pounds for a record, and al-Sayyidah Munirah gets only forty. So more people are buying Umm Kulthum's records than those of al-Sayyidah Munirah." This was the way artistic achievement was evaluated!

A questionnaire was printed soon in the same newspaper, asking the readers to vote for the favorite singer. I came out third. But, curiously, I didn't mind. I felt the newspaper was right. I believed I had a great deal more work to do in order to develop into the first-ranked singer. The important thing was not that I was ranked third but that I was determined not to remain in third place.

Eventually, a very fine article was published about me, by someone I had never met, Shaykh Mustafa Abd al-Razzaq. It appeared in *al-Siyasah* and it was the first article that I felt understood what I was trying to do in my work: to revive the old, marvelous traditional *tawashih*, the great tradition of singing of our past. I felt honored to be the instrument by which these glorious songs and poems could once more be transmitted to the people and understood by them.

When one of my records, "If I Were to Forgive and Forget," sold half a million copies, my fortunes took a turn for the better. And, not long after, I was sitting in one of the casinos on the Corniche in Alexandria. Opposite us was a cabaret. It was a beautiful, calm, cool evening in Alexandria. I could not believe my ears when the strains of "Aba al-Zahra' " came floating to me across the Corniche from that cabaret. The nightclub singer was actually singing a song composed by the great poet Ahmad Shawqi in praise of the Prophet Muhammad. That night, I felt a strange contentment. All those evenings with drunken audiences, all the long years of work, the fatigue, the long walks in the rain and cold of the Delta—they were worthwhile. An audience would sit and listen quietly to this great song, "Aba al-Zahra'," even in a cabaret.

· · · · · · · · · · · ·

Although father was basically a simple man from the country with a limited education, his horizons were broad. He was flexible and adjusted to new ideas and attitudes in ways I now realize were quite extraordinary.

For example, when I began to sing, it was my father's idea that I should wear modest clothes, the coat and the headscarf, for he felt this kind of attire was appropriate not only to my status as a young, respectable girl but also to the music which I sang, mainly religious in the beginning. In those days, respectable girls did not ordinarily become singers, and my modest dress was one of my father's solutions to his ambivalent feelings about having me, the daughter of a religious shaykh, singing in public. But when we came to Cairo, he soon saw that this garb was no longer appropriate, and he was the first one to suggest that I might wear dresses (still long, modestly cut, and with long sleeves) to sing in instead of the coat and *tarhah*.

My father also was responsible for changing the composition of the group which accompanied me. In the countryside, four men, wearing shaykh's robes, sang with me: my father, my brother, and two friends of ours. We had no musical instrumentalists with us. In Cairo, my father saw musical groups which combined vocalists with instruments, and he decided to form a new kind of group. As early as October 7, 1926, I was accompanied by an orchestra which my father had assembled from among the best musicians of the time: Muhammad al-'Aqqad, *qanun*; Sami Shawa, violin; and Muhammad al-Qasabji, oud.[12] The concert was a great success, and the press unanimously stated that the musicians were "masters of the art of Oriental music." From that time, I sang with an orchestra.

I took lessons on the oud myself, at my father's insistence; my teacher was Mahmud Rahmi and he would spend the whole day teaching me, while my father sat with us and listened. My father's musical instincts were good. Some of the vocal exercises which he taught me were later adopted at the conservatory in Cairo. He insisted that I should go to bed early and get up early on the days I was not performing. He devised a diet of certain basic foods which I had to eat, and I often drank a kind of eggnog made of hot milk, cane sugar, and an egg. Certain exercises had to be done every day.

My father insisted on high standards and continual development. He never thought that I had reached my goals but said I could always improve; the music can always be improved, he said. Generally, I agreed with my father, but occasionally, as I grew older, I disagreed with him.

Once we had decided to buy some land. This was not the first time; we had bought a small piece of land before but had lost it, because the contract was not written properly. Now we were interested in a parcel of fifty acres, which is a large and valuable piece of land in the Delta. It was being sold at auction by the bank, since the previous owners had not succeeded in making the mortgage payments. I begged my father not to buy the land unless all taxes and debts had been paid, because until this was done the land would never be legally ours. I asked that this clause be inserted into the contract, so that we would not be cheated again. I did not want my savings of ten years to be lost because my father was willing to take the "word of honor" of the lawyer. So I refused to sign the contract, and my father slapped me, hard.

I was not a child anymore, and I did not cry. I simply said, "Now, I will never sign the contract unless the clause which I demand is added. I know enough now to never accept anybody's word of honor until it is written down on paper."

After some embarrassed consultation between the lawyer and the owner and the bank officials, the clause I wanted was inserted. I signed.

My father never mentioned this incident again until almost a year had passed. "You remember, Umm Kulthum, the day we disagreed about buying the land? I have to tell you that you were right and I was wrong. When I went to the bank today, they told me they were ready to confiscate it several weeks ago because the previous debts and taxes had still not been paid. This would have cost the owner even more, so he paid off everything and, as of today, the land is ours, free and clear."

I was growing up.

.   .   .   .

Everything I have achieved in my life I owe to my mother, my father, and to Shaykh Abu al-'Ila.

Shaykh Abu al-'Ila made me understand for the first time *what* I was singing. He was for me a great example of belief in art, determination to overcome obstacles, and firmness in his standards of music. My debt to him is no less than to my father and mother.

From my mother I learned humility, the importance of being true to oneself, and the importance of having faith in God. She was a great lady. She transformed the poor and miserable days of our childhood into happy days; from poverty she created wealth. She loved us all.

My father was a poor man, also, but he gave me something greater and more important than the largest fortune, he gave me his constant love and his undivided attention. He gave me confidence in myself, the will to succeed. He taught me also that success is good, but not if it is achieved at the price of one's ideals and self-respect.

These are the ideas and people which have helped me.

Conclusion

Umm Kulthum remains a legend in the Arab world today and is generally considered the "mother of Middle Eastern music." For years her concerts were sold out at least three months in advance. In the little theater near the Azbakiyah Gardens and in the Cinema Radio, where she regularly sang in Cairo on the first Thursday of the month during the winter season, many of the theater seats were held by the same people year after year. So well did Umm Kulthum know her audience over the years that, if one of the seats in the theater was empty, she would ask, "Is the Umdah Muhammad of Tanta not well? I did not see him at the concert tonight." The concerts lasted four hours on the average, and Umm Kulthum is known for her tremendous physical stamina and vitality as well as for the glorious range of her voice. As she grew older and more secure in her own artistic judgment, she began to help in the preparation of the music and the words which she sang.

From her early singing of religious *tawashih* with her father, she became famous for her interpretations of secular *tawashih*, many of which were written for her by Shaykh Abu al-'Ila. She was also known, during the middle years of her career, for her mastery of *maqam* and her sure touch for the proper transitions and artistic improvisations possible between one *maqam* and another.

Umm Kulthum's struggle to achieve high standards in her art as well as in her personal life earned her awards from her own country and medals and decorations from nations all over the world. Her achievement has raised the status of entertainers generally and women entertainers in particular. Her work helped to open the way for a whole new generation of contemporary entertainers in Egypt and throughout the Middle East.

Notes

1.   The Ministry of Waqfs could be identified generally as a charitable foundation; it supports religious activities, education, libraries, the poor, etc.
2.   A *mawlid* is an annual celebration in honor of a saint or revered religious person.
3.   One *piaster*, or *kursh*, equalled about five cents at that time. A *millieme* was one-tenth of a piaster. The family's cash income was probably supplemented with payments in kind (oil, sugar, chickens) and perhaps some produce from their own kitchen garden.
4.   This was the chanting of religious stories and poems. The chanting of the Koran is *tartil*, which Umm Kulthum also learned.

5.   'Id al-Fitr is the Muslim feast which ends Ramadan, the month of fasting.

6.   *Qarun* is a mythical or legendary king of great wealth mentioned in both the Koran and the Bible (where he is called Korah in Numbers XVI).

7.   The *kuffiyah*, a head scarf worn by men, is held in place by the *'iqal*, a circle of black cotton rope.

8.   *Maqam* means literally a musical mode, and singers who have mastered the various modes of Middle Eastern music "play" with different modes as they sing words, phrases, or poems. The art lies in the transition and improvisation of one mode with another and may be compared to the art of plainsong and Gregorian chant in western music.

9.   *Muwashah*, pl. *tawashih*, means literally "a postclassical form of Arab poetry, arranged in stanzas." It is used also to refer to poems which are sung but follow the same meters. Several types of *tawashih* exist, the religious *tawashih* and the secular *tawashih*.

10.   A compendium of Arabic literature compiled by 'Abu al-Faraj al-Isbahani (A.D. 897–967).

11.   *Kitab al-Amali*, a dictionary of Arabic philosophy compiled by al-Qali 'Abu 'Ali Isma'il ibn Qasim (A.D. 901–967).

12.   A *qanun* is a stringed instrument somewhat like a zither; an oud is a descendant of the lute.

11 Halidé Edib Adivar

HALİDE EDİB ADIVAR

Turkish Nationalist

A.D. 1883–1964

Halidé Edib Adivar was born in Istanbul in 1883, into a well-to-do, traditional Turkish family. She grew up in the old aristocratic society of the Ottoman Empire. Her father, Edib Bey, was secretary to Sultan Abdul Hamid and worked in the palace; her mother, whose ancestors were learned religious men, died when Halidé was very small. Halidé was cared for by her maternal grandparents until she was four, when her father married again. Educated at home by English governesses and Turkish religious shaykhs, Halidé then went to the American College for Girls. Her father engaged a well-known scholar, Salih Zeki Bey, to coach her in mathematics. Although Salih Zeki Bey was nearly her father's age, Halidé married him in 1901 after graduation from the American College. Two sons, 'Ali Ayetullah and Hassan, were born of the marriage. At this time, the first movements toward reform by the "Young Turks" were beginning. Halidé and her husband both wrote for the liberal newspaper *Tanine*, Halidé specializing in literary criticism and articles about women's emancipation. She also began to write novels, which enjoyed great popularity. Divorced from Salih Zeki Bey in 1910, she continued to write and became a busy public speaker, particularly on the subject of

---

Photo: Halidé Edib as a young woman

the education of women and their participation in national life. She says herself that the period from 1910 to 1912 "was a prelude to my final plunge into nationalism which took an intense form after the disaster of the Balkan War."

Many modern Turkish historians list Halidé Edib with the "most prominent intellectuals of the time," who were responsible for organizing the nationalist movement.[1] In 1912, she was elected the only woman member of the Ojak, the Turkish nationalist club with branches all over the countryside. In 1918, the Ojak congress chose a council of eleven to modify its constitution; Halidé was a member of the council and, as a result of her efforts, the constitution was changed so that other women members were eligible. During the First World War, she worked in Syria and Lebanon, organizing schools and orphanages for the thousands of refugee children left homeless. A fellow nationalist and old family friend, Dr. Adnan Adivar, was also involved in these activities and they were married in 1917. Halidé and Dr. Adnan worked together during the long struggle for Turkish independence, he as medical doctor, she as one of the principal writers and translators attached to Mustapha Kemal Pasha's nationalist forces. Her stirring public speeches in the opening months of the nationalist struggle helped make her one of the first Turkish women to become a public figure and national hero. The excerpts which follow describe Halidé's early childhood and the formative years of her youth and early womanhood.

From the Autobiographies

Several instances of sudden consciousness of herself flash into her memory as she muses on her first self-acquaintance. There is the background: the big house in Beshiktash, on a hill overlooking the blue Marmora at a distance, and near at hand the hills of Yildiz with the majestic white buildings surrounded by the rich dark green of pines and willows which are pointed out to her as the residence of his Majesty Abdul Hamid.

She is not, however, interested in what the distance held, for the old wisteria-covered house, peeping through the purple flowers, with its many windows flashing in the evening blaze, is dominating her. The garden is on terraces, and there are tall acacias, a low fruit orchard with its spring freshness and glory, and a long primitive vine-trellis casting an enchanting green light and shade on the narrow pathway beneath it. This is the place where she moves and plays. There is a little fountain too, with a pair of lions spouting water from their mouths in the evening hours—making the only music in the twilight there. In the early morning, pigeons, ever so many pigeons, walk round her, and she quietly watches granny feeding them with crumbs. The wonderful smell, the wonderful color-scheme, and the wonderful feeling of stepping into the world for the first time in that garden.

There is another flash, which faintly lights up another house, not granny's any longer, but her father's own house near-by. . . . An intense uneasiness and an obscure feeling, perhaps of undefined fear. The woman whom she calls "mother" is lying in semi-darkness beside her, in a large bed, clad in her white gown. There are those two long, silky plaits, which seem to coil with the life of some mysterious coiling animals, and that small, pale face with its unusually long, curly black lashes resting on the sickly pallor of the drawn cheeks. This mother is a thing of mystery and uneasiness to the little girl. She is afraid of her, she is drawn to her, and yet that thing called affection has not taken shape in her heart; there is only a painful sense of dependence on this mother who is quietly fading out from the background of her life. The only act of that mother which the little girl remembers is when she finds herself sitting on the rather specially comfortable lap and the pale face with its silky lashes is lighted by the tender luster of the dark eyes while the woman dexterously plays with the little girl's tiny hands and takes each finger

[Excerpts chosen and adapted by the Editors from Halidé Edib Adivar, *Memoirs of Halidé Edib* (New York and London: Century, 1926), and *The Turkish Ordeal* (New York and London: Century, 1928). Reprinted by permission of Hawthorn Books, Inc.]

and cuts the nails—rather low—for it hurts. But no howling is possible as long as that low voice, with, as it seems, some warm color caught from the eyes, murmurs, "There is a little bird perched here" (this is said to the palm); "this one caught it" (this is to the thumb); "this one killed it; this ate it; and this little one came home from school and cried, 'Where is the bird? Where is the bird?' "[2] Oh, the soft tickle of that touch and the hidden caress in that voice!

· · · · · · · · · ·

The light is once more turned down, and now there is no mother. The little girl stupidly wanders about, understands nothing, knows nothing, feels lonely and abandoned. Every evening the father sits by a small round table. One single candle flickers, and his tears fall on the candle-tray, while the servants walk about on tiptoe and pull the little girl away by the hand.

'Ali is the man-servant who takes care of her; he is her *lala*, that indispensable personage in every old Turkish household, for which no English, no European, equivalent can exist, for it arose from roots wholly foreign to them, wholly Oriental. The *lala* was the natural outcome of the marked separation between the indoor and outdoor life of that day and world. Indoors was the delicate, intimate rule of women; out of doors was the realm of men. They could play there their proper role of protector, and one felt happy and secure in their presence. As child, and as child only, one could share to the full the freedom of the two worlds, and one's *lala* was one's natural companion into all the open-air places of experience. Then too he brings with him into memory that *je ne sais quoi* of the old-world service—devotion, attachment, pride, possession even—which the modern Turkish world has forgotten but which made so much of the warmth and color of the old household life. In the *lala*'s strength one was secure; on his devotion one could rely—tyrannously— and from his innocent familiarity one could learn the truths and fables which only fall from the lips of primitive affection. But to return. The little girl's *lala* is 'Ali, a quiet big man with a great deal of affection if she could specify that strange feeling yet. He is kind and grave and buys her colored sweets in the street, a thing which is strictly forbidden by her father. The woman who cooks and serves the meals is called Rassim, a dark and ugly creature with a face entirely covered by marks of small-pox. Rassim is in love with 'Ali, and 'Ali's brother Mustafa is the other man-servant. After the mother disappears the little one is in the men's sitting-room most of the time, and this is the way they must have talked, although she only realized the meaning of their words much later:

Rassim: "The old lady is lost to everything in her mourning. She cannot move or think, so now I can do what I like with the child."

'Ali: "Stop that talk. I will make thy mother cry, if thou touchest a single hair of her head."

Rassim: "But she's telling tales about us all the time. Thou knowest how she goes and mimics everything thou or I do so that everyone knows what we are doing."

'Ali: "What does *she* know? Poor little mite! Thou liest, Rassim."

Rassim: "*Vallahi* [by Allah], I don't"—she grinds her teeth at the little girl—"if she lets out anything more about us two I will let the crabs loose on her."

'Ali: "What are the crabs for?"

Rassim: "They are good for consumption. We had them to grind and put on her back, but she died before we could put them on."

'Ali: "How is Bey Effendi [the master]?"

Rassim: "Still crying by the light of that single candle. It is the portrait of the other man that they found on her breast when she died which has done the mischief."

'Ali: "Thou must have put it there, thou pig!"

Rassim: "No, *vallahi*! If she had not had the portrait how could I have put it anywhere? O 'Ali . . . his name was 'Ali too. All the 'Alis are tyrants."

Then she sings the old song:

'Ali, my 'Ali, my rose, come thou to the rosebush; if you comest not, give me a peach (i.e., a kiss), O 'Ali.

My 'Ali is gone to market; the evil eye will touch him; he who wishes 'Ali dead, may he lie in the grave instead.

Then she puts her arms around 'Ali and kisses him, which action is always followed by shaking the little girl and looking into her wondering eyes: "Halidé Hanim, thou art not to tell, never, never."

What is it that they do not want her to tell? When and how she has ever told anything she does not know, but she answers: "I *will* tell, Rassim Dadi;[3] I *will* tell."

Then follows the usual fighting between 'Ali and Rassim because of the little girl, and Mustafa looks on, with that disagreeable grin on his face.

The next morning she runs down to the kitchen in her night-dress, her feet all bare. She has a queer quivering feeling down her back, and her mind is full of crabs, whatever they may be.

"I *will* tell, Rassim Dadi," she screams defiantly on the last step, and before she can run up-stairs again she is caught and set in the middle of the kitchen while a large basket full of something is poured out on the floor, and there the little creeping horrors are all round her feet.

The helpless terror, the speechless agony of fear, the hair damp on her forehead, the staring eyes that hurt! She has no remembrance of the end of this terrible event, but she knows well the stories her granny used to tell later about Rassim's cruelty to herself.

"I rescued the poor little creature," granny would say; "I was coming to the house that morning, and from the garden I heard the child screaming. I rang, and Rassim never thought it was I, so she opened the door, and I found the child laid on the mat, her mouth filled with black pepper, which Rassim had been stuffing her with, and struggling to get away. I could have beaten Rassim, the wretch! But the little one continued defiant to the last. 'I *will* tell, Rassim Dadi,' she kept on screaming, while Rassim, wild with rage, kept on shouting, 'Say thou wilt not tell.' "

But all that is strangely forgotten, and the only thing that can be seen through the haze is a somehow connected vignette of the little Halidé sitting on the lap of a wonderful old man, with burning eyes and a flowing white beard, who caresses her hair with a gentleness so queer from those rough hands. "Poor little mite!" grandfather keeps saying.

Her next and last impression of the house in Yildiz is quite different. Rassim had been dismissed because of her cruelty, 'Ali and Mustafa had gone, and an old lady housekeeper and a young Circassian boy were living in the house, the housekeeper looking after her father and Halidé herself. Her father was going regularly to the palace again as in the old days. His tall groom with that lovely big bay horse used to stand by the door in the mornings, and the little girl would ride the horse before her father came out, her small feet dangling and the groom leading the horse by the bridle very gravely up and down the street. At last the father would come down-stairs and ride away followed by his groom on a white horse, while the little girl strained her eyes to get the last look of them as they disappeared round the turning of the long, stately road to Yildiz Kiosk.

She missed 'Ali badly, and even Rassim who had been so cruel she missed too. The atmosphere of excitement and disorder had gone. No one talked of a picture on a dead woman's breast and a man's tears. The father was mostly away in the palace, staying even at night, when it was his turn to be on duty.

It was now that the event which is somewhat like a symbol of her lifelong temperament occurred.

On the long divan, covered with white cloth, sat the old lady housekeeper, a kind and hard-working creature, leaning over her darning continually; the young Circassian sat at the table, lost in his books, for he was getting ready for a school education. (Her father had a mania for taking poor young men under his protection and sending them to school.) She, the little girl, was left to herself. There was no one scolding her or filling her mouth with black pepper for telling about things she did not know. There was complete silence. The father was no longer shedding tears by the flicker of a single candle. Her loneliness seemed suddenly to have taken the form of a tangible hardness in her throat. The woman with the long coiling plaits and wonderful eyes was no more. What was this silence about? Why had she no one to cuddle close to and go to sleep with? There was no answer to her unspoken questioning. Still only that dead silence. The next moment she stood in the middle of the room and spoke her mind out.

"I want my father!"

"He is at the palace."

"I want my father!"

"He will come back to-morrow."

"I want my father!"

"He cannot come, dear. The gates of the palace are closed at night, and the whole place is kept by guards."

"I want my father!"

Gradually the little voice rose and rose in hoarse and piercing howls of pain which she herself internally noted as strange. On and on it went, rising and howling till the Greek neighbors came in one by one to help the old lady housekeeper to calm and soothe her, their voices making a still greater noise than the little girl. The place was a Christian quarter— Armenians and Greeks were the only neighbors—and the Greeks of Constantinople talk louder than anybody else, especially if they are women. But there were twenty wild beasts ranging in the little girl's breast, making her howl with pain till she caught sight of a pail of cold water brought by a Greek woman to stop her crying.

"She may catch cold."

"But she will burst if she goes on like that."

"O Panagia" [holy Mother], "pour it on her head."

And pour it they did, which gave the old housekeeper the extra trouble of changing her clothes, but for the rest caused her a sudden catch in her breath which stopped her for an instant only to begin louder and louder, wilder and wilder, the next moment. . . . It was the symbol of the force of her desires in later years, the same uncontrollable passion for things, which she rarely wanted, but which, once desired, must be obtained at all costs; the same passionate longing although no longer expressed by sobbing or howling.

Finally the old lady housekeeper and the Greek women beg the young Circassian to take the child to the palace.

It was almost midnight as the young man carried her in his arms through the guarded streets of Yildiz. He stopped at each tall soldier whose bayonet flashed under the street oil-lamps.

"Who goes there?"

And the young Circassian placed the little girl in the lamplight and showed her swollen face: "It is Edib Bey's daughter. She would have died with crying if I hadn't promised to bring her to her father. Her mother died. . . ."

And the soldier, who probably had seen the mother's coffin pass not long ago, let them go on.

The little girl began to watch calmly and with pleasure the dimly lighted white road, the long shadows of the guards, while she heard the distant bark of the street dogs. She was not going to be knocked down by loneliness and dead silence any longer.

Before the gigantic portals which led immediately to the quarters where her father worked she and the Circassian youth were stopped once more. No one was allowed to pass the palace gates after midnight. . . . But sometimes a little girl and her heart's desire are stronger than the iron rules of a great despot. The guards are human and probably have little daughters of their own in their villages. There is a long wait. A man in black dress comes to the door. He looks at the little girl by the lamplight and lets her pass on. At last they reach the father's apartment. He looks at her with astonishment and perhaps with pain. He has just jumped out of bed because there is a rumor of some little girl at the palace door crying for her father. . . . On a bed opposite the father's lies a fat man with an enormous head who is blinking at the scene. (He is Hakki Bey, later on the famous grand vizir.) Every one no doubt expects her to jump into her father's arms, but her attention is caught by the quilt on her father's bed. It is bright yellow . . . and the night is closed in her memory with that bright patch of the hated color. . . .

[After her father remarried, Halidé moved in with her stepmother, and was reasonably content. She spent time also at her grandmother's house and many relatives in both establishments were about to love and entertain a little girl. One of these was Teizé,[4] a distant relative who had been a governess at the palace and was taken in by Halidé's grandmother. She became very close to Halidé.]

At this period of my life it seems to me I was hardly aware of the activities of the grown-ups at home. My life was centered in my story books, the outside world, my lessons, and Ahmed Aga, when a sudden event startled me and made me feel intensely my family circumstances.

One incident might have suggested to me the possibility of the event, if I had been a few years older. Teizé read me a letter in her room one morning. It was a polite and formal demand of marriage. As I was accustomed to seeing girls marry before they were twenty and had been fed up on stories of child marriages, I never connected Teizé with this very youthful phase of life—as I always regarded it. I was a little stupefied and did not make out the reason of her reading it. In some dim way I felt that she was expecting something of me, but I sat and stared stupidly till she said, "If I marry I go away of course." Then I realized that it was my personal calamity she was announcing, and all of a sudden I began to cry quietly and helplessly. Granny suddenly appeared and scolded Teizé, so far as it was in her to scold any one, for reading such a letter to me. The incident evidently affected me more than it was in me to express, for granny told me much later that afterward I developed a habit of walking and talking in my sleep which made her very anxious, and we paid a visit to Arzié Hanum. She had a regular consultation with the peris, breathed some prayers over my head, burned some pungent things in her silver bowl, and made me inhale some smoke.

She said I was troubled in the spirit and probably had the evil eye, and that I must not be pressed with much study. Every evening before I slept granny sat by my bed and made me say the two *surés* of the Koran, and in addition I repeated after her: "I lie on my right and turn to my left. Let angels witness my faith. There is no God but Allah, and Mohammed is his Prophet." I must confess that these simple words soothed me to a curious degree.

One day soon after, Abla [the stepmother] [5] went to spend a week with some old lady friends in Beshiktash, and in her absence father married Teizé. I cannot say that the event either pleased or comforted me, although there was no longer the danger of her leaving me.

The event was received coldly by the household, and with the marriage ceremony there settled upon the hitherto serene atmosphere of the house an oppressive feeling, a feeling of uneasiness and wonder at the possibility of unpleasant consequences, which never left it again. Sympathy and pity, as well as conjectures as to how Abla would receive the news, filled all our minds, and I fancy a rather violent scene was expected.

If there is an ecstasy and excitement in times of success, there is a deeper feeling of being singled out for importance when a great and recognized misfortune overtakes one. When a woman suffers because of her husband's secret love-affairs, the pain may be keen, but its quality is different. When a second wife enters her home and usurps half her power, she is a public martyr and feels herself an object of curiosity and pity. However humiliating this may be, the position gives a woman in this case an unquestioned prominence and isolation. So must Abla have felt now. The entire household was excited at her return. As she walked up-stairs and entered the sitting-room, she found only Teizé standing in the middle of it. But the rest must have been somewhere in the corridors, for every one witnessed the simple scene of their encounter. Teizé was the more miserable of the two. She was crying. Abla, who had somehow learned what awaited her homecoming while she was still away, walked up to her and kissed her, saying, "Never mind; it was Kismet." Then she walked away to her own room while her servant Jemilé wept aloud in the hall. Hava Hanum, whose heart was with Abla, probably because of her own past experience, scolded Jemilé: "Is it thy husband or thy lady's who was married? What is it to thee?"

Although this dramatic introduction to polygamy may seem to promise the sugared life of harems pictured in the "Haremlik"[6] of Mrs. Kenneth Brown, it was not so in the least. I have heard polygamy discussed as a future possibility in Europe in recent years by sincere and intellectual people of both sexes. "As there is informal polygamy and man is polygamous by nature, why not have the sanction of the law?" they say.

The rooms of the wives were opposite each other, and my father visited them by turns. When it was Teizé's turn every one in the house showed a tender sympathy to Abla, while when it was her turn no one heeded the obvious grief to Teizé. It was she indeed who could conceal her suffering least. She would leave the table with eyes full of tears, and one could be sure of finding her in her room either crying or fainting. Very soon I noticed that father left her alone with her grief.

And father too was suffering in more than one way. As a man of liberal and modern ideas, his marriage was very unfavorably regarded by his friends, especially by Hakky Bey, to whose opinion he attached the greatest importance.

He suffered again from the consciousness of having deceived Abla. He had married her when she was a mere girl, and it now looked as if he had taken advantage of her youth and inexperience. One saw as time went on how patiently and penitently he was trying to make up to her for what he had done.

Among the household too he felt that he had fallen in general esteem, and he cast about for some justification of his conduct which would reinstate him. "It was for Halidé that I married her," he used to say. "If Teizé had married another man Halidé would have died." And, "It is for the child's sake I have married her father," Teizé used to say.

"She would have died if I had married any one else." Granny took the sensible view. "They wanted to marry each other. What has a little girl to do with their marriage?"

Whatever theories people may hold as to what should or should not be the ideal tendencies as regards the family constitution, there remains one irrefutable fact about the human heart, to whichever sex it may belong. It is almost organic in us to suffer when we have to share the object of our love, whether that love be sexual or otherwise. I believe indeed that there are as many degrees and forms of jealousy as there are degrees and forms of human affection. But even supposing that time and education are able to tone down this very elemental feeling, the family problem will still not be solved; for the family is the primary unit of human society, and it is the integrity of this smallest division which is, as a matter of fact, in question. The nature and consequences of the suffering of a wife, who in the same house shares a husband lawfully with a second and equal partner, differs both in kind and in degree from that of the woman who shares him with a temporary mistress. In the former case, it must also be borne in mind, the suffering extends to two very often considerable groups of people—children, servants, and relations—two whole groups whose interests are from the very nature of the case more or less antagonistic, and who are living in a destructive atmosphere of mutual distrust and a struggle for supremacy.

On my own childhood, polygamy and its results produced a very ugly and distressing impression. The constant tension in our home made every simple family ceremony seem like a physical pain, and the consciousness of it hardly ever left me.

The unhappiness even manifested itself in the relation between granny and Hava Hanum. The latter criticized granny severely for not having put a stop to it before things had gone too far, and granny felt indignant to have the blame thrown upon her by a dependent for an affair she so intensely disliked.

Teizé, with her superior show of learning and her intellectual character, must have dominated father at first, but with closer contact, the pedantic turn of her mind, which gave her talk a constant didactic tone, must have wearied him. For in the intimate companionship of every-day life nothing bores one more than a pretentious style of talk involving constant intellectual effort. Poor Teizé's erudition and intelligence were her outstanding qualities, and she used and abused them to a maddening degree. When, after her dull and lonely life, she gave herself, heart and soul, to a man, the disillusionment of finding herself once more uncared for rendered her very bitter; and she either talked continually of her personal pain or else of some high topic, too difficult to be understood by the person she was talking to. Somehow her efforts to dethrone her rival from the heart of her husband lacked the instinctive capacity of the younger woman's, and it was only granny and poor me that sympathized and suffered with her in a grief which did not interest any one else.

The wives never quarreled, and they were always externally polite, but one felt a deep and mutual hatred accumulating in their hearts, to which they gave vent only when each was alone with father. He wore the look of a man who was getting more than his just punishment now. Finally he took to having a separate room, where he usually sat alone. But he could not escape the gathering storm in his new life. Hava Hanum not inaptly likened his marriage to that of Nassireddin Hodja. She told it to us as if she was glad to see father unhappy. The hodja also wanted to taste the blessed state of polygamy, and took to himself a young second wife. Before many months were out his friends found the hodja completely bald, and asked him the reason. "My old wife pulls out all my black hairs so that I may look as old as she; my young wife pulls out my white hairs so that I may look as young as she. Between them I am bald."

The final storm, kept in check for some time by the good-mannered self-control of the ladies, broke out in the servants' quarter. Fikriyar and Jemilé were always running down each other's mistresses. Fikriyar called Abla common and ignorant, and Jemilé called Teizé old and ugly. "Besides, she is a thief of other women's husbands," she added. One day the quarrel grew so distracting that the ladies had to interfere, and for the first time they exchanged bitter words. That evening father went up to Abla's room first, and he did not come down to dinner. The next morning it was announced that father was going with Abla and her little girls to Beshiktash to the wisteria-covered house, and we, the rest of the composite family, were to take a house near the college,[7] and my education was to begin seriously.

It was in 1893 or 1894 that I went to the college for the first time. I was perhaps the youngest student, and my age had to be considerably padded in order to get me in; and no amount of persuasion was available to have me taken as a boarder, so that father's plan to remove me from the influence of "that woman" as he now called Teizé had to be postponed. . . .

[After graduating from the American College in 1901, Halidé married Salih Zeki Bey, bore two sons, and began to write. During the constitutional revolution of 1908 and in the years following, she became involved with the new nationalist newspapers, among them *Tanine*. Her writings advocating the education of women earned such bitter recrimi-

nation from the reactionary party that, when the Unionists were over-
thrown in March 1909, she literally had to flee for her life.]

Salih Zeki Bey went out hastily to find out about the extent and importance of the rising. The next thing I remember about the day is the
coming of my father with Dr. Djemal, an old friend from Sultan Tepé.
The counter-revolution, they reported, was a very serious one.
Mehemed Arslan, the deputy from Lebanon, had been lynched, and
Nazim Pasha, the minister of justice, shot before the door of parliament
by infuriated soldiers, who took them for Hussein Jahid and Ahmed Riza
Beys. The soldiers were shooting their officers, as well as any one else
whom their organizations pointed out as a liberal or a reformer.

Tewfik, the son of Auntie Peyker and Hamdi Effendi (the young officer
who had returned from Europe after the constitution was declared, but
had joined the opposition and was now with the reactionaries), sent
word that I must escape to some safe place and that my name was on
their black-list. Dr. Djemal asked me to leave the house in disguise and
hasten, but I thought that I was safe in my own clothes in Istamboul, for
no one would know me there. I took the boys with me and immediately
started with my father and Dr. Djemal for Scutari, where I could find a
refuge more easily. As we drove along the Sublime Porte firing was
going on, and the people were moving like condemned shadows, while
solitary soldiers were running hither and thither. We took a boat from
Sirkedji, the only one that was available.

I left the boat at the landing in Scutari and had started to walk into the
town, holding tightly the hands of the little boys, who were convulsively
clutching at my skirts, when suddenly a human hurricane hurled itself on
us and flung us apart. It was soldiers from the Selimié barracks, who,
after killing their officers, were rushing down to take the boat and join
the counter-revolution. I found myself flattened against a shop, 'Ali
Ayetullah was pushed into a coffee-house, and Hassan was thrown
against a wall. They were trembling and half fainting with fear but were
miraculously unhurt in the brutal stampede. It was my first contact with
the mob.

In the meantime father's house, as that of a Unionist, although neither
an important nor a very well known one, was in danger. Some Unionist
houses were attacked. During the day and the night, Sultan Tepé, so
lonely on the top of the green hill, was a scene of shouting, rioting,
drum-beating, and firing, while the rifle-shooting from Istamboul rose to
a frenzied pitch. The mob with lanterns and drums continued their
demonstrations all night, and each time they approached we expected
the horror of the final moment. The whole night I sat watching and wait-

ing, the babies crawling around my knees, clutching me as the firing and shouting became louder.

The next morning strange-looking men stood by the door and watched the house. Opposite the garden walls of Sultan Tepé is the tekké[8] of the Euzbeks; the sheik as well as his children were friends of my father. That evening in the dusk a young man from the tekké jumped over the garden wall and came to the house without being seen by the men at the door. It was he who said that I must escape, for a cousin of theirs, an influential reactionary, was trying to find out if I was in my father's house. An hour or two later under the cover of the night I escaped with the boys through the back door to that holy refuge. The young men of the tekké kept armed watch that night, and I rested two nights in that quiet and comparatively safe shelter, but as the reaction grew wilder and as the city was moved more and more by the spirit of massacre, I was no longer safe. When the reactionary cousin, knowing the liberal tendencies of the youth of the tekké as well as my father's friendship with the sheik, began to inquire whether I had taken refuge there, I had to leave the sanctuary and seek refuge in the American College, which was then in Scutari.

In leaving the tekké I had to take further precautions. As I had grown up in the place, every one knew me, and the boys as well as I had to be disguised. I put on granny's loose black veils and dressed the boys in the oldest clothes of the gardener's children. I walked along the hills above Sultan Tepé, and Nighiar, my sister, who was a student in the college, came with me; before we had gone far from the tekké, the sight of two unusually brutal men running on the hills frightened her so much that her knees gave way. I could not help laughing in spite of my own anxiety, for she fell on her knees like a young camel.

On reaching the American College, Dr. Vivian, who had Dr. Patrick's place for the time, received me with great kindness. Her calm strength and friendly reception brought back to my mind for the first time since the beginning of the horror the imminent danger in which the new ideals and the country stood. These I had forgotten in my terror. Before I could greet Dr. Vivian I sank on a chair and began to sob passionately.

I stayed in the college four nights, hidden in the very room in which as a little girl I used to sit and repeat my childish lessons to Miss Dodd. All that seemed ages ago now, as I read the papers and listened to the incessant firing in Istamboul. There was a rumor that an army was coming from Saloniki to suppress the counter-revolution. How strange it sounded! A hundred years ago another Turkish army had marched from Macedonia under Alemdar Moustafa Pasha to save the young reformer

Selim and his reform from the mob and the army which had risen against it. Was history going to repeat itself in another form?

.   .   .   .

During my stay in the college the street massacres, an anarchy, and the lack of any control over the mob became so dangerous that my family sought for me a safer refuge out of the country, and I had to leave for Egypt with my little boys in the midst of the counter-revolution of 1909. . . .

[After the situation had calmed down, Halidé returned to Turkey with her sons.]

In 1910 I was having serious domestic trouble. I felt that I was obliged to make a great change in my life, a change which I could not easily force myself to face. Salih Zeki Bey's relation with and attachment to a teacher looked serious enough to make it seem conceivable that he contemplated marriage. A believer in monogamy, in the inviolability of name and home, I felt it to be my duty to retire from what I had believed would be my home to the end of my life. But knowing Salih Zeki Bey's passing caprices of heart and temperament I wanted to be absolutely sure, before breaking up my home, of the stability of his latest attachment. I therefore took the little boys with me and went to Yanina near my father with the intention of waiting there for a few months.

At my return Salih Zeki Bey told me that he had married the lady, but to my great surprise he added that polygamy was necessary in some cases, and he asked me to continue as his first wife. There was a long and painful struggle between us, but at last he consented to a divorce, and I left what for nine years had been my home.

It was a cold April night when I drove with the boys to Fatih, to the big old-fashioned house of Nakie Hanum, where I stayed till I found a suitable house. What now seems an almost ordinary incident in a woman's life was then of supreme importance and the cause of great suffering to me. My foolish heart nearly broke. I think the women of Turkey must be more used to divorce nowadays, for one hears little of broken hearts in the many divorce cases that now take place there.

.   .   .   .

I had been in low health for the whole year, feeling feverish and very tired, but I had not paid much attention to it. A medical consultation, however, showed that it was rather a serious chest weakness, and my continual fever and troublesome cough as well as my severe headaches obliged me to stay in bed for three months.

Salih Zeki Bey's second marriage had aroused so much personal curiosity that every eye probed me hard to see how I bore my own trouble after having written so much about other people's. I remember one fat woman in particular among my acquaintances who used to come with stories about the love-making of the new couple and watch my face with obvious curiosity. I neither questioned nor commented; I had a strange feeling of wonder at her apparent desire to see me suffer. I passed the test of vivisection rather successfully I believe, for my calmness and apparent lack of interest made her after a time drop the subject. Still it was a great pity that every one spoke of me as having consumption at this moment of my life, for consumption is ridiculously associated in the public mind with disappointed love.

I allowed myself no sentimental self-analysis or morbid philosophizing at this time, such as I had occasionally indulged in during the other serious illnesses I had gone through. I meant to conquer all physical ills, and I meant to make a home for my sons equal to the one they had had to leave, and to surround them with a happy and normal home atmosphere. I was determined to live, and not to leave them to the sort of life which children have when their mother is dead or crushed in spirit.

As I write these lines I feel as if I were writing of the life of a young woman who has passed away. I see her lying on a simple bed of high pillows; I see her struggling to write her daily articles or short stories; and I hear her cough continually. Then the evening lights blaze over the waters, the little boys come back, and she makes painful efforts to conquer her wild desire to kiss and hug them. They chatter about the American school they attend, and finally they go down to dine with granny, while she is left alone in the twilight room, with the utter mysterious loveliness and strange longings of the evening. She looks at pain with a quizzical smile, while she listens to the voices of the evening in the streets. The sellers of yogurt, cadaif, the chanting of beggars, the footsteps of workers who pass down to Koum-Kapou, and at last the call of childish voices and the patter of small feet scampering in the dusk in those large, lonely streets.

My own favorite among the voices belonged to a blind Arab beggar, and it was only on Friday evenings that he came. I knew that he leaned against the corner of the house, one hand against his cheek, while his guttural melody lengthened into an infinite wail, which yet had something of the desert and its lonely passion as it penetrated the evening air. It was mostly a religious chant, a wail and a complaint in wondrous

simple melody, calling to the Prophet, "*Ya Resoulallah, Ya Resoulallah.*"
The "Allah" was long and died away in a hissing sound. In no other
musical experience have I ever had this almost uncanny contact with the
musician. I was perfectly aware that he felt some one listening to his
guttural melody, for sometimes he would stop for a moment and murmur searchingly and low, as if he were trying to reach out for the soul-
contact which had snapped for a moment: "Where art thou? Art thou
listening?"

Then his stick struck the pavement, and he staggered on silently in the
manner of the blind.

Six months later when I was traveling and for the first time was not
there to hear him, he said to the cook, who gave him the usual coin,
"She is not up-stairs any more."

In the autumn of 1910 I was once more going on with my lectures,
and the cough and fever had gone. Besides my lessons and writings I had
become a busy public speaker. . . .

[About this time, Halidé became part of the Ojak (or Turkish Hearth)
association to which Kukalp-Zia (Zia Gokälp)[9] belonged, one of the
fathers of Turkish nationalist ideas.]

There was also at this time some change in my household. Mahmouré
Abla, with her five children and her husband who had returned from
Adrianople, came to live with me. Nighiar, my sister, who graduated in
1912 from the college and had become a teacher to Nakie Hanum's
school, came to me also.

There were seven pairs of childish feet that wore out the oil-cloth on
my stairs but brought a new world of life, youth, and joyful bustle to the
house.

Granny was living with me as usual, but I had lost the old sense of
nearness to her for the moment. I was constantly out for lessons and
lectures, the club demanded much of my time, and my circle of friends
had had a great deal happen to it.

My writing I had to do after ten o'clock at night when the noisy little
house slept and left me quiet in my room. Granny also enjoyed those
quiet hours; she came to me for talks then. She was much shocked by
the new women. Their talk, their walk, their dress, and their general
aspect hurt her. She felt lonely, like a stranger in a world where she felt
she had stayed too long, like a visitor who has outstayed his welcome;
it was as if the newly arrived guests had taken all the room, and they
looked ever so different from her. She suffered because they shook their

arms as they walked, looked into men's eyes, had loud voices, and smoked in public; above all they did not iron their clothes as she did every morning. In spite of every difference we found certain inner contacts where we met on common ground and understood each other.

In the middle of a difficult passage when my heroines had to be tended through their hysterical outbursts and follies (I had a special capacity for describing folly) she walked into my writing-room and said, "Let us talk, Halidé; I have not opened my mouth for days." Sometimes we did talk to her heart's desire, but at times I could not talk; the heroine or hero absorbed me more than granny, and then she walked back to her room with a sadness which spoiled my work, even kept me awake with remorse. She was eighty years old by this time but still appeared in good health, and always clean and dainty with a very correct taste, her clothes beautifully ironed; and she never missed any of her five long prayers daily.

Now and then she spoke of her longing for the old house with the wisteria, the spacious rooms with many windows, and the blazing lights of Istamboul seen through clean white curtains, with simple divans about. The chairs and heavy curtains and the little rooms of my house distressed her. I must have had some secret longing also, for we set out in search of big old houses with large gardens. We both knew that I could not change my house in Fazli Pasha. It had its own associations, its particular scenery; it had helped me to stand on my feet at a moment when I was broken physically and spiritually, and I had written the youngest and most passionate if not the best of my work there.

Once we found a house in a little street behind Sultan Ahmed which answered the description—the double stairs, the wisteria, the bath-room with old and beautifully carved basins, and the pointed door covered with red cloth and golden clasps.

We did not take it, but we talked of it, of the bath, of the double basins, and of Sultan Ahmed Mosque, from which one could hear the evening prayers and see the lights on its minarets in Ramazan nights. . . .

[During the First World War, Halidé was asked by Djemal Pasha, an influential Unionist, then governor of Syria, to help establish a series of schools for children to replace the French schools which had been closed by the Turks. First, she sent her sister, Nighiar, to set up an elementary school in Beirut. Later, in 1916, Halidé and Nakie Hanum, together with a staff of teachers, set out to organize schools and orphanages in Syria and Lebanon.]

Two days before I started I went to visit my father in Broussa. An incident that happened at the station in Galata illumined me both as to my own nature, in its most angelic and resigned mood, and as to the ways of governments in war.

A strict examination for gold was made of every passenger during the war. The Turkish population somehow never feels real confidence in paper money, and there was enough secret dealing in gold to justify the application of strict measures. There were a great many Anatolian women who traveled over the country for trading purposes, and they managed to smuggle all sorts of things, the discovery of which would have baffled any government. I saw them waiting their turn before the barrack where the examination was made. As I walked with Nakie Hanum toward the place, a rather dirty-faced but highly painted woman with a German accent came toward us and asked us to follow her.

"I am the government examining inspector for gold smuggling. Come with me to this office," she said, and opened a door to a very big room.

" I would rather go and be examined with the crowd," I answered.

"Now no jabbering; no Turkish ways," she said, with a ridiculous assumption of authority. "I represent the government and do what I please."

I made an instant decision to keep my temper under control and go through the disagreeable process with extreme *sang-froid*, so we walked in. At the end of the room stood a tall man with his hands in his pockets. Although he wore civilian clothes, he was the commissary of the station.

I waited for a moment, expecting the man to leave the room, but he did not do so, though the woman was getting ready to examine us intimately.

"The gentleman must leave the room before you begin," I said quietly.

Evidently she was a woman picked from the worst and lowest classes, and she spoke as her class would speak. "He is a great man," she shouted. "It is an honor to be examined in his presence. You Turkish women are unbearable—"

"You leave out the Turkish women," I said.

The man then spoke in a jeering tone, "She is a noble Austrian, and I am in command. Be careful about the way you talk to her."

"If you were the sultan, and she an Austrian royal princess, I would not be examined till you leave the room."

I am, generally speaking, a mild little person and keep my temper under control, but I was now struggling with something within me as I had never struggled before. I last remember the woman laying hands on me and trying forcibly to undress me. . . . Then a complete gap. I have never understood this gap, but I am afraid of it as showing incalculable possibilities within me.

The next thing I knew three policemen were entering the room. The man and the woman were not in the room any longer, while Nakie Hanum was smiling queerly.

"Will you please walk to the police station in this building?" said one, while I thought that all the three looked at me with open sympathy.

"What for?" I asked.

"For slapping a woman."

I looked at Nakie Hanum with surprise, but she nodded her head confirmingly.

There was a long table with five policemen sitting in a row, while the tall man, termed the great man by the woman, dictated with much gesticulation. The room was full of large mirrors. In one of them I caught the image of the woman.

"She has left her finger-marks on my cheek," she shrieked in a sort of refrain.

I caught my own image also in one of the mirrors, and it frightened me with its ferocity. I was crimson to the whites of my eyes, and I seemed to look like an angry tiger.

Part of the report he dictated was in this sense:

"As she seemed to belong to a high class, we took her to the room of the commissary, and with due respect the woman inspector tried to make the usual examination for gold. She immediately made seditious and rebellious utterances against the government, used most abusive language, and finally beat the inspector, who is a noble Austrian."

I remember him walking up and down, pleased with his eloquence.

"Sign," he said at last.

"I will not," I said.

"I will arrest you if you don't."

"You may. I can only sign something which is true, and if you allow me to dictate my own statement I will sign."

The policeman sitting in the middle had a long fair face with very kindly eyes. He said something in low whispers to the "great man" which made him consent with some reluctance.

I told the story shortly and simply, and finally added that if those they thought entitled to special treatment were exposed to this sort of thing it horrified me to think of the treatment which the common people must receive. This I signed.

Writers always enjoy a certain consideration, and the idea of this story possibly appearing at some future date in the Turkish newspapers was probably not a welcome prospect to the bully, but to his honor he did not flinch. On the contrary, he added a new threat: "I shall say that you

have attacked me with an umbrella, and if this lady"—pointing at Nakie
Hanum—"had not been present you would have beaten me." I had no
umbrella, and if we two, Nakie Hanum and myself, were put together,
lengthwise and crosswise, we should still not have been as large as his
powerful frame.

I went home that evening realizing sadly and fully the meaning of
"seditious and rebellious utterances," which I so often saw given as
reasons for delivering over people to courts martial.

The next morning Ahmed Bey, the chief of the police, apologized
through the telephone, and thanked me for enlightening them about
the undesirable process used in gold examination without the knowledge of the government. As I went to Broussa the next day I found both
the process and the woman inspector changed. . . .

[After the war, the movement for Turkish independence began in
earnest. Halidé found herself speaking to larger and larger groups.]

These months were months of almost continuous public speaking for
me. But the meeting of the revolution was to be in Sultan Ahmed, the
Friday after. And whenever people speak in Turkey about the Meeting
they mean the one at Sultan Ahmed on June 6, 1919.

I entered the Hippodrome through the narrow street called "Fuad
Pasha Turbessy." I cannot tell how many people accompanied me. I
could hardly stand on my feet, so fast and loud was my heart thumping:
it was only when I entered the huge square that this violent thumping
was stopped by the mere surprise of the spectacle. The minarets of
Sultan Ahmed mosque rose into the brilliant white flutes of magic
design. From their tiny balconies high in the air the black draperies
waved softly, flying like long, black detached ribbons in the sky. Down
below, just in front of the mosque railings, rose the tribune, covered
with an enormous black flag on which was inscribed in huge white letters, "Wilson's Twelfth Point." Not only the square but the thorough-
fares down to St. Sofia and Divan Yolou were blocked with a human
mass such as Istamboul had never seen and will probably never see
again. "Two hundred thousand," said the staff officers.

Besides this mass of humanity, hardly able to move, railings, domes,
roofs, and the grand old elms in the yard of the mosque were filled with
human bunches. How I reached the tribune I have no idea. Two soldiers
with bayonets walked at my side, and four more marched in front,
opening the way in as friendly a manner as they could—I have an unfor-
getable impression of their kindness and brotherly feeling on that day.
I do not know whether these soldiers were asked to escort me or

whether they had sprung from nowhere and wanted to help me in their own way.

As I set foot on the tribune I knew that one of the rare, one of the very rare, moments of my life had come to me. I was galvanized in every atom of my being by a force which at any other time would have killed me, but which at that crisis gave me the power to experience—to know —the quintessence of the suffering and desire of those two hundred thousand souls.

I believe that the Halidé of Sultan Ahmed is not the ordinary, every-day Halidé. The humblest sometimes can be the incarnation of some great ideal and of some great nation. That particular Halidé was very much alive, palpitating with the message of Turkish hearts, a message which prophesied the great tragedy of the coming years.

Flutelike voices from the minarets chanted, and hundreds of low bass voices, the voices of a myriad of ulemas and religious orders, took up the refrain from below—that refrain which is the hallelujah of the Moslem Turks: "Allah Ekber, Allah Ekber, La Ilahek Illa Allah, Vallahu Ekber, Allah Ekber, Ve Lillahil Hamd." As Halidé was listening to this exquisite chant, she was repeating to herself something like this:

"Islam, which means peace and the brotherhood of men, is eternal. Not the Islam entangled by superstition and narrowness, but the Islam which came as a great spiritual message. I must hold up its supreme meaning to-day. Turkey, my wronged and martyred nation, is also last-ing: she does not only share the sins and the faults and virtues of other peoples, she also has her own spiritual and moral force which no mate-rial agency can destroy. I must also interpret what is best and most vital in her, that which will connect her with what is best in the universal brotherhood of men."

Halidé's voice could not have been heard beyond a certain area, I am sure. She must have seemed a mere speck to those human bunches above and to the human sea below. But there was a profound and almost uncanny silence as she began to speak. Each one seemed to listen to his own internal voice. And Halidé was perhaps nothing more than a sensi-tive medium which was articulating the wordless message of the Day.

She began by pointing out that years of glory and beauty looked down from the minarets, and when she said this she was appealing to their sense of continuity in history . . . She said,

The aggressive policy of the allied powers of Europe has been applied during the last generation to the land of Turkey always un-justly, sometimes even treacherously. The European powers would have found a way to send armies of conquest to the stars and the moon had they known that Moslems and Turks inhabited those heavenly bodies. At last they have found a pretext, an opportunity to break to pieces the last empire ruled by the crescent. And against this decision we have no European power to whom we may appeal. But surely even those who have no share in Turkish booty are just as responsible—more responsible—in the inhumanity of this decision. They were all sitting at a court whose ostensible object was the defense of human and national rights, yet all that court did was to sanctify the spoliation of the defeated peoples. And these men who call the Turks sinners have sinned themselves so deeply that the great waves of the immaculate oceans cannot cleanse them.

But the day will come when a greater court of justice will try those who have deprived the nations of their natural rights. That court will be composed of the very same nations whose governments are now against us. Those peoples will condemn their own governments then for having been unjust to other nations in their name, for there is an eternal sense of what is right in the heart of every individual, and nations are made up of individuals.

Brethren and sons, listen to me. You have two friends: the Moslems and those civilized peoples who will sooner or later raise their voices for your rights. The former are already with you, and the latter we will win over by the invincible justice of our cause.

Governments are our enemies, peoples are our friends, and the just revolt of our hearts our strength.

The day is not far off when all nations will get their rights. When that day comes, take your banners and come and visit the graves of your brethren who have fought and have fallen for the glorious end.

Now swear and repeat with me:

"The sublime emotion which we cherish in our hearts will last till the proclamation of the rights of the peoples!" . . .

When she repeated the sentence—which became afterward something like a national slogan—"The peoples are our friends, the governments our enemies," she was expressing the proper sentiment of a Moslem nation, highly conscious of its democratic principles. When she was asking them to take the sacred oath, which they were to swear three times, that they would be true to the principles of justice and humanity, and that they would not bow down to brute force on any condition, she was formulating that moral characteristic without which no people can survive in the human family of the new world which is to come.

"We swear," answered thousands of voices. And there was a mighty swaying and a continual thunder which made the frail boards of the tribune sway under feet. In the meantime, the Allied aeroplanes flew in and out of the minarets, policing the crowd. They buzzed like mighty bees and came down as low as they could in order, I believe, to intimidate the crowds. But no one was conscious of brute force: there was that in the heart of the crowd which comes to a people at moments, a thing which is far above machines and death; and had the aeroplanes fired, I still believe the crowd would have stood in absolute stillness, in absolute communion with the spirit of the new revolution which was coming to life. The last time she stood and gazed in front of her, she saw that there were a mighty crowd of mutilated soldiers forming the head of the mass. All of them were dressed with religious care. A younger group holding each other's hands formed a semicircle around the tribune to prevent the crowd surging forward.

The tension was broken at last by a young student of the university, who started to cry out in a hysterical voice, and who all of a sudden fell and fainted. "My nation, my poor nation," he had sobbed. That woke Halidé from her trance, and becoming her ordinary self she hurried down from the tribune to help the sufferer.

And my story comes back to first person again, for that unnatural detachment which had created a dual personality was no more. At the foot of the steps an apparition in green robes and a turban took hold of me. It was a simple Anatolian hodja, with a round beard and black eyes streaming with tears.

"Halidé Hanum, Halidé Hanum, my daughter," he cried quietly, holding my hands. I made him sit on the steps of the tribune, and he leaned his old face on my hand and went on crying. As some one else was speaking at the time, I sat down also and patted his hand. I think I was also crying. Then I pushed him up the platform, very gently. "Go and pray," I said. And he did go up and pray, in Turkish, very simply and beautifully, I thought, and that ended the meeting.

Conclusion

From this time, Halidé Edib was a public figure of great political consequence and was in considerable danger. Fearing for the future of her two sons, then about fourteen and eleven, she arranged that they be taken to America to school by Charles Crane of Robert College. The day after the children left, Halidé and Dr. Adnan left for the Nationalist front, disguised as an old hodja, or Turkish religious leader, and his veiled wife. They traveled by carriage, horse, cart, and on foot to Anatolia, then to Angora. She was sentenced to death in absentia, and her house and possessions were confiscated. All during the battles for independence she worked closely with Ataturk (Mustapha Kemal Pasha) who was to emerge as the leader of the new Turkey. Although she had some doubts about Mustapha Kemal's methods, she served faithfully in the Turkish army, as a noncombatant private and then corporal, translating and writing dispatches, counting soldiers and guns. She became an expert with horses and guns.

Ataturk introduced many reforms relating to the position of women in Turkish society. Among them were (1) the abolition of polygamy; (2) the abolition of the veil; and (3) the passage of a number of laws granting equal rights to women in several areas: the vote, equality rights in divorce, equal inheritance rights, requiring the woman's consent to marriage, and the right to hold public office.

During Halidé Edib's lifetime her influence was great; it continues to be today. Her novels are still read in Turkey and young people, both men and women, speak of her as a much admired and revered sister. Her life spanned one of the most dramatic periods in Turkish history, from the crumbling of the old Ottoman Empire to the emergence of an independent nation. Her example helped prepare the way for the appearance of a new kind of Turkish woman.

Notes

[Notes from the original are indicated by the initials H.E.A., which follow them. Others have been prepared by Sharon Bastüg.]

1. Kemal Karpat, *Turkey's Politics*, p. 27.
2. The little finger game about the birds is still very common, somewhat equivalent to our "this little piggy went to market . . ."
3. *Dade* or *dadi* means "nanny" or "governess."
4. "Teizé" (modern spelling "Teyse") is a kinship term meaning "mother's sister." It is used as a polite term of address for women considerably older than oneself.
5. "Abla" is a kinship term meaning "older sister," also used as a polite form of address for women somewhat older than oneself.
6. The word *haremlik* does not exist in Turkish. It is an invented form, no doubt due to a mistaken idea that *selamlik* (literally, the place for salutations or greetings, i.e., the reception room and, therefore, among Moslems, the men's apartments) could have a corresponding feminine form, which would be *haremlik*. The word is, however, a verbal

monstrosity. *Harem* is an Arabic word with the original sense of a shrine, a secluded place (cf. Harem sherif, the Holy of Holies in the Ka'aba at Mecca). Hence it came to be identified with the seclusion of women, either by means of the veil or by confinement in separate apartments; and hence, again, it came to be used for those apartments themselves.— H.E.A.

7.   The American College for Girls, as it was then called; an institution founded by American missionaries for educating girls in the Orient. It is now represented by the Constantinople College for Girls, but it is no longer connected with any missionary societies. It was at first housed in an old picturesque Armenian house in Scutari.—H.E.A.

8.   *Tekké* is an institution or, literally, a building corresponding to the mosque of standard Islam. *Tekké*(s) are found among a religious sect called the Alevi, supposedly a Shi'ite sect but with a number of unique characteristics. One of these is the use of the *tekké* instead of the mosque. The *tekké* is a combination school, clubhouse, and religious building. Another unique characteristic of the sect is the ban on eating rabbits, which they consider to be the animal most nearly related to humans. The Alevi are widespread in eastern Turkey and also widely discriminated against. At the same time they are noted for being extremely progressive and free-thinking, especially with respect to the rights of women.

9.   The Turkish nationalist referred to is Zia Gokälp, a well-known Turkish sociologist.

Reference

Karpat, Kemal. *Turkey's Politics*. Princeton: Princeton University Press, 1959.

12

Huda Sh'arawi

هدى شعراوى

Founder of the Egyptian Women's Movement

A.D. 1882–1947

Biographical Sketch by the Editors

Huda Sh'arawi, founder of the women's movement in Egypt, is recognized throughout the Arab world as an early leader in the field of women's rights. Born in 1882 in Minia, the capital of Upper Egypt, Huda Sh'arawi grew up in a wealthy household with its own reputations and traditions for doing good. Here she was prepared and educated for a life of public service.

Since only one school for girls existed in Egypt at that time, Huda Sh'arawi was educated at home by tutors in both Turkish and French, the languages of a "lady" of the time.

In addition, she often slipped into the study when her only brother was having his private Arabic lessons; in this way, according to Aminah al-Sa'id, she learned to read Arabic. Thereafter, she read everything she could find in his library—in economics, philosophy, literature. She wrote beautifully, was widely read, and was fluent in several foreign languages. Says Muhammad 'Abd al-Ghani Hasan, "It is strange that Huda, who helped so many young girls become educated, supplied them with the means to enroll in schools, and worked so hard to improve the schools and institutes for girls, did not herself ever benefit from them. The

Photo: Huda Sh'arawi and Nabawiyah Musa, Cairo, 1923

school came to her house: both male and female tutors instructed her from childhood."[1] In 1910 she opened a school for girls, the first to offer general education rather than vocational training, such as midwifery. Aminah al-Sa'id recalls that all women who wished to attend this school were required to bring to the police station a document certifying that they were of good moral character. No women did so, but they sent their daughters to Huda Sh'arawi's school.

Huda Sh'arawi first came to public attention during the nationalist demonstrations in Egypt against the British. These took place at the end of World War I, when it appeared from the proceedings at the League of Nations that the Allied promises to the Arabs would not be kept. Sa'ad Zaghlul, an Egyptian political activist, was arrested by the British authorities in Egypt because he refused to retire from politics and be confined to his house in the countryside of the Rif.

When Zaghlul was arrested, demonstrations erupted throughout the country and many concerned women gathered at Huda Sh'arawi's house on March 16, 1919, to discuss what might be done.

First, they decided to send a letter to the British high commissioner, and Huda Sh'arawi herself signed a letter to Lady Burnett, wife of the British high commissioner, who was personally known to Madame Sh'arawi. The letter to Lady Burnett stated:

Dear Madam:

In these sorrowful times that my country is passing through, I would like to remind you of our conversation last summer when we discussed the results of the miserable war, just ended [World War I]. At that time you assured me that Great Britain was innocent and meant no harm by participating in this war. Great Britain, you said, did not participate, except to serve the cause of justice and humanity and to defend the freedom of the oppressed nations and to protect their rights. Would you tell me whether this is still your opinion today?

What do you think, Madam, of your government giving itself the right to impose curfews in a time of peace [here in Egypt] and to banish persons who have committed no crime except to want to live freely in their own country [an obvious reference to Sa'ad Zaghlul]. What can you say about your own soldiers who roam the quiet streets of Egypt with revolvers and machine guns, firing at unarmed people if those people's voices are raised to ask for justice and liberty?

Do all these deeds, Madam, result from Britain's efforts to serve justice and humanity?

If not, I beg you to explain the real meaning of your words spoken during our conversation together last summer. Remember, also, Madam, that if a group of young Egyptian boys throw stones at store windows, they are only following the example set by your own "civilized" soldiers not long ago.

Please, Madam, accept my heartfelt sentiments of sorrow and my personal regards.

Huda Sh'arawi[2]
March 16, 1919

The petition to the British high commissioner was presented formally at his office by more than 350 women, led by Huda Sh'arawi. The petition follows:

Your Excellency

We, the women of Egypt, mothers, sisters, and wives of those who have been the victims of British greed and exploitation, present the following petition to Your Excellency. We deplore the brutal, barbarous actions that have fallen upon the quiet Egyptian nation. Egypt has committed no crime, except to express her desire for freedom and independence, according to the principles enunciated by Woodrow Wilson at the Paris peace conference [of 1918] and accepted by all nations, those neutral as well as those involved in the World War.

We present this petition to Your Excellency in the hope that you will convey it to your government, for she has taken upon her shoulders the fulfillment and implementation of the promises made to Egypt [at the League of Nations].

We ask and beseech you further to inform your government of the barbarous actions which have been taking place in Egypt, when your soldiers have been firing on civilians, children, and unarmed men. Why? Because these people have objected, in peaceful demonstration, to your forbidding of Egyptians to leave the country and present their own case at the peace conference, as other nations have done. They were also objecting, in peaceful demonstration, to the British arrest and deportation of some of our Egyptian men to the island of Malta.

We hope, Your Excellency, that our petition, a petition from Egyptian women, will gain your acceptance and approval so that you will then return to the support of the principles of liberty and peace.[3]

[*The petition was signed by hundreds of women, including Huda Sh'arawi.*]

The high commissioner's response is not recorded, nor is that of his wife.

On Monday, March 24, 1919, to suppress the continuing demonstrations, two British airplanes bombed the city of Asyut, in Upper Egypt. Many were killed, including several women. A further demonstration on April 10, 1919, took place in Cairo and resulted in the deaths of other women, whose funeral procession was held the next day, April 11. On April 12, the women of Cairo participated in the funeral procession of the men who had fallen in the demonstrations, and the sight of hundreds of veiled women marching on the streets of the city allegedly so moved the men that they began to shout "Death to Imperialism." Accordingly, the British army opened fire and many were killed.

Several stories are told about this latter demonstration. One chronicled by Ijlal Khalifah is that the sight of the veiled women marching in the procession frightened the British. Some say that Huda Sh'arawi, who participated in this procession, stepped forward and spoke to the captain of the British cavalry troops sent to put down any demonstrations of violence.

She is supposed to have said, in perfect and eloquent English, "Here I am, standing in front of you. Why don't you shoot me as you shot our other Egyptian women? We want freedom for our country. We will not accept your domination or the disgrace of such domination, oh, you cavalier!"

The British cavalry officer, astonished by the woman's courage and also no doubt by the sound of his own language coming from that veiled face, is supposed to have ordered the men to hold their fire.

Despite all British efforts, the riots and demonstrations continued throughout Egypt. When Zaghlul was arrested, the British hoped to calm the people; no publicity about Zaghlul was supposed to appear, but, according to Mustafa Amin, the women managed to keep Zaghlul's cause alive by an ingenious method: day after day, women would bring small notes of money from their homes and come to Madame Zaghlul's house, where they spent hours writing "Yahya Sa'ad" (Long live Sa'ad Zaghlul) on every bit of paper money they could find. Then the money was placed into circulation, and "Yahya Sa'ad" became a national refrain. Needless to say, the British were not pleased.

Memos and petitions went back and forth to the British, and one of the most important was that sent to Lord Allenby by Huda Sh'arawi, now rather famous due to her earlier participation in demonstrations and her petitions to the authorities, calling for Egyptian independence. This letter, sent on Christmas Day, 1921, follows:

Your Excellency:

If you think that you have the power to extinguish the voice of the Egyptian people and to banish the man [Zaghlul] in whom they have put their trust and whom they wish to speak in their name, then I ask you to reconsider this point of view.

For now you have one voice raised, but soon you will hear 14 million voices, demanding their rights and their freedom and deploring injustice and aggression.

If you rely on power alone, Your Excellency, to destroy our rights, I ask you to reconsider this point of view as well. For power passes, but right remains.

We will continue to object to the plots and conspiracies which Your Excellency perpetrates against us. For these conspiracies will only arouse the anger of the people and the anger of God.

> On behalf of the Egyptian woman,
> Huda Sh'arawi
> December 25, 1921[4]

The first women's association in Egypt was formed by several women teachers in 1920, with Huda Sh'arawi at its head. After Egypt had gained a measure of autonomy in 1923, Madame Sh'arawi went as Egypt's representative to the International Conference of Women in Rome. When she returned from this trip to the west, Ijlal Khalifah says, "she began to think about the inherited traditions which did not allow her to appear unveiled in her own country. When she landed in Alexandria that year, she took off her veil and never wore it again. She faced a great deal of criticism from reactionaries, but she maintained a general air of modesty and dignity and paid no attention to the criticism."[5] However, her husband, a wealthy cousin, divorced her as a result.

Huda Sh'arawi established the Women's Union in 1924 which consisted of a school and a workshop as well as a club. She founded a magazine, *The Egyptian Woman,* which was published in both Arabic and French, to acquaint all women with the goals of the Women's Union: education for women; raising the minimum age of marriage for girls; equality of job opportunities; abolishment of prostitution; and establishment of orphanages, women's centers, and workshops where unemployed women could earn wages. Dar al-Itihad, headquarters of the Women's Union, was the center of conferences, lectures, and meetings on subjects of interest to women.

The first secondary school for girls was established in 1927, and the first co-educational university classes were held in 1929. By this time the veil was being discarded all over Egypt. Madame Sh'arawi's husband asked her to remarry, and, according to Aminah al-Sa'id, she did so for the sake of her children.

Huda Sh'arawi always was interested in promoting the use of the Arabic language at a time when French was the fashionable, political language spoken in Egypt. In 1929, she was searching for a young girl to give a speech in classical Arabic at a charity ball. She asked the head-mistress of the first public school to select some girls for this occasion. Three were recommended to recite; one was chosen. Her name was Aminah al-Sa'id. From that time on, Aminah al-Sa'id became an assistant to Huda Sh'arawi. For the last seven years of Madame Sh'arawi's life, it was Aminah al-Sa'id who read her public speeches.

During her long life, Huda Sh'arawi maintained her reputation for kindness, intelligence, dignity, modesty, and untiring efforts to improve the lot of women in Egypt. She was known for her interest in gifted women and encouraged many artists and writers from different socio-economic groups by sponsoring their education and arranging publica-tion and exhibits. The poetess Mayy Ziyadah was one of Madame Sh'arawi's close friends. Another friend characterized her thus: "Huda gives her time, her money, her energy to everyone, but never discusses it. I think that is because to Huda a good deed is done for God and that is all there is to it!"

Huda Sh'arawi attended International women's conferences in 1935 in Istanbul and in Copenhagen in 1939. In 1944 she helped form the All-Arab Federation of Women, which set the example for the Arab League, organized two years later. One of her last acts was to attend a confer-ence on the use of atomic weapons, held in 1946; she was one of the first women to call for the abolishment of all atomic weapons. Huda Sh'arawi died in December 1947, but her example paved the way for a new generation of Egyptian women—women involved in all aspects of national life.

The Aims of the Egyptian Feminist Union as Stated in Its Constitution[6]

The aim of the Association is to achieve the following goals:
1.   Raise women's intellectual and moral level so that they may realize their political and social equality with men according to law and according to traditional mores.
2.   Demand free access to schools of higher education for all girls who wish to educate themselves.
3.   Reform practices relating to marriage in order to permit the two

parties to become acquainted with each other before becoming engaged.

4.   Attempt to reform certain legal practices concerning marriage, the false interpretation of which is against the spirit of the Koran, and thus preserve the woman from the injustice which causes the practice of bigamy to take place without reason and repudiation of the wife to be made often without serious motives.

5.   Pass a law limiting the minimum age of marriage for girls to sixteen years.

6.   Conduct an active campaign in support of public hygiene.

7.   Encourage virtue and combat immorality.

8.   Combat superstition and certain practices which are not in accord with reason.

9.   Conduct a campaign in the press to encourage the ideas of the Association.

Notes

We are indebted to Karen Haynes for recording some of Aminah al-Sa'id's personal reminiscences of Huda Sh'arawi, which have been incorporated into the sketch.

1.   Muhammad 'Abd al-Ghani Hasan, *Mayy, Adibat al-Sharq wa-al-'Urubah*, p. 164.

2.   Ijlal Khalifah, *Al-Harakah al-Nisa'iyah al-Hadithah*, pp. 157–158.

3.   Ibid., pp. 152–154.

4.   Ibid., p. 186.

5.   Ibid., p. 237.

6.   Ibid., p. 235; Bahiga Araba, *The Social Activities of the Egyptian Feminist Union*, pp. 51–52.

References

Araba, Bahiga. *The Social Activities of the Egyptian Feminist Union*. Cairo: Elias' Modern Press, 1973.

Khalifah, Ijlal. *Al-Harakah al-Nisa'iyah al-Hadithah*. Cairo: al-Matba'ah al-'Arabiyah al-Hadithah, 1973.

Hasan, Muhammad 'Abd al-Ghani. *Mayy, Adibat al-Sharq wa-al-'Urubah*. Cairo: Alam al-Kutub, 1964.

13 Zahrah Muhammad

زهره محمد

A Rural Woman of Morocco

A.D. 1927–

Edited Interview by Susan S. Davis

Many westerners think of Morocco as an extension of the Sahara Desert, but this is true only for the country's southernmost part. The region where Zahrah lives is more typical: It Is a fertile agricultural area in the foothills of the middle Atlas Mountains, not far from the city of Meknes. Although there was more herding in the area when Zahrah was young, during French colonization much of the land was turned to farming, and now wheat, lentils, chickpeas, olives, and several kinds of fruit trees are grown locally. There are many villages scattered throughout the area and Zahrah now lives in a large one near an even bigger town, although she lived in a tent when she was first married. Her story spans approximately the years from 1930 to 1972.

What follows is the story of the life of Zahrah, the wife of Muhammad, as told to me in a tape-recorded conversation one afternoon in a Moroccan village. Zahrah had been a good friend and informant during my almost two years of field work in the village, and I had heard many of the incidents previously. I asked if I could record her life story, and she agreed. Because her story is recorded and thus available for reference, I have tried to stay as close as possible to Zahrah's own words in

Photo: Zahrah and her husband, Muhammad

my translation, except for changing names of persons and places to pro-tect the anonymity of the persons involved. I have omitted a few parts of her story because it was too long, but, otherwise, when phrases are repeated, when tenses are changed, and when there are pauses, it is because that's how Zahrah talks.

I would not suggest that Zahrah is "the typical Moroccan woman," since I do not believe that any such creature exists. Whether she lives in an urban or a rural environment, her economic status, personality, and position in the life cycle are all factors in determining a Moroccan woman's overall situation, and great differences do exist. Zahrah can be seen to some degree as typical of an older (40–55) village woman who is neither poverty stricken nor wealthy and who is quite assertive and out-going—as women her age are apt to be, when they become mothers-in-law after their long apprenticeship as daughters-in-law.

My thanks to Zahrah for sharing her story.

My Life/Zahrah Muhammad

Well . . . I'm going to tell you about when my father was alive—may God have mercy on his soul—when I was very small. The first thing I remember is when my father—God have mercy on him—was there, when I was seven years old.

At that time my father had a lot of land. He had farm land, he had sheep, he had cattle, and he had hired workers. There were people who washed clothes, people who milked cows, people for everything. The land was ours alone, and my father's land . . . he had land near the Selou River and he had land here. Then my father sold the land to a Christian; he sold him the land near Selou. And, when he gave him the deed to the land, he also gave him the deed to our land; he gave him everything at one time. He gave him the deeds to everything; he gave him the papers for that land and for this land. He only sold one piece of land, and he gave him the papers for the two pieces of land. And when he asked him to give him back his papers, he said to him, "You sold me everything."

That Christian, he didn't throw us off the land; he left us the land. He said, "I bought everything; everything, I've bought." And he stayed on that one piece of land and we stayed on the other piece of land. But that Christian . . . sure, we were on the land; sure, if he said, "You sold it to me" . . . everything was still ours. We grazed our animals and we farmed and we ate and drank; he didn't say a word about it. He couldn't say a word, that Christian. At the time when my father died, he left my mother to farm the land. My mother remained, farming the land; she farms today and she farms tomorow, and she shares with some people and she gets into arguments. They find our cattle and sheep grazing and they take them from us and lock them up in the corral. They always take them and say they ate up their wheat. They don't stake them—the animals are grazing and they round them up and take them to the corral. We go and pay a fine of money, and only then are they let out. The people who round up the animals are the laborers working for the Christian; whoever didn't like us would take them. The people who didn't like my mother would take them. Can you imagine that?

We remained that way with my mother for a long time. Then my mother went and got married. When my mother married, my sister's husband came from Meknes and said to us, "If you all want to come with me, come with me now. You have your own water, you have your own sheep, you have cows, you have wheat. Don't wait until you finish everything and then want me to take you; I'll take you with me now while you still have something to eat." My sister's husband took us to Meknes.

The sheep and the cows—my sister's husband took everything. He borrowed donkeys from some people and took the wheat; he took it to the train station and took it to Meknes and he took us, too, to Meknes. We stayed with my sister in Meknes in a big rented house, and that sister had six children. And there were how many of us: Kibbur and 'Ali and me and Mustafa and Dawiyah. I was the oldest.

After a little while, my mother comes and took my sister's husband to court because of us. When we went to the court house, the judge kept my brother Mustafa and he kept Dawiyah. He kept Mustafa to run errands for him and he kept Dawiyah to run errands for him and we remained.

My mother went in order to take us away from my sister's husband and to bring us back. And he said to her, "You went and got married . . . it's your own fault." He didn't want to give us to her; he said, "Why did you go and get married and leave them?" She went and married that pagan and left us all alone in the house. When she got married, she didn't take even one child with her.

With the new husband she had only one boy and she lost him; he died. Well, now we were staying with my sister. What could we do? There we were living with her and the wheat was ours. But the good flour and the good bread she makes for her children; and us, for us she makes bad bread. She makes two kinds of bread: she gives us bad bread and they get good bread. Still, we continued staying with her; they drink tea and they don't give us any. They eat stew; only if they have some left over do they give us some, and we stayed like that. I used to cry and cry.

We had a lot of wool and we had blankets and rugs . . . My sister took everything; everything she took. In the evening, when it got to be five in the evening, she'd say to me, "Get up. C'mon, let's go." I was small at that time, like Aminah [about 12]. She'd load me with those ten or fifteen kilos of wool; we'd take it and we'd sell it and we'd sell a rug or two. And the money . . . she takes everything. And me . . . I didn't know anything. Even if I was angry about it, I didn't want to say anything to her. She's older than I am and she would defeat me. And I don't know where to go or anything.

My sister's name was Saidah; she was my sister only from my father [a half-sister]. We stayed with her like that; we stayed with her and after a while they came and asked for my hand and she married me off. It was in Meknes that they came and asked for my hand and she married me off. When she married me, she kept the money. They gave her a lot of money. She kept all the money and told them to come back in a month. The day the month was up, they came. She said to them, "About that money, my sister . . . my sister spent it. My sister doesn't have any money; give me some more so we can have a wedding for her." She got more money, and only then did they have the wedding and I left there. When I left, my brothers and sisters remained there. I got married and I came here; I was married to Muhammad.

The man I married before that—I didn't stay with him. My mother gave me to that man when I was still small; my mother hadn't remarried yet. My father died, God bless his soul, and my mother gave me while I was still small. And that man would bring one big basket of grapes and he brings henna [the leaves, for dye] and he brings things . . . I take it and I dump it all out and I let the chicken eat that stuff; he ate it all up! And if he brought meat, I didn't want to eat it. When he had the wedding, I ran away and went to this woman's home and stayed with her; it was in the same village.

They came and caught me; they brought me back. I ran away again, and they slapped me into irons, on my legs they put a chain—on my legs they put iron rings like those for animals. A girl friend helped me and we took them off one leg and I hung it around my neck and I had the iron ring in my hand and I ran away from the village until I got to the farm. It was the farm on which that Christian lived; the Christian who took my father's land. When that Christian saw that iron on my leg, he took it off. And he telephones Meknes and took me away from that man . . . that's that. From that time, I never went near that man again; that was it. That man didn't take *anything* from me. Well, that was it. When I stayed with my mother a little while, my mother married and we went to Meknes.

Then the day I got married to Muhammad, I came here to this village. We children all went to Meknes; then they brought me from Meknes to here. My brothers and sisters stayed with my married sister for about three months. My mother goes and takes my sister to court. They always used to go to court and sit in front of the judge and my mother got them away from her. The judge said, "Their mother has the right to take them even though she was married again . . . Even if she was mistaken, now she's thought about it and she can take her children wherever she wants. You have your own children; you don't need her children. You, if you had no children, you could keep them. But since you have children, you can't keep your siblings. Those are your siblings and your mother should take them."

We, we never went to the judge's—only my siblings that stayed there.

Dawiyah stayed with the judge and Kibbur stayed right with the judge. My brother Mustafa disappeared; he didn't remain at all. We didn't know where he went.

Well, from then on there was only us and my mother. My mother stayed in Meknes with 'Ali. Then 'Ali went to the Sahara; he went when he was young. He went with a mason; he used to help him with his work. [Later] he went to Europe and he doesn't come to visit at all anymore.

Before he ever went to Europe . . . I got married and stayed in my house with my mother-in-law and with my father-in-law. I spent about four years in the village, in a tent.

I spent about four years and didn't have any children at all. And Muhammad's mother up and starts to pick on me and she keeps blaming me and everything and I keep crying. I say to myself, "I don't have anything. I'm going to leave." None of my family was near me and my mother was there in Meknes and just renting from people and where would I go? And I keep thinking, and I stayed there with them. My father-in-law would come—he was a nice man—he'd come and he'd find them . . . now, let's say our tent is like it's here, ours is here and there's another tent as far away as Malikah's house, down the street. They'd buy sugar and go over there and make tea and they'd leave me here, my mother-in-law and the wife of my husband's brother. The wife of my other brother-in-law died; he was named Dhan and that's why we named our son Dhan.

They'd leave me all alone so they could . . . I mean . . . so I'd go away. I used to remain all by myself like that. After a while, one day I found I was pregnant; at that time I found I would have a child. I knew that I was pregnant. And when my mother-in-law's sister came to visit us, she said to me, "Poor dear." She told me, "I am going to the *suq* [market]." I said to her, "If you're going to the *suq*, I will give you something to bring me some ground beef." "No, no," she said to me. "You've never told me to give you some ground beef. When you said, 'ground beef,' it must mean something special." I said to her, "No, I'll just give you something to bring me ground beef." I had sold some eggs and I gave her the money. She went to the market and bought the ground beef for me and brought it to me, the dear thing—may God have mercy on her soul—and she lit a fire in the brazier and roasted the meat and gave it to me.

"Good God," I said to her. "Give some to the men and everything!" She said, "I'm not giving any to anyone. It's your ground beef, you bought it yourself, you'll eat it all alone."

I just wanted them to taste a little bit. But if I could find a way, no one would eat any; it was only my mouth that says that [about sharing]. Well, sir, I ate that ground beef, but, me, well, sir, I didn't get filled up at all. I have a rooster and I'm going to up and slaughter it.

Yes, I ate that meat. My husband's brother said to me, he said, "You have a rooster and I have a rooster and my mother will give a rooster; then we'll slaughter the three roosters and we'll cook them, and you go ahead and eat." I told him, "O.K." We slaughtered the roosters. I slaughtered my rooster . . . I have another rooster. My brother-in-law's rooster was slaughtered. I left the other one not slaughtered. People went to get water. My mother-in-law told me, "Go get some water." I went to get water, and she took my other rooster and slaughtered it. When I came to cut the meat with her, I saw cuts on the legs. I marked them on their legs by cutting them a little, so I would know my own chickens—there were a lot of chickens. When I came and took hold of the meat to help her cut it, I found two of the roosters marked. I said to her, "You went and slaughtered my roosters." She told me, "No, not yours." Well, sir, my husband came and found me and said to me, "What's the matter with you?" And he started to beat me. I got angry about that chicken and I didn't eat a bit of it at all, not even a single bone. They cooked it and gave it to the men and they ate it. And I remained.

I remained crying and then I got the fever. Now I kept on crying and crying until I wanted to go crazy. I kept just crying and crying and crying and I don't eat, I don't do anything. I passed some ten days and I'm crying. Then a woman comes, Muhammad's aunt—the sister of Uncle Abbas [her father-in-law]. The good woman makes something and brings it to me. She made a bowl of couscous or something else on other days or oranges; she hides it and gives it to me and I eat as if it were stolen . . . because the others weren't nice to me.

Well, sir, after a little while my stomach got bigger. What luck! What am I going to do? My father-in-law went to jail and we remained in the house. Muhammad stayed and farmed; they have land and he plows his land. He plowed the land for his father. He wasn't going to—they had fought about a donkey—but he decided, "Okay, I'll plow for you." He continued plowing for him, he's plowing, and on and on and on, and my mother-in-law was living a little ways from us. My month got closer. I brought in some wood for fuel and she came, my mother-in-law, and picked it up and took it. The wife of my father-in-law came [he had two wives] and said, "Why did she take the wood?" I told her, "My mother-in-law took them," and they up and started fighting. One beat the other with the iron shovel until the blood was running. They went to court, they tried everything. One bit the other right here, so hard her teeth met through the skin. The co-wives were fighting, my mother-in-law and the wife of my father-in-law. My mother-in-law left and the wife of my father-in-law stayed with us. She had left before my father-in-law went to jail.

Well, sir, I remained like that. One *suq* day, I got labor pains. It was Thursday that day. Well, my mother-in-law didn't go to the *suq* early. Then they up and went to the *suq*. I said to myself, "Shall I tell her I have the pains? No, no—I won't say anything." I didn't want to say. I say, "Oh, God, don't let them be present for the birth."

They went, they all went, they went to the *suq*. All the people went to the *suq* and I remained all by myself. I go out of the house, I go in from the other door and I go out of the tent and go up to the cane hut; I come back to the tent. Then I call a little girl, my sister-in-law—she died; they called her 'Azzah and we named 'Azzah [her daughter] for her; she was 'Azzah Bint 'Ali. I said to her, "Go, sister, find me that Aunt 'A'ishah—I have the pains."

'A'ishah was a woman there. And that woman, she comes. That woman came and, in just the time we've been talking, I had the baby. I had the baby and she covered me and that's that. Then they up and lit the fire and cooked bread and made tea. When the others came back from the *suq* . . . they found I had the baby! They came at about this time [early afternoon]—and found me; I'd given birth. They were upset; they felt cheated.

Well, I stayed at my father-in-law's at that time . . . Every day I have a rooster; every day he slaughters a rooster for me . . . that was seven roosters. They had the baby christening for me; only then did I decide to stay with them; I was with them a long time.

I didn't lose the little girl [first child] until she had spent some three years, until she started to walk well, about like little Fatimah. Well, sir, I tell you, that little girl, I nurse her and I nurse her; since I don't get pregnant, I let her keep nursing. Then one day I weaned her, when she was probably two and a half or three, I weaned her. I went to sleep—we were harvesting and it was hard work and everything—and she nurses. She nursed and that milk killed her [a common belief]. She died and I remained, I told you, until I finished four years, that one [child] that came after that girl. I finished four years and people are saying to me, "Someone did something [magic] to you. You gave birth by yourself. You caught cold . . ." Everyone has a word to say. Then one day, there I am pregnant with Aminah, and I didn't do anything at all [magic]. I didn't do a thing. I didn't use pills or medicine or the *fqih* [religious teacher] or anything. I just got pregnant, that's all; I got pregnant with

Aminah. I spent a month and a half, and I knew I was pregnant. That year there was a drought; I got pregnant with Aminah the year of the drought. That year there was no harvest. There was no wheat. People were . . . It was America that used to give us wheat; there was only a little wheat.

After I had Aminah I remained probably some two years, two and a half years or more . . . then again I got pregnant with Dhan. When I got pregnant with Dhan, that girl nursed again, the milk from Dhan. It was Aminah, and she just almost died. She was sicker than the first little girl . . . So I go to this foreigner's place, the one who had the farm near us; Muhammad was a worker for him. I went to see his wife and she gave me a piece of paper. She told me, "You go to the doctor." I went to the doctor. When I went to the doctor I didn't give him the paper—I forgot it. When he had examined the little girl, he said, "Give me the money," and I remember and I pull out the paper—not until he brought the injection and was going to give it to her. He saw the paper, he put down the shot, and he went and brings another shot. He gave her two shots. He gave her one really good shot. He gave her shots Wednesday and said, "Thursday come and I'll give her a shot and another Friday." But I only returned on Thursday, that's all . . . and she got well. She had nursed, it was her stomach . . . She used to go to the toilet and just drip blood, only blood would flow.

Well, again I went on like that; we went on like that, staying there . . . and after a little while . . . When I gave birth to Dhan, I had him in the tent, in the tent. We hadn't moved down [here] yet.

Houses . . . there were houses in the village early on. My father didn't have a tent. There was Qasim bin Zituni, the father of that Si Muhammad; he didn't have a tent; there was Black Hamid who didn't have a tent. There were people who had houses, the people who were well off; they had nice houses.

The others have tents; they use them to move with the cows and the sheep. Now, when spring arrives, we move the tents from the place where we're living and we go, like to Dahir Maziz. There there's good land; just land that has grass and has flowers. We build the tents there and we bring our cows and we stay with them until the grass grows up, until the springtime is past . . . Then only do we return to our place. We leave the chickens and we leave the huts; if there are some or if there's some of the harvest, if there's some, it remains at the place and we just move the tent only. Every day we come to feed the chickens and go again. It's like if we went just to the place where the horsemen play like that. Now we take the tent and build it and we take the cows and the sheep and everything over there . . . because in that place, there's mud in it, and we take the sheep away to a place where there's no mud; one where there's good grass and everything. We stay with the animals until they eat well in the springtime, and we milk them there and we churn the milk there . . . and there are even times when some go and some stay at the house. Then you go down there to those sheep and in the evening you do the milking and you send for someone to bring you a donkey and they bring big earthen jars and they bring it all home . . . that's what we used to do.

And my father—may God have mercy on his soul—wasn't like that. My father used to have a house. They had big jars in which they used to churn buttermilk; now, there were people who do the milking, eight women or six women. Every evening they come and milk; not for money, like now it's gotten that way. They take milk, they take butter-milk, they take butter, and that's all. They don't live with us; each has her own house. It's just that when it's milking time, like now for you, your neighbor al-Ghaliyah will come and milk with you, Qasim's wife will come, that—ah—Zuhur will come and Malikah will come and all your neighbors will milk for you. And when the milking is done, they give each one her share of the milk. Again, if it were the time of the tithe of wheat coming up, they'd give it to them first; when they thresh wheat, they give to them. If it was a holiday or a big feast they'd give to them . . . and, if they wanted to [give], at the [animal] sacrifice. Now, it's become everything using money. At that time, you don't have a sheep, you'll come to me and take a sheep, without money, so you can cele-brate the feast. More than twenty or thirty sheep my father used to give, every year, to people so they could feast; people from our village. Just ask Zituni! Many people take a sheep; whoever doesn't have a sheep, he takes one. Also, that Uncle Abbas—Muhammad's father—he had sheep and he had goats. There used to be people who don't do the sacrifice for the feast. They always go to him and he gives them the [animal] sacrifice.

There are some who want to pay back the sheep; he says, "I got the sheep from other people; in the summer I'll buy one," and he buys it. There are some who get it free. Those things were not like they are now. Now, if you want meat, you buy it with money. They won't give you even a chicken; now you won't see even a chicken. At that time . . . like now, when we circumcised Si Muhammad, he'd probably get twenty or so chickens. You'd bring him a chicken and I bring him a chicken and like al-Ghaliyah brings ten eggs and another one brings a chicken and everyone will bring something to that boy. Only after he's circumcised do they slaughter the chickens. You give him broth to drink, give him the drumstick, another brings him something else. You give him the broth, give him the drumstick . . . not like now in the city. Now, if you don't buy a thing, you don't eat it.

There was plenty of wheat and plenty of milk and there was plenty of everything. The woman who has nothing used to have in her house six or seven hundred kilos [of wheat]. She always makes couscous of wheat. A person never used to buy grain at the *suq*. All the people that there are . . . they only buy grain at the *suq*. Now it's gotten so that everything is at the *suq*. There are only a few who have things at home.

At that time there was wheat and until the rainy season begins the wheat is still on the threshing floor. Who . . . one would be lucky just to find someone to thresh it for him. The wheat sat there until it got rained on. Lots of people thresh and lots of people eat and lots steal and there's still wheat left.

But, really, now when the Christians have come and there are machines and there are tractors, and there's all this . . . It's not like at that time.

There was plenty of everything at that time; it's just fabric that wasn't plentiful. A woman used to wear just a robe [a rectangular piece of cloth which is wrapped around the body and fastened into a loose-fitting "dress"]. And the woman who was considered elegant, you'd find she'd have two robes; that woman was good and important. They were just like my robe here, of this cotton. But there was *just* this robe; no pantaloons, no nothing. That's all—nothing else. My mother-in-law always had just a robe—that's all. Those who wear the *shamir* or the *dafinah* [more-tailored women's "dresses"] . . . until now, now they just are starting to wear them.

They used to make *hayk*[s] [cloaks] by themselves . . . Well, now that fabric has become plentiful, they go around in the streets with it; whoever wants, buys fabric . . . whoever wants buys sweaters, whoever wants buys pants. Whoever used to wear sweaters? or pants? No one!

Well, on our feet we used to wear leather slippers [*bilgha*], always slippers. They weren't bought; everyone knew how to make them at home. The farmers—at the time of plowing they made sandals of the skins of cows. The men made those for themselves and they plowed in the fields wearing them. Until now, they still make them. But the slippers used to come from Marrakesh; people always buy the slippers.

And for the wedding, if you get married. Now, you buy slippers for yourself and you buy slippers for the bride and you buy her father's brother slippers and you buy her father slippers and you buy her brother slippers if she has a brother. You just buy everyone slippers;

you "slipper" the whole tent. The groom buys all that. At that time there was only the "slippering" to do.

The father of the groom . . . the father of the groom buys for the father of the bride and he buys for her brothers . . . And if she still has her mother, he furnishes all of them with slippers.

Again, if the groom is going to have the wedding . . . he has his sister, he has his sister's daughter, he has his father's brother's wife, he has his mother's sister . . . He'll buy them *dafinah*[s] or he'll buy them slippers. Now, he buys for his sister and he buys for his mother's sister's daughter, and he'll say that he bought for her. And when it's time for the wedding, people are going to give him offerings of money because he bought them those things. They offer him more money than it cost him to buy those clothes. If he buys her slippers for $2.00, she'll give him an offering of $6.00. If he bought her slippers for $1.00, she'll give him an offering of $2.00 or $3.00. That's what they used to do. Like now, take the son of Bin Ayyad. The son of Bin Ayyad, when he got married, bought some twenty-two *dafinah*[s]; he bought one for al-Ghaliyah herself. Really, he bought Aminah a *dafinah*. All of them, he bought them *dafinah*[s] because of the offerings, so they would shower him with offerings.

And people come . . . you must come if he gave you a *dafinah*; you won't stay home, you'll have to go, you must. It's shameful for you to stay home and he bought you something.

Well, now everything has gotten full; now everything has become plentiful. It used to be, say, the woman who has a robe . . . I used to have a robe, and on *suq* day three people come asking to borrow it from me in order to go to the *suq* in it. They would cover themselves with it.

Us, we didn't used to go to the *suq*; it was us who didn't go to the *suq*. When a woman was still young, it was shameful for her to go to the *suq*. Her father-in-law or her mother-in-law go to the *suq*; us, we never saw the *suq* until we moved to Mawlay Ahmad . . . just then we started going to the *suq*. Honest to God, I never ever went to the *suq*. From there, I never ever saw what the *suq* looked like.

Well, I stayed there a long time; everyone of my children, I gave birth to them there. I gave birth to Khadijah there, I had Dhan and I had Aminah and I stayed there so long without children, so long, and I never went to the *suq*. Now, when we came here we began going to the *suq*; we go and we shop. It used to be we didn't shop at all; only the men shop, they do whatever they want. He brings you potatoes or he brings you meat or he brings you soup or whatever he brought you; you cook it—it's your business.

And the robe, like I told you, in the morning I'm still sleeping and a woman comes and called me and says to me, "Sister, give me your robe; I'm going to the *suq*." My mother's brother's wife—now she's an old lady—she used to go to the *suq* and come and ask for my robe. There was that nice D'lafiyah—may God bless her—an old lady and she comes to borrow my robe. Even though they have work clothes, that robe is nice and clean. Always that robe from my wedding; I was never careless with it. It's always hidden. I always wash it and leave it hidden. Well, now, if a wedding came up or a party, I cover up with it; and if there weren't any, I leave it there, hidden. Like your *qaftan* [a dressy garment] you want to keep hidden . . . like that *qaftan*, is how it was with that robe I had.

We used to go . . . if we went, we go to a wedding . . . if we went to a wedding, we go with our husbands. Like if the wedding was in Wala Harun or here in Mawlay Ahmad or in Zagharun or wherever . . . we don't go alone; we all go. Even if it was nearby, we all would go. Even though it was a village, we go, man and woman, to the same place. It wasn't bad, in our tradition. Now it's become so that men sit by themselves and the women by themselves.

If they used to sing and dance, they used to do it with a man beside a woman. You've seen the Berbers on television? It was like that they used to do in our village. A woman stands here and a man here and a woman here and a man here. All the young girls, even if they don't know how to dance, enter in. She just wears her robe and stands there and all. And the older women . . . there's nothing hanging over them. If she wants to dance, she goes ahead and dances, and if she doesn't want to dance . . .

If you were young and just married, it's okay to go . . . if you're next to your husband, it doesn't matter. You go with your husband. You stand with him . . . wherever he stands, you stand next to him. There's nothing he can say about it. If there were strange people from some place in our village—if there was a wedding and strange people came—you don't go. You sit with the women until your husband calls you.

Then, again, if a bride got married, they don't leave her in the house. Now, it used to be if a bride got married, the groom would take the bride away. They take the groom probably some three kilometers or two kilometers, and they take the bride and they take her bed and her husband embellishes ['*izih*: deflowers] her there, just in the wilderness; then, they bring her back and then they check her blood [as proof of virginity]. There wasn't one of those big tents or anything. How many brides I've seen with my own eyes! Now, for example here, the best man comes and he carries the bride on his back, and another best man carries two pillows and he carries a rug. Well, they go and take her far away and they take the groom there and he embellishes her there in the wilderness and they bring her back. In the early days it was this way, but now they've started to say it's shameful; they say why should the woman be embellished out in the open country?

When she was with child, the woman used to remain without pantaloons, without clothing against the cold. They don't say the cold would hurt her, or anything else. She eats whatever she ate, and when the labor pains come . . . even if she's going to empty the water jar for them, she has the baby right there, or she goes to get water and she gives birth in the wilderness. All by herself; she isn't afraid.

When I was going to have my first baby, I knew that I was going to give birth, but I didn't know what it would be like. But I sent for the woman, that's all . . . and when I sent for the woman, I wasn't afraid. She was a midwife. She lived in our village, and I know that she's a midwife for people.

And there was also at that time . . . now, it used to be if you went to visit someone . . . If I came to visit you, I can't come unless my father-in-law gave me permission or someone came with me. I won't go even though we were out in the country. We used to live in just tents, we don't have rooms or anything. For the woman, her boundary is the edge of her tent. You don't come to visit me and I don't go to visit you . . . even if you know them very well. If there was some party or a wedding or if someone was sick, it's okay. But to just go—you can't. Even if you want to go visit her, she won't come to visit you. The old people are with you; you can't leave them and go.

And if you asked . . . if he wants to, if he feels like it or it pleases him, he'll let you go. And if he doesn't want to, he won't let you go. Even if you go with him to the fields, say he's harvesting and you're gathering the wheat with him, and if a woman came and he saw you talking to her, he'd say, "Why are you talking to her?" Even though it's only a woman, not a man. Well, that's just what the old people used to do. Old people used to be naïve, not like us.

And there was also at that time, it used to be, even if you had sugar in the house, you can't make tea, you can't make coffee . . . you can't make anything. You can't make anything at all if the man didn't make it, and if he didn't give you any, you don't drink any. Not until the man comes. And he'll be away, wherever he was; he'll come and finally make tea and he and the guests will drink. Just what's left is what he'll give to you; he'll just give you the teapot, and if there's some left he makes you some tea . . . only then will you drink. If he didn't give you any, you don't drink. And you aren't going to complain loudly and say, "I didn't

get any at all,'' or take the tray and make tea yourself . . . that's shameful.
It's the man who makes tea, and now . . . everything is topsy-turvy
[laughing].

We . . . , one always says it's good now; better than the way it was at
that time [laughing]. Say you had eggs, you have chickens, and the
peddler came to the village; say he peddles beads and *suwak* [walnut
stick used as toothbrush and gum-rouge]. You'd say to yourself, "I'm
going to buy something.'' You can't go, even if you have something to
buy with. You'll look for a woman to go and buy for you. If you would
go out, he would see you; if you were still young, you don't go outside.
It's shameful for you to go out and see the peddler, even if there's
something you need in the house, you send . . . you call some woman,
or some unmarried girl to call a woman for you; you give her money
and only then she buys for you; you . . . you don't go and buy. Even if it
used to be like that . . . they were strict in their time.

Now, at that time my brother-in-law was with us and Mawludah was
still a virgin [unmarried] and we're grinding; we have a stone mill and
we grind by hand. Every day we grind whatever we're going to eat.
Now, today's flour we cook tomorrow, and tomorrow's flour we cook
the day after tomorrow. Every day we grind flour in the evening and we
grind early in the morning. We went to grind flour and he came and
found us singing and he chased us away from the mill—my brother-in-
law, Muhammad. He chased us probably about six kilometers, and he's
catching up with us and we're going, running away. He wanted to beat
us. We left the mill uncovered and we left the flour uncovered. He said,
"Do I have dancing girls [prostitutes], that you're singing in the house?
They're singing and people are passing next to the tent! Goddamn your
father!" Now, that's finished. Now, that's finished. Now everything has
gotten . . . [trails off and stops].

They used to get married without a written contract. And now, these
people take her [the bride] with a contract. And he who wants to marry
without a contract, he marries without a contract. Even in the early days,
the contract existed; I have a contract—from the early days. I have a
contract in Meknes; I had a contract and my mother took it, and I told
her to give it to me. Then we gave it to my father's brother and again I
returned it to my father's brother—I used to call my sister's husband
"father's brother" [uncle]. That contract got lost on us, but our contract
is in Meknes.

Now, when Muhammad [her husband] came here, he said, "I'll end
up running and going to Meknes. You'll just look for the contract and
when you want to get it out, I'll just end up going back and forth. I'll

get the people that know us and we'll make a [new] contract." And he went and rounded up twelve people and took them to the judge's, and I didn't go with them at all. He made the contract and at the same time he had a family record of births [*hala madaniya*] made, and he brought home the contract.

I have two paper . . . I have two papers. And this contract here, Muhammad has had translated two times, this one here. He translated it and gave him one translated contract, written with white writing and the paper is black. There's one with white paper and black writing; when he translated it again, the picture came out black. I have the contract; if there wasn't a contract, we can't do the family record of births. Because of the birth record, we up and redid the contract. We did it before Dhan [oldest son] entered school. If there's no birth record, the children aren't even considered . . . and education, too. Now if I'd gone to Meknes and complained, I would have gotten my other contract . . . if I'd made a fuss about it.

That's the contract with Muhammad. That other man, that I told you I went and ran away to the Christian's place, they didn't negate that thing [marriage contract]. The day that I married Muhammad, they called that man and he came and I did the divorce paper, and only then did I get married to Muhammad. Because that first man [husband], he was the owner of the contract. Well, now I have the contract. Now, I have the contract in Meknes and I had gone to look for it . . . My sister's husband is still there to find it for me; he's there in Meknes.

My sister died; there just remain her children, in Casablanca and Salé. And because of what my sister did to me, that's why now I don't want to visit her children. I have my sister's children in Salé; my sister's two married daughters and their children. And I have my sister's children in Casablanca. And that one who's in Mecca is my sister's daughter. And another son of my sister . . . Muhammad, he's in Europe. Yes, there are my sister's children.

Now it's only . . . the thing is that I got used to it here and I don't feel like leaving. If I would go, they would be *very* happy to see me. I went to see them one time, me and Dawiyah. Just ask them; this Ruqiyah nearly went crazy over us! She works for a government minister for $90.00 a month. She cooks in Rabat; she cooks very well—there's no one who knows how to cook like she does. She didn't want to cook for the king, and she cooks for this one minister, that . . . they call him Ghashshash, or they call him . . .

They live in . . . Kiran [a Salé neighborhood]. They, my sister's daughters, live in Kiran, a place they call Kiran. Muhammad knows the place;

he knows where they live. And we . . . I *could* go to visit them . . . it's just my idea, now I'm used to it here and I can't leave my son and I can't leave the house, and that's that. But if I *were* to go visit them, they wouldn't let me go back. After this week passes, I'll go, God willing. After the feast is over, we'll see . . . I'll probably go now.

14

Umm Ahmad

أم أحمد

A Village Mother of Egypt

ca. A.D. 1902–

Biographical Sketch by Lucie Wood Saunders

The Delta of Egypt lies at the mouth of the Nile, where it flows into the Mediterranean. Here, along the branches of the Nile, is located the richest and most intensively cultivated land in the country and some of its most densely populated rural areas. The majority of the people in the Delta live in villages and cultivate small plots of their own land or work for others on larger estates. Kifr al-Hana, with a population of about 2,400, located fifty miles northeast of Cairo, is a village like many other Delta villages, and Umm Ahmad is like other village mothers in many ways.

A small woman with brown eyes that sparkled suddenly with lively interest or with affection, Umm Ahmad was about sixty years old in 1962. She had lived in Kifr al-Hana all her life, except for rare visits to other villages. Twice married and the mother of adult sons and a daughter, she had explored, comprehended, and maneuvered within all the domestic roles that women hold in her village, becoming wiser than many in her social relationships while maintaining her capacity for love. Umm Ahmad was also well acquainted with the body of knowledge generally available to village women and she could discuss many sub-

---

Photo: Egyptian Delta village women

jects cogently and well. Her experiences are unusual in a few respects, but she shares most of them with other old women in Kifr al-Hana, and these experiences indicate the changes in women's roles which come with age; they also suggest some of the possible interpretations of these roles.[1]

Umm Ahmad, her youngest son, and his wife lived together in 1962. She spent most of her time tending their shop, which had the largest stock and the most customers of any in the village. In an agricultural community that divided itself socially and economically into two major segments—the rich, who have access to enough land and other resources so that the men do no physical labor, and the fellahin, who cultivate, care for animals, and do other labor—Umm Ahmad's household was counted in the latter group and considered to be in comfortable circumstances. Their two-story house of mud brick was two rooms wide. The larger front room was used for the shop, and here, as well as in the entrance hall, Umm Ahmad visited with kin or friends. In the back of the house, meals were cooked daily by the son's wife, under Umm Ahmad's supervision; the family all slept in the smaller front rooms and on the oven in winter. Upstairs, Umm Ahmad kept household supplies in one room while her son's wife's furniture occupied the other. Umm Ahmad was always busy and she recalled her memories of the past as she responded to visitors' comments on different aspects of village life.

Umm Ahmad was one of three daughters and she remembers living well as a child in a household where there was plenty of food. Under their mother's direction, she and her sisters alternated tasks, taking turns working in the house or in the fields, carrying stable dirt to the fields or taking food to people working there. The girls were well prepared for the life they would encounter as wives to fellahin men, to whom they were married at about the age of fifteen. When Umm Ahmad was married, her father added funds of his own to the bride price and bought his daughter dresses, jewelry, and household furnishings. Umm Ahmad recalled that the things bought for her were a small and a large copper *tisht*,[2] a copper tray and pan, a straw-filled pillow, a mattress and comforter, a big wooden box, one silk dress, two cotton dresses more colorful than the blue flowered dress that she wears now, three head scarves, a pair of red slippers, two slips, two pairs of panties, and a veil with gold on the nose piece of the type which women wore many years ago. She and her husband had eleven children, of whom four lived to be adults. She said that sometimes she became pregnant within a few months of the birth of her last child, and twice she had to nurse two children at the same time because they came so quickly after each other. She sometimes had to put the latest baby in a basket which she would hang from the ceiling and rock as she could because she had so little time to cradle them in her arms. Like other mothers, she expected her children to have learned to behave courteously by about the age of six and to be able to help her.

Umm Ahmad said that she, like all fellahin wives, swept, baked, washed clothes, made dung cakes for fuel, made butter, made cheese, and milked. She had raised chickens in the house. She had worked in the fields cutting clover, pulling weeds, resetting wheat and cotton, thinning wheat and cotton, cutting wheat at harvest, picking cotton, opening the ditches for irrigation, herding the water buffalo, carrying lunch to the men, and sometimes turning the Archimedean screw (a hand-operated irrigation device). She recalled that once, when she and her first husband were working in the fields at night, she was watching the water buffalo turn the irrigation wheel when she heard strange sounds from the road and the beast began to low in a peculiar way. Suddenly the water stopped flowing and terrible sounds came from the canal. She called her husband, who tried to unstop the canal, but it was no use; thus they knew that the sounds emanated from ghosts. Terribly frightened, they went home quickly, saying a verse of the Koran to protect themselves.

Until her husband died, Umm Ahmad spent her time working in the house, cultivating their fields, and bringing up their children. She did not work for wages as some village wives do. She did not talk much about her affinal relations or her own parents and siblings during this time. Like all newly married villagers, she and her husband lived with his parents, until the older people died. The jealousy that developed between Umm Ahmad and her husband's sister during this period of co-residence before the sister married continued when both were old women in 1962. If they saw each other at social gatherings or during rare visits, old disputes were likely to be continued and the two women could quickly begin arguing vehemently about past events, such as the quality of Umm Ahmad's bridal clothing.

Umm Ahmad remained unmarried for some time after her first husband's death and she continued to stay in the house where they had lived together. During this period she had to assume an independent economic role because her four living children were still young. She and her children had inherited thirty-five irats of land from her husband on which they raised cotton, wheat, and corn.[3] They also owned a water buffalo. Umm Ahmad cultivated the land with her sons and began to plan how she could manage the major feat of social and economic organization that every fellahin household faces, that is, arranging and financing the marriage of her children. When her oldest son was sixteen, she decided on a wife for him and, since her husband had no brothers, her own brother represented her in making the arrangements for the bride price. However, her brother was not expected to contribute to the bride price; Umm Ahmad managed that herself. She sold the water buffalo and the wheat crop; she borrowed LE 5 [Egyptian pounds; about $12.00] from her sister and with this she paid the bride price. During the celebrations of the marriage, she received gifts of money amounting to LE 16 as well as presents of sugar, rice, and macaroni. She sold the food that she did not use for the wedding feasts and bought a buffalo calf with this and the cash she received. In about two years, she found a wife for her second son and agreed to pay LE 50 as bride price. She sold the water buffalo for LE 40 and the cotton crop for LE 10 and so was able to pay the girl's father. During the celebrations for this son's marriage, she received presents of LE 17 in cash, which she used to repay the debt still owed her sister, and in addition she bought another buffalo calf.

Then, for awhile, Umm Ahmad lived with her married sons, their wives, and her two unmarried children. Soon, however, she agreed to marry again, herself, and her new husband moved in with them. Her children disliked him from the beginning, especially the two youngest children who did everything they could to annoy him. Finally, he said he was going to take her away from her children, and he moved with her to the house a few doors away—where Umm Ahmad and he lived until he died two years later.

After her second husband died, she moved back with her married sons and her other son and daughter. Umm Ahmad said that trouble started immediately, with quarrels nearly every day with her sons' wives. She said the source of the trouble was the two wives, who quarreled with her and between themselves. They would, for example, bring a quantity of flour for her to measure so each could make bread, and she would divide it equally between them; then they would quarrel so much about who had the most that she would have to weigh it out again. One of the wives was clever and baked quickly, using little fuel, while the other was so slow that Umm Ahmad would bake for her and this, naturally, would anger the first wife. Finally, her sons were drawn into the quarrels; first each sided with his wife against the other, then both sided with their wives against their mother. She concluded, like all other village mothers, that it is very difficult to live with one's sons' wives.

Her younger married son died suddenly, and his wife returned to her father's house. Umm Ahmad began to arrange for the marriage of her third son, for whom she had found a wife. Her brother again took the role of the father in the marriage arrangements, but Umm Ahmad had the responsibility of financing the marriage, and she sold the water buffalo for this purpose.

When the youngest son's wife came into the household, Umm Ahmad again had two young women to help with the work. Her daughter, Habibah, remained in the house and Umm Ahmad was able to spare her all the drudgery of housework as she had done when the previous wife was there. The household lived comfortably, supporting itself by cultivating the land and selling the products of the water buffalo. Umm Ahmad organized her sons' wives' work as she had before, by alternating assignments between the house and the fields. Each wife washed her own clothes and her husband's, and Umm Ahmad sent one of them to market with Habibah until Habibah was old enough to go alone. Umm Ahmad's only housework was cooking fancy dishes for special occasions since a woman gains prestige from doing this. She also managed household funds. After the butter was sold in the market every week, the sons' wives and Habibah would bring the money to Umm Ahmad. Her sons also brought her all the money from the sale of the crops. Everyone ate together, since Umm Ahmad provided the money to buy the food. She also provided funds for seed and fertilizers. Once a year, at the feasts, she went by bus to the capital of the district, about six miles away, and bought two outfits of outer clothes and underclothes for each person in the household. She allowed her sons' wives to keep for themselves the money they made by raising pigeons and selling dung cakes.

Umm Ahmad maintained the household in this way until the time came to marry her daughter, Habibah. She and her sons agreed to marry her to a young man from a prosperous household, and Umm Ahmad took the unusual step of selling three irats of land to match the amount of bride price in order to provision her daughter exceptionally well. She used all the presentations of money that she received at the celebrations to buy unusually large quantities of wedding foods, in contrast to her careful husbandry of these funds when her sons married. She sent baskets of cakes and twenty-five large pastries (*fatir*) with her daughter when she went to her groom; she sent three chickens on the Thursday after the wedding and four on the tenth day afterwards. Umm Ahmad had always been accused of spoiling Habibah and it was clear that she wanted to protect her in her new house.

The allocation of so large an amount of household funds to someone who was leaving angered her sons' wives, who grumbled continually about it and gradually convinced their husbands that Umm Ahmad was depriving them. Eventually, her sons insisted on dividing the common property; each son took his share, Habibah was given hers, and Umm Ahmad kept seven irats. The corn from that year's harvest was divided equally, each took all the milk from the cow for three full days, and then the cow was sold and the money divided. The two sons sold their shares of the land and moved to Sharqiyah, the neighboring province, leaving Umm Ahmad alone in the house.

Within a year, however, her sons returned asking for help. Part of their money had been stolen and they were unable to complete the payment for the land they were buying in Sharqiyah. Umm Ahmad pitied their situation and sold her land, dividing the price between them. They returned to Sharqiyah to finish paying for their land and then re-sold it. Both brothers then returned to the village, the older buying a small piece of land and living separately while the younger, Muhammad, moved in with Umm Ahmad and bought the stock for a shop. Each son agreed to contribute LE 1 per month to support his mother, and she ate separately from Muhammad. With these developments, Umm Ahmad relinquished the economic base of her managerial functions in the household, and her relationships with her sons began to shift. She had lost access to capital and was dependent for subsistence on her sons' sense of obligation. Her only means of achieving her desires in inter-personal situations was by maintaining their respect for her sagacity, reminding them of their obligation to her, and asserting the rights of deference that come with age. The change in role developed slowly.

In Kifr al-Hana, when the father of the family is dead, adult brothers are considered responsible for their sister's behavior. Umm Ahmad, however, continued to have a decisive voice in transactions involving her only daughter, Habibah; her strong feeling for Habibah was well known and her sons must have been aware that she would take extreme steps on her daughter's behalf. Thus, when she supported Habibah's pleas that she be divorced from her husband, Muhammad and his brother recognized that they would be well advised to do as they were asked. Habibah had been complaining bitterly for some time, saying she was deprived of food in her husband's father's house, and was not even offered a sample from the food her own mother sent as presents on feast days. Her husband's people also worked her too hard in the fields, she said.

Umm Ahmad did not want her daughter to suffer, but she knew also that the arrangements for divorce would mean that her daughter would forfeit all the furnishings she had taken with her at the time of marriage and would also forfeit the right to have her own daughter with her. But Habibah got her divorce and returned home to live happily with Umm Ahmad. Soon, however, she had to be married again. At the end of three months a suitor appeared and Umm Ahmad and Muhammad agreed with him on the bride price and the marriage date. This man was not able to provide the marriage presents specified in the agreement, and before the wedding took place Umm Ahmad's first husband's sister and her sons came to visit. They suggested another candidate for Habibah's second husband, an old man who was kin to the sister's first husband. Umm Ahmad decided to accept this plan because the man was said to be kind and a kinship connection already existed with him.

The marriage was arranged. Habibah went home with her second husband three days after he had brought the clothing specified. The man did not want a celebration, since his first wife had recently died, so Umm Ahmad made a big basket of cakes for Habibah.

Soon after his sister's remarriage, Muhammad, unknown to his mother, began to negotiate for a second wife, and he brought her home early in 1961. His first wife, greatly angered, moved out and he had to maintain her in a separate house. Since his second wife was young, Muhammad asked his mother to live with them, thus Umm Ahmad once more assumed the management of the household, controlling household supplies and allocating household tasks to her son's wife.

By 1962, Umm Ahmad had assumed the social behavior of an older woman. This meant that she had considerable freedom of behavior in public situations. She spent most of her time in the shop making quick sales of tea or occasional exchanges for an egg, or chatting at length with more leisurely buyers who came inside the shop, prepared to spend more time in purchasing flour, potatoes, or other major commodities. Because of her age, there were no restrictions on her conversation with men, so she talked freely with everyone who came into the shop. In the evening, when Muhammad made tea for visitors in the shop, she was served first in deference to her age, and young relatives kissed her hand when they visited. She did not need permission, as a young married woman did, to put on her worn black overdress to go out occasionally to socialize with other women at celebrations of marriages, births, or circumcisions and *zars* [or exorcism ceremonies]. She went out also to pay sympathy visits after deaths and to listen to funeral recitations.

Age did not bring public political or religious roles for Umm Ahmad or any other old woman in the village. Women do not hold public office here and, in fact, in 1962 public offices remained restricted to a small number of relatively rich men. Indications that the socioeconomic correlates of leadership were beginning to change in response to the revolution were evident, but they had not yet changed basically. Umm Ahmad had started voting a few years earlier when other village women did. Religion was important to her but her practice of it was private. She prayed regularly at home and fasted on certain holy days in addition to keeping the fast of Ramadan. She also was charitable to the poor. She was not well informed about Muslim beliefs, nor were any other women. She was, however, knowledgeable about all kinds of cures for disease, whether these were medicinal herbs or magical practices, and she had some knowledge of the beliefs in spirits underlying the latter.

Unlike old widows who lived alone and had no business, Umm Ahmad was seldom without company. She talked with her son's wife if no one else was around; her daughter, who came every day; or her other son and Habibah's husband, who came to see her everytime they were in the village. Most customers chatted briefly, but younger women who came to buy sometimes stayed to ask her advice or to seek her support. Her wide net of interaction and her reputation for being a woman of good sense tended to make her opinion significant in shaping public views. One day, for example, two co-wives came to the shop, one in the morning and the other in the afternoon. The older complained that she had been insulted by the second wife as she sat outside her parents' house where she had taken refuge. Later, the second complained that her co-wife tried continuously to make trouble between her and her husband. Umm Ahmad soothed both of them, saying that a husband was not worth quarreling about and that they should learn to live peacefully. Later, she commented that the first wife did not act sensibly, because she had let her husband get control of her marriage furniture; she, as the wife offended by his remarriage, had a right to this furniture. Umm Ahmad advised her at the time to get a divorce and take her property. In this, as in other instances, Umm Ahmad felt that it was important for a woman to be strong in a domestic situation. She sometimes said that women rule here, but she always implied that they must guard their rights so they could rule.

By 1962, in contrast to her public role, Umm Ahmad's domestic sphere of action was becoming somewhat more restricted through changes in her relations with her son Muhammad. Essentially, he was exploring the potentialities of his role as an adult man, while she had to learn the limitations of her role as an old woman. Two major domestic events revealed these trends, one involving Habibah and the other herself and Muhammad.

Habibah often expressed appreciation for her old husband's kindness and consideration, noting that he urged her to buy foods that she liked, encouraged her to seek remedies when she complained of physical discomfort, and gently covered her at night when the blankets fell off. Late in the first year of her marriage, however, she began to quarrel with him frequently and to complain of his appearance. After an especially severe quarrel, he complained to her brothers that she had been seen near her former husband's house. Her brothers questioned her and she denied all wrong doing but they struck her twice with a stick anyway. Umm Ahmad threw herself between her sons and daughter, threatening to leave them and take Habibah with her to beg in the streets if they struck her daughter again. The brothers were shamed and desisted, the old husband said it should all be forgotten, and Habibah cried bitterly. That same day, Umm Ahmad went to consult with a shaikh in another village about Habibah's relations with her husband. The shaikh found that magic had been made against Habibah and her husband by the man's daughter, and he gave Umm Ahmad an amulet for Habibah to wear, in order to remove the effects of the magic. Habibah wore the amulet and from that time on she and her husband had no more major problems; she said, however, that she now hated her brothers.

The second incident which indicated that roles were shifting involved a serious quarrel between Umm Ahmad and Muhammad. About eight months after his second marriage, Muhammad began going to the coffeehouse every night to gamble at cards. His mother argued that, since he had three women to support, he could not afford such behavior. But, in defiance of her admonitions, Muhammad went off to the coffeehouse as usual the next night, and Umm Ahmad was forced to recognize that she had no means to stop him. A week later, she and Muhammad had a major break. This began when Muhammad ordered his second wife to get a bundle of straw and she refused, saying that she had a backache. He then told Umm Ahmad to get the straw and she refused saying that there was no reason for her to do so when he had two wives who could. He then went to his first wife, who refused on the grounds that his second wife was at home enjoying good food so there was no reason for her, the first wife, to help him. He returned to the house and ordered his mother to get the straw. She did so, though she said it was a hard job for one her age. Then she left the house and went to her other son. She told him that she was badly treated and wanted a house for herself. After Umm Ahmad had spent five days with this son, Muhammad came with her brother, who assured her that Muhammad was sincere in his apology and promised that it would never happen again. She agreed to return to the house, and Muhammad beat his first wife, whom he now blamed for the whole incident.

But Umm Ahmad's relations with Habibah did not change as she aged. She said once that she did not want her daughter ever to say that she had not done everything she could for her and that this had been her guiding principle throughout life. Umm Ahmad supported and advised Habibah in her many searches for magical means of achieving pregnancy. She also helped her with preparations for holding a *zar* ceremony, though she commented privately that spirits do not really possess human beings, and the *zar* is mainly a refreshing experience for nervous people. Umm Ahmad played an important role in advising Habibah on the socioeconomic aspects of her domestic situation. The major incident in which her advice was crucial was when Muhammad and Habibah's husband wanted the girl to sell her gold earrings so they could buy a cow as a shared investment. Umm Ahmad told Habibah not to do this, and the two men gave up the idea. Somewhat later, Umm Ahmad advised Habibah to sell the earrings in order to buy a calf in partnership with her husband and Muhammad. She told her to get a receipt from her husband for the amount of money she contributed and to use the remaining money for another pair of earrings. Habibah did as her mother advised, thus continuing to hold some capital while making a potentially productive investment. Umm Ahmad recognized clearly that a woman's postion is strongest if she has some independent economic resources, though she herself was not able to apply this principle in her relationship with her sons.

In 1965 when I last heard from Umm Ahmad, she was living alone in the same house while Muhammad had moved with his second wife to a newly reclaimed area.[4] He had taken most of the stock in the shop with him and opened a shop there for his wife to run while he worked at an irrigation pumping station. He had left Umm Ahmad with about LE 10 worth of merchandise, and she continued to run her shop on a reduced scale. Her business had declined further with competition from another shop. Both sons contributed LE 1 a month to her. She continued to see Habibah, who now had fewer problems since giving birth to a daughter.

Conclusions

What do these incidents in Umm Ahmad's life show about her domestic relationships, her perception of her roles, and the relations between men and women in this village? A somewhat unexpected aspect of her domestic role is the managerial capacity which she is expected to show in middle life. A woman must manage her sons' wives' work in house and field, and she must manage household expenditures and savings. Umm Ahmad exerted an unusual degree of economic and managerial control because her husband's death gave her the sole responsibility for financing the marriages of her three sons. Village practices did not lead her to expect financial assistance from her husband's kin or her own. Rather than in asserting control in particular relationships, she was concerned mainly with managing her household in order to attain basic social goals for her children.

Umm Ahmad's influence on her sons' behavior depended in part on her control over economic resources, a relationship that old men also recognize, with the result that they rarely relinquish land to their sons. Umm Ahmad's confrontations with Muhammad indicate that household management is significant in governing a son's behavior only when it relates to funds which the mother controls. Without economic resources, Umm Ahmad's rights as an old woman derived from her age and her status as her son's mother. Respect was her due, and consideration of her feelings a reasonable expectation. But to elicit appropriate behavior from her son when he failed to show it, she needed to assert the rights of age and status. For this, she could rely on the support of public opinion because these rights were generally recognized in the community.

Umm Ahmad's life was similar to that of other village women in that she managed her household, financed her children's marriages when she was left with the sole responsibility, developed ability in social relations, and acquired a store of knowledge about the supernatural as well as mundane matters. Her experience is suggestive of some aspects of the structuring of relations between men and women in Kifr al-Hana. Clearly, if women control economic resources they can affect men's behavior significantly. Furthermore, women are expected to become managers in the domestic sphere and, thus, may have more practice in managerial skill than many landless men who spend their lives working for others. All women have some rights and the means of defending them. Something of the recognition of the potentiality of women's roles and their possible economic activity leads to Umm Ahmad's assertion that "women rule here." That she scarcely ruled in 1962 was masked by the deference behavior elicited, in most situations, by her age, and the knowledge that her daughter was securing the basis for a strong position in her own household.

Notes

1.   The research on which this paper is based was supported by the Social Research Center of the American University at Cairo. Mrs. Sohair Mehanna al Attawi of the Social Research Center was my research associate, and her role was a major one in the field research process.
2.   A *tisht* is a large basin. An object of value and an important household utensil, it is part of the equipment of all village brides. Umm Ahmad's memory for the amount of her possessions was always exact.
3.   An irat is a unit of land measurement; 24 irats equal one feddan (1.038 acres).
4.   People from densely populated rural regions such as this were offered the opportunity to buy land on a long-term basis in areas near Alexandria which had been reclaimed in government projects.

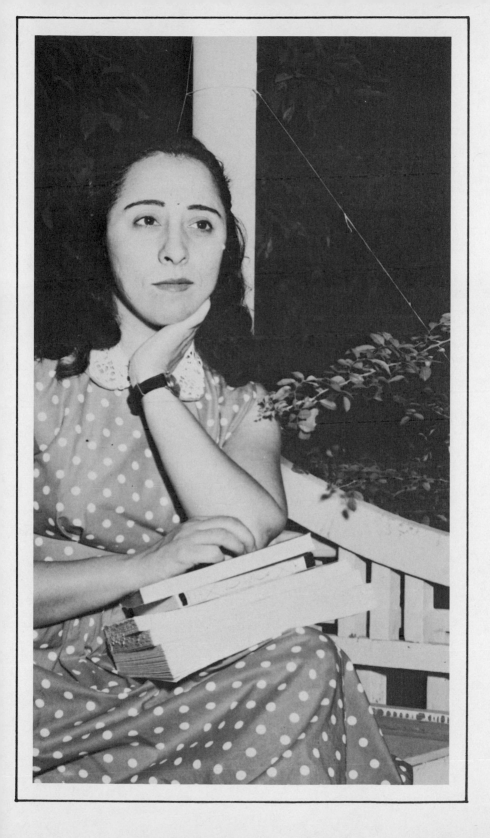

15

Nazik al-Mala'ikah

نازك الملائكة

Modern Poet of Iraq

A.D. 1923–

Nazik al-Mala'ikah was born in Baghdad in 1923. A long tradition of poetry and letters is found in her family, for her father and grandfather were both poets. She studied Arabic literature at Baghdad University and later attended Princeton University, where she received an M.A. in comparative literature. Upon her return to Iraq from the United States, she assumed a leading role in the free verse movement, through both her poetry and her critical work. She has published many critical essays and numerous collections of poetry, including *'Ashiqat al-Ayl* (Lover of the night), *Shadaya wa-Ramad* (Splinters and ashes), *Qararat al-Mawjah* (The bottom of the wave), and *Shajarat al-Qamar* (The moon tree). In recent years she has become disenchanted with some aspects of the free verse movement in Arabic poetry and has rejected several of its new forms. She has taught at Baghdad University and now lives in Kuwait.

Photo: Nazik al-Mala'ikah, 1958

The Beginnings of the Free Verse Movement/Nazik al-Mala'ikah

The year 1947 marked the beginning of the free verse movement,[1] which was born in Iraq and from Baghdad spread throughout the Arab world. Because of the extremists who answered the call, the movement soon seemed about to engulf all other styles of traditional Arab poetry.

The first free verse poem published was one of my own, "The Cholera," composed in one of the classical quantitative Arabic meters, *al-mutadarik* (al-Khabab). To illustrate, I quote a few lines:

Dawn has come.
Listen to the footsteps of the passersby
In the silence of the early morning—listen, look at
the procession of mourners.

Ten deaths, twenty, . . .
Don't count. Listen to those who are weeping.
Listen to the voice of the wretched child.
Dead, dead, the count is lost.
In every house a body lies, mourned by those who grieve,
No moment of eternity. No moment of silence.
This is what the hand of death has done.

Death, death, death . . .
Humanity is complaining, complaining of the deeds of death.[2]

[Nazik al-Mala'ikah, "Bidayat al-Shi'r al-Hurr wa-Zuru Fuhu," in *Qadaya al-Shi'r al-Arabi* (Baghdad: Manshurat Maktabat al-Nahdah, 1954). Translated by the Editors.]

[Tala'ah al-fajru
Isghi ila waq'i khuta al-mashin
Fi samti al-fajr, isgh, unzur rakba al-bakin
'Ashratu amwatin, 'uahruna
La tahsi, isgh, lil-bakina
Isma' sawta al-tifl al-miskin
Mawta, mawta da'a al-'adadu
Mawta, mawta, lam yabqa ghadu
Fi kullimakanin jasadun yandubahu mahzun
La lahzata ikhladin la samt
Hadha ma fa'alat kaffu al-mawt
Al-mawtu al-mawtu al-mawt
Tashku al-bashariyahtu tashku ma yatakibu al-mawt.]

A copy of the magazine containing "The Cholera" reached Baghdad in 1947, and in the second half of the same month Badr Shakir al-Sayyab published a collection in Baghdad entitled *Azhar Dhabilah* (Withering flowers). In the collection was a free verse poem, in al-Ramal meter, entitled "Was It Love?" In a footnote to this poem al-Sayyab commented that this poem was "a sample of the verse that varies in meter and rhyme."

Al-Sayyab writes:

Is it love that I
Became a slave to wishing
Or is love to repudiate wishes
Or is love a meeting of mouths and a forgetting of life,
The disappearance of one eye in another in ecstasy,
Or like a gathering which comes together only to be
Diminished in the surge of the storm,
Or is it like a shadow in a stream . . .

However, the appearance of these two poems did not attract much attention from readers. As far as my own poem was concerned, Majallat al-'Urubah commented only on the transition in the style of meters. Two years passed in silence. No free verse was published in any periodical.

In the summer of 1949 my collection *Shazaya wa-Ramad* (Splinters and ashes) appeared, and a number of free verse poems were included. In a long introduction to the volume, I pointed out the importance of the innovations in this poetry, and I tried to explain the differences between this style of writing and the two-segment line style.[3] Then I gave an example of the selection of beats.

The appearance of *Splinters and Ashes* created a great uproar in the Iraqi press, and many heated discussions took place in Baghdad literary circles. Many of the reviewers wrote angry and scornful commentaries, forecasting that the call for free verse would fail completely. But throughout this uproar, the majority of the public and of the poets themselves remained silent. Acceptance of the new forms came about in a quiet way. As soon as the first early difficult months of the movement had passed, free verse suddenly began to be written by young Iraqi poets and to be published in newspapers. The call for free verse was being answered and was reaching a wider and wider group.

'Abd al-Wahhab al-Bayyati, an Iraqi poet, published a first book in March 1950. Its title was *Mala'ikah wa-Shayatin* (Angels and devils). The volume contained poems of free meters.[4] Following this, in the summer of 1950 another collection appeared, that of Shadhil Taqah, *al-Masa' al-Akhir* (The last evening). Then came *Asatir* (Legends), by Badr Shakir al-Sayyab, in September 1950, and, from this time on, collections appeared one after the other, all containing poems in free verse. Thus the call for free verse began to resound more strongly, so much so that some of the poets began to abandon completely the old traditional form, which included the two-segment line [or balancing hemistiches]; they began to write in a totally new way.

Circumstances of the Free Verse Movement

The free verse movement began in rather difficult circumstances and had many obstacles to overcome. Some of the circumstances were general and involved the total idea of a new movement; some are linked with free verse itself. As for the general circumstances, the free verse movement was like any new movement in arts and letters. At first, it was not yet fully developed as a style, somewhat hesitant, with the roughness of beginnings, the rawness of green fruit. This early period was a necessity, but the movement is still experimental and one must say that the movement's honesty and zeal to achieve new forms does not excuse individual poets from slipping now and then and stumbling into error. But any literary movement which emerges suddenly in certain times and circumstances is bound to go through long years of development before it puts down solid roots, refines its tools, and comes to full maturity. Such a movement does not emerge fully grown; it must pass through stages before it crystallizes. Today its faults appear to us more clearly, as we see it from a distance and have explored more completely our new experiences, our new cultural maturity, our widening horizons.

As for the special circumstances surrounding the beginning of the free verse movement, one must remember that this was the first time an Arab audience was confronted with Arabic poetry written entirely in free verse. We say this, in spite of the fact that some well-known scholars have stated that the free verse movement had its origins in Andalusian *muwashshahat* poetry, and in the *band*, or one-line segment poem, which was created by Iraqi poets during the past two centuries or shortly before. As for the Andalusian *muwashshah*, the known pieces which survive are organized into stanzas, and each segment has a fixed length. Thus, even if the poem is somewhat flexible in terms of its over-all length it has certain limits which indicate that the *muwashshah* is far from free verse, for free verse is the verse of meter alone, and the *muwashshah* is the verse of segments as well.

As for the *band*, or one-line segment type of poem, it is common knowledge that this style is relatively unknown to the average reader. I, myself, never heard of it until 1953, despite my own intensive concern with Arabic poetry. Texts on versification do not refer to the *band*, neither the familiar literary works nor the volumes used by teachers in their classes. The great and famous poets who wrote during the peak periods of Arabic poetic achievement did not use this form; only the later Iraqi poets utilize the *band*, a technique somewhat akin to the dialect of friendly and familiar correspondence.

We make these points, not to downgrade the aesthetic value of the *band* or *muwashshah*, but to show that free verse did not come from those directions. Further, the existence of the *band* did little to help Arab readers accept free verse when it appeared. The important point is not whether such styles of poetry existed before but how the audience and the poets of today are becoming aware of free verse, and how it is affecting their thoughts and attitudes.

Perhaps the most obvious evidence that the movement was a product of our particular period of time lies in the fact that the majority of readers continue to reject and refuse it. Among them are many who cannot be overlooked, who think that free verse has the name but not the quality of poetry, for it lacks rhythm and therefore is more like ordinary prose.

These are the special circumstances in which free verse emerged. We should not forget that a literary movement which springs up suddenly in such a way lacks an important quality, the quality of a traditional art which has developed gradually. Thus, a movement like free verse lacks a set of rules to support it, a basic direction to follow so it does not fall into error. But, in order for the movement to develop such forms and directions, one must be willing to take risks and make sacrifices. A poet faithful to his art may have difficulty in writing in this controversial style, fully aware that he is entering a new area which may not prove fruitful and which may ruiñ his reputation as a poet, a reputation, and fame, that has taken years of work to build.

As a result of all these general and special circumstances surrounding free verse, it is easy for the pioneer poet to fall into repetitive similes or images which become boring simply because the pioneer has not yet mastered the techniques. He may follow in the manner of his other colleagues without adding any innovations of his own and produce not an intelligent imitation but a poem which indicates that the poet is unaware of what he is attempting! For one must remember that the only rules which exist for free verse are the poems of others, and these are still relatively few. A poet who admires a certain poem's meter and rhyme will try to compose his own work on the same model and will sometimes be unable to avoid falling into an imitation, not only of the earlier poem's meanings and ambiance, but also of its mistakes. This is one of the many dangers which have been apparent in free verse during the early period. No sooner had some of the characteristics of free verse been demonstrated in some of the work of the new writers, than poems were written that were similar in subject matter, diction, mood, and image. An error in one poem crept into other poems in an alarming way, as though it were a rule to follow, not a mistake to be avoided.

But the problems of the free verse movement were not confined simply to errors of circumstances; they arose from many other directions which we will consider in the following paragraphs.

Misleading Characteristics of Free Verse

On the surface, it appears that free meters are easy to compose; great possibilities exist to make the poet's task of expression easy and to create a ready musical atmosphere which enables the poet to inject this natural music into his poem without great effort. But sooner or later every mature poet discovers the truth and will not be deceived by appearances. At first glance, what appears to be easy in these verses and rhymes is later found to be dangerous, a way full of pitfalls which are easy to fall into. These pitfalls are a source of great anxiety to the serious poet, for he can see that, unless he takes great care, his verse is in danger of becoming corrupted, fragmented, banal, and, finally, of no literary value whatsoever.

We will discuss these deceptive characteristics of free verse, namely, freedom, music, and spontaneity.

1.   The glittering freedom which free meters offer to the poet is, in truth, a dangerous freedom. The poet comes to his work, unrestricted by specific lengths for line segments or fixed patterns for his rhymes. As he begins, the ease of it captivates him; no rhyme exists to irritate him, no specific number of *taf'ilat*, or feet, stands in the way of his thought. He is free, free, and quickly he can become intoxicated by this freedom. And, while in this intoxicated state, it is easy for the poet to forget other things about poetry which he should not forget! It is as though he is screaming to the goddess of poetry, "No half freedom for me! None of that! All or nothing!" And in this manner, the poet releases himself even from the bounds of balance, the unity of the poem, the rules of its structure, the links of its meanings. The glittering freedom becomes total chaos.

2.   The music that the free meters seem to possess inherently plays a

great part in misleading the poet in his task. This is the hidden ghoul of free verse. In its shadow and under its influence, even a well-meaning poet may write something rough and undigested, a thought fragmented almost without his being aware of it, for the quantitative musical meters and their fluency deceive him and hide the faults of this characteristic. The poet may not see that this music is not the created music of his own poetry but is superficial music which exists inherently in the meter itself. Free meters are new in our literature, and everything new has a special exuberance about it. So does the poet fall victim to the music of free meters and rhymes, letting them form his poem, rather than using these rhymes and meters himself for his own ends, making them work to raise the standard of the poem and give it new and excitingly different shapes and colors.

3.   The spontaneity of free verse is a characteristic which surpasses the previous two factors in complexity. This spontaneity results from the oneness of the meter which is found in most of the free rhymes. Free verse relies on the repetition of the meter, which may differ in its number from one line to another. This fact helps the rhyme to gush forth continuously, like the rushing of a stream down a slope, which stems logically from the lack of natural stops (waqafat) in the poem. As poets know, stops have an important place in the rhyme scheme. Sometimes the poet does not realize the importance of these stops until he suddenly misses them. At this point he is forced to double his efforts and gather together all his power and strength to avoid the poem's downhill transition without a single pause, from one meter to another. We can demonstrate this tendency by noting the use of stops in the style of al-Khalil's rhymes and meters and comparing this usage with what free verse offers in this area.

In al-Khalil,[5] the sixteen meters consist of two segments, or hemistiches, which have stops at the end of the second segment, a sharp, inescapable stop. The words in the line finish and with them the meaning finishes.[6] Thus the limits of each line are quite clear, and each line is clearly distinguished from the line which follows. But free verse does not have such fixed stops; the poet is not forced to finish his meaning at the end of a line but may extend his meaning to the following line or the one after that. The question of stops, then, is left to the poet's own inclination or taste. He may stop whenever he wishes and here the problem begins. We have observed that beginning poets writing free verse do not always know how to use it and write entirely without stops. Thus, when one reads such poetry, one goes on as if running breathlessly forward without end. More mature poets recognize the great responsibility which such freedom places on them and see that free meters do not give them any help at all. On the contrary, the entire burden of the poem falls on the flow of meaning and on the way the words are connected within the poem. This is not an easy task.

Consequences of Spontaneity in Free Verse

The spontaneity which we have described leads to two further characteristics in the poetry, which may be counted among its faults.
1.   The sentences tend to become extremely long, as in the following example by Badr Shakir al-Sayyab:

As though some sorcerers extended their pale lean fingers
To the sky
Pointing to a flock of crows blown by the wind
To the end of the lighted horizon
Until the executioner mounting his block goes far
Beyond his goal.[7]

Together these lines contain one idea or image, an image which proceeds without a single stop.
    Another example is a poem by 'Abd al-Wahhab al-Bayyati:

I wonder if the stray shadows behind him were aware of
    the singing
They wandered on and on in a half dream and awakened to
    the sky
Telling stories of young girls searching for lovers with
    their singing behind the walls of the night.[8]

Together these lines constitute a question, and it is difficult to cut through the long lines to get to the meaning. For the tone of questioning with which the poem begins ("I wonder if . . .") should not end before the words "the night." Such length of expression is a fault, one which is encouraged by the nature of free verse and one against which the poet must continually be on guard. In sum, if we examine all the restrictions found in the free meters of free verse, they are scarcely less than the restrictions placed on the poet by the old meters; they may even be greater. In both kinds of poetry, the stop is necessary but for different reasons. The free verse poet must formulate his own strict rule in expressing his ideas, in order to compensate for the obligatory rules placed on the old poetry by the two-segment line, or hemistiche style.
2.   Generally, it appears to us that free verse, because of its flow and

spontaneity, simply does not want to end, and there is nothing harder than ending these poems. The reason for this is the lack of stops. In the two-segment line, or hemistiche, the obligatory stop helps the poet greatly, for the segment is itself a stop. What remains for the poet is to complete his ideas within the limitation imposed on him by the form. Any strong and firm expression can do the job and end the poem, especially in poems of description and monologue and, perhaps, lyrics. In free verse, no natural stops exist, and the poet, even if he is using the strongest and firmest expression he can create, still feels as though the poem has not ended but continues to flow on. Thus it is necessary for the poet to go on feeding the poem, lengthening it, despite the fact that he has finished what he wants to say. The difficulty is more acute in poems of description and monologue, for the free meters are more suited to narrative and dramatic subjects.

Weak Endings in Free Verse Poems

From a study of the ways in which free verse poems are ended, one can see that the poets sense the difficulty of ending the natural flow of free verse though they may not actually be aware of it. Thus, they take refuge in some superficial and unacceptable techniques, such as ending the poem by repeating the first stanza. Buland al-Haydari, for example, begins and ends his poem "My Friend" with this stanza

My friend
Why don't you take your past and get out of my way
For we are empty and we are finished.
We remembered much but now we have forgotten.[9]

The ending is not mere chance, for the poet uses the same technique in many other poems, including "Depth," "I'll Never See Her," "Old Love," and "Tomorrow We'll Return." This technique is not unique to al-Haydari, for it creeps into the poetry of 'Abd al-Wahhab al-Bayyati[10] and we notice it in Badr al-Sayyab[11] and in Shadhal Taqah.[12] The recurrence of the technique indicates that all these poets sense the difficulty of ending free verse poems; they take refuge in the superficial method above, a method which is in fact only an escape for the poet from using the natural ending. Still, he is forced to this escape mechanism by the pressures of free verse. The repetition here is nothing but a kind of hypnotism the poet uses to numb the senses of the reader so he will believe that the poem is really finished.

Another method used to end free verse poems is that utilized by Badr

Shakir al-Sayyab in his poem "The Grave-Digger." The end of this long poem is as follows:

The lights of the city still glitter from afar
And the grave-digger continues his work
He avoids the new grave,
As he stumbles along,
Dreaming of a rendezvous
And of wine.[13]

And at the end of another poem, he writes:

Your shadow appears from afar while it's waving goodbye,
And I continue my struggle alone

I call this the "continuing" ending, which is used not only by al-Sayyab,[14] but by Buland al-Haydari as well:

The two hands go round
Tick! Tock!
Oh, coward!
Oh, coward, when is he going to wave goodbye?
And I continue struggling alone.[15]

The continuing ending is hypnotic, just like the repetition of the last stanza, cited above. It leaves the meaning in a comfortable continuity, as though the poet is saying to the reader, "and things went on and on forever in the same way" or, in other words, "see, in this manner the poet's role ends and it is therefore fitting that the poem should end also."

Much of the responsibility for using such techniques must be applied to the nature of the spontaneity of free verse itself. However, the mature poet should not be excused, simply by the nature of free verse, from ending his poem in an acceptable artistic manner.

Defects of Free Meters

If, as we have stated, the three good qualities of free verse, that is, musical quality, freedom, and spontaneity, offer pitfalls for the poet, what, then, are the effects of the real defects of free verse? The most apparent defects spring from the structure of the meters. We can explain them in the following way:

1.   Free verse offers the poet a choice of eight different meters from among the sixteen different meters of classical Arabic poetry. Here the poet immediately feels the narrowness of the range available to him, for the Arab poet is accustomed to a choice of sixteen different meters, each with its variations. These variations permit great possibilities, allowing for a variety of color in the meter and rhythm. Free verse is limited to half the number, a notable decrease.

2.   Most free verse depends on six meters of the eight available. These six depend on one pattern of taf'ilat (feet) and this creates a monotonous tone, especially in a long poem. In general, I think free verse is not suitable for legends and epics. Epic poems need continuous variety, not only in the length and number of lines but also in the pattern of feet; otherwise the reader becomes bored. Given this limited number of meters and the possibility of repetitiveness in the work, the poet must expend great effort in order to vary the poetic language, to arrange the thoughts in an interesting way, and to spread the centers of meaning throughout the poem. All these elements may, if used well, reduce the monotonous tone induced by a dependence on too few meters.

Flexibility of Free Verse and Its Future

To summarize, free verse should not totally dominate our contemporary poetry. Its meters do not suit all subjects, because of the limits imposed on it by the one-foot rhythm pattern, the lack of stops, and the ability for spontaneity and musical quality. We have no intention whatsoever of downgrading free verse, but some caution is necessary for those who have surrendered entirely to its charms. Long years of experience with free meters show that banality and mediocrity may lie behind the superficial attraction of the meters, unless the poet takes great care.

Actually, the movement began to divert from its earliest stated goal, which was to free poets and poetry from the structures of the past. This is not too surprising. However, there is no need for pessimism about the future of the movement. Historically, this particular poetic movement does not differ from any other movement calling for freedom, whether it is national, social, or literary in character. Throughout the centuries, we have witnessed hundreds of examples of people's revolutions, when an exaggeration in the implementation of the spirit of the revolution led to chaos and degradation at first, until the movement settled into a more stable pattern. Thus, despite some tendencies toward mediocrity, we feel confident of the future of the free verse movement.

In 1954, I wrote in *al-Adib* that the movement of free verse "will progress in the coming years until it reaches a dead end, but today it is at its peak. No one is responsible, and certainly not the movement itself, if poets with little talent or education write deplorable poetry on these free verse models."[16]

That was eight years ago, and I see now that the forecast is coming true. If it is appropriate for me to make a new prophecy about the position of literature in the Arab world today, I would say that the free verse movement will reach a point of ebb in the coming years and that many of those who have answered its call will reject it. This does not mean that the movement will die. Free verse will continue as long as Arabic poetry continues and as long as there are human feelings. The extremes which we see now will resolve into more solid stability, and in the long run Arabic literature will benefit from the movement. As for the poets who were victims of the pitfalls of free verse (and for every movement it seems there must be victims), the credit accruing to them will lie in the fact that they kept Arabic poetry from plunging over the precipice completely and disintegrating into chaos. They gave us clumsy examples of a poetry groping for new goals, but these examples saved us from falling into similar pitfalls and these poets have thus served as the unknown saviors of contemporary Arab poetry.

[*The following two poems illustrate some of Nazik al-Mala'ikah's own achievements, using free verse methods she discusses in her essay.— Eds.*]

The night asks who am I?
    I am its secret—anxious, black, profound
    I am its rebellious silence
    I have veiled my nature, with silence,
    wrapped my heart in doubt
    and, solemn, remained here
    gazing, while the ages ask me,
                  who am I?

The wind asks who am I?
    I am its confused spirit, whom time has disowned
    I, like it, never resting
    continue to travel without end
    continue to pass without pause
    Should we reach a bend
    we would think it the end of our suffering
                  and then—void.

Time asks who am I?
    I, like it, am a giant, embracing centuries
    I return and grant them resurrection
    I create the distant past
    From the charm of pleasant hope
    And I return to bury it
    to fashion for myself a new yesterday
                  whose tomorrow is ice.

The self asks who am I?
    I, like it, am bewildered, gazing into shadows
    Nothing gives me peace
    I continue asking—and the answer
    will remain veiled by a mirage
    I will keep thinking it has come close
    but when I reach it—it has dissolved,
                  died, disappeared.

[Nazik al-Mala'ikah, "Who Am I?" from Mounah A. Khouri and Hamid Algar, eds. and trans., *An Anthology of Modern Arabic Poetry.* Copyright © 1974 by the Regents of the University of California. Reprinted by permission of the University of California Press.]

The Viper

Where shall I go?
I'm weary of the ways,
I'm bored with the meadows
And with the persistent, hidden enemy
Following my steps.

Where can I escape?
The trails and roads that carry
Songs to every strange horizon,
The paths of life,
The corridors in night's total darkness,
The corners of the bare days . . .
I've wandered along them all,
With my relentless enemy behind me,
Keeping a steady pace, or sitting firmly
Like the mountains of snow
In the far north,
Fixed like stars
In eyes from which sleep has fled
(Flung by the hand of sadness
Into the wound of insomnia)
Fixed the way time is fixed
In that hour of waiting.

Which way can I turn?
Whenever my feet try to flee,
To climb over the mountain's peak,
My enemy gives back to me
What the day's efforts have destroyed:
The fetters of memory.
I do not ask freedom from my fetters,
For what freedom can there be
While my frightful enemy's eyes
Spit out autumn
On a soul that longs for spring?
And there, behind the wisping fog
Lies that horrible viper,
That ghoul! What liberation can come
While the shadow of his hand
Veils my cold forehead?

Where can I escape?
My enemy's hateful, hooded eyelids
Cast across my path
The cloud of an unbearable, dead tomorrow.

Where shall I go?
What bend in the road can I find
To separate me forever from my merciless enemy?
He scoffs at my beseeching,
He does not seem to hear my weeping,
And he laughs cynically at my terrible bewilderment.

Where, where can I escape?
Where can I go
On my constant monotonous flight?
My enemy does not answer,
He no longer responds to my fearful call.
And why should I cry, or call?
Is there any refuge near or far?

I will travel behind the sky
Past the frontiers of hope,
And suddenly one evening
I will hear the sound.
"Go ahead! Go ahead!
This is a lost road
Beyond the boundaries of place.
Here you will not be troubled by the viper's murmur
For this is a remote labyrinth,
Perhaps fashioned by an ancient hand
For a strange-natured prince.
Then the prince died and the trail was left
To the twitching hands of total loss."
I hear the sound all over the fields
And I go on.
Perhaps I shall wake here
From the blackness of my constant shameless nightmare.
Perhaps my enemy will lose his way.

Oh, how beautiful it is to walk
Without those deadly steps behind me,
Their frightening echoes faint and dying
Along my tortuous, twisting way.
He will never come.
No, he won't come.
He won't come.

But I hear . . . yes, a laugh full of hatred.
He has come.
Why should I go on?
I will say goodbye to my brief dream of freedom,
And yet, carrying its cold form with me,
I find I must go on.

So I will go on,
And my merciless, hidden enemy
Will follow me along each new road,
Past every evening,
And in the sorrowful black nights
He will be there.
I see him now on the distant horizon,
Looking at me
By the light of the moon,
With my unknown future,
My distant yesterdays.

Where, where can I escape
From my relentless enemy?
He is like destiny,
Eternal, hidden, everlasting,
Eternal,
Everlasting.

[Nazik al-Mala'ikah, "Al-If'wan," in *Shadaya wa-Ramad* (Beirut: al-Maktab
al-Tijari, 1959). Translated by the Editors.]

Notes

1.   Free verse, in English prosody, has been defined as "verse, which, although more rhythmic than ordinary prose, is written without rhyme" (M. H. Abrams, rev., *A Glossary of Literary Terms*, p. 39). The term means something rather different in Arabic poetry, as is indicated by the essay which follows.

2.   I composed it in October 1947, and it was published in the literary magazine *Majallat al-'Urubah* in Beirut, December 1947. The magazine commented on the poem in the same issue. I wrote this poem to express my feeling toward Egypt during its cholera epidemic. I tried to express the sounds of the horses' hoofbeats as they dragged the carriages full of dead bodies through the streets, the victims of the plague in the Rif of Egypt. The necessity of expressing this feeling led me to discover free verse.—N.M.

3.   "In the traditional *gasidah* [Arabic poem], each line must consist of an exact number of feet (*tafa'il*), four, six, or eight, which the poet may not increase or decrease throughout his poem. Also, each line must be divided into two equal and balancing hemistiches (*shatrani*). Finally, all lines of the poem must end with exactly the same kind of rhyme, built upon the same rhyming letter" (Mohamed al-Nowaihi, "The Battle of the New Poetry," *Texas Quarterly* 9, no. 2 [Summer 1966]: 148). Very simply put, such poems exhibit terminal rhyme of the pattern *aabacada*, i.e., an enclosed couplet followed by open couplets.

4.   In Arabic, *al shi'r al-hurr*, that is, meters or combinations of meters chosen by the poet himself. As Mounah A. Khouri has stated, "al-Mala'ikah advocated the need for a free verse, in which the meter is based upon the unit of the *taf'ilah* (foot) and the freedom of the poet is secured through his right to vary the *taf'ilat* or the lengths of his lines as he feels most appropriate for the expression of his message" (Mounah A. Khouri and Hamid Algar, eds. and trans., *An Anthology of Modern Arabic Poetry*, p. 16).

5.   An earlier, traditional poet. Abu Abd al-Rahman al-Khalil ibn Ahmad al-Farahidi al-Uzdi (A.D. 718 or 719–791 or 792) was a well-known man of letters of Basra, honored as a grammarian and lexigrapher. Although not a poet himself, he established rules of Arabic prosody and set meter and rhyme patterns which are still used by poets today.

6.   In most classical Arabic poetry, each line of the poem has its own unity. See Ibn Khaldun, *The Muqaddimah: An Introduction to History*, 3:381–382.

7.   Badr Shakir al-Sayyab, "The Grave-Digger," in *Haffar al-Qubur*, p. 3.

8.   'Abd al-Wahhab al-Bayyati, "Stray Shadows," *Majallat al-Adib*, September 1952, p. 41.

9.   Buland al-Haydari, "My Friend," in *Songs of the Dead City*.

10.   'Abd al-Wahhab al-Bayyati, "The Game Is Ended," *Majallat al-Adib*, October 1952.

11.   Badr Shakir al-Sayyab, "In the Dark Village," in *Legends*.

12.   Shadhil Taqah, "Harvest of Fire," in *The Last Evening*.

13.   Al-Sayyab, "The Grave-Digger."

14.   Badr Shakir al-Sayyab, "The Last Rendezvous."

15.   Buland al-Haydari, "Attempt," *Majallat al-Adib*, July 1952, p. 16.

16.   Nazik al-Mala'ikah, "The Free Verse Movement in Iraq," *Majallat al-Adib*, January 1954.

References

Al-Nowaihi, Mohamed. "The Battle of the New Poetry." *Texas Quarterly* 9, no. 2 (Summer 1966): 148–157.

Ibn Khaldun. *Muqaddimah: An Introduction to History*. Translated by Franz Rosenthal. 2d ed. Bollingen Series, no. 43. Princeton: Princeton University Press, 1969.

Khouri, Mounah, and Hamid Algar, eds. and trans. *An Anthology of Modern Arabic Poetry*. Berkeley: University of California Press, 1974.

Norton, Dan S., and Peters Rushton. *A Glossary of Literary Terms*. Revised by M. H. Abrams. New York: Holt, Rinehart & Winston, 1957.

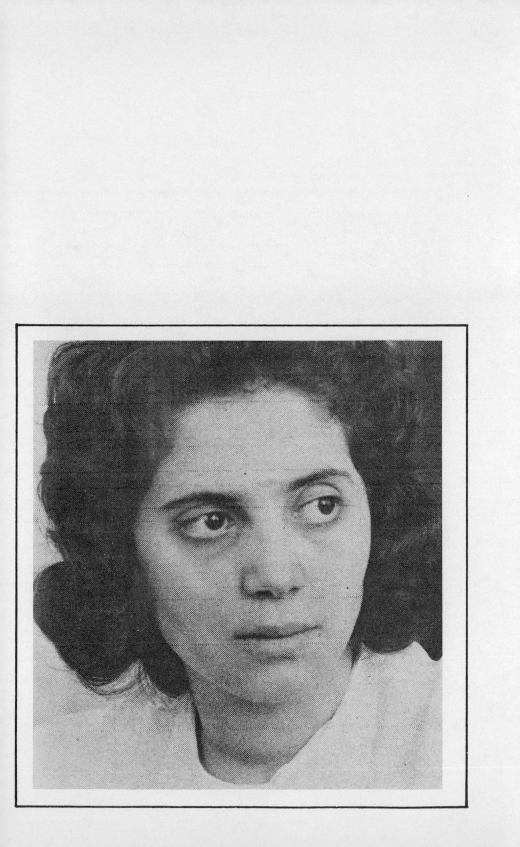

خلقتم مني شخصية
رحتم تحاسبوني ع

كان في مرادي ان
ولكن معرك الجزا

16

Jamilah Buhrayd

جميله بوحيرد

Legendary Algerian Hero

A.D. 1937–

**Two Interviews: January 8 and 15, 1971
by Walid 'Awad for <u>Al-Hawadith</u>**

Nations need legends, we are told. People need heroes to look up to, someone great, someone who transcends the events of daily life. Yet the hero, himself, becomes isolated from other people, as he is lifted to an eminence which no ordinary human attains. Even the great philosophers and poets have been placed, by their contemporaries, in situations of which they were not a part. As the years passed, history put words into their mouths which they never uttered.

But what about living legends? How can heroes, who live on after the legend, co-exist with living people? This was the question that opened my meeting with Jamilah Buhrayd, the Algerian hero whose name is associated with the Algerian revolution, the revolution of the million martyrs.

I was sitting with Jamilah Buhrayd in the lobby of the Phoenician Hotel in Beirut, during her recent visit to Lebanon. I must introduce her by giving my impressions as a man.

Photos: Jamilah Buhrayd before the revolution, 1950's, and later, 1970's

Age: 34. Figure: good, well proportioned. Coloring: skin almost fair; a rosy, clear complexion. Hair long, black, and glossy. She wore tight trousers, a long-sleeved high-necked gray wool sweater. And around her neck a gold chain with a Koran at the end of it. For Jamilah is religious. Her faith is deeply rooted. This at least we know from the volumes that have been written about her. The first book was done by Jacques Ferjis, then her lawyer, now her husband; titled simply *Jamilah Buhrayd*, it was published in French.

Jamilah herself does not read or write Arabic. French is the only language in which she can converse with people who do not understand the rapid Algerian dialect of Arabic. But those who know the nature of Algeria under French imperialism will find an excuse for Jamilah's lack of her native language.

"Arabic," explains Jamilah, "was not the first language in my school in Algiers, L'Ecole Daudivan. The first language was French; after that in importance came German, and Italian, and, finally, Arabic. I feel ashamed of myself when I sit down to write a letter to an Arab friend, for, if I tried to write in Algerian dialect, I would have difficulty choosing the letters. So I end up writing in French."

Jamilah and I conversed in French. I was still thinking about heroes and I addressed her as a hero, thinking this would please her. But she shook her head in a surprised way and said, "Me? A hero? Who told you that?"

I said, "I have read the poems, the books that have been written about you, the defense of your lawyer, Jacques Ferjis."

"Oh," she said, "don't call him Jacques. Call him Mansur. That's his name now."

"Sorry," I answered, "Mansur."

She smiled and said, "Those writers you speak of, they gave me titles I don't deserve. In those days heroism was a national duty, assigned to all Algerians."

I answered, "Now I can add one more virtue to those the historians have given you: humility."

"Oh," said Jamilah, breaking suddenly into Algerian dialect which I could barely understand, "I swear I'm not a hero. Nothing. The hero is Algeria. As for me, well, I was only one person in a large group. The leader of our group in the Qasbah district of Algiers would assign each of us a job to be done in a certain place at a certain time. And we would do it. My job was to plant bombs. I carried death with me in my handbag, death in the shape of time bombs. One day I was supposed to put a bomb in a café managed by a Frenchman. I did it. I was unlucky. I fell into their hands. They arrested me. They locked me in a cell."

I said, "Perhaps the heroism lay not in throwing the bomb but in your endurance of the worse kinds of torture to extract the names of your comrades, like 'Ali 'Ammar. And you didn't give them the names. Perhaps that was the heroism."

Jamilah was silent. She looked down and covered her face with her right hand. The mention of her comrades seemed to cause her pain.

Jamilah was trying to hide tears. But she controlled herself and said, "You keep asking about heroes. Well, I will tell you from my own memories about 'Ali 'Ammar. He and a nineteen-year-old girl called Hasibah Bu 'Ali and an eighteen-year-old boy were all members of our cell, the highest in ranks of the underground movement of the Fronte de Liberation Nationale (FLN) in the city of Algiers. General Lacoste, the Frenchman assigned to destroy us, had made a map of the places where the movement was known to have been. One by one, he discovered the hiding places. This particular day, a shoeshine boy who worked with us heard that Lacoste had located the headquarters of our cell, in a house in the Qasbah. He rushed to tell us and the three—'Ali, Hasibah, and the other boy—hid in an opening in the wall. Lacoste's men came into the house; they knew the three were hiding but did not find the wall. So they put a time bomb in the house and over their megaphones they announced that the rebels had seven hours to surrender or the house would be blown up. And everyone cleared out of the house, the children and the families, and the hours ticked by, but the three behind the wall preferred death to surrender. You ask me about heroes. They were heroes."

This time her eyes did fill with tears, eyes that were big and luminous, just as the poet Nizar Qabbani described them, "like two candles of the temple." Jamilah's tears spilled over, she tried to control herself once more, and I quickly changed the mood by asking, "Did you read Nizar Qabbani's poem about you?"

Jamilah said, "I've heard of it."

I was somewhat surprised. "That's all? You've just heard of it?"

"I told you I can't read Arabic," said Jamilah. "But people have read it to me."

"Shall I recite some of the lines to you?"

"If you like."

"Here is how the poem begins:

Jamilah Buhrayd.
Jamilah Buhrayd.
Cell number 19.
In the military prison of Buhran.
And the age is 22."

Jamilah interrupted me. "My cell wasn't number 19. The poet was wrong."

"What was the number of your cell then?"

She smiled. "Well, actually I don't remember, but it wasn't 19, I'm sure of that."

I tried to explain what Nizar was doing in his poem. "You see, Nizar Qabbani wanted to complete a metaphor, a picture, and number 19 must have fit into his picture. He wasn't exactly trying to be a mathematician."

She straightened up and leaned forward. "Yes, perhaps," she answered, "but don't you see, my friend, Nizar Qabbani and the others who wrote about my case, they created a legendary sort of figure that's hard for me to recognize as me. Jamilah of the writers and poets, the one you made a movie about, is one thing; Jamilah the real person is something else."

"Not a legendary figure?"

"Not exactly," she said. "I can't help but smile when I look at that legendary figure called Jamilah. Who is she? Where does she live? What does she think about? I don't know. Perhaps she lives only in books. As for Jamilah whose address is Shakespeare Street, Algiers, and who is married and is the mother of three children, she's really just an ordinary human being." She stopped. "Luckily, the poets didn't spoil that Jamilah's life and happiness, like they sometimes do to legendary figures. But I'm not that figure. I'm me, Jamilah, the Jamilah that God, not the poets, created."

"What about the prison of Buhran's Jamilah?"

"A legend. A legend."

"But we love that Jamilah. We don't want to give her up. She's part of our struggle. She's one of our heroes."

"All right," Jamilah said. "That's fine. But please don't keep calling me a hero. The word's too big for me."

I changed the subject. "Tell me about your early life."

"Well, I went to school when I was six. I thought I was French, for we learned French lessons from French teachers and we memorized French poems. I used to come home and shout out my lessons, that France was my country, the Gauls were my ancestors, just as they were the ancestors of the French. My mother knew better of course; she knew who owned the land of Algeria and who were our real grandparents; but my mother spoke no French and so she did not understand what I shouted out all day long. Then . . . well, when I got older I dreamed of becoming a seamstress. That was my ambition in life."

"Seamstress? Jamilah Buhrayd a seamstress? It seems unbeliev-able. How could you move so easily from an atmosphere of silk and velvet to one of gunpowder and brutality?"

Jamilah bent her head, and now, for the first time, I noticed the mark of a deep scar on her forehead.

"Well," she said, "you have to think about the early period, before the 1954 revolution, and then the period of revolution, those ten years, as a second period. When I talk about Jamilah the seamstress I'm talking about the early period. All the French schools in Algeria were like mine; they taught us with the assumption that we were French. Paris was the capital, the mother of us all. The French parliament was our parliament, Vincent Auriol was our president, the French flag was our flag. Algeria? At that time, it didn't exist. It was *French* Algeria. And we carried around our French identity every day in school. It wasn't easy to get rid of that identity; we'd had it all our lives." Jamilah began to laugh. "You know, my friend, I promised myself I wouldn't discuss the past with you today. And here I am doing it!"

"Why not?" I answered. "You accuse the writers and poets of imagining you the way it pleases them. The truth is lost. Why can't we go back and search for that reality? Remember, Jamilah, there is a whole generation of Arab boys and girls who have grown up with the legend of Jamilah. Not just in Algeria, either. These are the young people who demonstrated in the streets in the late fifties, marching to the French embassies in all the Arab capitals, carrying banners, 'Set free Jamilah!' 'Jamilah Buhrayd, the Arab Joan of Arc!' Can the real Jamilah Buhrayd really ask us to forget all that? Can you tell us it's all a deception? Or can't you tell us the way it was, so we can see the reality, too, as you do?"

Jamilah looked at me for a long moment, then she began to speak. "Yes," she said. "I will try and explain how it began for me. When I was very small, seven or eight in the vocational school where I wanted to learn to be a seamstress, my uncles were always being questioned by the authorities. I didn't know why. I only knew that my mother was always anxious about her brothers and delighted to see them when they dashed into our house in the Qasbah, even though she would weep and tell them how afraid she was for their safety. I didn't really understand what was going on, why my father, a peaceful businessman, was so different from my uncles. They were involved in the struggle for independence, even then. But I didn't know that. I was the only girl in the family with five brothers. I was much influenced by my mother, who devoted all her life to caring for us." Jamilah paused, then added, "Maybe that's why I wanted to learn to sew, so I could help my mother make our clothes, my brothers' and mine. There were so many of us."

"Did you want to finish your training in Paris?"

"Paris? Why Paris?"

"Because Paris is the capital of fashion design."

Jamilah's face changed. "It was the capital of imperialism."

"So you were affected by the fever, too, that was going around Algeria, then, the fever of independence from France?"

"Yes," she said simply. "When I was fifteen, I guess, I began to realize that there was something else besides this French identity which I had had all along. There was something called Algerian identity; it was different, it was ours, but we had no real picture of it. I don't know exactly when I began to realize about a freedom, independence, but I think it was the death of my friend Aminah that changed me, from Jamilah the schoolgirl with long braids who wanted to be a seamstress, to a . . ." Here Jamilah suddenly broke down. I realized that the fighter Jamilah sat before me, weeping, and I could not help her. And I did not want to force her to go on, for she could not. But the reader should remember the story of Aminah, one of the group working under 'Ali 'Ammar, the engineer who made the bombs. Like Jamilah, Aminah carried bombs in a fashionable French handbag and the police guards thought she was going shopping or to meet a friend. But one day she was discovered and she took poison rather than risk the torture we had heard about. But this time, also, the massacres in the Qasbah had taken place. Jamilah's mother and father were dead, as well as her uncle Shaykh Mustafa Buhrayd. This was the period when the violence was increasing, when the soldiers were scouring the Qasbah looking for the persons who were involved in the deadly cycle of bomb throwing which panicked the whole city of Algiers and which forced the French government to recall some officers and to send out General Lacoste, a former hero of the Resistance, to break the Algerian underground movement. Until this time Jamilah had not been active in the FLN, except to collect contributions and distribute leaflets. Her uncles, however, had always been active. Now all her neighbors were active. Why shouldn't she suddenly become more active, too?

In her confession, Jamilah stated that with her own hand she had put a bomb in the Bar Simone when the Bocas Band was playing and French soldiers and their girl friends were dancing. But, when she was arrested, she was not carrying a bomb. She was returning from a mission she had just completed with a number of her comrades, including Jaffar, whom the French call the "Wolf of the Qasbah" because he was the most accurate and the most elusive of the bomb throwers.

That day the smoke of the explosion was behind Jamilah. She was on her way to her uncle's house in the Qasbah when she heard the soldiers calling her. She realized that her only chance lay in escape. The shadow of the prison of Qal'at Barbarossa lay ahead of her on the citadel of the city; the imperialist soldiers were behind her. She walked faster, but a single shot from one of the soldier's guns caught her in the shoulder and she found herself falling down onto the ground, with blood spreading over her clothes. The soldiers didn't call her Jamilah. They called her Layla. Every brunette Algerian girl was called Layla by the French soldiers. Jamilah was taken to Barbarossa prison and interrogated. Where did you get the bomb, they said. Who gave it to you? Who was with you at the Bar Simone? (This was the explosion designed to assassinate Officer Bayard, who had led the massacre in the Qasbah.) Did you know Jaffar? Who is Jaffar's leader? The officers questioned her repeatedly while the bullet fragments were removed from her shoulder by a French doctor. Jamilah said in her confession that she did not know what she replied. They tortured her, off and on, for seventeen days, and she does not remember what she said. All she was sure of was that she did not betray a single one of her comrades' names.

By now Jamilah had dried her eyes and said, "You know, my friend, there were thousands of Jamilahs, just like me. They all moved, like me, from the Qasbah to the French quarter. Carrying bombs in their handbags and throwing them into cafés. I'm not really sure why all the publicity ended up centering on me. For there were many women in the prison with me, subjected to the worse kinds of torture, and they didn't betray their comrades either. Each of them deserves pages and pages from the poets. All of us, all of us Jamilahs were parts in the whole. Individuals don't make a cause, you know. It's the principle that you believe in. Our aim was revolution, our aim was independence. We won both!"

I said, "But they tortured you horribly; they put electrodes on your body. This is what the Arab intellectuals said, when they presented your case before the liberal French public."

"I asked you not to dwell on the painful past. Please."

"The past, yes. But not the reality."

She nodded slowly. "Well, perhaps it was advantageous for our cause to exaggerate my days in the prison. Didn't it move the French liberals?"

"Yes, it did, and Jacques Ferjis was one of them."

"Not Jacques. His name is Mansur."

"Sorry," I answered.

"You see, Mansur is not really French any more than I am. He was born on the island of Union, near Madagascar, and he has French citizenship just as I did. He says what brought him to my trial and finally to my side was his outrage at such atrocities being committed in the name of France."

We paused a moment, then I said, choosing my words carefully, "They say that when you left the prison, you were half dead."

Jamilah smiled a little, "And how do you find me now?"

"As beautiful as your name." [The name Jamilah means "beautiful" in Arabic.]

"Am I half dead then?"

"No, of course not. You look in perfect health."

"Except for the fact that I am the mother of three children, which keeps me busy, I'm just fine. You know, my oldest, Nadyah, is eight. I adopted her, for her father was a martyr who died in the revolution."

"And the second?"

"That's Maryam. She's four and a half."

"Now I can see that the poets were a little bit right," I put in.

"How?" asked Jamilah.

I repeated some more lines of Nizar Qabbani's poem.

A ewer for water
A prison guard
And a pair of hands folded on the Koran.
In the morning light
A woman sits
Repeating, in a whispery voice,
Verses with a melancholy sound
From the surahs of Maryam
And al-Fatihah.

Jamilah said, "Well, that part is true. I was praying. But I didn't memorize the surahs of Maryam. I wish I could have, but I didn't."

I said, "Tell me about your third child."

"We called him Ilyas."

This name surprised me a little, for it is a Christian name and Jamilah is a Muslim. So I asked whether this name was given because of a vow Jamilah took before the boy was born or whether her husband had perhaps chosen the name.

Jamilah objected. "Come on, my friend. You should know that Ilyas is the name of one of the old prophets before Islam. My marriage to a Christian has nothing to do with it."

"And your children. How are they brought up?"

"As Muslims, as Arabs, as nationalists."

"And are they aware of your case?"

Jamilah said again, "I am not a *case*. Please. I simply played a small part in one period of the Algerian struggle."

"Do your children understand that period?"

"Yes," said Jamilah. "When I explain it to them they understand."

"Well," I added, "it's not strange to find a nationalist kind of child rearing in Jamilah's house."

"It's the same kind of house my husband was brought up in," she said quickly. "His family was by nature sympathetic to our struggle, and he remembers this, since he was a boy, long ago, in Africa."

I prepared to say goodbye. "You know," I said, "I don't want to give up my legend of Jamilah."

"Oh," she said, "down with legends, my friend! They have done enough to impede our progress already. Just remember, those of us who took part in the struggle, we perish. But it is Algeria who remains."

We shook hands.

"Write to me," she said. "My address is Shakespeare Street, Algiers."

I wanted to say, but to whom shall I write? Jamilah the legend or Jamilah the ordinary human being? Jamilah the Joan of Arc of the Arabs or Jamilah the mother of three and the wife of a Marxist lawyer? "Every person is only a small part of a whole, the cause," she had said. Was Jamilah then a Marxist? But what about the Koran she wore around her neck?

She was waiting. We were standing in the lobby of the Phoenician Hotel in Beirut and other people were milling about us.

I said, "Do you think heroism is inherited? Is it transmitted through mother's milk?"

"Oh, no," said Jamilah. "It's born of events, it's created in the middle of battles."

We said goodbye. But I did not tell her that I would write to her as Jamilah the legend. For I am from the east, and the east is a land which is nourished on legends and whose history itself is a legend.

January 22, 1971
by Khawlah Qal'aji for <u>Al-Hawadith</u>

Jamilah said, "There are certain incidents I can't forget, for they are beautiful, and their beauty comes from courage and belief and determination. It's hard to go back ten years. Really one musn't spend one's time discussing incidents and events of the past deciding which were turning points in the revolution, for now we are building a new country and we need to concentrate on that. Still, there is one incident I will remember until the day I die. That happened in prison. There were thousands of us in that prison, men and women. We would be arrested, put in the cells, and taken out now and then and tortured. Some died under torture. Some would be carried out to the courtroom for their trials. Some came back. Some did not. One morning two judges and the head of the prison passed my cell. I did not know why. They went through the long corridors of the prison, until they came to the cell of a man who had been sentenced to death that morning. He was to be moved to a special part of the jail. He was far from us, and he wanted to tell us all that he was to die, and he shouted out three times, very loud, 'Allah wa-Akbar [God, he is great!].' And all over the prison from all the thousands of cells, came the answer, 'God is Great! God is great! God is great!' and then the national song of Algeria.

We have rebelled. It's life or death.
And we have determined that Algeria live,
So bear witness to our vow!"

Jamilah wept. "I'm sorry," she said. "I will continue in a moment. . . . Thousands of us singing. You can't imagine how we felt at that moment. We sang to let our brother know we were with him." She dried her tears and said quickly, "Of course, at that moment we didn't cry, either. We didn't know whether we would be sentenced tomorrow or another of us would be arrested and tortured. But, that day, the thousands of us, singing, we were sharing the fate of our brother who was to die for Algeria at that moment. He believed that Algeria would live and be free. He was right. We don't fight now. We remember the fight and try to be worthy of it."

She wiped her eyes. "Now you know why I don't like talking to journalists, for talking about these memories is like a knife in my heart. Let me tell you we lost great men in the fight, men who are still with us in their memories, almost as strongly, as though they were living creatures. Who are they, you ask? Al-'Arabi bin Haydi is one. He was one of the first. There are many like him. I feel honored to have known him and taken part in the revolution with him."

What about the Algerian woman and her place in society today? After the battle for Algerian independence was won, many books were written, accusing Algerian women of retreating from their new freedom into conservatism. Among these books were *The Algerian Woman* by Fadéla M'rabet and *The Woman and Her Relatives* by Germaine Tillion. These two ladies, the Algerian and the French, explored the low status of women in the Mediterranean area. Just as Algeria was once a colony for the French, they said, so woman remains a colony which exists for the good of man. What did Jamilah think?

Jamilah said, "The Algerian woman certainly is not a colony. She exists, she lives, her existence was proved by her performance in battle, and she continues to prove her existence in working to build her country. You can find her everywhere, as a member of parliament, a teacher, an office worker. It's true we don't find as many women in politics as men, but women have always imposed their views in a quieter way without public fuss. I believe the role the Algerian women play today, rebuilding what has been demolished, regaining what has been lost, is as important as the role she played in battle. But I do think that no modern woman in the Arab east has appeared to take the place of such leaders as Mayy Ziyadah, Nazik al-Mala'ikah, Aminah al-Sa'id, and Bint al-Shati."

What about the younger generation, are they more free, in matters of sex, for example?

Jamilah shook her head. "The young women of Algeria don't have time to discuss the problems of sex right now. We are still in a struggle to make our new country work, to rebuild the destroyed family, to preserve our identity as a nation. In the future, perhaps, we will arrive at a kind of life where men and women relate on a more friendly, equal, and open basis. I hope so."

"And," she continued, "I don't think love is just sex. No. It's everything which is harmonious. It's deep feeling. It's the family. It's the country. That is love. If the younger generation forgets this, it is lost. The values are there. They search for peace, they say. But how can they see peace in a world where there is still Palestine and Vietnam? Palestine and Vietnam will not get their freedom by utopian talking and imagining. They will have to fight. And this action and this justice must come from women as well as men, girls as well as boys."

Today Jamilah works in her neighborhood as leader of a local organization which is striving to improve social conditions. She hopes to finish her studies but not now, for she is busy bringing up her children. "Maybe, when my children are grown up, I will go back to school," she says. "I believe that it's never too late to learn.

"You need to tell your readers," she concluded, "that the role of heroes is not finished at the end of the battle. It's the way they behave in ordinary life, their day-to-day actions, that is important, for this will influence others. Their lives must be based on ideals."

We finished our conversation. Jamilah left me, but I still see her today; I see her spirit in Layla Khalid and in Aminah Bakhur and tomorrow in some other Arab woman. Let us hope that we will meet another Jamilah before long, another young girl who will emerge, in a time of need, from the conscience of a proud nation.

[Translated by the Editors]

17

Jawazi al-Malakim

جوازى الملاكيم

Settled Bedouin Woman

A.D. 1931–

Biographical Sketch by Elaine Hazleton

The Hashemite Kingdom of Jordan, formerly known as Transjordan, is steeped in historical, religious, and political associations. The tiny area occupied by Jordan today, only 37,737 square miles, corresponds roughly to the biblical lands of Ammon, Bashan, Edom, and Moab; today it has a population of about 2,348,000. Conquered and inhabited by a series of invaders over the centuries, Jordan's independence as a country was finally recognized in 1923 by the British, following a series of uprisings by the Bedouin tribes of the area, principal inhabitants of the country. These were the uprisings made famous in the west by T. E. Lawrence in his book *Revolt in the Desert*. The present king, Hussein, terminated the country's longtime relationship with Britain in 1956, and since that time Jordan has relied heavily on aid from the United States, Saudi Arabia, and Iraq. It is bounded by Syria, Iraq, Saudi Arabia, and Israel.

Jawazi and Hassan came from the nomadic tribes of the northwestern Arabian desert. Even in their lifetimes the land they roamed has changed political affiliations several times, but this has only marginally affected the lives of the tribesmen. The range of their tribes was from north-

---

Photo: Bedouin woman

western Saudi Arabia across Jordan and into Syria. Recently the various governments have been trying to limit the nomads to one political state. The land claimed by their tribes now extends from the northern tip of the Gulf of Aqaba about seventy-five miles to the north. It is hilly desert with sparse rainfall only in late winter or early spring. The western edge of it is the Great Rift Valley, which the Arabs call Wadi Araba. The land is useful only for occasional grazing, unless irrigated. The ancient Nabataean capital city of Petra lies in this area.

Jawazi is perhaps not totally typical, since, as the wife of a shaykh, she enjoys a somewhat higher standard of living in Amman than other tribal members. However, her attitudes and values do reflect those of the nomadic peoples, who are gradually disappearing from their traditional camping and grazing grounds, forced by changing patterns of economics to seek their living in other ways.

Jawazi lives in a small house in Amman with her husband, Hassan, and their nine children. But, until she was nearly forty, she lived a nomadic life in southern Jordan, first with her father's tribe, the al-Ghalmijin, and then with the tribe of her husband, the al-Malakim. Hassan, whose father fought with T. E. Lawrence during the Arab uprisings of the 1920's, succeeded to the shaykhship in the early 1960's.

Jawazi speaks with pride of her mother's tribe, the Bani Hassan; her father considered it an honor to marry a girl of the Bani Hassan.

Jawazi, like her husband, Hassan, was born and brought up in a nomad's black tent, skillfully woven from the hair of local goats. Her father's tribe owned goats, sheep, and camels, and thus the family followed the rains and the grasses brought by the rains, in order to graze their animals. In the spring the tribe planted crops and camped close to the fields until the harvest was completed. Then they would follow the grasses once more.

In the tribal society in which Jawazi grew up, each person had his role to fulfill. It was not hard to learn what was expected, explained Jawazi, because each child had several years to watch and learn before he or she was expected to carry a full share or responsibility in the family unit. A boy stayed with his mother until the age of four and then he accompanied his father or another male member of the tribe as they tended stock, planted grain, or made and repaired the weapons and tools used by the tribe. When a boy was older, he was given responsibility for watering the animals and he was expected to learn to defend the tribe and the honor of his family. The family honor was considered of prime importance, and each member's reputation and behavior, of both men and women, reflected on the family unit as well as on the tribe. The social mores associated with an insult to a family or to the tribe were clearly laid out to the young people; Jawazi says she knew them well from the time she was very small. Every member of the family had a strict obligation to behave always in a way to enhance and uphold the honor of the family. If a feud were to begin, only the shaykh could negotiate a settlement.

A girl remained with her mother or older sister until the time of her marriage. Jawazi learned to sew, weave, grind grain, cook, and help care for the younger children. She wore knee-length dresses with trousers under them for warmth in winter. But she did not need to cover her face until after marriage and then only if strangers were present. When a girl was eight or nine she was allowed to accompany the other girls to the well to get water. Often the well was a considerable distance from the nomad camp, and the girls would take donkeys and bring back water in skins, as well as fuel for tribal use. Jawazi remembers what fun it was for the girls to ride the donkeys into the desert and be out of range of the watchful eyes of the tribal elders. The young boys were responsible for watering and keeping track of the animals, which also took them to the well. Thus, it was here that the social life of both boys and girls took place. And, although marriages were arranged by the parents before the couple had formally met, many couples met from time to time at a well. This is what happened with Jawazi and her future husband, Hassan. Even though they were of different tribes, they had occasionally seen each other and talked at a well while performing their duties. They had even arranged to meet at various times before Hassan finally asked his uncle, who knew Jawazi's father, to propose the marriage.

Jawazi and Hassan were married in the early fifties, near the ancient crusader castle of Shubak in southern Jordan. Jawazi was twenty-two, fair skinned, brown haired, brown eyed. She had sewed and worked for many months preparing her wedding finery, and her mother had saved jewelry and coins for her to wear. Like all nomad women after marriage, Jawazi wore coins of gold and silver both as ornament and as a form of personal savings. Her jewelry was her own personal property; her husband would not ask her for it, though she was free to use it as she pleased. The whole tribe respected the right of women to own their jewelry and protected women against the abuse of this right.

The Muslim marriage ceremony in the desert was simple and accompanied by the slaughter of lambs and sheep. A large feast was offered by the bride Jawazi's family. There was singing and dancing to the accompaniment of a *rababa*, a one-stringed instrument made of goatskin stretched over a wooden frame and played with a horsehair bow. Often the feasting for a wedding would continue for several days, as it did with the marriage of Jawazi and Hassan.

For the most part, each tribe kept to some general areas. Not all the families of a given tribe would camp together, and often families from neighboring tribes might camp close by. On festive occasions, such as religious feasts or weddings, many families from several tribes would camp together. These were memorable occasions for the whole family, especially the children. Highlight of the year was the 'Id al-Fitr after Ramadan, the month of fast. New clothes were prepared for each person, gifts of toys and candy were given to the children, and a great feast was prepared. Jawazi was expert at making *kusa mashi* (stuffed squash) and she loved to prepare it for this feast. Since the tribes and families changed camp every few weeks or months, the children were constantly making and renewing friendships. This turnover of relationships made the family unit quite close, since the members relied heavily on each other for emotional support as well as for survival.

After their marriage, Jawazi and Hassan lived with Hassan's family until they were able to afford a black tent of their own. At this time, Hassan was selected for the Desert Legion, an extension of the Jordanian army. The Legion patrols the desert on camelback, and members are carefully selected for their bravery and vigor as well as for their knowledge of camels and the desert. Since Hassan was assigned to the area around Shubak and Petra, he was able to be home frequently with Jawazi and their new young daughter. Soon they were able to assemble their own tent, household effects, and flocks of animals. In fifteen years of living in the tent, Jawazi bore five children.

Life was not easy in the Shirah Mountains, the area where the tribe tended to camp, but nomadic life also had its joys. Jawazi particularly remembers the spring and describes the flowers, the lambs, the green wheat, and the abundant water. Summers were spent in higher areas where the nights were cool and clear. Winter was the hardest time for the nomads. Often the snow would cover the grasses and there was little food for the animals. Also there was the constant danger of a tent collapsing on the family while it slept, burying them all in snow.

Jawazi and Hassan's worldly possessions during this period consisted of a tent, mats to sleep on, rugs and pillows, cooking utensils, and clothing. For cooking over an open fire, Jawazi used large copper pots and she served the food on a brass plate intricately carved with verses from the Koran. The adults ate together from the one large platter, each person using only his right hand to take the food. Hands were washed ceremoniously before and after each meal. The youngest of the adult men brought the water jug, soap, and towel to each person except the children, who ate later.

By this time Hassan was being groomed by his father to assume tribal leadership. He knew he must be acceptable to the members of the tribe, and there was much for him to learn. He accompanied his father to Shubak and to Amman to sell the wheat and barley grown by the tribe, saving some grain for seed and setting some aside on the chance that a bad year might come. Profits from the crops were equally distributed among the tribal families, who trusted the shaykh to arrange for their families' food and their marriages and to settle feuds, if necessary. Before becoming shaykh, Hassan had to have a respectable family of his own. He also had to make the *hajj*, or pilgrimage, to Mecca with his father.

During these years, Jawazi says, she and Hassan could see that their world was changing. In the open desert, where once had been only tribal lands and pastures, borders were being laid down, borders marking off from one another the new nations of Jordan, Syria, Saudi Arabia, and Lebanon. What place did the nomad have in these new countries? A nomad's skills brought little return in the modern marketplace. The wars that Hassan's father had fought with T. E. Lawrence had brought new people and ideas. Hassan could not help but be aware that those men who could communicate with the British were able to obtain more for their families.

Jawazi says that she listened intently to Hassan's stories of Amman, his descriptions of houses with running water and of better schools for children. Hassan told Jawazi that their children, if they were to succeed in this new world, would need a good education. Further, the Jordanian government was trying to persuade the tribes to give up their nomadic life, and it was offering subsidies to tribal people who would settle on farms or in the towns.

Then Hassan's father died and he became shaykh of the al-Malakim. He decided to settle down and moved his family to the small house on a hilltop in Amman where they still live.

Jawazi and Hassan both found it very hard in the beginning to live in the city. Jawazi missed the quiet of the desert. Hassan, too, had been the most respected man in his area, but in Amman he was just another Bedouin, whose neighbors came from many different parts of Jordan. There were also the Palestinians, who deeply resented being expelled from their ancient lands. The Palestinians and Jordanians of the cities spoke a different dialect of Arabic than Jawazi and Hassan, and Jawazi said she could not talk to people at first and felt like a stranger. City customs were also different. The urban Jordanians were much more protective of their girls, and all the women wore veils over their faces. It seemed that Islam was more demanding, Jawazi said, in an urban society. In the desert there was a freedom of spirit, she says, that did not exist in the city. Jawazi missed that freedom.

The family had moved from the tent to their house in Amman in the fall of 1968, and they were comfortable that winter. But the spring of the year was the hardest time of all for Jawazi. She had always loved the spring in the desert, making goat cheese, the lambing, sunrises over the hills, and the smell of flowers everywhere. But, she explained, by spring their children had made friends and were excited over their achievements in the new schools. Jawazi and Hassan realized that the children would not be happy in the desert again, and, even though they, too, loved the old life, they reminded themselves that they tended to forget the hardships. In the new society, Hassan said, the nomad was bound to be the loser eventually, and so for the sake of their children's future they decided to stay in Amman permanently. Jawazi bore four more children: four boys and five girls in twenty years of marriage. Although Hassan could have taken more wives, he has not done so. The practice of polygamy is needed for the nomadic life, they both feel, but is demoralizing to the woman in the city.

Jawazi and Hassan are both proud of their children. Their oldest child is the first girl of the tribe to go to a university. She graduated from the University of Jordan in June 1976. She speaks Arabic, English, and German and plans to teach school in Jordan. The oldest son plays the bagpipes with the Royal Jordanian Army Band, which received honors in Scotland last year. He is fluent in English, has finished high school, and hopes to study abroad when he has finished his army service. All the other children are in school in Amman except the two youngest, who are still at home with their mother.

Jawazi never went to school or received any formal education, but she is a proud and wise person. She explained that she wished the world to understand the value of the nomads' customs; they may be different from other customs, but they, too, are important, she says. She wants her children to love God and to be proud of their Bedouin heritage, but she wants them also to be flexible enough to fit into the world as they find it today. She does not expect her daughters to cover their heads or to follow customs of tribal dress; she says she wants them to be comfortable with their peers but at the same time remember and be proud of who they are. Both Jawazi and Hassan state that they expect to have some control over whom their children marry, and they are preparing dowries for their daughters.

Hassan and Jawazi are not rich, but they are moderately comfortable in their little house. In addition to the government subsidy, Hassan serves on the shaykhs' council to King Hussein of Jordan. As shaykh, he manages the tribal affairs, which also brings him a little income. He plays the *rababa* and sings Arabic poems; he even receives small royalties from records he has made of his music. He has had some traditional education and has also studied English at the British Council in Amman. Currently he is compiling a book of familiar Bedouin poems passed down orally for generations, and the Antiquities Service of Jordan gives him a small retainer to keep recording this literary heritage of his tribe.

Jawazi and Hassan continue to maintain many of their tribal customs. Guests are immediately served, first, with hot, sweet mint tea and, later, with Arabic coffee. They do not drink or serve alcohol nor do they eat pork, but they seem tolerant of those who do. Although the children all wear western-style clothing, Jawazi still wears a long dress, and Hassan wears his traditional garments, the *thobe* and the *kuffiyah*, and fingers his *misbahah* as he drives his Volkswagen bug around the city of Amman.[1]

Since she does not feel comfortable in short dresses or slacks, Jawazi sees no reason to wear them. She does not cover her face but often wears a scarf over her head, as she did in the desert, when she goes out in public.

Today many families of the al-Malakim have partially settled down around Shubak and Petra. They farm the same land every spring. Members of the tribe come regularly from the countryside to visit Hassan and Jawazi in Amman, and Hassan returns their visits. One of Hassan and Jawazi's sons will probably succeed his father as shaykh of the tribe. Hassan and Jawazi want him to be well educated so he can deal effectively with those in power, in order to protect the land and better the position of the tribe in the rapidly changing society of Jordan.

Note

1.   The *thobe* is a long full garment made like a shirt; the *kuffiyah* is a head scarf worn by men; the *misbahah* is the Muslim rosary, used for prayer.

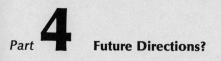

Part **4**   **Future Directions?**

18

Layla Ba'labakki

ليلى بعلبكى

Modern Lebanese Novelist

A.D. 1936–

Layla Ba'labakki was born in 1936 in southern Lebanon into a traditional Muslim family of the Shi'ite sect. She interrupted her university education to work as a secretary in the Lebanese parliament. Her first novel, *I Live*, was published in 1958, translated into French and other European languages, and compared by critics to the work of Françoise Sagan. She has also published a second novel, *The Two Monsters*; a book of short stories, *A Space Ship of Tenderness to the Moon*; and many articles in Beirut's newspapers and magazines. The short story reprinted here led to her trial on charges of obscenity and harming the public morality. Currently, she lives in Beirut and is completing a third novel.

Photo: Layla Ba'labakki

A Space Ship of Tenderness to the Moon/Layla Ba'labakki

When I closed my eyes I was able to see everything around me, the long settee which fills one vast wall in the room from corner to corner; the shelves on the remaining walls; the small table; the coloured cushions on the carpet; the white lamp, in the shape of a large kerosene one, that dangled from a hole in the wall and rested on the tiled floor. Even the windows we had left curtainless. In the second room there was a wide sofa; a table supporting a mirror; a wall-cupboard and two chairs upholstered in velvet. Since our marriage we hadn't changed a thing in the little house, and I refused to remove anything from it.

I opened my eyelids a little as I heard my husband mumble, "It's light and we alone are awake in the city." I saw him rising up in front of the window as the silver light of dawn spread over his face and naked body. I love his naked body.

Once again I closed my eyes; I was able to see every little bit of him, every minute hidden detail: his soft hair, his forehead, nose, chin, the veins of his neck, the hair on his chest, his stomach, his feet, his nails. I called to him to come back and stretch out beside me, that I wanted to kiss him. He didn't move and I knew, from the way he had withdrawn from me and stood off, that he was preparing himself to say something important. In this way he becomes cruel and stubborn, capable of making and carrying through decisions. I am the exact opposite: in order to talk things over with him I must take hold of his hand or touch his clothes. I therefore opened my eyes, threw aside the cushion I was hugging and seized hold of his shirt, spreading it across my chest. Fixing my gaze on the ceiling, I asked him if he saw the sea.

"I see the sea," he answered.

I asked him what colour it was.

"Dark blue on one side," he said, "and on the other a grayish white."

I asked him if the cypress trees were still there.

"They are still there among the houses that cling close together," he answered, "and there's water lying on the roofs of the buildings."

I said I loved the solitary date-palm which looked, from where we were, as though it had been planted in the sea and that the cypress trees put me in mind of white cemeteries.

For a long while he was silent and I remained staring up at the ceiling. Then he said, "The cocks are calling," and I quickly told him I didn't like

[From *Modern Arabic Short Stories*, selected and translated by Denys Johnson-Davies. Copyright © Oxford University Press, 1967. Reprinted by permission of the publisher.]

chickens because they couldn't fly and that when I was a child I used to carry them up to the roof of our home and throw them out into space in an attempt to teach them to fly, and both cocks and hens would always land in a motionless heap on the ground.

Again he was silent for a while, after which he said that he saw a light come on at the window of a building opposite. I said that even so we were still the only two people awake in the city, the only two who had spent the night entwined in each other's arms. He said that he had drunk too much last night. I quickly interrupted him by saying I hated that phrase—I drank too much—as though he regretted the yearning frenzy with which he had made love to me. Sensing that I was beginning to get annoyed he changed the subject, saying: "The city looks like a mound of sparkling precious stones of all colours and sizes."

I answered that I now imagined the city as coloured carboard boxes which would fall down if you blew on them; our house alone, with its two rooms, was suspended from a cloud and rode in space. He said that his mouth was dry and he wanted an orange. I concluded what I had been saying by stating that though I had never lived in any other city, I hated this one and that had I not dreamt that I would one day meet a man who would take me far far away from it I would have died of dejection long long ago. Pretending that he had not heard my last remark he repeated: "I want an orange, my throat's dry." I disregarded his request and went on to say that with him I paid no heed to where I was: the earth with its trees, its mountains, rivers, animals, and human beings just vanished. Unable to wait further, he burst out at me, "Why do you refuse to have children?"

I was sad, my heart was wrung, the tears welled up into my eyes, but I didn't open my mouth.

"How long is it since we married?" he asked. I uttered not a word as I followed him round with my eyes. He stiffened and continued, "It's a year and several months since we married and you've been refusing and refusing, though you were crazy about children before we married; you were dying for them."

He swerved and struck the settee with his hands as he burst out, "Hey chair, don't you remember her entreaties? And you lamp, didn't you hear the sound of her wailing? And you cushions, did she not make of you tiny bodies that she hugged to herself and snuggled up to as she slept? Speak, O things inanimate. Speak. Give back to her her voice which is sunk into you."

Quietly I said that inanimate things don't feel, don't talk, don't move. Angrily he enquired: "How do you know they're dead?" I replied that things weren't dead, but that they drew their pulse beats from people.

He interrupted me by saying that he wouldn't argue about things now and wouldn't allow me to escape solving the problem as I always did. Absent-mindedly I explained to him that the things around me, these very things—this settee, this carpet, this wall, this lamp, this vase, the shelves and the ceiling—are all a vast mirror that reflects for me the outside world: the houses, the sea, the trees, the sky, the sun, the stars and the clouds. In them I see my past with him, the hours of misery and dejection, the moments of meeting and of tenderness, of bliss and of happiness, and from them I now deduce the shapes of the days to come. I would not give them up.

He became angry and shouted, "We're back again with things. I want to understand here and now why you refuse to have children." No longer able to bear it, I shouted that he too at one time refused to have them. He was silent for a while, then he said, "I refused before we were married, when it would have been foolish to have had one." Sarcastically I told him that he was afraid of them, those others, those buffoons in the city. He used to beg for their assent, their blessing, their agreement, so that he might see me and I him, so that he might embrace me and I him, so that we might each drown the other in our love. They used to determine for us our places of meeting, the number of steps to be taken to get there, the time, the degree to which our voices could be raised, the number of breaths we took. And I would watch them as they secretly scoffed at us, shamelessly slept with the bodies they loved, ate three meals a day, smoked cigarettes with the cups of coffee and carafes of arak, and guffawed as they vulgarly chewed over stories about us and thought up patterns of behaviour for us to put into effect the following day. His voice was choked as he mumbled: "I don't pay attention to others. I was tied to another woman."

Ah, how can I bear all this torture, all this passionate love for him? He used to be incapable of confessing the bitter truth to her, that he didn't love her, wouldn't love her. Choking, he said that it wasn't easy, he wasn't callous enough to be able to stare into another human being's face and say to her, after nine years of getting up each and every day and finding her there, "Now the show's over," and turn his back and walk off. I told him to look at my right hand and asked him if my blood was still dripping from it hot on to the floor? "You were mad," he mumbled, "mad when you carried out the idea. I opened this door, entered this room and saw you stretched out on this settee, the veins of your hand slashed, your fingers trailing in a sea of blood. You were mad. I might have lost you." I smiled sadly as I pulled the shirt up to my chest, my face breathing in the smell of it. I said that my part of the play required that I should take myself off at the end, and the form of absence possible for me, the form I could accept and bear, was a quick death rather than a slow, cruel crawling, like that of the turtle in the film *Mondo Cane* that lost its way in the sands, held in the sun's disc, as it searched for the river-bank. He repeated sadly that he didn't know I was serious about him. I asked him sarcastically whether he was waiting for me to kill myself in order to be sure that I was telling the truth. I told him that I had lost myself in my love for him; oblivious to all else, I slipped unseen, like a gust of wind, through people's fingers, scorching their faces as I passed through the street. All I was conscious of was the weight of bodies, the height of buildings and of his hands. I asked him to draw closer and give me his hand which I craved to hold. He remained standing far off, inflexible, and at once accused me that after all that misery and triumph I was refusing to become pregnant from him, had refused again and again and again, and that from my refusal he understood I no longer loved him.

What? I cried out that he could never accuse me of that. Only yesterday I was stretched out beside him and he gave himself up to deep sleep while I was open-eyed, rubbing my cheeks against his chin, kissing his chest, snuggling up under his arm, searching in vain for sleep. I told him frankly that I was upset by the speed with which he got to sleep, and by my being left alone and awake at his side. He hastened to deny this, saying that he had never been aware of my having remained sleepless. He believed that I dozed off the moment he did. I revealed maliciously that it wasn't the first time he had left me alone. I then related in full yesterday's incident, telling of how he had been asleep breathing quietly, with me stretched close up against him smoking a cigarette, when suddenly in the emptiness of the room through the smoke, I had seen a foot fleeing from under the sheets. I moved my own but it didn't move and a coldness ran through the whole of my body. I moved it but it didn't move. It occurred to me to shout. I moved it but it didn't move. I hurriedly hid my face in his hair. I was afraid. He moved and the foot moved. I cried silently. I had imagined, had felt, had been unable to tell the difference between his foot and mine. In a faint voice he said: "In this age people don't die of love." Quickly seizing the opportunity I said that in this age people didn't beget children. In olden times they knew where the child would be born, who it would be likely to resemble, whether it would be male or female; they would knit it woollen vests and socks, would embroider the hems, pockets and collars of its dresses with coloured birds and flowers. They would amass presents of gold crucifixes for it and medallions with "Allah bless him" on them, opened palms studded with blue stones, and pendants with its name engraved on them. They would reserve a midwife for it, would fix

the day of the delivery, and the child would launch out from the darkness and be flung into the light at the precise time estimated. They
would register a piece of land in the child's name, would rent it a house,
choose companions for it, decide which school it would be sent to, the
profession it would study for, the person it could love and to whom it
could bind its destiny. That was a long, long time ago, in the time of
your father and my father. He asked, "Do you believe that twenty years
ago was such an age away? What has changed since? What has changed?
Can't you and can't I provide everything that is required for a child?" To
soften the blow I explained that before I married I was like a child
that lies down on its back in front of the window, gazes up at the stars
and stretches out its tiny arm in a desire to pluck them. I used to amuse
myself with this dream, with this impossibility, would cling to it and
wish it would happen. He asked me: "Then you were deceiving me?"

Discovering he had changed the conversation into an attack on me so
as to win the battle, I quickly told him that only the woman who is un-
fulfilled with her man eagerly demands a child so that she can withdraw,
enjoy being with her child and so be freed. He quickly interrupted me:
"And you were unsatisfied?" I answered him that we had been afraid,
had not travelled to the last sweet unexplored regions of experience; we
had trembled in terror, had continually bumped against the faces of
others and listened to their voices. For his sake, for my own, I had defied
death in order to live. He was wrong, wrong, to doubt my being madly
in love with him.

"I'm at a loss. I don't understand you," he muttered. I attacked him by
saying that was just it, that he also wouldn't understand me if I told him
I didn't dare become pregnant, that I would not perpetrate such a
mistake.

"Mistake?" he shrieked. "Mistake?" I clung closer to his shirt, deriving
strength from it, and slowly, in a low voice, I told him how scared I was
about the fate of any child we might cast into this world. How could I
imagine a child of mine, a being nourished on my blood, embraced
within my entrails, sharing my breathing, the pulsations of my heart and
my daily food, a being to whom I give my features and the earth, how
can I bear the thought that in the future he will leave me and go off in a
rocket to settle on the moon? And who knows whether or not he'll be
happy there. I imagine my child with white ribbons, his fresh face
flushed; I imagine him strapped to a chair inside a glass ball fixed to the
top of a long shaft of khaki-coloured metal ending in folds resembling
the skirt of my Charleston dress. He presses the button, a cloud of dust
rises up and an arrow hurls itself into space. No, I can't face it. I can't
face it.

He was silent a long, long time while the light of dawn crept in by his face to the corners of the room, his face absent-minded and searching in the sky for an arrow and a child's face. The vein between his eyebrows was knotted; perplexity and strain showed in his mouth. I, too, remained silent and closed my eyes.

When he was near me, standing like a massive tower at a rocket-firing station, my heart throbbed and I muttered to him that I adored his naked body. When he puts on his clothes, especially when he ties his tie, I feel he's some stranger come to pay a visit to the head of the house. He opened his arms and leaned over me. I rushed into his embrace, mumbling crazily: "I love you, I love you, I love you, I love you, I love you." He whispered into my hair: "You're my pearl." Then he spread the palm of his hand over my lips, drawing me to him with the other hand, and ordered: "Let us take off, you and I, for the moon."

June 15, 1964

Officer Adil 'Abd al-Rahim, chief of the Beirut vice squad, summoned the writer, Layla Ba'labakki, to his office and carried out an investigation concerning the subjects and words occurring in the writer's book *A Space Ship of Tenderness to the Moon*. The questioning concerned two sentences:

He lay on his back, his hand went deep under the sheet, pulling my hand and putting it on his chest, and then his hand traveled over my stomach . . .

He licked my ears, then my lips, and he roamed over me. He lay on top of me and whispered that he was in ecstasy and that I was fresh, soft, dangerous, and that he missed me a lot.

The writer replied that her book did not endanger traditions and morality but simply "stated facts that each of us lives." She further explained that she does not consider the word an end in itself but as a means, a means to reveal or uncover the way we face truth in our lives and to help us probe deeply into human problems. She admitted that she wrote the story and stated she would defend every word and every letter.

After the interrogation was completed, the Lebanese author left the office. The disposition of the case was this: the public prosecutor would be asked his opinion in the matter, since the accusation against Miss Ba'labakki, that she had damaged public morality, still stood.

Yesterday (June 14), members of the vice squad embarked on a campaign to confiscate Miss Ba'labakki's books. They visited each bookstore known to carry the book and confiscated the remaining copies.

June 18, 1964

The public prosecutor of the Court of Appeals called the author, Layla 'Ali Ba'labakki, in accordance with item 532 of the criminal law, accusing her of harming the public morality in her book recently published under

[Layla Ba'labakki, *Safinat Hanan ila al-Qamar* (Beirut: al-Maktab al-Tijari lil Tiba'ah wa-l-Tawzi' wa-al-Nashr, 1964). Translated by the Editors.]

the title *A Space Ship of Tenderness to the Moon*. The public prosecutor of the Court of Appeals, Mr. Sa'id al-Barjawi, assigned the case to the court in charge of monitoring publications (Makhamat al-Matbu'at). The trial of Miss Ba'labakki was ordered to begin. Under item 532 the public prosecutor demanded the imprisonment of Miss Ba'labakki for a sentence of one to six months plus a fine of ten to one hundred liras.[1]

June 27, 1964

The Court of Appeals concerned with cases relating to publications opened the case of Layla Ba'labakki, author, under the chairmanship of Judge Adib Afish and with the following members as advisors: Mr. George Najim and Mr. Nadim Marun Abbud. The representative of the public prosecutor's office was Mr. Sa'id al-Barjawi.

At 10:15 A.M. Saturday (yesterday) Miss Layla Ba'labakki arrived in the court, accompanied by her defense lawyers, Mr. Muhsin Salim and Mr. Rashad Salamah. A large group of writers and intellectuals, journalists, and lawyers was also present. The trial began by establishing the identity of the accused, Layla 'Ali Ba'labakki. The general prosecutor read the accusation and asked the presiding judge of the court, Mr. Adib Afish, to ask the accused, Layla Ba'labakki, to reply to the charges. She replied: "I admit frankly that I wrote the book *A Space Ship of Tenderness to the Moon*. I believe its contents do not touch or endanger the public morality. I am surprised at this accusation, especially since nine months have passed since the publication of the book."

Presiding Judge Afish: Does the public prosecutor wish the proceedings of the court to be secret?

Public Prosecutor Barjawi: Yes, Your Honor, I do ask for this, for the sake of the security of the public morality.

Defendant Ba'labakki: Your Honor, I demand that the trial be open to the public, for I believe that the contents of my book do not offend the public morality in any way.

Defense Lawyer Salim: The public prosecutor is fully within his rights to request that the trial be held in secret. But what can be gained by conducting the trial in secret? This is the first time in the history of Lebanese court proceedings and in the history of Lebanese literature that an author, well known not only in Lebanon and in the Arab world but also in Europe, has been tried in a Lebanese court. We ask the honorable court not to accede to the public prosecutor's demand and to consider, before making its decision, the whole issue of the public's right and freedom to know. Freedom for the general public is an idea to which Lebanon has long been devoted, as the court knows. Thus, it is the right of the citizens of Lebanon to have public access to the proceedings of this trial.

Defense Lawyer Salim, continuing: Your Honor, I am not afraid of a secret trial, but I am afraid of the interpretations which public opinion may place on a secret trial. The public will question why Layla Ba'labakki was tried in such a manner. Thus, once more I ask the court to reject the demand of the public prosecutor and to conduct the trial in public.

Public Prosecutor Barjawi: Now that I have heard the request of the defense, I will leave the matter to the court.

Presiding Judge Afish: The court rules that the trial will be conducted in public.

Public Prosecutor Barjawi: The prosecution repeats the original accusation against the defendant and requests a verdict of guilty for the items mentioned previously in the arguments for the prosecution.

Presiding Judge Afish: The court asks the defense to present its arguments.

Defense Lawyer Salim: The defense has a subsidiary demand before presenting the arguments in this case, for this is the first case of its kind and I believe it is important to surround it with all possible safeguards. I ask that a committee be formed of well-known Lebanese intellectuals. These experts would be assigned to read the book under discussion, *A Space Ship of Tenderness to the Moon,* as well as other of the author's books. I believe such a committee would be able to explain better than I that the work under discussion is a work of literature; that its goal is to elevate literature in general and its aims are as far as possible from arousing sexual desire in the reader and thus harming public morality. In the nine months since the book was published, the general public has supported the author, Layla Ba'labakki, despite the fact that people have been divided into two groups on the issue, both for the book and against the book.

Public Prosecutor Barjawi: The prosecution agrees with Defense Lawyer Salim that public opinion is split concerning the book under discussion. But most people of literature have rejected the work on the grounds that it contains some sentences and phrases which arouse sexual desires. Therefore, the public prosecutor agrees to form a committee of well-known intellectuals to inform the court that the author. Layla Ba'labakki, has intended, in her book *A Space Ship of Tenderness to the Moon,* to arouse sexual desire and harm the public morality. Therefore, I repeat the original accusation against the defendant.

Presiding Judge Afish: The court has decided to include the subsidiary demand as falling within the boundaries of the case. Now the court asks the defense to present its arguments.

Defense Lawyer Salim: We ask that the court be recessed for a week so that we may summon witnesses and gather material.

Presiding Judge Afish: I see no reason for introducing witnesses, particularly since the accused, Layla Ba'labakki, has admitted she wrote the book in question.

Defense Lawyer Salim: We ask permission of the court to present five defense witnesses in order to establish the character of our client, Layla Ba'labakki.

Public Prosecutor Barjawi: Your Honor, I ask the court to refuse the demand of the defense to summon witnesses.

Presiding Judge Afish: The court refuses the demand of the defense to bring witnesses. I charge you now to begin your defense.

Defense Lawyer Salim: Your Honor, I respectfully begin by stating first that I believe the office of public prosecution and the office of the defender of public morality committed a grave error in summoning Layla Ba'labakki to their respective offices to question her concerning words and phrases in her book *A Space Ship of Tenderness to the Moon*, which the public prosecutor asserts are offensive to public morality. I submit that it would have been much more humane and much more according to the dignity of their offices and the dignity of my client had she been called before the court of justice (Qasr al-'Adil) to be questioned by one of the investigating justices, rather than being questioned in the police station like one of the ladies of easy virtue who actually do harm the public morality. The public, I submit, is rather bewildered to read in the Lebanese and foreign press that Layla Ba'labakki, an author, an artist, a human being, a creative force, has been treated like a common criminal in her own country. Is it right for such acts to be allowed? People ask what crimes my client is supposed to have committed. Is such treatment just? Second, Your Honor, it is common knowledge that no book can be published until permission has been obtained from the designated authorities. I present here, for your perusal, the papers to prove that my client was granted lawful permission to print and publish the book under discussion, *A Space Ship of Tenderness to the Moon*. Further, I am most surprised that it has taken the public prosecutor nine months, nine months since the book was first published, to institute proceedings against the author and to take upon itself the confiscation of the work.

The defense submits that Layla Ba'labakki, the defendant, was subjected to unjust and illegal treatment. Accordingly, we ask that the charges against her be dropped.

On the issue of the book itself, Your Honor, I would like to remind the court that the defendant is a serious writer. What is a writer? A person who tries to communicate his or her thoughts and emotions to other people through the medium of words. The author or writer is, in a sense, a camera, but one which photographs life with words, creating pictures in which we may see her thoughts and feelings clearly. Thus it is important, Your Honor, for the court to look at this book of two hundred pages as a whole, rather than singling out two sentences in the work as representative and stating that these two sentences alone are harmful to public morality.

Finally, I would like to state that my client, Layla Ba'labakki, belongs to the literary school of realism. She lives her works; she has developed her own methods to depict life and she does this with the literary freedom which we have always enjoyed and which has no boundaries in Lebanon. For all these reasons, therefore, I ask for a verdict of not guilty for my client.

Defense Lawyer Salamah: I, too, reject the claims of the office of the public prosecutor, and I ask for a verdict of not guilty for our client, Layla Ba'labakki.

Presiding Judge Afish: Does the defendant wish to speak?

Defendant Ba'labakki: Yes. I wish to say that I do not consider myself guilty of the accusations or at fault in any way. I had not the slightest intention of offending or harming the public morality. It is true that I write in a realistic manner and I try to delineate the bare facts of life with as much honesty as possible. I would also like to remind the court that the authorities granted me permission to publish the book under discussion, *A Space Ship of Tenderness to the Moon*. Thus I plead not guilty.

[The court was adjourned until Thursday, August 23, at which time the sentencing was scheduled to take place.]

August 23, 1964

The clerk of the court summarized the case in the following manner:

In the name of the Lebanese people, the court of appeals in Beirut, the court in charge of cases concerning publications, is now in session in the Fourth Civil Room.

After examining the papers of this case and after what has been said before this court, the facts may be summarized as follows:

According to the proceedings of the office of public prosecution in Beirut, number 10848, dated June 1964, Layla 'Ali Ba'labakki was accused of writing, at a date not long past, the book *A Space Ship of Tenderness to the Moon,* containing expressions and sentences which are not in accordance with public morality.

In the course of the trial of Miss Ba'labakki, the defense attorneys asked that a committee be formed of well-known intellectuals who would examine the book and give their opinion of it on condition that this opinion would not influence the court. The public prosecutor left this request to the discretion of the court. Accordingly, the court agreed to include this subsidiary demand in the basic proceedings of the case.

Concerning the request to form a committee of intellectuals, the defense first requested the formation of a committee to read the book in question and give their judgment, although the court need not abide by this judgment.

The two defense attorneys, Mr. Salim and Mr. Salamah, presented the arguments for the defense and asked for a verdict of not guilty for their client, the accused Layla 'Ali Ba'labakki. The public prosecutor repeated his original accusation and asked for a verdict of guilty.

Many discussions have taken place in the course of the past two months between the judge and his advisers, the prosecutor and the defense lawyers, and the findings of the court may be summarized as follows: There is no disagreement between the text of the law in such cases and the *ijtihad*.[2] However, the judge and the judge alone retains the right of weighing the facts and exhibits, and the manner of judging the case is left to his discretion, also, relying, if he wishes, on outside opinion in matters requiring knowledge, in this case, artistic knowledge. It was decided that this advisory opinion proceeding should be carried out by one or more specialists, who would appoint the members of said advisory committee, on the basis of artistic qualifications and capacity for objective judgment. This was recorded as Item 278-279 and all that follows is under civil [as opposed to *shari'ah* or Islamic canon] law.

The first matter of business was to investigate whether the defense's demand for an advisory committee was appropriate under the law. Since the defense requested from said committee an opinion beyond artistic evaluation, this could be interpreted as having wider influence. The committee could then be accused of participating in the final verdict, which is not permitted by law. As far as evaluating the book and deciding whether or not the phrases in it constitute a felony—this is to be decided by the court. Thus, the defense demand for an advisory committee of specialists was considered unnecessary and was rejected.

The lawfulness of the accusation. The defendant, Layla 'Ali Ba'labakki, has asked for a verdict of not guilty, alleging that her book *A Space Ship of Tenderness to the Moon* was permitted by the designated authorities to be published and distributed. The book was distributed and sold to

Lebanese and non-Lebanese bookstores and was sold by them. Thus, she considers the confiscation and the charging before the court as illegal. The defense has submitted proof that permission to publish was obtained: photocopies and receipts which show that the publisher abided by item 20 of the law of publications, September 14, 1962, leaving four copies of the book immediately upon publishing with the Office of the Ministry of Culture and Guidance, as specified. Although it is true the author and publisher abided by the letter of the law (item 20 of the publication law), this does not protect them from possible prosecution in the following two instances:

1.   If the book contains any libel or slander of individuals
2.   If the book contains any material which can be construed as a violation of the law of publications, item 56, which controls publications of books

In the first instance, the right of accusation belongs to the individuals allegedly libeled or slandered. In the second instance, the right of accusation belongs to the office of public prosecution. The Ministry of Culture and Guidance does not have the authority to prosecute; that belongs to the office of the public prosecutor. As soon as the public prosecutor's office saw the police report of the interrogation of Miss Ba'labakki, they asked the permission of this court to confiscate the remaining copies of the book. Thus, the confiscation of the book and the accusation of the author and publisher constitute an action within the law and fall within the scope of the powers of the public prosecutor.

Further, the law of publications (56), especially clause 6, states, "It is prohibited to publish any report, book, letter, essay, photography, or news item which is not in accord with public morality"; the accusation by the public prosecutor of June 18, 1964, states that the defendant has written in her book *A Space Ship of Tenderness to the Moon* phrases and sentences which do not accord with public morality. The accusation does not specify the phrases which were so judged, apparently being satisfied to accept the opinion of the police investigating officers, who underlined the allegedly offensive phrases in red ink. The court wishes to state that it also considers those phrases objectionable. Thus, on the basis of all these considerations, and in the light of the original accusation, the three following issues must be discussed before a verdict can be reached:

1.   The concept of public morality
2.   Whether the two sentences, which were underlined in red ink and which read as follows: "He lay on his back, his hand went deep . . ." (p. 53) and "He licked my ears, then my lips . . ." (p. 54), in the author's

book should be singled out or whether the work should be considered as a whole

3.   The purpose of the author in writing such sentences and whether criminal intention exists or not

The concept of public morality. The Lebanese legislature does not give a detailed definition of public morality either in clause 6, item 56, of the law of publications, or in item 532 in the criminal law concerning public morality. General phrases rather than specific details appear, and for good reason, since the law itself and the concepts within the law, such as that of public morality, are subject to change and development according to the time; in this case they are also subject to change and development according to the writer's purpose, the period of time during which he lives, and the reader's receptivity to what the writer sets forth. Thus, in a case like this one, interpretation of the law is left to the wisdom and discretion of the court. The court must debate the merits of the work, view the material from different points of view and try to set it in various perspectives, before attempting to give the work a legal description which would be a basis for pronouncing a verdict of guilty or not guilty on the charge of "endangering public morality."

[At this point there was placed on exhibit a book entitled *Journalism before the Jury,* by Albert Gilles, published in French.]

The consideration of the work as a whole or in part. We have stated already that some phrases in this book have been underlined in red Ink by the police, and the public prosecution accepted this judgment viewed in isolation; on the surface they do indeed appear to be harmful to public morality. But the court is inclined to believe that any artistic work should be viewed in its entirety, rather than in its separate parts. Only in this way can the artist's over-all intention and motive (our third issue) be ascertained.

The author's purpose and intention. Now the court proposed to examine in some detail the stories in the defendant's book *A Space Ship of Tenderness to the Moon* in order to determine whether the author's intention was serious, or whether it was simply to divert the reader and to arouse his sexual desires and thus harm the public morality. First, let us consider the defendant herself, Layla 'Ali Ba'labakki, the daughter of a conservative Lebanese village family, who left her home and traveled to Paris, where she remained for some time, in an environment totally different from that of her own people. As she lived in this strange environment, she observed the peoples' life styles, their confusions, their troubles, their silences. Each day she tried to learn more about this new society, to discover its particular truths. Trained from childhood in letters, coming from a tradition which used words to express enlightened thoughts, Layla 'Ali Ba'labakki was moved to put down on paper the things she had seen and felt in her real and her subsequent imaginary trips to the strange society in Paris, and thus she wrote the book in question, *A Space Ship of Tenderness to the Moon*.

In terms of precedent, the case falls under *Pandecte and Presse*, part 45, page 762, paragraphs 827 and 832, of the legal code. Using this as a basis for discussion, in order to examine the stories of the defendant, the court finds that most of these stories do not seem to have the intention of arousing sexual instincts. On the contrary, the author struggles to picture reality, in its ugliness as well as in its beauty. Her story "The Cat" ("al-Qittah"), for example, is nothing if not a moral tale with a severe lesson that any reader may examine with benefit. Her story "I Was a Mare" ("Kuntu Muhrah") illustrates the different kinds of traditions which are still part of Lebanese culture and cherished as such. These differences in tradition may also lead to tragedy, as the author demonstrates in "Anger Will Never End" ("Lan Yantahi al-Ghadab"). Further, she shows us that learning from human experience may have its dangers, as in "al-Tajribah."

The defense lawyers, Mr. Salim and Mr. Salamah, have pointed out, as the author has done herself, that Miss Ba'labakki considers herself as belonging to the literary school of realism, and perhaps it is these "realistic" phrases which have caused her to be accused of writing things harmful to public morality. The court wishes to state that realism in human life can be traced to the most ancient period in our history, to be more precise, to the moment when man was created by God, in his naked reality, and, later, hid his nakedness with fig leaves. On the whole, the court believes that so-called realistic phrases used by the author are only a means to express a kind of example (*hikma*), as in the lessons or examples we receive from the following works of literature:

1.   The myth of man receiving the Covenant from God, the rainbow in the heavens, and man's unworthiness to receive it
2.   The legend of the isolated cave in the desert (Saw'ar), its walls stained red with blood which stained the entire land of Canaan
3.   The tale of Egypt's Pharaoh, in which his loved one, tempting the Pharaoh to lust, writhes on a bed of Lebanese cedar wood, her naked body fragrant with the scents of the land of Ethiopia
4.   The story of the virgin of Israel, guardian of a dying kingdom, bringing to old age and coldness the warmth of her body . . .
5.   The legend of the rose of Sharun, the lily of the valley . . .

Throughout the ages, poets and men of literature have used realism for their own ends, sometimes abandoning it altogether, more often employing it. This trend can be seen with the poet who, in describing his wanderings, composed the first *mu'alaqah* from which we trace the beginnings of Arabic poetry; then in the work of the youth of Quraysh, who was ruined by lust and self-indulgence. We see it displayed in the work of al-Nawasi [Abu Nuwas], when he celebrates in his *al-Khamriyat* his love for wine; in the verses of the blind poet of the *Dahliz* describing his hours of peacefulness; in Jahiz of the Eyes, called al-Jahiz, whose works reflect self-praise and boasting; by the author of *al-Yatimah* in his *Daliyatihi*;[3] and, finally, in the world-famous tales of Sheherazade, *A Thousand and One Nights*.

This realism that we find throughout the history of literature has, in most cases, been only a method to extract a kind of wisdom, a way of describing the experience of life, a means to reach a worthy aim. Thus, we cannot describe it as "being harmful to the public morality," especially when the intention of the artist is clear, and the ultimate goal one of artistic beauty.

Therefore, after all these points have been considered, the court views the defendant, Layla 'Ali Ba'labakki and her book *A Space Ship of Tenderness to the Moon* as follows: Her intention was to portray, realistically and truthfully, her characters as she saw them moving on the bare stage of life. She gave to acts and emotions their accurate names in order to dramatize the idea which she was presenting. Just as a human being exposes his real self in front of a mirror in order to see clearly, and hopefully improve, its faults and its uglinesses, so does the book in question use realism to help the reader see life more clearly. The stories in question do not arouse sexual instincts or harm public morality. The work is to be seen rather as a serious creative effort, a call to set people free from their narrow environments, a call for all of us to face the naked truth and its ramifications, to see good and evil and to learn to choose between them, not with eyes closed with the trachoma of tradition that has woven a veil of ignorance around us, but with eyes wide open toward the light.

And, therefore, the court finds that, since such efforts do not constitute a crime which is subject to punishment, the court's judgment is that all procedures against the defendant, Layla 'Ali Ba'labakki, should cease immediately.

Presiding Judge Afish: Thus, after listening to all the arguments, we submit the unanimous verdict of the court: to cease procedures against the defendant, Layla 'Ali Ba'labakki, to abrogate the payment of any fine, to overturn the original decision to confiscate the defendant's work, and, finally, to return the confiscated books to their owners.

An honorable judgment, stated before the public and in the pres-

ence of the public prosecution, on this date, August 23, 1964.
[Signed]: Associate Adviser Judge Abbud,
           Associate Adviser Judge Najim, and
           Presiding Judge and President Adib Afish

Notes

1.   One lira equals about 30 cents.
2.   *Ijtihad* is an Islamic legal term meaning, roughly, precedents of past cases.
3.   Famous poems in Arabic are known by their rhyme schemes; here it is *dal*, the letter *d*.

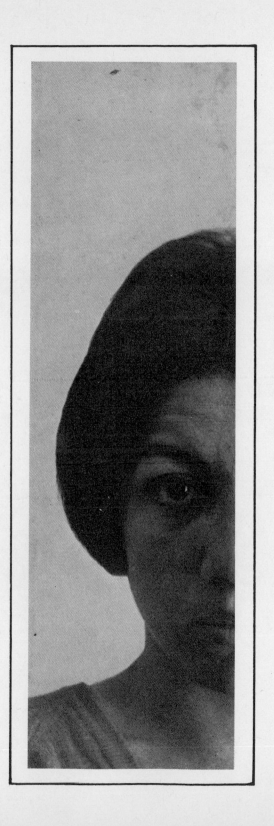

19

Furugh Farrukhzad

فروغ فرخزاد

Modern Iranian Poet

A.D. 1935–1967

Biographical Sketch by Michael C. Hillmann

Poetry for me is like a friend to whom I can freely
unburden my heart. It's a mate who completes me,
satisfies me.

Poetry is like a window which automatically opens
when I go to it. I sit there, I stare, I sing, I cry
out, I weep, I become one with the vision of
the trees . . . on the other side of the window there
is an expanse, and someone hears.

Poetry is a serious business for me. It's a
responsibility I feel vis-à-vis my own being.
It's a sort of answer I feel compelled to give
to my own life.

I don't search for anything in my poems; rather
in my own poems I discover myself.[1]

Photos: Furugh Farrukhzad

If a contemporary European or American poet were to describe poetry in the above terms, there would be nothing novel or striking in the view. But because the author of the quoted statements is Furugh Farrukhzad, an Iranian woman and important contemporary poet, a particular, two-fold significance accrues to them.

First, the promise of personal, intimate poems couched in personal, intimate terms flies in the face of the mainstream of traditional Persian poetry, a basically convention-bound and conservative craft with a thousand-year history. Though Furugh was not a shaping force in modern Persian poetry, which formally came into existence in the early 1920's, she, as a second-generation modernist, entered an arena where the battle lines between the forces of tradition and innovation and past and present are still drawn and the conflict persists.

Second, as a woman in a predominately Shi'ite Muslim society, Furugh's commitment to poetic statements of frankness and self-revelation flies in the face of an equally long standing and just recently challenged tradition of feminine circumspectness, public modesty, and conscious avoidance of attention and competitiveness in a male-dominated society. Furugh may not have been a feminist, but as a free spirit and poet, she was perforce at the forefront of the new consciousness of women in Iran, another continuing conflict of past versus present, religion versus secularism, and traditional mores versus changing attitudes and common sense.

Furugh's corpus of poems, fewer than two hundred, mostly short lyrics, composed during a period of about fifteen years from her school days through 1966, demonstrates the truth and consistency of her view of the nature and function of her craft, and—more importantly—establishes her as a first-rate modern Iranian poet. Thus, her work obviously deserves consideration, first, as poetry of perhaps lasting value.

But, here, in a volume focusing attention on Middle Eastern women and their roles as women in Middle Eastern societies, the critical evaluation of Furugh Farrukhzad's poetry becomes a peripheral concern. Instead, with ten selected poems in translation, a biographical sketch, and an attempt at a brief statement of Furugh's impact upon Iranian society as a person, this article aims at allowing Furugh Farrukhzad, a Middle Eastern woman, to speak.

At twenty, Furugh Farrukhzad published *The Captive,* a collection of forty-four poems composed between 1953 and 1955.[2] The collection featured an important preface by Shuja' al-Din Shafa who, in the course of predicting poetic greatness for Furugh, singles out the following poem as the most successful in the collection.[3]

Furugh Farrukhzad

Face to Face with God

From the prison confines of darkness
From the turbid cesspool of the world
Hear my needful clamor,
O able, unique God.

Rend this veil of blackness, and
Perhaps you'll see within my breast
The source and substance
Of sin and corruption.

The heart you gave me, it isn't a heart
Beating in blood; free it, or
Keep it empty of carnal desires,
Or encumber it with affection and fidelity.

Only you are aware and only you know
The secrets of that first sin;
Only you are capable of granting
To my soul the original bliss.

O Lord, O Lord, how can I tell you
Of my weariness with my own body and my vexation?
Every night on the threshold, as it were, of your glory
I have the hope of another body.

From my eyes snatch
The eagerness to run to another;
O God, have mercy, and teach my eyes
To shy away from the shining eyes of others.

Give me a love that will shape me
Like the angels in your heaven,
Give me a friend, a lover in whom I might see
A glimpse of the bliss of your being.

Some night rub from the state of my mind
The image of love and the picture of its treachery;
In avenging faithlessness
I want victory over its rival in a fresh love.

O Lord, O Lord, whose powerful hand
Established the foundation of existence,
Show your face and pluck from my heart
The zest for sin and lust.

Don't be satisfied with an insignificant slave's
Rebelliousness and seeking of refuge in another;
Don't be satisfied with the flood of her tears
At the foot of a wine cup.

From the prison confines of darkness
From the turbid cesspool of the world
Hear my needful clamor,
O able, unique God.[4]

"Face to Face with God" is not particularly typical of Furugh's early
poems in its address of God, but its representation of a desperate and
longing mood is typical. And, when the emotion and the images of
romantic imagery of "Face to Face with God" are focused on the specific aspects of a woman's love for a man, as in the following poem from
The Captive collection, the reader confronts a poetic speaker who is
open to the charge of ignoring traditional Iranian bounds of literary
decorum and who, as an "I" representing a woman poet, transgresses
bounds of traditional social mores as well.

The Hidden Dream

O, hey, man who has burned
My lips with the sparkling flames of kisses,
Have you seen anything in the depth of
My two silent eyes of the secret of this madness?

Do you have any idea that, in my heart, I
Hid a dream of your love?
Do you have any idea that of this hidden love
I had a raging fire on my soul?

They have said that that woman is a mad woman
Who gives kisses freely from her lips;
Yes, but kisses from your lips
Bestow life on my dead lips.

May the thought of reputation never be in my head.
This is I who seeks you for satisfaction in this way.
I crave a solitude and your embrace;
I crave a solitude and the lips of the cup.

An opportunity far from the eyes of others
To pour you a goblet from the wine of life,
A bed I want of red roses so that one night
I might give you intoxication.

O, hey, man who has burned my lips
With the flames of kisses,
This is a book without conclusion,
And you have read only a brief page from it.[5]

The poetic speaker in *The Captive* is a serious, searching, vital, loving
young woman. The poems contain no philosophizing, *ubi sunt* or *carpe
diem* themes, or full-blown descriptions of nature. Images drawn from
nature appear in these poems as part of a world in which love and the
giving which it means are all that matter or seem to exist. The speaker
reveals a whole spectrum of moods: anticipation, regret, joy, remorse,
loneliness, abandon, sensuality, repentance, doubt, and revery. But the
issue, timeless yet immediate, is love, love which makes the heart ache
and which can satisfy all needs. It is heterosexual love, women's love for
men, men seen in their various stances, from proud, possessive, uncom-

prehending, faithless conquerors of the body to selfless lovers of whom the speaker feels unworthy. Men in *The Captive* poems are there with strong chests, embracing arms, heads to be held in one's lap, lips to kiss. Lovemaking is often an end in itself, but it has meaning as such. Some men do not comprehend this, and others, who see the speaker as a promiscuous object, are wholly ignorant of love's magic and meaning and wholly unprepared to commit themselves to love's giving. *The Captive* poems are not joyous for the most part, but the reader feels in them the vitality, sensuality, and hopefulness of the youthful speaker emphatically portraying the significance of love. Parenthetically, it is interesting that the poems as a whole lack a specifically represented Islamic environment or palpably Iranian settings, even though the reader assumes that the reiterated sense of captivity which the speaker voices (obviously) reflects a climate of traditional mores both Islamic and Iranian.

The first poem in Furugh's second collection, *The Wall,* published in 1956, is a bold apologia of romantic, sexual love.

The Sin

I sinned, a sin full of pleasure,
In an embrace which was warm and fiery;
I sinned surrounded by arms
Which were hot and avenging and iron.

In that dark and silent seclusion,
I looked into his secret-full eyes;
My heart impatiently shook in my breast
In response to the requests of his needful eyes.

In that dark and silent seclusion,
I sat dishevelled at his side;
His lips poured passion on my lips,
And I escaped from the sorrow of my crazed heart.

I whispered in his ear the tale of love:
I want you, O life of mine,
I want you, O love-giving embrace,
You, O crazed lover of mine.

Passion shone like a flame in his eyes.
The red wine danced in the cup.
My body in the soft bed
Drunkenly shook on his chest.

I sinned, a sin full of pleasure,
Next to a shaking, stupefied form;
O God, who knows what I did
In that dark and quiet seclusion.[6]

The moment described in "The Sin" is called a sin, but the speaker's representation of the moment, with her implication that she, the woman, was the lover toward a man depicted as beloved, seems positive and vital, the natural urgency and pleasure of it all an implicit questioning of how such a moment can be thought of as sinful.

Furugh's questioning becomes more general and encompassing in the following poem from *The Wall*:

At night on the damp road
    our shadows seem to flee from us
          far from us down
              the slope of the road
              into the ominous haze of the fading moonlight
             cold and heavy, above the vine branches
    they softly move toward each other.

At night on the damp road
              in the silence of the aromatic earth
    sometimes they cling impatiently to each other
    our shadows . . .
              just like flowers intoxicated with the wine of last
                night's dew
             as though in their bitter separation from us
    they eagerly murmur melodies
             which we force angrily back into the silence of
                our breasts.

But,
    far from the shadows,
              unaware of tales of their attachments,
                    their separations,
                    their unions,
    our weary bodies in their stagnant standstill give shape to life.

At night on the damp road
    how often have I said to myself
        does life within our shadows assume colors, or
        are we ourselves the shadows of our shadows?

O you thousands of wandering spirits,
              sliding about me on the waves of darkness,
        where is my shadow?
        "The light of terror gleams in the crystal of my silent cry."
        where is my shadow?
        where is my shadow?

I don't want
　　　for a moment to separate my shadow from myself
I don't want
　　　her to slip far from me on the paths, or
　　　　　　fall heavy and weary under the feet of passers-by.
Why must she in her searching confront the lips of closed doors?
Why must she rub her body against the door and wall of every house?
Why must she travel hopelessly in a cold and alien land?
O . . . O sun
　　　why do you keep my shadow at a distance from me?
　　　I ask you:

　　　　　　Is darkness pain or pleasure?
　　　　　　Is a body a prison or a field of freedom?
　　　　　　What is the darkness of night?
　　　　　　Night is the shadow of whose black spirit?

What does the sun say?
What does the sun say?
　　　Weary
　　　Bewildered
　　　Astonished
　　　　　　I race down the road of endless questions.[7]

In the only comprehensive study in English of Furugh's poems, Girdhari Tikku compares the basic thrusts of Furugh's separate collections of poems. According to Tikku, *The Captive* poems depict the psychological state of a person "in a world of tradition and dogma with no or little hope of a fuller experimental life," whereas in *The Wall* the reader confronts "the situation of a mind which has tried to break through the traditional restrictions," only to discover a world "surrounded by a wall where communication does not become possible simply by the dropping of traditional restrictions."[8] Furugh's third collection, *Rebellion*, published in 1956, represents for Tikku a sort of natural development out of the poet's earlier poetic issues in its attempt at defining "human identity" and at "facing the philosophical question of free will and predestination."[9] Whether or not Tikku's view embodies some reading into the poems, he nevertheless forcefully draws attention to stages in Furugh's developing and expanding awareness and convictions and reminds readers that the issues in her poems may be considerably more complex than mere appreciation of the significance of the titles of the three consecutive collections: *The Captive, The Wall,* and *Rebellion.*

In the following poem from *Rebellion,* the reader easily discerns one aspect of how far Furugh has progressed from *The Captive* and statements in it, such as "Face to Face with God."

Divine Rebellion

If I were God, I would summon the angels one night
To let loose the disc of the sun in the furnace of darkness.
Out of anger I would tell the servant gardeners of the world
To separate the yellow leaf of the moon from the branches of
                    night.

At midnight behind the curtains of my own great hall
My angry, rough hands would turn the world upside down.
My weary hands, after thousands of years of silence,
Would throw the mountains down into the open mouths
                    of the sea.

I'd release the shackles from the feet of thousands of
                    feverish stars;
I'd spread the blood of fire into the silent veins of the
                    forests;
I'd rip the curtains of smoke so that, in the blowing wind,
The daughter of the fire would dance drunkenly in the
                    embrace of the forest.

I'd blow into the enchanting flute a nocturnal wind
So that creatures would rise up from river beds like
                    hungry snakes,
And weary from a life of slithering on a damp chest,
They would descend into the heart of the dark whirlpool
                    of the night sky.

I'd quietly tell the winds
To set into motion the intoxicating boat of the red perfume
                    of flowers across the strait of fevered night;
I'd open up the graves
So that thousands of wandering souls might once again
                    hide themselves within the enclosure of bodies.

If I were God, I'd summon the angels one night
To boil the water of heaven in the furnace of hell,
And with burning torch in hand drive out
The flock of ascetics from the green pastures of heaven.

Weary of divine asceticism, in the middle of the night
       in Satan's bed
I'd seek refuge in the slopes of a fresh sin.
I'd choose at the price of the golden crown of divinity
The dark and painful pleasure of the embrace of a sin.[10]

    The thirty-five poems in Furugh's fourth collection, *Another Birth*, were composed in a period of nearly six years from 1958 through 1963, and the publication of this volume and subsequent poems truly signaled "another birth" for Furugh as a poet and a person.

    First, the later poems exhibit marked differences in superficial form from Furugh's earlier collections. None of the later poems exhibit quatrain stanzas, which constituted the basic formal divisions in her earlier compositions (i.e., of eighty-six poems in her first three collections, seventy-five are series of quatrains). The later poems also exhibit a predominance of verses of unequal length (as opposed to verses of uniform length in terms of quantitative metrical patterns in earlier compositions), an abandonment of regular patterns of end rhyme, and less adherence to traditional patterns of quantitative meters. In these regards, Furugh's later poems constitute a departure from traditional verse forms and prosody almost as marked as her earlier break from traditional verse in terms of subject matter and diction. Nevertheless, there persist in Furugh's later poems palpable links with and echoes of traditional verse and the Iranian literary past that help give many of these poems a true ring and body, in contrast with the products of some other contemporary Iranian poets that often seem mere grafting of kinds of western verse and modes of thought onto the Persian language. This sort of lack of development of new forms without recourse to and regard for the cultural context from which they spring signals for one critic a lack of depth in much of contemporary Persian verse.[11] But this is an indictment from which Furugh's later verse is surely excepted.

    Second, Furugh's later poems reveal maturity both in command of language and in a broadening of concerns and vision. These dimensions of Furugh's growth as a poet are easily seen in the many poems from *Another Birth* and the posthumous *Let Us Have Faith in the Beginning of the Cold Season* translated elsewhere, poems such as "The Bird Was Only a Bird," "Daybreak," "Earthly Gospels," "Gift," "I Feel for the Garden," "I Was Dying of You," "In the Cold Streets of the Night," "Journey Poem," "O Bejeweled Land," "One Window," "Poem," "The Rose," "Someone Who Isn't Like Anyone Else," "Those Days," "Upon the Earth," "The Wind-Up Doll," and "The Wind Will Carry Us Away."[12]

The following brief samples from Furugh's later poems illustrate aspects of how they represent for her "another birth."

In his important compilation called *New Verse from the Beginning till Today,* Muhammad Huquqi singles out Furugh's "My Heart Is Heavy" for a detailed explication.[13] This brief lyrical statement illustrates the departure in form in Furugh's later poems from the quatrain sequences which her earlier poems exhibit, and its eleven lines appear in sections of unequal length (i.e., 2, 4, 3, 2). The poem lacks end rhyme and a consistent pattern of quantitative rhythm (although a large number of *u*-combinations occur).

My Heart Is Heavy

My heart is heavy, O so heavy.
I move to the porch, and
    extend my fingers over the stretched skin of night.
The linking lamps are dark, O so dark.
No one will introduce me to the sun, or
    escort me to the celebration of the sparrows.
Bear flight in memory, for the bird is mortal.[14]

For the speaker of this poem all avenues are blocked; the attempt to relate to and free oneself from night futile. It is a moment that may epitomize a whole life or constitute the essence of a life of attempted love and hopelessness. But, as the following poem reveals, it is not being alone that is responsible for one's sense of loneliness and futility.

Night comes
and after night, darkness
and after darkness
eyes
hands
and breathing and more breathing
and the sound of water
     which drips drips drips from the faucet

Then two red points
from two lighted cigarettes
the clock's tick-tock
and two hearts
and two lonelinesses[15]

    Furugh moves from the vision of hopelessness and despair in "My Heart Is Heavy" and "The Couple" to doubt and possible optimism, respectively, in the next piece, a brief section from the highly regarded title poem of *Another Birth*:

Another Birth

Life perhaps is a lengthy street
          where a woman walks
                    everyday with her basket.

Life perhaps is a rope
          by which a man hangs himself
                    from a porch.

Life perhaps is a child
          returning from school.
Life perhaps is the lighting of a cigarette,
          a moment of rest in love making, or
          the absent look of a passer-by
          who tips his hat and
          says "good morning"
          with a meaningless look
          to another passer-by.[16]

And in the following deceptively simple poem, the readers confront a
bitter-sweet, nostalgic recollection of an Iranian girl's youth:

Friday
    quiet
    desolate
    like old alleys, sad
    with its sick, lazy daydreams
    with its surreptitious, long yawns.

Friday
    no expectations
    surrender

The house
    empty
    oppressive
    with doors shut against the onslaught of youth
    with darkness and visions of the sun
    with loneliness and guesses about the future and doubts
    with its curtains, books, cupboards, and pictures

O how peacefully and pridefully it passed by
    My life like a strange dream
        in the heart of those quiet, desolate Fridays
        in the heart of those empty, oppressive houses
    O how peacefully and pridefully it passed.[17]

And in a final poem from among Furugh's later works, the horrors of one sort of future, a future Furugh never succumbed to, are graphically portrayed:

The Wind-Up Doll

Oh, yes, more than this,
One can remain silent more than this.

For hours and hours, with the vacant stare of a corpse,
One can gaze at cigarette smoke,
        at the shape of a tin cup,
        at a faded flower in a carpet,
        at an imaginary line on a wall.

With stiff fingers, one can
     draw aside the curtain, and
     watch the rain pouring down onto the street,
        a child standing under an arch, kite in hand,
        a decrepit cart noisily and hastily leaving the
              empty square.

One can remain perfectly still
          next to the curtain,
          both blind and deaf.

One can exclaim,
    with a voice potently false and alien,
    "I love . . ."

In the powerful embrace of a man,
One can be a beautiful, healthy female commodity
         with a body like smooth leather
         with two large, firm breasts.
One can contaminate the purity of a love
      in bed with a drunk
          a madman
          a vagrant.

One can cleverly ridicule every startling mystery.
One can solve crossword puzzles all alone
        and with the discovery of a useless
        answer keep oneself occupied, a useless
        answer, yes, in five or six letters.

One can genuflect for a whole lifetime
                with bowed head
                at the foot of a cold sarcophagus of a saint.
One can find God in a nameless grave.
One can find faith with an insignificant coin.
One can rot in the precincts of a mosque
                like the book of homilies of an old prayer reader.

Like zero in division, addition, and multiplication,
One can always achieve a constant result.
One can see in the depths of the pupils of your eyes
                a colorless button from an old shoe.
Like water in its own container one can dry up.

One can hide the beauty of a moment with embarrassed shame
                like an unbecoming black-and-white snapshot
                at the bottom of a trunk.
In the empty frame of a day,
One can hang the portrait of a person condemned,
                                defeated, or
                                crucified.

One can cover cracks in the wall with masks.
One can merge with even more useless designs and pictures.
Exactly like a wind-up doll,
One can see one's own world with two glass eyes.
One can sleep for years in a felt-lined box
                on lace and tinsel.

One can, in response to every obscene squeeze of a hand,
                exclaim without reason:
                        "Oh, I'm so fortunate!"[18]

Furugh Farrukhzad was born in Tehran in January 1935,[19] one of five
children of Colonel Muhammad Farrukhzad and Turan Vaziri Tabar.
Furugh's formal education was exclusively at girls' public schools in
Tehran: six years of elementary school, three years at Khusraw Khavar
High School, and a brief period of study of painting and sewing at
Banavan Technical School. She never received a high school diploma.
    At thirteen or fourteen, Furugh began composing poetry in the tradi-
tional *ghazal* verse form, but she never published any of these *ghazals*.
At sixteen, she married Parviz Shapur, a government employee, who has

more recently become a satirist and caricaturist of some local distinction. A year later, in 1952, Furugh's first collection of verse, called *The Captive*, apparently appeared. The famous collection with the same name but including poems composed in 1952 and after appeared in 1955.

Furugh's only child, a boy named Kamyar, was born in 1953, and shortly thereafter the family moved to Ahvaz where Furugh's husband had been transferred. Furugh is still remembered in Ahvaz as a daring young woman, petite, attractive, with beautiful eyes, one of the first women there to wear tight-fitting clothes on the street. Rumor had it that she had her paramours in Ahvaz as well. In any case, Furugh's marriage to Shapur dissolved by divorce in 1954, before her twentieth birthday, with Shapur gaining permanent custody of Kamyar.

By the time she returned to Tehran and *The Captive* appeared in 1955, Furugh was a well-known literary figure and the subject of some controversy. *The Captive* featured a preface, cited earlier in another context, by Shuja' al-Din Shafa, who therein addressed himself to the furor over Furugh's "immorality" and "scandalous" candor. Furugh's early poems and rumors about her personal life and disregard for traditional mores had had an impact upon the reading public. Shafa termed the whole question of "morality" in poetry irrelevant to literary judgment and added that it might be hypocritical as well. As he argued, with all the sins of omission and commission found in private and public life, how can people be truly indignant or scandalized at the obviously honest and artistically rendered revelation of a woman's private "sins"? [20]

The Wall, Furugh's second collection of poems, appeared in 1956, dedicated thusly to her ex-husband:

To Parviz, in memory of our common
past and with the hope that my insignificant gift might be a compensation for his innumerable kindnesses. [21]

Such a dedication may imply that, contrary to the popular view, the failure of Furugh's marriage may have been Furugh's own doing rather than the result of any incompatibility caused by her husband. One might guess that Furugh was not a woman able to breathe and grow in a conventional marital situation, but that she could only learn this about herself through the experience of a marriage. A poem called "The Wedding Band," composed in the spring of 1955, depicts at least one of the views Furugh entertained about marriage. In this poem, a girl wonders aloud about the secret or meaning of the wedding band on her finger. Her husband replies that it is the band of good fortune and symbol of life.

Everyone else offers congratulations and best wishes. But the girl has doubts about what the band signifies. Years later, the girl, now a dejected woman, sees in the gold of the band the death of her hopes of husbandly faithfulness and wails: "This band is the band of servitude." [22]

But the popular view was that Furugh was misunderstood and mistreated by Shapur and thus had no recourse but divorce. Furugh's younger brother, Firaydun, now a well-known singer and television personality in Iran, later observed bitterly that Furugh's only recompense for always referring to Shapur in favorable terms was the latter's refusal to allow her to see her son, a deprivation which was the cause of great and lasting sorrow for Furugh. In any case, Furugh never remarried, and her son, Kamyar, remained with Shapur and grew up a stranger to his mother.

Back in Tehran, Furugh, now in her early twenties and well known in literary circles, was already being acclaimed as only the second woman poet of real or supposed greatness in the history of Persian literature, the other being Parvin I'tisami (1907–1941), whose life and works have recently been reviewed for English readers by Heshmat Moayyad in a thorough and illuminating essay called "Parvin's Poems: A Cry in the Wilderness." On the subject of the inevitable comparison between Parvin and Furugh, Moayyad writes:

Between her and Furugh . . . stands a difference in thought equal to centuries. Parvin, like a pearl within an oyster, carefully protected by her father and educated under the classical rules of etiquette to the extent that an Indian scholar during a visit to Iran did not succeed even in speaking to her, must necessarily show a shy, completely reserved deportment, even an almost timid apprehensiveness about the absolute purity of her thinking and disposition, while the other, Furugh, courageously and unscrupulously breaks all the barriers of social norms and frees herself from all fetters and chains put on women and marches in front of radical modernists like a standard-bearer of freedom with a degree of self-defamation.

Both felt the misfortune of women equally strongly, the one withdrawn and introverted and only discernible behind her fables and strife poems, while the other steps out in public and candidly proclaims her needs and sufferings. [23]

In the summer of 1956, Furugh traveled to Europe for the first time and upon her return published her impressions of Europe in a series of articles in *Firdawsi* magazine. The trip seems to have had a great effect upon Furugh's personality, and some critics feel that her experience in Europe gave her the broader, more mature vision embodied in her later poems. Furugh, herself, subsequently intimated that the trip served in part as an escape from the stifling atmosphere of Iran and from the opprobrium that her early poems and personal life style had generated among a number of Iranian readers. Her younger brother, Firaydun, whom Furugh visited on this and subsequent trips to Europe, later characterized Furugh's 1957 trip to Europe as a necessary escape and respite. In any case, during her 1956 and 1957 trips, Furugh became acquainted with Italian and German, which apparently she learned to speak and read quite well. She apparently learned English, as well, but did not achieve fluency in the language until the middle 1960's.

In 1957 appeared *Rebellion*, Furugh's third collection of poems, which she later characterized, along with *The Wall*, as "the hopeless threshing of arms and legs between two stages in life . . . the final gasps of breath before a sort of release." [24] Presumably, the freedom or "release" Furugh describes here refers, in large measure, to her relationship with Ibrahim Gulistan, short-story writer and cinematographer, which began in 1958. At that time, Furugh became Gulistan's assistant in his film company, having been introduced to the latter by Sadiq Chubak, Iran's most prominent writer of fiction, who seems to have been a sort of literary confidant and sounding board for Furugh during the period between her divorce and her meeting Gulistan. Furugh and Gulistan apparently fell in love shortly after meeting, and their relationship apparently continued till Furugh's death nine years later. Gulistan, married and a father, seems to have set Furugh up in an apartment in North Tehran and appeared as her escort at parties among friends and in public. Naturally, Furugh's relationship with Gulistan did not go unnoticed by the press, and both of them were severely criticized for their scandalous behavior.

Gulistan's influence upon Furugh during the last eight years of her life was pervasive and decisive in the development of her interest and talent in film making. In personal terms, on the basis of impressions their friends provide, Gulistan was a strong and steadfast friend and lover, whose own firmness, discipline, and self-confidence undoubtedly helped to enable Furugh, negatively, to survive the opprobrium which she, as a free spirit, had constantly to face and, positively, to find further avenues of expression for her distinctive personality. Some indication of what Furugh thought of their relationship can be surmised both from the naming of her fourth collection of poems, *Another Birth*, and from her dedication of the volume to Gulistan.

As for Gulistan's role in the growth and maturation of Furugh as a poet, despite his public denials, there seems to be no doubt that

Another Birth and subsequent poems owe a great deal to Furugh's association with Gulistan. As Chubak puts it: "Through Gulistan, Furugh was
drawn to study and reading, i.e., searching out and reading good books
. . . What I mean is perhaps something like the science of reading,
choosing books, knowing books . . . The influence and knowledge of
Gulistan had a considerable effect on the development of Furugh's
artistic personality . . ."[25]

In 1959 Furugh went to England to study film production. Back in Iran
she had her first experiences in filming documentaries and began the
editing of a film called *The Fire*. From this time on until her death she
was active in film production, sometimes acting, sometimes producing,
sometimes assisting and editing. Films with which her name is associated include *Courtship* (1960), a short film on Iranian courtship customs commissioned by the National Canadian Film Corporation to
Golestan Films; *Water and Heat* (1961), which portrayed the social and
industrial "heat" of the Abadan environment; and *A Fire* (1961). *The
House Is Black* (1962), a documentary made by Furugh and three colleagues on the leper colony in Tabriz, received the grand prize for documentary films at the 1963 Uberhausen Film Festival in Germany. This
was a most significant award for an Iranian producer, especially a
woman. The same winter, *Another Birth*, Furugh's fourth and most important collection of poems, was published in Tehran and was received
with great acclaim by the devotees of modern Persian verse. Furugh,
herself, was much pleased by *Another Birth* and felt it represented her
first mature work as a poet.

In the spring of 1964, Furugh assisted in a film called *Brick and Mirror*.
That summer, the anthology *Selected Poems of Furugh Farroukhzad*
appeared, and she traveled again to Europe, in Italy, Germany, and
France. In 1965 UNESCO produced a half-hour film about Furugh's life
and in the same year Bernardo Bertolucci produced a fifteen-minute film
biography. She accepted an invitation to Sweden in 1966, to produce a
film there, and she was planning to play the title role in a Tehran stage
production of Shaw's *St. Joan*, which she herself had translated into
Persian.

But one Monday afternoon in February 1967, just after her thirty-
second birthday, Furugh died in an automobile accident. Gulistan buried
her in a plot next to his mother and set aside contiguous plots in the
same cemetery for himself and his wife.

Furugh's death shocked the Iranian literary world and even had the
effect of changing the minds of some people previously disapproving of
her personal life style and unappreciative of her poetic output. Special

issues of *Arash* and *Firdawsi* magazines appeared in her honor, and annual remembrances have continued to appear in the press on the anniversaries of her death. A volume of selected poems, letters, biographical and critical essays, and eulogistic articles was published in 1968, and in the same year *From Nima Onward*, an anthology of modern Persian verse, previously prepared by Furugh and including some of her own poems, appeared. In 1974, a posthumous collection of poems, composed after *Another Birth*, appeared under the title *Let Us Have Faith in the Beginning of the Cold Season*. All of Furugh's collected poems have gone through numerous printings.

On the basis of the external details of Furugh's life and if one can assume that her poems are a mirror of her views about her life, the visage of a very particular sort of person emerges. Furugh was a most inquiring, searching, active person who seems to have committed herself fully to all ventures. Her vitality and constant activity may, however, have been her only real happiness; or, in other words, the involvement kept her too busy to reflect upon unhappiness.

For, on the basis of her poems, her letters, and the recollections of relatives and friends, Furugh was not a happy person. Circumstances conspired to make happiness difficult, and some of the circumstances had to do with the confrontation between Iranian society and her personal predilections, needs, and goals as a woman. It takes no reading into the details of her short life to discover the cruel ironies that she constantly faced.

Born of an upper-middle-class family whose second son spent years pursuing higher education in Germany, Furugh, for whatever reasons, didn't even finish high school and was married before her seventeenth birthday and was a mother before her eighteenth. A teenager of talent in verbal and visual arts, Furugh's Maecenas was her own determination. A divorcee at twenty, Furugh, for whatever reasons, was not allowed ever to see her son. Of her father, Furugh said in later years that he was a man one could only say "Hello" to. Is it not possible that this father who seems to have been unable to communicate with a female offspring in terms of equality gave his daughter in marriage to another man equally unprepared to deal with a real partner? Later, it must have hurt Furugh that the attention given her poetry focused on its morality and the sex of its author rather than on its own terms as poetic statement. And, as a free spirit—*whore* is the word one Iranian male scholar uses with a smile to describe Furugh, quickly adding that he doesn't think the worse of her for it—she surely must have suffered greatly when her giving of self intellectually and physically to men for whom she felt love was construed by some of them as a "lay." An added burden was her apparent inability to develop close relationships with some women, many of whom probably saw her as a threat or a disgrace to their sex.

Furugh's tragic and untimely death at thirty-two gave her poetry a special poignant popularity, just as the womanly frankness in her early poems of the fifties had first drawn another sort of "unliterary" attention to her. Both factors have certainly colored and continue to color much critical judgment of Furugh's works in Iran and per se constitute part of the impact which Furugh's person and poems have had and will continue to have upon Iranian readers. Nevertheless, since her death there have been a number of dispassionate and incisive assessments in Persian of Furugh's impact and importance as a poet and a person.

One is Muhammad Riza Shafi'i Kadkani's brief article written on the occasion of Furugh's death.[26] According to Kadkani, Furugh's special genius and distinctive poetic personality emerge only with *Another Birth*, her fourth collection, a book which he argues will assuredly give Furugh permanent recognition as the most important woman poet in the thousand-year history of Persian literature, and as one of two poets of prominence in the present century. Kadkani sees three characteristics of Furugh's poetry as particularly decisive and distinctive in her poetic achievement. The first is a tendency to create what Kadkani calls "pure poetry" and a distinctive way of presenting images that vividly and exactly portray the abstract view of the poet. Second, Furugh's poetry is the first example in Persian literature of straightforward lyric statements embodying the perceptions of a woman as an individual with respect to aspects of love relationships. In this regard, according to Kadkani, Furugh is the pre-eminent spokesperson for the current generation of liberated Iranians and is unparalleled in her depiction of typical moments and moods in the lives of the members of the group—loneliness, alienation, surrender, and silence. Thus, although Furugh's vision is individual and specific, it concomitantly stands as an expression of the mood(s) of a large number of urban, literate, mostly younger Iranians. A third characteristic distinctive of Furugh's poetry combines simplicity and conversational informality—no sense of restraint in choosing words, her choice consistently a matter of determined appropriateness to the context at hand (rather than the use of words conventionally associated with Persian verse)—and the broadening of the range and potentiality of quantitative rhythm through the use of her particular diction.

Of the three characteristics cited by Kadkani, the second, her distinctive subject matter, would seem to be the focal aspect in determining Furugh's impact as a poet upon Iranian society. And if, as Furugh herself implies in saying that poetry is for her a medium in which she comes to self-knowledge, Furugh's poetry may be taken as a testament and mirror of her life and personality, a nonliterary dimension is added to the significance of its particular subject matter and content. This suggestion is developed into a most stimulating thesis by Riza Barahini in a brief article on the third anniversary of Furugh's death, wherein Barahini, who views Iranian history as a "masculine history," asserts that Furugh was the founder of "feminine culture" in Persian poetry.[27] Prior to Furugh no woman poet in Persian had ever composed love poems with men as the love object, and after her none can escape her influence. According to Barahini, Furugh's works cause the development of a feminine tradition in Persian poetry, and she will have a permanent place in the Persian pantheon for this reason rather than for inherent qualities of form and technique in her verse. Furugh's verse, says Barahini, is "poetry of content" rather than of form and technique, and it is "poetry of feminine content" which is rare in any age and has the capacity for permanence.

Notes

This article is an excerpted version of a lengthy critical study of the poetry of Furugh Farrukhzad being prepared for publication in 1978. Some of the research reflected in this article was undertaken during the summer of 1975 in Tehran, Iran, while I was being supported by grants from the Joint Committee of the American Council of Learned Societies and the Social Science Research Council and from the Center for Middle Eastern Studies at the University of Texas at Austin. Their support I hereby gratefully acknowledge.

1.   Furugh Farrukhzad, "Harfha'i bi-Ja-yi Muqaddamah" [Comments in lieu of an introduction], in *Barquzidah-'i Ash'ar-i Furugh Farrukhzad* [Selected poems of Furugh Farrukhzad], pp. 6–14.

2.   A volume of verse by Furugh called *Asir* [The Captive] was apparently published in 1952 and is referred to as "the seventeen years of experiences of a fearless woman" by Amir Isma'ili and Abu al-Qasim Sadarat (*Javdanah, Furugh Farrukhzad* [The immortal one, Furugh Farrukhzad], p. 283). But this is not the famous *Asir* subsequently printed and reprinted, because all the poems in the latter *Asir* are dated after 1952.

3.   Shuja' al-Din Shafa, Preface to *Asir*, p. 6.

4.   Furugh Farrukhzad, ibid., pp. 141–144. The Persian original, dated April–May 1955—Ahvaz, is a composition of eleven quatrains with verses in a quantitative metrical pattern of --u-u-uu--- and an *abcb* end-rhyme scheme. All translations in this article are merely impres-

sionistic prose renderings of the original poems. They neither exhibit scholarly accuracy nor embody literary appeal.

5.   Ibid., pp. 115–117. The Persian original is a composition of six quatrains with verses in a quantitative metrical pattern of -u---u---u- and an *abcb* end-rhyme scheme.

6.   Furugh Farrukhzad, *Divar* [The wall], pp. 11–15. The Persian original is a composition of six quatrains of verses with a quantitative metrical pattern of u---u---u-- and an *abcb* end-rhyme scheme.

7.   Ibid., pp. 149–154. The Persian original is a composition of nine stanzas of unequal length and verses of unequal length lacking a pattern of end rhyme. The pattern of quantitative meter is -u---/u---/u---/u--- (slash marks indicating the number and kind of feet exhibited by lines of different lengths). In preparing the translation of this poem, I made use of an unpublished translation by Afzal Vossoughi.

8.   Girdhari Tikku, "Furugh-i Farrukhzad: A New Direction in Persian Poetry," *Studia Islamica* 26 (1967): 149–173.

9.   Ibid.

10.   Furugh Farrukhzad, *'Usyan* [The rebellion], pp. 49–53.

11.   M. R. Shafi'i Kadkani, "Shi'r-i Mu'asir az 'Umq-i Insani Tuhi-st" [Contemporary verse lacks human depth], *Farhang-u Zindigi*, no. 9 (September–October 1972), pp. 32–35.

12.   A complete bibliography of translations of individual poems from Furugh's works is contained in *Twentieth Century Persian Literature in Translation: A Bibliography*, comp. M. C. Hillmann.

13.   Muhammad Huquqi, *Shi'r-i Naw az Aghaz ta Imruz, 1301–1350* [Modernist verse from the beginning till today, 1922–1971], pp. 200–202.

14.   Furugh Farrukhzad, *Iman Biyavarim bi-Aghaz-i Fasl-i Sard* [Let us have faith in the beginning of the cold season], pp. 85–86.

15.   Furugh Farrukhzad, *Tavalludi Digar* [Another birth], pp. 123–124. The original Persian is a composition of thirteen lines divided into two sections of eight and five lines.

16.   Ibid., p. 165, lines 7–15 of a sixty-eight–line composition.

17.   Ibid., pp. 69–70.

18.   Ibid., pp. 71–75.

19.   The biographical material presented here derives mainly from various articles in Isma'ili and Sadarat, *Javdanah* and from conversations with acquaintances of Furugh in Tehran.

20.   Shafa, Preface to *Asir*, p. 4.

21.   Farrukhzad, *Divar*, p. 3.

22.   Farrukhzad, *Asir*, pp. 149–150.

23.   Heshmat Moayyad, "Parvin's Poems: A Cry in the Wilderness," in *Islamwissenschaftliche Abhandlungen Fritz Meier*, pp. 171–172.

24.   Farrukhzad, "Harfha'i," p. 6.
25.   Sadiq Chubak, quoted in Isma'ili and Sadarat, *Javdanah*, pp. 196–197.
26.   M. R. Shafi'i Kadkani, "Akhbar—Marg-i Furugh Farrukhzad" [News—the death of Furugh Farrukhzad], *Rahnima-yi Kitab* 9 (1966–1967): 657–660.
27.   Riza Barahini, "Farrukhzad, Bunyanguzar-i Maktab-i Mu'annas-i Shi'r-i Farsi" [Farrukhzad, the founder of the feminine school of Persian poetry], *Firdawsi* 20, no. 950 (1970): 20.

References

Barahini, Riza. "Farrukhzad, Bunyanguzar-i Maktab-i Mu'annas-i Shi'r-i Farsi." *Firdawsi* 20, no. 950 (1970): 20.

Farrukhzad, Furugh. *Asir*. 7th ed. Tehran: Amir Kabir, 1973–1974.

———. *Divar*. 5th ed. Tehran: Amir Kabir, 1973–1974.

———. "Harfha'i bi-Ja-yi Muqaddamah." In *Barquzidah-'i Ash'ar-i Furugh Farrukhzad*. 3d ed. Tehran: Kitabha-yi Jibi, 1973.

———. *Iman Biyavarim bi-Aghaz-i Fasl-i Sard*. Tehran: Murvarid, 1974.

———. *Tavalludi Digar*. Tehran: Murvarid, 1970.

———. *'Usyan*. 7th ed. Tehran: Amir Kabir, 1975.

Hillman, M. C., comp. *Twentieth Century Persian Literature in Translation: A Bibliography*. Washington, D.C.: Imperial Embassy of Iran, 1976.

Huquqi, Muhammad. *Shi'r-i Naw az Aghaz ta Imruz, 1301–1350*. Tehran, 1972–1973.

Isma'ili, Amir, and Abu al-Qasim Sadarat. *Javdanah, Furugh Farrukhzad*. Tehran: Marjan, 1972.

Kadkani, M. R. Shafi'i. "Akhbar—Margi-i Furugh Farrukhzad." *Rahnima-yi Kitab* 9 (1966–1967): 657–660.

———. "Shi'r-i Mu'asir az 'Umq-i Insani Tuhi-st." *Farhang-u Zindigi*, no. 9 (September–October 1972): 32–35.

Moayyad, Heshmat. "Parvin's Poems: A Cry in the Wilderness." In *Islamwissenschaftliche Abhandlungen Fritz Meier*. Wiesbadan: Franz Steiner, 1974.

Tikku, Girdhari. "Furugh-i Farrukhzad: A New Direction in Persian Poetry." *Studia Islamica* 26 (1967): 149–173.

20

Fadéla M'rabet

فضيلة مرابط

Modern Algerian Journalist

A.D. 1935–

Fadéla M'rabet was born in Constantine, Algeria, into a religious family with a long tradition of relationship to the *'ulama,* or elders of Islam. Her father, however, was involved in radio, and she, herself, after graduating from the University of Algiers in science, began a career in radio. She had a program on Radio Algiers exclusively for women. Her first book, *La Femme Algérienne,* was based on reactions and interviews with Algerian women immediately following the revolution and the subsequent granting of Algerian independence in 1962. Her second book, *Les Algériennes,* from which the following selection is taken, appeared soon afterward. Her third book, *L'Algérie des Illusions,* was published in 1973. She now lives in Paris.

Photo: *Fadéla M'rabet*

Chapter 1. *Tartuferies*

I fear the way in which you will divide the spoils.—*The Prophet*

In accordance with our traditions . . . *with respect for the Algerian personality* . . . and *in an Arabo-Islamic framework*[1]—these phrases are
used more and more frequently in contemporary discussions of the evolution of the Algerian woman.

But what do they mean? Let us try to understand.

Actually, the phrases are not as simple as they appear: it is generally
stated that the Algerian woman ought to develop in *accordance with our
traditions,* but no one who uses the phrase has explained what it means.
I have searched in vain through official texts, speeches, newspapers, and
summaries of traditions. I have found . . . well, Molière (in spite of himself), who says, through Orgon, "There's the colonial tradition, of
course," but then one must be joking or a hypocrite to mention that in
these days, but then there is Tartufe: "This is a man . . . who . . . ah! . . .
a man . . . well, of course, a man would say that . . ." But, finally, I have
found a spokesman who declares, in *Révolution Africaine*: "Our problems are complicated, but their bases are clear . . . the young Algerian
woman should remain attached to good traditions but rid herself of bad
customs and bad traditions . . . she does not confuse . . . traditional traditionalism with colonial traditionalism!"[2]

Good for the young Algerian woman! However, those of us who do
not share her perspicacity are obliged, in order to understand what tradition means, to first note what has gone on, in our country, for generations, from great-great-grandfather to great-grandfather, from great-
grandfather to grandfather, from grandfather to father, from father to
son . . . and so to daughter.

It is *tradition,* for example, to marry a girl very young; at two or three
years, in former times, she was already promised; and "when it was a
question [in modern civil codes] to fix an age before which marriage
would not be permitted, it was not possible to find, in the doctrine of no
matter which [Muslim] rite,[3] an opinion sufficiently authorized so that
one could justify such a reform. All rites, in actuality, authorized the
marriage of minors, even of babies."[4]

It is not even unusual to promise a child before it comes into the

[Excerpts from Fadéla M'rabet, *Les Algériennes* (Paris: François Maspero, 1967).
Translated by Elizabeth Warnock Fernea.]

world; the child is not yet born, but the women (mothers of sons) are already bargaining among themselves; "If it is a girl, you keep her for me," they say to the mother.

"In 1930, at Lafayette in Guergour province, a little girl of nine was married to her cousin; a short time afterward, he invited her and her mother to a party given by himself, dismissed the mother, and consummated the marriage, despite the resistance of the interested parties . . ."; in 1925, at El Kseur, "a little boy of eight married a little girl of 11."[5]

Tradition: "colonial tradition," or postcolonial? In the spring of 1965, in the south, I saw a child of twelve already married and a mother; sickly herself, she carried her child with difficulty. And when I asked the *qadi* of this oasis at what age girls were married, he replied, "According to what law?" And when I did not seem to catch his meaning, he continued, "But of course, according to Koranic law or Algerian law?" Very subtly, he added, "From the age of six, one can promise a girl and write the contract, but it is at the age of sixteen, naturally, that the marriage is then consummated and registered with the authorities."

At the age of sixteen, really? In 1967, Algerian marriage was characterized, as always, by great precocity and great frequency: at the age of fifteen 10 percent of the girls and 1 percent of the boys were married; at twenty, 73 percent of the girls and 20 percent of the boys; at forty-five, 98 percent of the women and 94.9 percent of the men.[6]

Many of the marriages are officially registered after they have already taken place, and this is another *tradition*.

Thus, the law of May 2, 1930—which applied only to Kabyles and fixed the age of marriage at fifteen for girls and eighteen for boys— encouraged "a great number to marry according to their own customs, to disguise the ages of the couple, or to make a marriage declaration before the required age is attained."[7]

Well before the promulgation of the "Khemisti law,"[8] the charade had been readied, and in 1965, as in 1930, people did as they pleased. "Ahmed and Z. Said celebrated the marriage, one of his daughter [14], the other of his son [18], with the customary Muslim *fatihah*, while awaiting the legal age to declare the marriage. The court sentenced them to one month in prison, suspended sentence."[9]

Tradition decrees that marriages be without love, be arranged by families between cousins,[10] and that the fiancee only be notified at the last moment; if the father no longer exercises his theoretical right of coercion (*djabr*) and thus the consent of the bride is necessary, it is *tradition* that her agreement be signed for her by a designated male (the nearest agnatic relative, as *wali*, or representative); and good taste decrees that the young girl should not refuse to give her consent.

"In spite of everything," I said to the *qadi*, "if one of these girls, aged sixteen, for example, came to you, in tears, begging you not to give her to a fiancé of seventy, what would you do?" He coughed, cleared his throat, scratched his head—such insolence must be an unusual occurrence for him—then said, "Well, I would bring them together, I would listen to the father's arguments, and those of the daughter, and after that, I would make a decision."

It is still *tradition*, not only in the rural areas, but also in the suburbs of Algiers and in Algiers itself, for the wedding nightgown to be exhibited after the marriage has been consummated. If there is nothing to exhibit, the classic result is that the unhappy girl, not understanding what has happened (and for good reason: some women naturally have no hymen), is sent back to her father's house.

But even when the "merchandise" happens to be good, the honeymoon does not last, and these marriages are not always happy. Sometimes the husband, dissatisfied, suspects his wife of deceiving him (jealousy, among us is, in fact, a *tradition*); for some little thing, or for nothing, he mistreats his wife, even beats her, and, if he is finally stopped, justice, by *tradition*, almost approves his actions.

Thus, an Algerian peasant, working in the fields a kilometer from his own house, sees his two nephews leaving his house. Convinced that his wife has made a fool of him, he runs in and cuts her up about the head and nose; is not this normal behavior?

"This man," explained the lawyer, "avenged his honor *according to custom*. He only cut her head and nose. Only a small scratch will remain when the wound is healed. I am happy that this woman is not dead. None of us can ignore the ways in which dishonor is avenged in the different countries of the world. Each country has its *customs*. He could kill her. He did not do it. That is in his favor . . . Honor is very much respected in Islamic countries, a man is attached to the customs of his country, of his religion, of his *mechta* [land] . . . He has *traditions* of honor— . . . Knowing that he has been made a fool, he avenges himself . . . It is not an act of savagery."[11]

Whether or not all this was true—the judge, after half an hour's deliberation, sentenced this good traditionalist to five years in prison—suspended sentence.

Honor, decidedly . . . "Yesterday evening B. Aissa, aged 47, living at Tifrit [three kilometers from Akbou] killed his sister, aged 48, with a hatchet. Questioned by the police, he stated he had killed his sister to defend the honor of his family."[12] But let us return to the ordinary husband.

Traditionally badly married, he is not obliged to kill his wife or even cut up her nose; he can abandon her very easily, or repudiate her, which is less risky and this is another *tradition*. "If the Koran does place conditions for regulating and reducing this arbitrary practice, the 'irregular' repudiation still survives and has been confirmed by traditional law as well as by certain modern situations."[13]

Tradition is alive, in fact: more than thirty cases of abandoned families on the court docket in one day in Algiers, in the winter of 1966; fifty in the spring of 1967; this does not include the suits against husbands and fathers who, obliged to pay support, quickly "forget" and disappear.[14]

But not all men disappear, for *tradition* offers another solution to the discontented: take a second, a third, a fourth wife. Polygamy is quite usual in rural areas. I know a small area of Aurés where almost all the men have at least two wives.

What about polygamy on the national level? One can only give approximate figures: "just before the war of liberation, polygamy in Algeria was practiced by only 3 percent of men over sixty. However, some people estimate that, just after independence, polygamy increased slightly."[15]

Whatever the figures, even if only a few Algerians have four wives at the same time, many marry one woman, divorce her, remarry—and begin again: "successive" polygamy such as this is more frequent. And divorces are more numerous.[16]

Still, let us admit that marriage, more or less forced, with a cousin more or less a child, and which is more or less expensive (a dowry of 5,000 Algerian dirhams is not unusual),[17] is not a catastrophe; the husband does not use his wife as a field hand, does not take a mistress, does not beat her, does not lock the cupboards with a key when he leaves the house (like my neighbor's husband, who weighs her store of potatoes daily!); he does not figure expenses down to the last penny. Even then, what is the wife's role, in this so-called life without a history?

Tradition answers: bear children. "In 1917, there were about 6.5 children per married woman who had completed her family";[18] if one counts the miscarriages and abortions, that means about a dozen pregnancies per woman. To be pregnant or to ready herself to bear children: that is the woman's basic occupation—and it is well known that the woman's sterility (which is like a living curse) or her tendency to bear only girls constitutes a more or less sufficient reason for her to be returned to her father's house.

Childbearing on this scale exhausts the woman,[19] but *tradition* has no pity: in addition to bearing children, the wife needs to occupy herself with the house, the cooking. "It is the natural order of things that [a woman] be above all keeper of the hearth," declared the students in their message of greeting at the First Congress of the UNFA [Union Nationale des Femmes d'Algérie].[20]

The newspaper *El Moudjahid* consistently develops this theme; for example, on March 10, 1967, a letter from a reader was published, in large type, four columns wide, under the title "On the Meeting of Two Civilizations": it reminds us that "man ought to find in woman a pleasant companion, who will comfort him after his long day of hard work, who will lighten his leisure . . . To work in the home . . . this is, of all tasks, the most noble, for it takes place in intimacy . . . Thus it would not be prudent to systematically advise women to work outside the family home . . ."

Should girls, then, be educated, for what, in the end is not *traditional*? The question of girls' education continues to be debated; although such education certainly exists, it is important to note how long the girls actually stay in school. For example, in a little village, of seventeen girls admitted to school, two passed into the sixth grade and one into the fifth.[21] Should such girls wish to go out in public with their husbands, *tradition* will oppose it. The Algerian women who "show themselves" in public are still rare, and, at official functions, one searches in vain for the wives of our leaders; if it is absolutely necessary to have a female escort —as was the case when our ex-president received M. and Mme. Sekou Touré—one borrows a well-known figure for the occasion: a deputy, for example, or a representative of the Women's Union . . .

Not to learn anything, not to see her fiancé before marriage, to be married very young and condemned to *reproduce*; not to have any social life, not to take part in the conduct of public affairs—these are then some of our *traditions*, solid traditions, which long preceded colonialism and continue to survive long after independence.[22]

The Algerian woman, then, is supposed to conform to these traditions in order to evolve? The word itself, *evolution*, means change, change from one form to another, breaking with other forms, then the emerging of a new person and access to a new way of life. To speak of "evolution according to our traditions" is to say that one can change without innovating, can transform oneself by simply modifying oneself, to remain oneself while no longer being oneself, to be still something without remaining anything!

Actually, there is no such thing as "traditional evolution"—the term makes no sense, and this is probably why the definition is such a secret; is the whole idea then only a screen or pretense?

Before answering our question, we need to examine the other arguments often invoked in favor of tradition and see if they are of the same poisonous stamp.

If evolution ought to be "in line with our traditions," it should also, or at the same time, be in accord with "the Algerian personality"; the latter term is often used; even if it is only a variation on the preceding term, it does have the merit of being a little less obscure and of revealing its hidden meaning more easily.

People have not, it is true, set out simply to *develop* the idea of an evolution "specifically Algerian," "in harmony" with our "profound being," but at least we find, here and there in the press, some clear enough indications of its meaning.

For example, in the journal *Humanisme musulman* (August 1965), M. El Hachimi Tidjani, its founder, director, and principal editor, sets out to define the *components of our personality*:

What first strikes us is this: "The reply is not so simple—the epithets which can be applied to us are not always free of ambiguity . . . thus we are Algerian, but without being very different from other inhabitants of the Mediterranean basin . . . Further, we are Arabs and have been arabicized, but at the same time we are defined as Muslims, with Africans and the people of Bandung. And if we are oriental in terms of our origin, religion, language, culture, and history, we are equally western in terms of geography, economy, and history."[23]

Clearly, this is a bit much and an obviously insupportable position; shall we hasten to cut away, to clarify, purify, remove "these ambiguities"; in short, to separate Algerian reality from the less flattering appearances which mask it; so that M. Tidjani, who feels "a powerful need to strengthen the essence" of the Algerian personality, will attempt to define it. . . .

. . . The "components of our personality," states M. Tidjani, are "values," and these "values" are "the conscience of our historic continuity and our participation in universal culture"; and "our religion and our language." Later, he adds, "True nationality cannot be reduced to a simple identity card, consecrated and called national. On the contrary, it is a combination of elements, such as the Muslim religion, the Arabic language, or a Berber dialect, common experience, common hopes and economic interests, and, finally, a desire to live together."

There is no need to quibble with M. Tidjani about the "components" which he would consider discussing, such as our "common hopes" or "our desire to live together." Beneath the surface of these elegant phrases lies one fundamental and most important characteristic: written in large capital letters, it is the religion of Islam.

The "Algerian personality," then, is defined by M. Tidjani within a strictly religious framework and in exclusively religious terms. Thus, *El Djeich*, the journal of the ANP [Alliance Nationale Populaire], in July

1966, speaks of "reinforcing the Islamic personality"; in relation to this, M. Malek Bennebi, a former defender of ideas (specifically Algerian) on the "*colonisabilité*" of the Arabs, writes as follows:

"All political activity, if it is to call itself Algerian, should remain faithful to its spiritual sources, to the message of the dead . . . The message of our dead and their pact—this is the source from which our political activity should draw its mystique. Thus, in formulating our political policy [polity] in three words: socialism, Arabism, Islamicism, President Ben Bella has performed an act of faith."[24] These proposals are surely those of 1964 . . .

But in 1966, *Révolution Africaine* also spoke of a "return to sources" which, for Algeria, will be "irreversible."

Is the definition clearer? We know now at least that "Algerian personality" means "Islamic personality," a personality which is not to be made but "reconstituted," not created but "resuscitated," according to the "pact" which M. Bennabi and others have made with the dead.[25]

But with what dead? Our dead are numerous, thirteen centuries of them, doctors, lawyers, interpreters of our traditions, reformers, fault finders, theologians, and those who are anonymous. To which sources exactly are we to return? To the *Risala* of Al Qayrawani (10th century), for example, or to *L'Abrégé* (Mokhtasar) de Khalil (14th century)?

Or, following Ghazali (17th century) and Ibn Taymiyya (14th century), can one perceive "the essence of Koranic revelation," distinguish between what is an article of faith (*aqidat*) and a cultural proscription (*ibadat*), on the one hand, and, on the other hand, all that relates to morality (*akhlaq*) and to social life (*moamalat*) from that which depends "on the conditions of the time and place?"[26] While we await the response of the interpreters of our theology, our "Algerian personality" remains rather indefinite.

Still, if none of our theoreticians have yet decided what the Algerian personality is, some have indicated what it is not; and, once more returning to sources . . . Spinozists ("all determination is negation"), they define the Algerian personality by a series of exclusions.

The Algerian personality excludes, first, all imitation of western styles and fashions. The press often criticizes "the long hair, bell-bottom pants, and miniskirts that we see."[27] In order to prepare better for the celebration of International Woman's Day, *El Moudjahid* opened its columns, in February and March 1967, to readers, largely bigots who seem both obsessed and obscene in their attitudes:

I do not see in what way these girls in miniskirts can make a contribution to what our country should be.

If there is any element which prevents full emancipation, it is a
small minority of girls who are permitted to wear the miniskirt and
the short hair coiffure. [?]

Our socialism rests on the pillars of Islam and not on the emancipation of the woman with her makeup, her coiffure, her finery,
which causes unbridled passions to burst forth; the effect of these
passions is detrimental to humanity as a whole (causing discord,
and quarreling, the crimes which generally are caused by women).
I do not say that man himself is a saint, but that he is confused and
upset.

If the Algerian woman really allows herself to wear the miniskirt,
it is because there is no longer any honor and respect in our
country. Women have misunderstood emancipation; the country
will not develop because of making miniatures [*sic*] and
coiffures . . .

Women's *toilette* today has become a scanty, tight sheath which
outlines her shape suggestively. It no longer reveals femininity,
but the female sex itself.

This latter statement, of course, is the point of the article, and *El
Moudjahid* then has the good taste to publish, in the name of "the defense of our sacred Islam," the following paragraph:

Without the slightest hesitation, the women let a good part of
their thighs show, to say nothing of their . . . (begging your pardon) and this in public, and even in the presence of or in the face
of their parents, for they do not even take the trouble to cover
themselves . . . put themselves in order . . .

What virtuous indignation! "Put ourselves in order." Since men set
the example, we can cite some of them: under the title "A Happy
Change in Dress," *El Moudjahid* published the following letter January
4, 1967:

During the last fortnight . . . I have noticed a tendency to wear
certain traditional garments; it is not unusual to see young men on
the streets of Algiers wearing burnooses and *djellabas*; I believe it
is clear that the month of Ramadan and fasting encourages a certain return to sources, which translates itself into these changes in
dress . . . In our opinion, this is indeed a pleasant change . . . One
can only regret that this evolution [*sic*] . . . will probably only last
for the duration of Ramadan.

Evolution—or masquerade? "I know many women, and some of them
the most modern of all in their attitudes," writes an Algerian woman
frightened by modernity, "who, though they are usually unveiled, use
the veil still as a garment of fantasy, coquetry, . . . to wear to weddings,
for example."[28]

Robes, trousers—according to habit, apparently, and since the habit
makes the monk, the "Algerian personality" thus forbids any adoption
of fashions or mores which might be called western, for these can only
be perverse: "outward signs of maladjustment accompanied by corrupt
ideas and a degraded mentality . . . it is true that a glass of alcohol has
never killed anyone, still . . . one must denounce such obvious relaxa-
tions" in traditional behavior.[29]

Europe connotes *debauchery*: this accusation constantly recurs in the
press of the Maghreb [Algeria, Tunisia, and Morocco], particularly when
it discusses evolution, its *plat de résistance*.

Take, for example, the review (dishonest, in our opinion) of G. Tillion's
Le Harem et Les Cousins, by the editor-in-chief of *Jeune Afrique*. He
presents the "pseudo-liberated" Europeans as people obsessed with
sex: "The western woman has gained the right to adultery and to a
sentimental nomadism . . . this victory . . . leads her frequently to the
psychiatrist's office . . . and drives her to pursue, via a succession of
lovers, a moral stability which is almost no longer accessible to her . . ."[30]

A healthy spirit . . . : wearing a gandura, austere, and without complexes, the "Algerian personality" does not draw its sustenance from a
foreign culture; if it tastes such culture, it should only be with a light
touch of the lips. "The modernists who wish to consider themselves
people of the future, manifest wild infatuation with everything that is
not Algerian: foreign language and culture, the history of France, the
USSR, China, Yugoslavia, American music, Guinean folklore" (Tidjani).

Since foreign culture is so "depersonalizing," we must take care not
to read too much, among others, from the works of . . . Frantz Fanon.

"[The Algerian woman] cannot write a hymn of battle, a song of work for the Algerian people," according to M. Bennabi, "because she has not immersed herself in the roots of her own subjectivity . . . It was not Ghandi's English companions who composed the great hymn which led the Indian masses to liberation . . . It was not an American who composed *L'Internationale* and *La Marseillaise* . . . Fanon lacked the touch with which he could have made the Algerian soul reverberate . . . In order to speak a people's inmost language, one must share their beliefs. Fanon was an atheist."[31]

He was even—how can M. Bennabi forget it?—"from Martinique."

Rejecting the fashions and the morals of the west, protecting oneself from all "infatuation" with foreign culture, or assimilation, the "Algerian personality" must keep at a distance everything which, like a virus, might be associated with these fashions, these morals, this culture. And how can this personality possibly discover itself, if its representatives continue to shamelessly mix their genes with those of the foreigner? The "Algerian personality" cannot accommodate itself to mixed marriage; it refuses such a thing absolutely; this is a categorical imperative of our "essence."

An Algerian woman, Z.O., presents her views on this matter in an article which needs to be quoted in its entirety.[32] As an introduction she uses some lines from the poet Lamoud:

Greet the doctor and don't forget his wife:
He is called Salomon and his wife, Madame Balkis.
He has a child—may God give him a long life!
In whose being the French and Arabs do battle.
But don't blame him if he betrays his country,
For he is half *Salah* and half *Maurice*.

The fact that the child "betrays" his country can be passed over; this is some kind of "mistake"; but how was the father able to transgress his Algerian personality so basically? "Is he not aware that here, in each house, lives a young girl, perhaps several young girls, of more perfect beauty, more noble religion, higher morality, and purer origin?"

[How could he have married] one of those poor women, who share neither his language, his ways of life, nor his nationalist sentiments . . . this foreign woman will gradually make him lose his Arabo-Islamic personality, will make him share her language, her faith and her mentality . . . How can we avoid this evil—if such foreigners become mistresses of our households and mothers of our children? How can our youth ignore or pretend to ignore the fact that the best women on earth are our women, and that the most noble woman in the world is the Arab woman?

Yes [continues Z.O.], youth will not find anyone better than the Arab woman, a woman who lives exclusively for her man. She accepts unhappiness so that he may be happy, she tires herself so as to allow him to rest, she loses her health so that he may safeguard his; if he falls ill, she sacrifices both sleep and nourishment to care for him; if he is in financial difficulties, she sells her jewels and goods to come to his aid; if he commits mistakes or indulges in acts of egotism, she demonstrates her respect by her forbearance, her virtue, and she closes her eyes . . .

If he is attracted to another woman, she does not look for another man. If he strays, she remains faithful; and she does not abandon her home and her children to go off with a lover, like western women do.

So much pleasantness and no equal contempt or disdain? Z.O. finally can no longer continue in this vein, and she bursts out: "When will the consciences of our youth awake? When will the truth appear to them in all its glory? . . . Our young people must have a pure origin, roots of good quality, blood, soul, a well-rounded education, which excludes a mélange of bloods, the confusion of spirit, the absence of education . . ."

What is happening to "the virility, the splendor of Algeria, the national Arabo-Islamic character of our vigorous youth? What state of mind can our young people be in, when they [see] their sisters in the arms of foreigners, who are their enemies and the enemies of the entire Arab nation? Must they all be lost?"

No, one cannot choose "for a wife the daughter of one's enemy . . . those poor women of Europe who attach themselves to our young men like leeches"; no, one cannot forget that "numerous women of France, Israel, Germany, and Italy were found in the mountains with the troops of Challe, Bigeard, Salan, and that they aimed their bullets at our young soldiers."

Thus, all mixed marriages are forbidden, by "a true and authentic patriotism," for the sake of the honor of our country.[33]

Motivated by the same "patriotism" as Z.O., concerned, as she is, to "base the new society . . . on our Arabo-Islamic traditions," and to "struggle with all strength against detrimental foreign influences," officials of the National Union of Algerian Women [UNFA] have taken an official stand against mixed marriage.

The *Rapport d'Orientation* of the First Congress, November 1966, denounced "a sign which ought to cause anxiety: the continuing of Algerian marriages to foreigners. The same situation is found among many students, the future leaders of Algeria, who are obliged to spend long periods of study abroad and who often return with foreign spouses.[34] The UNFA and the country's leaders ought to pay attention to this problem, which will obviously influence the evolution of our society and its future."[35]

The *Résolutions finales* return to the same question:

The Congress ought to fight against . . . influences which are incompatible with the Algerian personality—to dedicate itself completely to the protection of the nuclear family . . . by creating structures which . . . conform to [the] Algerian personality and to [the] Arabo-Islamic culture.

This is why we disapprove of mixed marriage, insofar as it greatly upsets the balance of the family [structure].

Mixed marriage poses other problems which ought to prevent future leaders who have made mixed marriages from being appointed to responsible positions, particularly in foreign affairs.

So! We have been instructed: in order to refashion an "Algerian personality," we must divest ourselves of all foreign elements. We must "slough off" these influences, clean ourselves up, disinfect ourselves.

Let us then break up with our foreign husbands (or those of foreign origin: militants who are naturalized or converted are no different); take off our skirts, dresses, and suits, and you, my brother, put on *babouches* [slippers] and a *gandura* [traditional full-length garment], cut your hair short or, even better, shave your head! Carry worry beads in your hand and, even if you are a minister in the government, by all means repudiate those foreigners—French, Swedish, German, Yugoslav, Bulgarian, Russian, or Italian—whom you, to the detriment of the specific Arabo-Islamic-Algerian personality, dared to marry.

Prohibit, as the South Africans do, any "melange of races," and, like the Sioux of North America or the Toba of South America, give up worrying about introducing weaknesses into our race. Let us marry each other and remarry each other with our cousins.

Veiled and wearing burnooses, let us throw to the dogs the works of Frantz Fanon, "who does not touch the origins of our subjectivity," and the works of Kateb, Dib, Senac, and Ait Djafer as well, these authors who stubbornly speak French. And let us throw out the works of Molière (Tartufe will be the first to go, surely) and those of Gogol and of Shakespeare . . . For knowledge of the culture, the fashions, the mores, the men and women of foreign countries denudes us of our real essence, alienates us from our true personality . . . let us just be ourselves!

Ourselves—but what will we really be? Once we have purified, disinfected, scrubbed ourselves clean, what will our personality be?

Islamic! Yes, I well understand that. But Islamic in what way? Like the Turks, the Malayans, the Irano-Indians (not likely the latter, for India is "a land of syncretism—Bahai, Ahmedi—and of tolerance")[36] Black Africans, Arabs—and if Arab, Middle Eastern or North African Arab? "Oh, no, Algerian!" And there we are again, scarcely any further ahead than before, and probably less further ahead: dressed like the others, who are no longer the same others, our heads empty and our hearts dry, waiting for M. Tidjani and M. Bennabi to, hand in hand, come and "stir [our] soul, henceforth an Algerian soul, into a sacred trance" which . . . what . . .

Let us conclude, then, as follows: In cloaking evolution in the veils of tradition, in acclaiming the singularity of a nature which one has difficulty in defining, in scraping in lost depths "for the roots" of our "subjectivity," in placing in the same category Fanon, anisette, and Rouget de Lisle, and in equating open culture with mental neurosis, long hair with revolution, debauchery with modernity, and western women with prostitutes one is simply stacking the cards and confusing the issues.

In telling women what they ought not to do, not to wear, not to read, not to look at, and not to love, and by not explaining to them, in concrete terms, what they *can* become, one is opposing oneself, objectively, to all progress: one is simply continuing and maintaining the confusion, the hate, the sectarianism, and the prejudices which already exist. Such a passion for the past reveals a fear of the future, and this "fidelity to the dead" is an affront to the living—and to the dead themselves.

What gave the past its vitality, this past to which traditional intellectuals refer [declares J. Berque], is that the past was involved with the problems of the period, it was then modern, open to the world. A tradition which tries to cut itself off from cosmopolitan influences, to restrict itself to a more and more insular *specificity*, is not a living tradition . . . Such a tradition expresses itself, not in creative or affirmative terms, but in terms of response and memory [*réponse et ressentiment*]. Such a culture defines itself as against something. It no longer exists; it simply reacts. When one defines oneself only as against another, this means that one hesitates to exist or live.[37]

And that one is afraid to see women actually existing as independent persons.

Perhaps it can be argued that we are taking these confused proposals and definitions too seriously; for, when people speak of "sacred tradition," of "specific personality," one understands this to mean, "basically," *religion*. We suspect, then, that basically the Algerian woman, in her evolution, should remain faithful to Islam. Thus, it might be well to examine the question from this point of view.

But, again, this in itself is ambiguous; for "to evolve in terms of our religion" could mean, in the larger sense, to evolve while continuing to observe the fundamental precepts of Islam (the "five pillars") or, in a more narrow sense, to evolve while conforming to the Koranic proscriptions regarding women.

In the first sense, there are no *special* difficulties. If the Muslim woman may be defined as she who professes that "there is no God but Allah and Mohammed is his Prophet," who recites her five daily prayers, gives alms, fasts one month per year, and eventually makes the pilgrimage to Mecca, she can—just like the man—abide by these canonical obligations and still evolve: in theory, there is nothing in these rules which will retard or prevent her eventual emancipation.

Perhaps, in practice, some problems will arise. If one is allowed to say at night the prayers which the necessities of work have prevented one from performing at the proper moment during the day, to delay until more affluent days the expensive pilgrimage (at least 4,000 D.A. [Algerian dirhams, about $800.00]), other accommodations are less easy to accomplish.

For example, the fast during Ramadan is required by the faith, but can a developing country afford such a period of fast, a fast which will lower the rate of natural productivity as well as contribute to many other problems (damage infants' health through the mothers' weakness, diminish the strength of adults who are already undernourished, create higher absenteeism on the job, more natural abortions [up to 50 percent]—cut down on the amount of blood plasma in the hospitals, add to accidents on the job, in automobiles . . .)?

Will a scrupulous observance of the faith, and of the fast in particular, curb our society's evolution? If the question is posed, it is on the broadest possible scale, at the level of collective development; and it is then as much as that she is a member of the larger national community—and not just that she is a female—that the Algerian woman finds herself involved (favored or rejected) in the community's answer to this question.

For if one considers women's evolution as occurring outside the general social process, that is something else: without taking into account those inevitable "arrangements" between heaven and earth in which the history of religions abound; without re-interpreting the dogmas of former times in terms of the present. A view of women's liberation as being regulated, uncompromisingly, by the letter of the Koran is a very different matter indeed.

Those who refer to evolution in this latter sense take care, most of the time, to state clearly, "according to the Koran . . . religion says that . . ." They use these terms as if to give more weight to their proposals, but they never indicate the surah or verse of the Koran upon which they rely, or even that their particular citations may be shortened or "sweetened." Are they ignorant of the Koranic text? Confused? Dishonest intellectually?

For example, Laila Hacène asserts, with hardly a single piece of supporting evidence, that "Koranic laws are not designed to keep the woman in an inferior position." Designed or not to . . ., what do they actually say?

Our spokeswoman continues, in a still more interesting vein, "Due to the influence of existing social structures, the Koran, in some points, favored the man more than the woman. At the time, the consequences were not particularly grave, and certainly nothing is to be found in the Koran which could be construed as degrading or scornful of the feminine condition."[38]

But if there has been "degradation" despite [the Koranic surahs], is it that the Koran has been totally ineffectual and the Muslim a bad practitioner of his faith? Why? Leila Hacène says nothing at all about this and adds, in order to clarify everything, "For slight inequalities, the Koran brought compensation . . ." Well, then, is it equality or inequality?

Why not the one rather than the other? Ah, but all of our commentators seem uneasy in their responses. Afraid of being challenged by the texts, they waver, retract what they have already said, and manage to lose the argument in subtle *distinctions*: this is the case, for example, of M. Zoheir Ihadadan.

In a long article, "Emancipation or Depersonalization,"[39] M. Ihadadan admits, "It is wrong to pretend that Muslim doctrine affirms equal rights for man and woman. We find the contrary to be true; the restrictions are numerous; a woman cannot be an imam or a judge, or be placed at the head of a State; two women are necessary as witnesses to equal the testimony of one man. These examples testify to a certain inequality."

True, and, if the author were to push his analogy further, he would have to admit that, according to Islam, a woman is inferior to man, and that thus there is no evolution possible "within the Arabo-Islamic framework." He may think this, but such statements are not appropriate to be published on the eve of a religious feast.[40] He refuses both what he calls "depersonalization" and "emancipation" and is therefore obliged to invent a compromise solution; sure enough, he does so!

After having suggested that his examples "testify to a certain inequality," he adds: "But one should note that this position is that of doctrine. It is more difficult to state what the position of the Koran is in this matter, or the position of the Prophet."

What? Muslim doctrine is not that of the Koran? But then, it is not Muslim? So what is it?

M. Ihadaden foresees this objection: "The distinction which we make between the Koran and doctrine could be contested, since the Koran is a source of doctrine. But the doctrine draws its tenets from other sources, in its sections concerning women, and it has neglected the spirit and the sense of the basic principles contained in the Koran!" Take heed, then, all jurists, doctors, reformists, *qadis*, shaykhs, and others accused of heresy and traffic in doctrines!

But by what other doctrines is this "doctrine" allowed to be indoctrinated? With what impure sources (foreign perhaps; oh, *spécificité*) is it mixed? M. Ihadaden does not reveal his . . . sources. And, finally, what good does it do to propose a "doctrine" for the Algerian woman which owes less to the Koran than to the male's desire to be superior?

"It is not a question of superiority or inferiority," he concludes, "but of natural differences in aptitude. It is a fact that a man is stronger than a woman; it is a fact that he can do the most difficult tasks; it is also a fact that a woman admits herself defeated by work which necessitates a sustained physical effort and which is not congenial to her nature."

It is also a fact that M. Ihadaden has not had to compete with a Soviet woman worker in the mines of the Urals or in Siberia; or on the mat with a female judo expert; or in the laboratory against Madame Curie; or, in daily life, with all the peasant women who, despite work in the fields, carrying wood and water, and tending the household, still have the energy to care for six children. It is a fact, finally, that M. Ihadaden does not hesitate to use the most worn out cliches and, as a partisan of no "depersonalization," has the nerve to imitate a . . . Lyautey and say, "It is a question of differences and not of inequalities."[41]

But let us leave the "doctrinaire" types to argue about their sources, and let us return to the Koran itself.

No ambiguity is to be found here concerning the nature of woman and her role: addressing itself only to men, the Koran says that "Allah has given wives [to them]" (16,74), that "among his signs is that of having created wives [for them]" (30,20).[42]

Created for man, woman has as her basic function the satisfaction of men; they are sources of pleasure, the warrior's repose: ". . . [Allah has created] for you wives to bear you issue . . ." (30,20), and, more explicitly, "Your wives are a field for you to plough. Go to your field as you wish . . ." (2,223).

Created for men, for their satisfaction, women are inferior to them; it is true that they have "rights equal to their obligations" but these rights are not the same as those of men, for "men have dominance over them." (2,228).

M. Aniba's "explanation" of this verse constitutes another clever evasion: "This precedence has nothing to do with the qualities of the man and the woman but applies mostly to the function of the masculine partner, who is responsible for the happiness and well-being of the family group. It is only a question of a prerogative conferring the administrative direction of the family on the man."[43] But what is this "prerogative" based on if not on the pre-eminence (and the precedence) of the man?

Another verse of the Koran, which M. Aniba does not quote, confirms this: "Men have authority over women, because Allah preferred certain among you over certain others, and that men spend of their goods, in favor of women . . . Those of whom you suspect a lack of docility, scold them! Relegate them to their rooms! Beat them . . ." (4,38).

Even if "authority" means equally "protection, capacity to act in the name of,"[44] even if one translates the word *qawwamuna* as "direction" or "guidance" (men are guides or directors of women),[45] it is always women who are in need of being protected and directed—acted for more than acting. The fact is that truly "Allah preferred certain among you to certain others"; it is by virtue of a divine decision that women are inferior to men by nature.

From this inferiority, a number of consequences result; some of them follow:

———A Muslim man may marry a woman of the Book (Christian or Jewish; Koran, 5,5), but a Muslim woman may marry only a Muslim.[46]

———A Muslim may "marry of those women are pleasing [to him] two, three, or four" (4,3), and having "relations with [his] wives and [his] concubines if [he is] above reproach" (60,29,30); and Allah has "declared lawful for [him] . . . [the] slaves that have been given to him in the course of wars" (33,48). But a Muslim woman may never have more than one husband.

——A Muslim man is free to do as he pleases, dress as he wishes, and lead his life in his own way, but a Muslim woman "becomes mistress of herself only when she becomes an old woman"[47] or only when she marries, but "the majority as far as marriage is concerned is little more than an illusion, for the woman escapes her dependence on [her parents or tutors] only to fall under that of her husband."[48]

——A Muslim man is not required to be faithful to his wife (since polygamy and concubinage are permitted to him); but a Muslim woman ought to be faithful to her husband always, and it is enough that she be merely *suspected* of adultery in order to merit punishment.

——A Muslim man, throughout his conjugal life, has the right to correct his wife, but a Muslim woman is never allowed to "correct" her husband.

——A Muslim man may dispose of his goods and use them as he wishes, but in the Malikite rite (ours in Algeria) a Muslim woman cannot dispose of more than a third of her goods without the permission of her husband.

——A Muslim man may repudiate his wife at any time and without providing the slightest motive as justification for this unilateral act; as for a Muslim woman, in the Malikite rite, her only recourse is to ask for a divorce before the court, for a duly proved reason.

——Divorce by mutual consent is recognized, yet the Muslim woman, to extract repudiation from her husband, should present him with a gift (khul).

——In case of divorce, it is the father, or his nearest male relative, who keeps the child; if the children are very young, they can be left in care of the mother (on condition that she not remarry), although the cost of child maintenance is borne by the father alone.

———In the strictest sense of the terms, the wife is not even obliged
to nurse her children; "Repudiated wives are obliged to nurse their
children until the age of two, *if the father wishes that the nursing
be completed*" (2,23). The mother no longer exercises the right to
the guardianship of her children (the law recognizes only *la tutelle
testimentaire*).

———Finally, a Muslim woman can inherit, but the share is always
less than a man: "If a man dies without children, but leaves a sister,
half of what he leaves goes to the sister . . . If he has brothers and
sisters, the male share is equal to the share of two sisters" (4,75).

This is equality?
No doubt, for, since "God is good and merciful," women are supposed to be well treated; although they may be inferior and submissive,
they have some rights, and the men have duties toward them.
During his lifetime, the Prophet treated his wives with great tenderness. Many verses in the Koran exhort men to respect their female con-
sorts: "Say to the believers that they should lower their eyes modestly
and be chaste" (24,30); not to abandon them without some provision for
their support: "If you repudiate your wives, provide for them in relationship to your means, in the manner in which you live; do not be un-
generous to them, in order to place them in difficulties; if they are
pregnant, provide for them until they have delivered. If they are nursing
a child of yours, support them, and bestow that support upon them in a
convenient manner" (65,6).
There is no doubt that women are persons. Their consent to marriage
is required: "O you who believe, it is not right for you to take women
against their wishes" (4,23); they keep all rights to their own property:
it is the husband, even if the wife is very rich, who must provide the
maintenance for the family; they share in inheritance, and, if they live a
pious life, they have a place, like men, in paradise: "The one, man or
woman, who does good works while he is a believer, that one will enter
the Garden, and he will not be wronged by so much as a particle of a
date stone" (4,123 [*sic*], 124).
But despite the promise of a happy hereafter and a relatively comfortable material existence on earth, the Muslim woman is still, ontologic-
ally, inferior to the man. This is not a "detail" which can be considered
negligible or re-interpretable: for a believer, this inferiority is fundamental. Because it proceeds from a divine preference, this inferiority is
the mark—natural, ineffaceable—of the woman.
This status, stated in the Koran, represents definite progress *for the*

seventh century; one may speak justifiably of the "feminism" of Mohammed; in an era when girls were buried alive and women treated like cattle, the Prophet's proscriptions were, assuredly, revolutionary. But, just like Christian nations who have not ordered their lives according to evangelical principles, the peoples of Islam have not applied the most progressive tenets of the Koran in all times and places: they have been continually twisted and circumvented.

In the field of economics, Maxim Rodinson has demonstrated this well. He points out: "The prohibition against *riba* [usury] is not very practical . . . the legal doctors have been ingenious, in inventing ways by which the theoretical prohibitions may be circumvented. These methods have a special name in Arabic: *hiyal*, or tricks, ruses. Special books are devoted to listing these ruses, such as those of Abou Bakr Ahmed Al Khaccaf, who died in 874." [49]

But there are no books to explain how the message of the Prophet can be twisted or circumvented for the benefit of women; this is because there has been no need for such volumes. The jurists have always been men, the majority of women did not know the law, and it was quite natural that the law could be broken without causing any problems for anyone. Throughout the centuries, the Muslim woman has been deprived of her rights and of her goods; in contrast, those Koranic proscriptions which do not have economic repercussions or affect the man's position (the idea of inferiority, beatings in case of *supposed* or *feared* intractableness) have been applied according to the letter and continue to be so applied.

If, throughout history, Islamic theology has been revised or left untouched according to practical needs of this kind, how then can the Algerian woman accomplish today what she has not been able to accomplish for thirteen centuries?

The greatest potential revolutionary will pause when she considers the historical record, when she tries to explain to herself the needs of the social group which has produced her; and even in very favorable circumstances she may not have enough strength to begin the process of women's liberation according to a model which might have some possibility of being realized.

What miracle, in 1967, is going to give her this power which she lacks? And how will she bring to an end the traditions which, long before now, have been inextricably entwined with sacred Revelations—traditions which are no longer, within the group conscience, distinguishable from Revelation itself and which have contributed toward the "freezing" of women's role in a status of predetermined inferiority (whether by the Book itself or by social mores)?

Even supposing that thirteen centuries of restrictive interpretations and retrogressive practices could be abolished by an act of magic and that the basic ideology would as a consequence acquire new vigor, still that ideology would not have today the same revolutionary significance it did in the time of Prophet.

Certainly, *in the seventh century,* one can see that for a woman to be the third or fourth wife, when before she did not have this title or the rights conferred by that title; to be able to inherit a quarter or a half share, when before she had received nothing; to give her consent to marry when before she had been taken against her will . . . surely one can see that these were changes for the better, and generous changes.

But—*in the twentieth century*—it can hardly be considered revolutionary to live with a co-wife, when monogamy is stipulated by most of the laws; to be relegated to domestic tasks or to the lowest ranks of hired labor, when the equality of men and women has become a basic demand; when, in some countries, women direct business enterprises, are engineers, scholars, astronauts; to be "protected" when, in other areas of the world, women plan their own lives according to their individual tastes and wishes; to let the fathers choose the husbands of their daughters and the husband the house where the couple will live, all because men, being men, have "pre-eminence."

Let us be just, though. Is it not true that the majority of Algerian women today do other things besides having children and keeping house, "lowering their eyes" (24,31) when they go out, and "covering themselves with their veils" (33,59)?

Yes, that is true, but it is also true that many women are abandoned without legal process, deprived of all support and all inheritance, beaten by drunken husbands or harassed by street urchins.

"We are here to help in the cases of abduction of young girls, or in cases of rape," states a lawyer. "No mother of a family can walk alone without being accosted by people of a questionable type; no woman student can return home from school without being harassed by . . . street urchins."

El Moudjahid comments, "Not a single day passes without disappearances, even kidnappings, crimes, and offences of all kinds which never are reported to the police . . . We must sound a cry of alarm."[50]

If we continue to hold to the proposition that the evolution of the Algerian personality must take place in "the framework of our religion," then it is the men who must evolve; it is the man's behavior that needs to be adjusted to the precepts of the Koran; for, in terms of our religion, the Algerian woman, in a sense, is already "evolved," and has been for centuries.

And if one understands by the words *healthy evolution* only that people "will not steal, [that] they will not fornicate, [that] they will not kill their children, and [that] they will not commit infamous acts" (60,12) and when one speaks of the evolution of women as conforming to our religion, one can see only too well that it is the very idea of evolution itself that is being rejected.

When the jurists attempt to readjust the precepts of the Koran to the demands of the modern world (with regard to polygamy, support of the wife by the husband, adoption . . .) and try to place evolution in a Koranic context, they are really attempting to return to the past, trying to construct a framework within which it is impossible to realize the stated goals of our nation: "To wish to reduce the claims of conscience to the exigencies of a revolutionary epoch is, in the strict sense of the word, reactionary."[51]

In just such ways are our Tartufes embarked on a campaign of sabotage and obstruction; they take refuge behind incontestable texts that the speakers themselves have not read; and they cite only what is necessary in order to give themselves the air of enlightened reformers.

But their campaign is badly orchestrated from time to time; the players are matched poorly with their instruments, and they strike false notes; as a result, religion, which the good apostles benignly present as the condition of "a healthy revolution," becomes an obstacle to all progress. These types (*boutonneux*)—to whom *El Moudjahid* gives an unexplainable publicity,[52] reveal the true meaning of their religious argument, as may be seen in the following comments:

Allow me to say that the Algerian woman's participation in the evolution of the nation is a catastrophe for the Muslim religion and a betrayal of the Koran—Allow me also to say that the debauchery and the confusions in the present administration are really due to women. In these cases, it would have been better had they remained sequestered.

Another commentary in *El Moudjahid*:

Insofar as the woman can render useful service, I do not see why one . . . should prevent [her evolution]. In some ways one must be in tune with the times. [Alas, alas, alas.] The evolution of the woman is inevitable, thus one must channel it.

Woman is not equal to man. Our working classes are deeply
Muslim, traditional, and conservative; otherwise, where would our
religion be? . . . Our socialism rests on the five pillars of Islam and
not on the evolution of the woman . . .

The evolution of woman has been a determining factor in the
degradation of Islamic manners and morals.

In order to assuage the current thirst for civilization, must one turn
upside down and drag through the mud all that remains precious
to us, our heritage, our honor, and our religion, these factors which
have always brought glory to Muslims and contributed to the
grandeur of Islam?

The fact of being submissive to her husband, of being serious and
going out in public veiled has never prevented woman . . . from
participating in public life, and from working . . .[53]

Fanatics with badly fitting masks? Or better-adjusted devotees? Whoever they are, it is curious that these good souls do not mention the
Koran when they are discussing the problem of woman's evolution; one
might ask why not, if the Koran is a rule of life, which one constantly
invokes in all areas of life? It regulates inheritance of property but says
nothing against private property; does it permit, then, agrarian reform
and collective farming?[54] Such a question apparently does not bother
the devotees. Our penal code, for example, is far closer to the French
code than to the Koran, but have our (religious) devotees ever protested
against it?
    We might make even graver accusations: have we ever seen con-
demned, in the name of religion, such things as abandoned families, the
increase in the divorce rate, the proliferation of bars and prostitution,
the traffic in corruption of all kinds?[55]
    How can a believer, in the true sense of the word, keep silent before
the moral crisis which our society is facing? Or keep silent—except
when the word *woman* is mentioned; then suddenly all is unleashed,
and people raise their arms to heaven, but I suspect that it is not love of
heaven which provokes this holy anger.
    What, then, are the reasons for such behavior? Why do we have these
litanies to "sacred tradition," these mystic trances which come over men
(and some women, as well, in imitation) whenever the problem of
women's liberation is raised?
    We must not exclude the possibility that some of these reactions

spring, *in part,* from a certain lack of understanding: someone may be against evolution because he does not know quite what it means or, further, because he is against what he thinks it means; the political context in which evolution is placed often tends to distort the whole idea.

This distortion extends to other ideas as well, as it did during the war of liberation, and one finds the same thing even in times of *independence!* For, if some understand independence to mean "agrarian reform and the socialization of the means of production," others understand it to mean "opportunities for looting and grabbing, taking over requisitioned villas, and in general an easy life without work."

Independence, which came to us in July 1962, signaled the beginning of autonomy and revolutionary dynamism; but it also signaled the rise of the petit-bourgeois arriviste mentality, wheeling and dealing, and the basic idea, "I push you out so I can put myself in." In 1967, five years later, the concept of independence is still not always totally clear; recently, the labor representative declared to the owner of the business where he worked, "We're independent now, and I can stay here."

When the new ideas arise from other cultural milieus and the "terrain" is not receptive, deeper and more frequent confusions are evident; this is the case with women's emancipation.

This idea was not born in Algeria, or in the Muslim world, because the material bases for the idea do not exist here; the economy is different to begin with, and the market depends on manual labor. The idea of women's liberation first took form in Europe and it was introduced to Algerian society as the kind of notion which conflicted with our traditions and our culture.

The experiences and incidents of the recent past must not be forgotten, such as the masquerades of May 13 (when Frenchwomen lifted the veils from a number of Muslim women), the prostitutes forced to burn their veils, the workers of Mme Massu (who set up philanthropic centers where young girls could do handwork). For a very long time, the Algerian saw the evolution of women in a context of aggression, and during the colonial period it meant at first only a tentative "de-nationalization"; then it became the focus of the colonial attack on the Algerian identity.

"It was in the years 1930–35," Fanon writes, "that the decisive battle began. Responsible French officials of the Algerian colonial administration were dedicated to the destruction of the people's own originality. Given power to proceed, step by step, toward the breakdown of the forms of existence capable of evoking, more or less, a sense of national reality, they directed the greater part of their efforts toward the wearing of the veil—. . . Get the women on your side, and the rest will follow."[56]

To unveil, to dress in the European manner (and, at the extreme level, to eat European food, celebrate Christmas and Easter, name one's children Peter and Paul): the evolution of women was associated with actions at first, the action and appearance of the occupier; to Algerians in the beginning, then, evolution meant disowning their faith and their community and compromising with the enemy, becoming Franci-fied.

If only the early model had demonstrated some indisputable superiority; if, stripped of its political meaning, evolution had only had something appealing or enchanting about it! But the *pieds-noirs* who felt that women's liberation was their own personal territory added touches which only vulgarized the idea; and it was a very obvious vulgarity, a vulgarity of glamor, language, and morals.

For foreign women, when observed from a traditional point of view, looked heavily painted and arrogant ("The French woman is generally more racist than the man and acts as a powerful force to discourage contact between the two societies").[57] They talked and laughed loudly, they drank anisette with men, they had parties on horseback. From a traditional point of view these foreign women could only be prostitutes.

Thus, even though the times in general were revolutionary, the idea of women's evolution did not gain much support, for it was associated in people's minds with the persons (foreign) who symbolized it,[58] and with the circumstances (colonial) in which it was first apparent. Today this memory is constantly kept alive by the behavior of certain Europeans, but also by that of some young Algerian city women who adopt, from the west, the most questionable appearances and only those appearances.

No counterpropaganda, no attempts at education or explanation, can erase such evidence or help to change these young women's ideas and judgments (no less than those of Algerian men) on the idea of what evolution means.

We see such outward manifestations in the magazines displayed on the newsstands, if they have not already been observed in the advertising of our national press: on November 11, 1965, for example, *El Moudjahid* carried an enormous photo (15 by 10 cm) of a nude woman sitting astride a chair. This accompanied the announcement of the film *The Scandal of Christine Keeler*.[59]

In Touggourt an artistic evening was organized by the *syndicat d'initiative* [chamber of commerce] in the spring of 1966. Prostitutes, picturesquely dubbed Ouled Nail, appeared on the stage with cigarettes between their lips. Why should we be surprised, then, that the public identifies all women who smoke with the Ouled Nail.

Generally, what can women's evolution signify in such contexts? No more than other ideas (*socialism, the people*) which one has never taken the trouble to define but has, on the contrary, tried to obscure; just as there is *"a specific socialism,"* . . . *a Muslim socialism* . . . *a scientific non-Marxist socialism,*[60] there is also a *"good evolution,"* an *"evolution according to our traditions,"* which should be *"prudent."*

Good or bad, slow or rapid, traditional or modern, what is this evolution, and what does one mean when one discusses it? The concept, which has never been narrowed down and defined, embraces the most contradictory characteristics and often those which one associates with the least possible evolution, for example, general debauchery, "sleeping around," night clubs, and the Riviera.

If so many Algerians see evolution in terms of the aggressions of the past and the scandals of today, they also project their dreams and desires toward the same idea and, when the sequels of colonialism turn out to make life difficult, those dreams and desires are reactivated by the frustrations of the present.

Like a sick or angry man who "sees red," many a man, gripped by true sexual obsession,[61] translates evolution into terms of debauchery; he invents in his own mind women who are in accord with his fantasy. Thus, walking out freely becomes "provoking," a woman's pleasant smile an "invitation," and ease in attracting others becomes "libertinism." In the end, not only western women are then equated with whores but also all Algerian women who are a bit modern in their behavior.[62]

By indulging in such fantasies, men are freed from their obsession while at the same time keeping their consciences clear; then they feel justified in shutting up their sisters, while at the same time they chase their neighbors' sisters: since the neighbors' sisters are "bad girls," why not? The whole combination of projection, transfer, defense mechanism, and autojustification is well known.

But this does not explain everything: to the historic reasons and the physiological and psychological compulsion must be added some very specific socioeconomic motivations, common to all men; these motivations express finally, in the end, the needs and the customs of a particular class.

Undoubtedly, the majority of men, ours as well as others, are interested in preserving the status quo; too many privileges are at stake, and for too long a time, for them to happily renounce the status quo. For centuries, woman has lived in the shadow of man ("directed," "protected"), and the man managed, organized, ordered; it is natural and normal that, when the old order is threatened, the privileged classes should protect that order.

But not everyone is equally privileged: if the peasant, who holds the purse strings, ill-treats his wife, and marries off his daughters, has some advantage over *them*, the landowner has greater advantage over the peasant; his fifty hectares of land, for example. If the small-time worker, who goes out with his buddies to the café and the cinema is more favored than his sequestered wife, he is still less favored than the high official with a car and a villa.

The worker and the peasant no doubt are interested in preserving their privileges as men; but the landowner and the official are even more interested in safeguarding their privileges. When one has nothing else, a woman is a good deal. Olive trees, flocks of animals, a position as cashier in a firm—these things are equally precious and it is these things which must be safeguarded.

For, if the oppression of woman is a particular case of exploitation of man by man, the profiteers and exploiters may all be lumped in one category: the bourgeois, who, in pretending to maintain the oppression of women, seek, in reality, to perpetuate oppression of other men; all this takes place under the cloak of Islam or its variants—"sacred tradition," "glorious past," "specificity." . . .

[The author then explains in some detail the bourgeois corruption and exploitation currently taking place in the Algerian government bureaucracy as examples of what she means.]

In Algeria, as in other areas of the world, the bourgeois are trying to revive the old myths only to delay the day of change.

Today our bourgeois dabble freely in the public money, hardly disdain either alcohol or night clubs, and do not hesitate to celebrate Christmas, with presents and, if not a crèche, at least with a fine tree ("the children, you understand").[83] They are contemptuous of Algerian schools and therefore place their offspring in Christian schools (on this point M. Tidjani does not object, nor does that other good apostle of Arabo-Islamism, the Moroccan Allal el Fassi).[84] And it is these bourgeois of ours who plagarize so easily western models, who have developed the fable of Algerian "specificity."

This is one fable: that after the passage through our land of, among others, Carthaginians and Romans, Vandals and Byzantines, Arabs, Turks, and French, some "purity" of our being remains. Another fable: that we share with all Mediterranean peoples (Jews, Christians, or Muslims) those customs and habits which constitute our originality—circumcision, the veil, the sequestering of women, marriage between cousins.[85] Is this a fable, or is it simply replacing the events of today with ideas from the past? And the final and most important fable is one that has been de-mobilized, for peace has returned; this fable is nationalism.

What is this specificity, if it is not the "being ourselves" of the colonial era? And to be ourselves then, was that not simply being against the other—the enemy? But the enemy is no longer there, and nationalism, when the country is not obviously threatened, loses some of its bracing virtues; one rejuvenates it, one calls it "specificity" and throws it to the people—like powder in their eyes.

Blinded, they do indeed remain themselves (in their poverty, their hunger, their rags; they visit the marabouts, fear the djins and the anger of heaven); and while the people are occupied with their superstitions, one can devote oneself to business. "The mafia of big businessmen, dealers, and other affluent types grieve for the past because it was of benefit to them . . . they play on the people's credulity with fetish-ism," writes *Alger Républican* in February 1964.

During this same period, *Le Peuple* published, under the title "Let Us Pose Real Problems," a piece signed by numerous personalities, among them no less than Colonel Si Hassan, a member of the Revolutionary Council:

Behind the fine pretext of defending the values of Islam, we can see a campaign, a campaign knowingly conducted in order to launch an attack on the process of socialization in which all the progressive forces of the nation are irreversibly engaged. Dreaming of a theocratic state in the service of certain caste and class interests, the promoters of this union[86] see as their goal the slowing of Algerian progress, and the blocking of any dynamic revolutionary who seeks to activate that progress.

In the same vein, Mostefa Lacheraf writes that all politics of caste, feudalism, or opportunistic bourgeoisie, seem to rely on a mystique which alone has the power to save all the world and direct the destiny of all; it will do this, of course outside the popular and democratic procedures.

This mystique is often only a confused messianism. In such situations one sees the birth of a system in which *constraint* is its principal safeguard, a system which, to justify itself ideologically, calls on a disparate mixture of religious-socializing doctrines; in this system self-serving traditions of the people are mixed with a pretended economic and social progress which is conceived in paternalistic terms . . . Messianism and mystique: obscurant pretensions . . .[87]

Those who invoke tradition are guilty of the same pretensions; they use the same mystifying technique, for the people, they think, do not know how to choose between the "good" and the "bad" traditions; and, if the people hold to one tradition, they will continue to respect the others. A good example of such thinking is the man who said that "there have always been poor people and rich people; the world is like that, one can do nothing about it." Yes, one must resign oneself, some to sleep, wrapped in cardboard, under the arcades of the former Rue de la Lyre, and others, to sleep, perhaps not in a golden bed, as in Ghana, but at least in a room "of rustic style."

And, since the people are not encouraged to look at things from the different points of view, to compare and criticize, we all become engulfed in outraged racism. The ego is set up for opposing itself to something; thus, the westerner, the foreigner, becomes that something, the other; the other is the nonspecific, then the absolute evil . . . and so on. The knot is tied.

Thus, we can see that the antifeminism of our reactionaries is set, very logically, within this context.

It is not possible for them to encourage the cause of women's liberation and at the same time maintain their other privileges. Women's liberation is not a problem which can be viewed in isolation; it is part of the whole in which it is implicated and which in turn conditions that whole; the bourgeoisie, who enrich themselves by exploiting this whole, cannot touch one of the forms of exploitation (woman by man) without placing the other forms in jeopardy. The problem must also be seen in economic terms, and, if one approaches it seriously, one can see that it is the total social structure which ought to be progressively changed.

Women's liberation requires, for example, that girls, the women of tomorrow, benefit, as of today, from an education as good as that being offered to boys; this would involve construction of schools: high schools, higher training institutes, mostly technical, which are *already* in insufficient supply throughout the country. So many investments![88]

Further, the access of many women to the world of work, tomorrow

and even today (many are unemployed and seeking work), would require that new jobs be created, and, to do this, factories and hospitals,
enterprises of all sorts must be constructed: still more investments.

This will still not be enough, for women workers will need to be freed
from the care of the children which prevent them presently from being
part of the labor force; nurseries must be opened, kindergartens; maternity services be provided, as well as a number of other group services,
such as low-priced restaurants, laundries, transportation, clinics . . .
Again, more investments.

Stating the situation in another way, one must be willing to invest on
the basis of loss—because, in contrast to an enterprise like a bar, or a
shop, or a hotel, no return will be forthcoming on the investment in the
immediate future. Enormous amounts of capital will be required; and
one must ask, Have the bourgeois even in rich countries ever organized
their investment on such a basis?

In France one accumulates property, one discusses for months the use
of a piece of land (shall one construct a wine market? a large school?).
Meanwhile people jostle each other at the entrances to hospitals,[89]
crowd into furnished rooms in Rue Mouffetard or into the hovels of
Saint-Denis.[90] Thus it should be clear that what is necessary is investment and spending without profit; before that can happen a radical
change in social structure must take place. Thus, women's liberation
cannot be realized in a capitalistic context.

Some might object that, despite this, Europeans are "evolved," that
European women are more "free" than Muslim women. Certainly they
are less enslaved, but their enfranchisement, relative as it is, can only be
understood if placed in *their* traditional framework.

For three centuries at least (from the sixteenth to the nineteenth), the
bourgeoisie of the west was revolutionary and objectively progressive;
with the capital from trade, the bourgeois constructed mills, then factories, and introduced fertilizer and machines into the countryside. They
industrialized and modernized Europe, and since they needed, for this
immense enterprise, many hands at low wages, they opened their factories to women (and to children). Liberation, yes, but also oppression:
object of pleasure to the husband, the woman became an instrument of
work (and, often, of pleasure as well) to the owner of the enterprise.

Economic progress, a general rise in the standard of living, and the
struggle of women, first as workers—these factors have indeed modified
the initial situation. But even if the European woman of the industrial
countries has achieved some rights, basically she remains an exploited
being;[91] the majority of women are paid less than men for equal work;[92]
the majority of women are excluded from qualified positions;[93] they are

prevented, through the absence of necessary services, from working overtime; still they work, on the average, more than ninety hours a week; and by the end of the month, in order to meet the bills, it is not unusual for them to prostitute themselves.[94]

The Algerian bourgeoisie is poorer (what an understatement) than their prototypes in Europe. They have less scope and vision, they are lacking in civic spirit, and they are incapable of organizing, even in their own interest, a beginning of economic development. They are also incapable, for even stronger reasons, of encouraging the process of women's liberation. As the problem has been stated, then, it is difficult to deny; this juggling, this stubbornness in insisting that all liberation must emerge from tradition; this preaching about a "return to sources": the only aim of it all is to protect the sources of income.

Let us look once more at these statements: *to evolve with respect for the past . . . to conform our personality to our Arabo-Islamic specificity*. Now, perhaps one can see more clearly the value of these arguments: where they originate, who they serve.

Of course not all who share this point of view are bourgeois, but whether this is from ignorance, inattention, or alienation does not matter; they are the agents of reaction, whose main purpose is now well understood: to prevent all evolution.

The reactionaries are equally interested in camouflaging the present. They speak of evolution in terms of the past, without ever analyzing the situation in which the woman finds herself today, a situation which must change if her position is to improve. They speak in this way in order to conceal the facts and also to mask all these who, in one way or another, seek to condemn the Algerian woman.

Notes

1.   For the information of European readers, I would like to make it clear that there is a fundamental difference between Arabo-Islamicism and Arabism, insofar as the first expression may be used with a reactionary meaning. The second expresses the revindication of freedom and dignity among the Arab peoples, in the face of the racism and imperialism of the capitalist west.

2.   September 8, 1966.

3.   At the end of the ninth century . . . four great schools of Muslim jurisprudence were established. They still exist:

The Malikites (in the Maghreb and North Africa) follow Malik ben Anas, who died at Medina at the end of the eighth century.

The Hanafites follow the Persian Abou Hanifa, who settled in Iraq and died at the end of the eighth century. This is the most "open" school . . . The official school under the Ottoman Empire, it persists in Turkey, Pakistan, and China.

The Shafi'ites (Egypt, Yemen, India, Indonesia) follow the Arab Ash-Shafi, who died in Egypt at the beginning of the ninth century.

The Hanbalites (limited to Saudi Arabia) descend from the great Ibn Hanbal, an Arab who died in Baghdad in the middle of the ninth century. A strict school, they reject all innovation and demand strict application of the law.

But it is well known that these four schools are all perfectly orthodox and that they differ only on points of detail in the legal interpretation of the Koran and the *Sunna*. Tradition . . . (V. Monteil, *L'Islam*, p. 67).

4. Y. Linant de Bellefonds, "Immutabilité du droit musulman et reformes législatives en Egypte," in *Revue Internationale de droit comparé, 1965*. Cited in M. Borrmans, "Codes de status personnel et évolution sociale en certain pays musulmans," *IBLA*, 1963. On the subject of the legal status of the Muslim, many suggestions have been given to me by M. Borrmans, to whom I wish to express here my deep gratitude.

5. J. P. Charnay, "La Vie Musulmane en Algérie, d'après la jurisprudence de la première moitié du siècle," *P.U.F.*, 1965, pp. 23–24.

6. I would like to thank here most sincerely Dr. J. N. Biraben, chef de service, L'Institut National d'Etudes Démographiques, Paris, who gave me these figures.

7. J. P. Charnay, "La Vie Musulmane en Algérie," p. 23.

8. Following the proposal of Madame Khemisti, a deputy, in 1963, the National Assembly passed a law fixing the age of marriage at a revolutionary sixteen for girls and eighteen for boys.

9. *El Moudjahid*, October 17, 1965.

10. Cf. G. Tillion, *Le Harem et Les Cousins*.

11. *El Moudjahid*, February 17, 1967. All italicized words in the quotations to be found in this article are mine.

12. Ibid., February 27, 1967.

13. M. Borrmans, "Codes de status personnel."

14. On abandoned families, see chapter 2 of *Les Algériennes*.

15. *Révolution Africaine*, December 20, 1964.

16. On divorce, see chapter 2 of *Les Algériennes*.

17. One Algerian dirham equals one new French franc.

18. According to Dr. J. N. Biraben.

19. On the condition of mothers, see chapter 2 of *Les Algériennes*.

20. *Révolution-Université* [sic], no. 4, December 1966.

21. "At the first level of education, the rate of girls enrolled is rela-

tively high, particularly in the early years of study (48 percent in CP 1, urban zone); it diminishes in number in absolute proportion as one progresses toward the upper grades. The end of the first cycle of study marks the greatest departure of girls enrolled in the Lycées" (*Bulletin statistique de l'Education Nationale*, no. 16, p. 7; no. 3, p. 11).

22.   Cf. appendix, *Quelques traditions . . . in Les Algériennes*.

23.   I quote the text as it is, without modifications . . . or corrections.

24.   Conference held in Algiers, Ibn Khaldoun room, February 1964. Cited in *Le Peuple*, nos. 19–28, March 1964.

25.   Not all Algerians, nor all Algerian intellectuals, agree with these absurdities. For example, in an interview which appeared in *Le Jour* (Beirut daily, May 27, and June 3, 1966), Mouloud Mammeri stated, very aptly: "In a century of space civilization, I find it rather vain to cling to particulars, which, instead of immuring us in a prison of our oneness, ought to be, on the contrary, instruments of our mutual enrichment . . ." He believes it to be a question rather of "realizing the city of our union, rather than the cliques of our particularisms."

26.   V. Monteil, *L'Islam*, p. 67.

27.   *Révolution Africaine*, September 1966.

28.   Leila Hacène, *Jeune Afrique*, July 17, 1966. In the debate sponsored by this magazine on the merits of G. Tillion's book, my young compatriot declared that "the superiority of the man . . . rests in the natural harmony of things." She cites, as examples of "democracy" in action, where this "superiority" is a "political reality" (women don't vote), the Swiss, that country of banks and of hotels—forbidden to Italians. She rejoices in the power to be cuckolded, although it costs too much for the husband (one year in prison for a man, two years for the woman, in case of adultery, according to our new penal code). Leila Hacène then concludes, logically, "I choose tradition."

29.   "Luxe et luxure," *El Moudjahid*, December 7, 1965.

30.   *Jeune Afrique*, no. 288. After this issue appeared (illustrated in an extremely disgusting way: as a representative of the "liberated" western woman, photograph of a poor shop girl; and, as representative of the "enslaved" Oriental, photo of a—courtesan;), the international weekly, as it calls itself, received numerous letters of protest, one of which, more pertinent than most, came from C. A. Julien. The editor, irritated, told this eminent historian to go back to his books, since the subject was one forbidden to Europeans. I, too, protested against these absurdities, which expressed their apartheid in a new formula. The editor-in-chief's response was: "I promise you that your letter, which contributes a great deal to the debate, will appear next September." That was in 1966. Surely a Maghrebi rendezvous!

31.   In the Conference already cited [n. 24]. "Immersed in the roots
of his subjectivity . . . touch which makes the soul quiver . . ." For those
who imagine, on the basis of these statements, that M. Bennabi is something of a deep-sea diver or a manufacturer of subjective pianos, I must
point out, in all seriousness, that he was the director of higher
education.

32.   *El Djeich*, Arabic edition, September 1965. Translated and reproduced in the *Revue de Presse*, no. 99. I would like to express my deep
gratitude to those in charge of *Revue de Presse*, who allowed me complete and free access to their library.

33.   This racist frenzy is apparent not only in Algeria; several years
ago, the National Union of Tunisian Women (UNFT) came out against
mixed marriages; and the Moroccan women have also done so. In *Al
Massa*, August 17, 1966, cited in *Revue de Presse*, no. 108, under the title
"The Danger of Moroccans' Marrying Foreigners," we read:

Although we have tried to discover the causes of such infatuations,
we suggest that money may be the principal lure; the young girl
lets herself be overwhelmed by the promise that her foreign husband will provide her with all the goods of progress of which she
dreams. The bitter truth is revealed a little later. The young girl is
shadowed then by immorality for, being Moroccan and Muslim,
she finds herself incapable of living in harmony with a foreign
man, who belongs to a religion other than Islam. In the end, she
loses the respect and esteem of her family and of her society. She
loses her dignity and her good reputation . . .
    This union compromises the young Moroccan woman's future
as well as her present. She bears children who are complicated,
dissolute, and who belong to no religion . . . Such children may
grow up psychologically disturbed . . . with feelings of bitterness
and hate . . . criminal instincts may take root in their hearts . . .
    How can she [the young Moroccan woman] allow herself to be
so insensitive as to betray, first, her immorality, then her impiety,
and finally her lack of social sense?

On the other hand, we must do justice to the Moroccans who are not
followers of Verwoerd. For example, we quote from an article by Zakya
Daoud in the revue *Lamalif* (October 1966, cited in *Revue de Presse*, no
109). After having noted that 30 percent of mixed marriages end in
divorce, she adds:

One asks too much of mixed marriages: one demands more of

them than they can give, for they are neither better nor worse than other marriages. They are marriages like others, with their sorrows and their joys, their little dramas and their great problems . . .

However, when they are successful, and this happens much more often than is generally believed by critics of such unions, mixed marriages are the best marriages, in the truest and fullest sense of the term. Out of difficulties, renunciations, compromises, and affirmations, which go on day after day and year after year, two human beings coming from different backgrounds have constructed, with much love and patience, something original. One young Breton woman has accepted the fact that she has not been able to visit her home in seven years; another young Danish girl has lived with her in-laws without a word of complaint and has learned Arabic perfectly in two months; another secretary takes Arabic after she has finished her day's work; a young Parisian has gone to live in the rural area, with no regrets . . .

[Zakya Daoud concludes that] mixed marriages and their offspring have a role to play; they are introducing a new element into Moroccan society, an element which ought to be beneficial if it is accepted and integrated into the society without preconceptions.

34.   Numerous instances of this are found: all purely subjective statements—no official number has ever been given, though some say that there are about 25,000 mixed couples in Algeria (the majority Algerian-foreign). This figure includes the French women, wives of Algerian citizens, who were repatriated as "Algerians."

35.   *Bulletin intérieur du FLN*, no. 4. The final resolutions return to the question: "The Congress should fight against influences incompatible with the Algerian personality and dedicate itself completely to the protection of the nuclear family . . . by establishing structures . . . which conform to [the Algerian personality] and to [the] Arabo-Islamic culture. This is why we disapprove of mixed marriages insofar as they greatly disturb the balance of the family structure."

36.   V. Monteil, *L'Islam*, p. 101.

37.   Interview in the Beirut journal *L'Orient*, November 11, 1964, quoted in *Revue de Presse*, no. 89.

38.   *Jeune Afrique*, July 17, 1966.

39.   *El Moudjahid*, March 20, 1967.

40.   The article was published in a special number on the occasion of the 'Id al-Kabir (a major Islamic feast).

41.   We know Lyautey's comment about Moroccans: "They are not inferior, they are other." How well stated!

42.   *Le Coran*, Blachère translation, Maisonneuve edition.

43.   *Humanisme musulman*, August 1965, p. 49.

44.   R. Blachère's note in *Le Coran*, p. 110.

45.   *Le Coran*, Hamidullah translation, Le Club français de livre.

46.   This clause has been revoked in all "modern" codes (Moroccan, article 29; Iraq, articles 17–18, etc.) or implied by them when they are not explicit on the subject (Tunisia, cf. Borrmans, "Codes de status personnel," and see appendix to *Les Algériennes*, p. 1).

47.   O. Pesle, *La Femme Musulmane dans le droit, la religion et les moeurs*, p. 92.

48.   Ibid.

49.   M. Rodinson, *Islam et Capitalisme*, p. 52.

50.   *El Moudjahid*, February 15, 1967.

51.   Rodinson, *Islam et Capitalisme*, p. 44.

52.   The letters quoted here were published in February and March 1967.

53.   Commentary in *El Moudjahid*, April 4, 1967.

54.   Rodinson, *Islam et Capitalisme*, p. 31.

55.   Why should we be surprised since these same people, or in this case their mouthpiece, dare to eulogize Nazism! In the August 1965 issue of *Humanisme musulman*, we can read the following on p. 17: "What is the Hitler movement? How did he use his somewhat antiliberal methods? Fundamentally, the Nazi movement was a reaction, certainly brutal, against a fact of life. Germany was decaying, it was necessary to save Germany. The Nazi regime was the only regime capable of saving Germany; the regime was Germany and its enemies were the enemies of Germany, and they had to be destroyed without mercy."

56.   F. Fanon, *L'an V de la révolution algérienne*, p. 15.

57.   P. Nora, *Les Français d'Algérie*, p. 175.

58.   They took good care of it, for the benefit of the Europeans, "progressive or not"; equating authentic Algeria with traditional Algeria, they refused to see, in a modern Algerian woman, a complete Algerian. They did not understand that, educated and unveiled, she could still be a citizen of the country. Is it necessary to point out that this narrow and contemptuous view, which equates Algerian-ness with traditionalism, is deeply reactionary?

59.   An exception, or a happy change in orientation? For the past fifteen days, toward the end of June 1967, the cinemas in the capital have shown only films from socialist countries.

60.   One should give credit here to Abdelaziz Zerdani, minister of labor, who, during a January 1966 conference of the local Union, UGTA, of central Algiers, denounced the confusions which are continued by such statements.

Speaking of these "specific socialisms," which are in the end only socialism in name, Zerdani stated, "if we insist on this point, it is to emphasize the emergence and growth of a number of plans or formulas called such names as *Islamic socialism* or *Christian socialism*. Recourse to such formulas only disseminates confusion and helps develop ideas which are basically opposed to socialist ideology and practice. It is from this base that reactionary and antirevolutionary slogans can develop and spread, which will prevent the true scientific approach to problems . . . Of these themes, we [mention in particular] . . . those tendencies which seek . . . to awake national feeling by the call, in all times and under all circumstances, on national values" (*El Moudjahid*, January 14, 1966).

61.   I do not know if there are, in these days, more ways to meet and attack women than before, but to read the "police record" of *El Moudjahid*, one might well believe this to be the case.

H. Abdelkadir, 35, raped a nine-year-old girl. Prison. Escaped. Raped again, a fourteen-year-old girl.

L. Mohammed, 22, raped a thirteen-year-old girl.

N. Ahmed, 24, kidnapped and raped a twelve-year-old girl.

G. Salah, 19, employee in a dry-cleaning shop, raped a fourteen-year-old girl behind the counter.

D. Mahieddine, 54, father of eight children, paramedic in an Algiers hospital, drugged two sick young girls (12 and 15) and then raped them.

I continue to maintain that what I wrote in *La Femme Algérienne* is still true: if it is disagreeable for a woman to walk on the streets of Algiers by day either alone or in a group, in the evening it is dangerous.

62.   Some end by recognizing this; such a young man approached me one evening when I was leaving the radio station. Very tense and aggressive, he began a detailed critique of *La Femme Algérienne*; he agreed, however, to discuss the subject with me and, little by little, he changed his mind. By the end of our conversation, he admitted his mistake. He was waiting for a *pépée*, a young girl in bell-bottom pants, cigarette between her lips, talking like a tough . . .

Many European readers equally "project," and understand my work in a way which reveals the concerns of their own milieux; A Frenchman asked if I was for free love in marriage, while a Dane (certainly drunk) explained to me that *La Femme Algérienne* was an invitation to eroticism! "Yes, yes," he insisted, "I read between the lines."

83.　This alienation is so widespread that the minister of national education has publicly denounced it . . . "Although we believe in all the prophets, the introduction of the tree and gifts at Christmas . . . smacks of blind imitation" (televised interview, January 10, 1967, cited in *Al Chaaf*, the Arabic language daily, January 11, 1967).

84.　The most affluent classes [have] a tendency to register their [children] in the schools run by the office of French universities and culture (*Statistiques Education Nationale*, bulletin no. 16, p. 17). I have myself witnessed pathetic scenes: the principal of a large Algerian high school pleading with the principal of a French high school ["Oh, it would be so good of you"] to register his own daughters in the French establishment. Not all our principals, obviously, are like this. And this is a tendency which is not justified; in the capital, at least, the local teachers are well qualified, and our pupils succeed as well on the French *bac* [exam] as on the Algerian *bac*.

85.　Cf. G. Tillion, *Le Harem et les Cousins*, p. 93.

86.　For example, a meeting was organized at the Maison du Peuple on January 5, 1964, by the Al Qiyam Association. More than three thousand persons signed a theocratic political resolution (calling for the closing of shops on Fridays, reserving jobs for Muslims alone). This association includes several teachers, workers, imams (one of whom held forth the day after the parade of November 1, 1965, on the indecency of holding female sports competitions), and a considerable number of merchants. These are the shock troops, as one can see, of the "specific socialism."

87.　M. Lacheraf, *Algérie, nation et société*, p. 303.

88.　In France, for example, in the preparatory classes of the largest schools, for every 16.060 boys there were 3.845 girls. Also certain establishments, like Saint-Cyr, Navale, Ecole de l'Air, or Polytechnique, are forbidden to girls. Cf. "Les intellectuelles," *La Nouvelle Critique*, no. 161, p. 24–25.

89.　Cf. *Le Nouvel Observateur*, January 10, 1967.

90.　Nearly one-fourth (22.6 percent) of the houses in France do not have running water. In rural communities, the figure is nearer to half (42.2 percent), close to 10 percent in the cities, and 12.5 percent in the Paris area. Nearly 8.5 million houses (60 percent) do not have inside toilets, and this reaches 80 percent in the rural areas and 43 percent in the Paris area. To possess a bath or shower, the INSEE notes, is a luxury reserved to 28 percent of French houses (*Le Monde*, October 1966).

91.   The Swedish woman appears to me more alienated than others; sex in Sweden has perhaps become "the opium of the people."

92.   At the Herstal plant (Belgium) where three thousand workers went on strike in the spring of 1966: "a driller earned 4.14 French francs per hour, a woman driller 3.18 francs; a packer, 4.38 francs, a woman packer, 3.24 francs; a man working on "machine parts," 5.07 francs, a "woman machinist," 3.64 francs" (*Le Monde*, April 20, 1966).

93.   Cf. *Le Monde*, November 1966.

94.   Cf. "Prostitution dans les grands ensembles," *Le Nouvel Observateur*.

21   Zaynab

زينب

An Urban Working-Class Lebanese Woman

A.D. 1937–

Biographical Sketch by Suad Joseph

Lebanon is a tiny country (4,000 square miles) on the extreme eastern shore of the Mediterranean Sea. An independent republic since 1945, Lebanon today has a population of around three million, a population swelled by an influx of Palestinian refugees as well as by the high national fertility rate. In ancient times, this country was an important center of international trade, with its historic ports of Tyre, Sidon, and Tripoli. Beirut, the modern capital, has replaced the older ports in importance, but Lebanon still gains much of its national income from trade and commerce. Although only a fourth of the Lebanese land is cultivated, most of the inhabitants outside the cities gain their living through agriculture, cultivating grain, vegetables, and fine fruits. But the majority of the population lives in the rapidly growing cities of Beirut and Tripoli.

For many centuries, Lebanon has been a meeting place of cultures and religions as well as traders and refugees. Its contemporary political system is based on proportional representation in government offices of the dominant religious sects. Traditionally, the president has been Christian and the prime minister Muslim. But seventeen different religious sects are legally recognized, and the situation is complex. In recent

---

Photo: Lebanese woman preparing kibbi

years, much conflict has erupted within Lebanon, particularly in Beirut and Tripoli, and the political system is currently in question as different political and religious groups vie for dominance.[1]

Zaynab, whose life history follows, is a working-class urban Lebanese woman who lives in Burj Hammud, a suburb of eastern Beirut.[2]

Zaynab, a thirty-four–year–old Lebanese Muslim of the Shi'ite sect, was equipped with an alert sense of self and place. She was outgoing, aggressive, joyful, witty, clever, and opinionated, known for her sense of humor and conviviality. At neighborhood gatherings in Burj Hammud, where Zaynab and her family live, she was usually one of the most vocal of those present. Conversations among female or mixed company often centered around her and frequently consisted of her parrying witty observations with other women or men. Neighbors had come to expect her quick twists of thought and often would instigate situations so that she would entertain them.

Abu Raymond, a former neighbor also known for his humor and good-natured cursing, had frequently engaged her in witty exchanges.[3] In the summer evening hours, they would shout from apartment to apartment in the narrow alleys of the neighborhood, at times abusing each other's sexuality, and generally entertaining the neighbors greatly.

A strong, healthy-looking woman who emanated over-all delight in the people and events around her, Zaynab attracted people. Although a few of her neighbors chose to avoid her boisterousness, in general she was well liked.

The first time I met Zaynab, in 1971, she practically kicked me out of her house. When I arrived, for a brief interview, she was busy washing, by hand, her husband 'Adil's clothes and those of their eight children. Barking that she had no time for my nonsense, she dismissed me and almost ushered me out the door. A municipal employee, who was accompanying me to make introductions, explained that I was a university student; I was doing a study of Burj Hammud, of which the municipality approved. I apologized for interrupting her work and said I would come back later, but then she insisted that I stay. Sitting me down and welcoming me, she rushed downstairs to her husband's bakery, produced a respectable assortment of pastries, and insisted that I eat and have coffee. Then she joked about her bad manners and told me she had thought I was a Jehovah's Witness.

At one time predominantly Armenian, Burj Hammud has a population of about 200,000, of which about 40 percent are Lebanese Armenians, 40 percent Lebanese Shi'ites, and the remaining 20 percent Palestinians, Syrians, and Lebanese of other religious sects. The Camp Trad neighborhood where Zaynab and 'Adil lived was settled in the 1930's by Armenian refugees from Turkey. It came to be called "camp" because the homes were originally tin shacks, giving the neighborhood a temporary appearance. Today the original name remains, although houses and apartments have been built along the narrow streets, and Zaynab's neighborhood is now very mixed, housing mainly Lebanese, Syrians, Palestinians, and a few Jordanians, Egyptians, Iraqis, and Greeks of almost every religious sect.

In 1971 Zaynab and 'Adil had been married for fifteen years, the first and only marriage for each of them. Except for three years in which 'Adil had worked abroad before his marriage, they had lived all their adult lives in Burj Hammud. 'Adil spent long hours working in his bakery below the apartment where the family lived, so he was usually on hand if Zaynab needed him. Occasionally she and the children helped him in the bakery. A relatively easy going man, 'Adil was willing to be persuaded by Zaynab in matters of joint concern. His leisure time was spent almost entirely with his family, since he was not the sort of man who frequented the coffeehouses, lingered on street corners, or passed time in other places, as some neighborhood men did. Rather casual about most things, he was not politically active and usually did not become involved in heated discussions of social and political issues—an activity which occupied a number of local men.

Zaynab was born in 1937 in the Mseitbi district of Beirut. Her mother had been born in Palestine, though both her parents were originally Lebanese Shi'ites. When Zaynab was three, her parents moved to Tabarayyah, Palestine. Both her father, who had a fifth-grade education, and her mother, who was illiterate, wanted their children to receive some education. Zaynab was accordingly enrolled in a private Jewish school and, by the time she had completed her schooling (in the third grade), she had learned some Hebrew, which she still remembered. During the Palestine War of 1948, she returned to Lebanon with her parents, who eventually came to live in Burj Hammud. Her father was a vendor in the Beirut vegetable market, and he bought a house in the Camp Sis neighborhood of Burj Hammud. He sold that house in 1953 and moved to Camp Trad, where he later bought the house in which he and his family were still residing at the time of my field work. By that time though, Zaynab's father was retired.

Of the eleven children in her family (10 living in 1971), Zaynab was the third oldest. Her oldest sister, who died in child delivery, had been illiterate, but the second-oldest sister had gone on to sixth grade and Zaynab and her younger sister had reached third grade. All her brothers had some education: one had reached fourth grade, one fifth, another sixth, and a fourth the seventh. One brother had even completed a university degree in the United States and was working as an engineer in Michigan. The sixth brother was in college in Michigan, and the seventh was planning to join his brothers and attend the University in Michigan when he graduated from high school in Beirut. One of the brothers, a boxer trainer, was living in Spain, and another brother, himself a boxer, was doing a tour of matches in the United States in 1973.

Zaynab had met 'Adil when her family moved to Camp Trad. They had lived near each other in Camp Sis but had not known each other then, although their parents were friendly at that time. As they came to know each other, Zaynab and 'Adil fell in love. She was nineteen at the time and he was seventeen. Both sets of parents objected to the romance on the grounds that Zaynab was older than 'Adil. Furthermore, Zaynab's parents wanted her to marry another suitor, one more established than 'Adil, who at that time was still working in his father's bakery. But Zaynab recruited the support of her mother's sister, and the aunt succeeded in persuading the parents to accept the match. Zaynab and 'Adil were married in 1956.

Their first home was a small apartment in a building owned by a friend of Zaynab's father. About a month later they moved into their present home, a somewhat larger apartment in 'Adil's mother's house, where they had a bedroom, living room, kitchen, and toilet. Umm 'Adil was divorced and kept one of the rooms in the apartment for herself. Zaynab and 'Adil supported 'Adil's mother and paid her fifty Lebanese pounds (about $16.50) in monthly rent. Umm 'Adil ate with them and they paid for her clothes and her utility bills. 'Adil bought the bakery business from his father in 1971, although his mother still owned the building.

Zaynab and 'Adil's apartment and belongings were rather typical in the neighborhood. They had electricity and running water but no heat or hot water. For warmth in winter they would gather around a brazier of burning charcoal. Their refrigerator saved Zaynab a lot of work, but she washed by hand. There was an Eastern toilet, or ground toilet, in the apartment but no shower or bath tub. Zaynab bathed her children in a large tin pan. The apartment was furnished with a sofa, six upholstered chairs, a clothes closet, and a china closet. They also had a broken coffee table and two old rugs. Since they did not own beds, they slept on mats, which were spread on the floor each night. They did own a radio and an electric iron but no television, record player, tape recorder, sewing machine, fans, or tables. Downstairs in the bakery they had a telephone and 'Adil maintained a stationwagon for his work. The apartment had a balcony, but very little sun came in and the house was often damp. Zaynab, who spent much of her time indoors, often wore a light sweater over her dress to keep warm. Her high activity level must also have toned down the effect of the dampness.

Zaynab and 'Adil did not seem hostile or bitter about their poor condition. When I asked her to describe their furnishings and list their property, she joked about her broken coffee table and created exaggerated names and descriptions for her old rugs and other belongings. She did this as much for her own amusement as for mine and her guests, Umm Raymond, her closest friend, and Umm 'Adil, her mother-in-law, who were sitting with us that day. But still, in their apartment of approximately forty square meters in area (about 125 square feet), the eleven members of the family (Zaynab had her ninth child in 1973) were crowded. They seemed to adjust by almost never being in the apartment all together, except at night. 'Adil worked long hours in the bakery. And six of the nine children (ages 15, 13, 11, 9, 8, 6, 5, 3, and 2 months) were in school and therefore not home much of the time.

Zaynab made the decisions concerning her children's schooling. She had enrolled two children in the nearby Catholic private school and four in a Shi'ite private school. One of the children had had polio and had never been in school, and two of the children were still too young. Zaynab's children performed on an average-to-mediocre level in school. Two had repeated a grade each and one had failed three times. They were neither well dressed nor particularly sloppy. They did not appear to have any outstanding characteristics and in general seemed quieter than many of the neighborhood children. When not in school, they played at home, near the house, or in the house of Umm Raymond. The older children also helped their mother with the housework and with the care of the younger brothers and sisters.

Like most of the people in Burj Hammud, Zaynab had a number of relatives living in the area. Her parents and four of her brothers lived in the same neighborhood and two maternal uncles lived in other parts of Burj Hammud. Her sister was in the Beirut district of Ashrafiyah, less than five kilometers away. 'Adil also had a number of relatives nearby; his mother lived in the same house, his brother on the same street, and a maternal uncle and two cousins in the same neighborhood.

Both Zaynab and 'Adil spent more time with her family than his. In his personal affairs, 'Adil relied on Zaynab's parents and siblings. He had borrowed money from Zaynab's father to buy the bakery from his own father. He turned to Zaynab's family not only in financial matters but also for personal and moral support. In some of my interviews with him, I suggested a number of potential problems that he might confront and asked to whom he would go for help under those circumstances. Of the twenty-four situations posed, he listed a member of his own family only once, whereas he named members of Zaynab's family ten times. This may have been partly due to internal problems in 'Adil's family. His father had divorced his mother and remarried; as a result both 'Adil and his brother, 'Atif, refused to speak to the father. 'Atif's wife, Layla, was unhappy living in Burj Hammud and seemed unable to tolerate either the living conditions or the people. An Egyptian Sunni woman with a college education, Layla was constantly ridiculing the people of the neighborhood and the Lebanese government. Although awed by her education, a number of people in the neighborhood disliked her. Zaynab herself was not impressed by Layla and said that her sister-in-law was conceited, arrogant, and selfish. The two women had had a number of arguments arising from Layla's disdain of 'Atif's family and the Lebanese in general. Since 'Atif's store was a principal outlet for the bakery, 'Adil maintained relations with his brother, but Zaynab refused to visit them or talk to them, even on holidays.

Zaynab was close to her immediate family, but, like an increasing number of urban Lebanese, she had no on-going relationship with her family's village of origin. She had been there only twice in her life and felt that she did not know it at all. Camp Trad was home to her, even though most of the relatives of the extended family still lived in the natal village near Sour. 'Adil also rarely visited his village of Nabatiyah. In the previous three years, he had been there only once.

Visiting was an important part of Zaynab's social life, as it was with most women in Burj Hammud. Much of Zaynab's leisure time was spent visiting and being visited by friends and relatives. Her closest friend was of course Umm Raymond, the Chaldean Catholic widow of Abu Raymond, with whom Zaynab had joked so often and so boisterously before his death in 1971. Umm Raymond lived downstairs, adjacent to the bakery, and the two women spent most of their time together cooking, sewing, washing, or just visiting. They continually helped each other in their daily work, advised each other on important matters, and acted as surrogate mothers to each other's children. 'Adil also was fond of Umm Raymond and respected her. I once asked 'Adil from whom he would seek advice if he and Zaynab were having marital problems. He immediately answered, Umm Raymond. Umm Raymond similarly turned to Zaynab and 'Adil. I asked Umm Raymond from whom would she borrow money if she needed it. For both small and large sums, she said that she would ask Zaynab. She also said that Zaynab was the first person she would turn to if she were depressed and needed to talk. In one incident in which Umm Raymond's son fought with youths from another part of Burj Hammud, Umm Raymond thought he was hurt. She became hysterical, shouting, screaming, tearing at her clothes. Neighbors from a number of houses rushed to help, but it was Zaynab who embraced Umm Raymond, comforted her, and succeeded in calming her. The two women visited each other's relatives, borrowed small sums of money from each other, and continually relied on each other for moral and emotional support.

But Zaynab also exchanged visits with many other people of the neighborhood, people of different religious sects: Maronites, Catholics, Greek Orthodox, Armenian Orthodox, Sunnis, Shi'ites, and 'Alawites. In one fairly typical week, she was visited by eight Shi'ites, three Sunnis, two Catholics, and one Greek Orthodox. The most frequent among her visitors that week was Nadya, a neighboring Sunni woman who averaged three visits a day. Nadya was having marital problems and sought Zaynab's advice as well as her good-natured humor. That same week Umm Raymond visited Zaynab an average of twice a day, 'Adil's maternal uncle came once each day, and Zaynab's mother came four times that week. The age range of that week's visitors was seventeen to seventy, although most of them were twenty-three to forty-five. Many of these visitors were illiterate and only one of them had up to a fifth-grade education. Ten of her fourteen visitors that week were female, half of whom lived in Camp Trad. Only one visitor had come from as far as five kilometers away.

The same week Zaynab herself visited seven people, of whom six were females. Only one, Nadya's sister, whom she visited twice, lived outside Burj Hammud. Zaynab's visits to Umm Raymond took most of her visiting time, an average of three visits a day. She had also visited an ailing Maronite woman across the street four times that week, while the remaining four people (a Greek Orthodox, an 'Alawite and 2 Shi'ites) were visited once each. All were people who had visited her that same week.

Social rules of friendship in Burj Hammud require an exchange of visits on occasions of births, deaths, weddings, and holidays. Zaynab did not overly extend herself on such occasions, but she kept up the basic obligations. Most of the people whom she visited on these occasions lived on her street. In the previous two years she had visited three households on occasions of childbirth (a Shi'ite and a Sunni neighbor and her own sister), nine households on occasions of deaths (2 Shi'ite, 1 Chaldean Catholic, 1 Greek Catholic, 1 Maronite, 1 Greek Orthodox, 1 'Alawite, and 2 Armenian Orthodox neighbors), and one for a wedding ('Adil's cousin, a Shi'ite). However, on the major Muslim and Christian holidays she made a brisk round of visits, usually accompanied by 'Adil. During that year she had visited seventeen households for each of the Muslim holidays of 'Id al-Fitr and 'Id al-Adha (12 Shi'ite, 4 Sunni and 1 'Alawite). Seven of these were neighbors, five were her relatives, four were 'Adil's relatives, and one was the mother of her neighbor Nadya. On Easter and Christmas she had visited fourteen households, ten of which were on the same street (1 Roman Catholic, 3 Chaldean Catholic, 5 Maronite, 3 Greek Orthodox, and 2 Armenian Orthodox).

Zaynab and 'Adil's financial situation was in some ways typical and in other ways atypical of the neighborhood. Unlike most residents, they had parents who owned buildings. Zaynab estimated that her father's building was worth 70,000 LP (about $23,300),[4] which would some day have to be divided equally among her and her nine siblings. 'Adil's mother's house, worth about 35,000 LP ($12,000), would have to be divided among five siblings.

In 1972, 'Adil had grossed between 800 and 900 LP per month (about $250–300), somewhat more than most of the other men in the neighborhood. But, during 1973, their income had been cut by several hundred Lebanese pounds, since bakery sales were down. They must have been relying on some savings to get by, for Zaynab said that in 1973 they were still spending about 500 LP (about $175) a month on food alone. Bread was an important part of their diet, as it is with most Lebanese poor. Each week the family ate 21 kilograms of bread for which they paid 10.50 LP ($3.50). They used a little more meat than was usual in the neighborhood, an average of 10 kilograms per week (29 LP; $9.75). Another 10 LP ($3.50) went every week for 10 kilograms of vegetables, and they consumed about 20 kilograms of fruit, which cost 35 LP ($11.75). Their weekly diet also included 3 kilograms of cheese (10 LP; $3.50), 30 eggs (3 LP; $1.00), 4 kilograms of yogurt and yogurt spread (lebne) (3.60 LP; $1.20), 1 kilogram of Turkish coffee (5 LP; $1.75), 3 litres of milk (5 LP; $1.65), ⅓ kilogram of tea (.35 LP; $.90), and 1–2 kilograms of grains and seeds (about 1–2 LP; $.30–.60). They also went through 14 packs of cigarettes weekly (17.50 LP; $5.85).

Clothes are rather expensive in Lebanon. During 1972 Zaynab and 'Adil had spent 736 LP on clothes for the children, 422 LP for 'Adil, and 268 LP for Zaynab, for a total of $475. Schooling for the six children also represented a large expense for them. Like most people in Burj Hammud, they had to send their children to private schools. In 1970 only two of the thirty-eight schools in Burj Hammud were governmental. The public schools served only 400 of the 16,658 students enrolled in Burj Hammud.[5] This represented only 2 percent of the students in local schools and only 0.5 percent of the 73,000 estimated school-age population.[6] As a result, Zaynab had to pay 1,322 LP or nearly $450.00 in the 1971–72 school year for her children's tuition, registration, fees, books, and supplies at private schools.

Entertainment and personal expenses of the household at times amounted to 100 LP a month, all of which was spent on 'Adil and the children ($350.00). 'Adil also spent in the neighborhood of 90 LP a month on his stationwagon for fuel and repairs, in addition to the yearly 275 LP registration fee, for a yearly car cost of $470. Like most Camp Traders, Zaynab and 'Adil went to doctors, hospitals, or clinics only at critical moments. From 1971 to 1973 they had used hospitals on two occasions, once for their polio-stricken son, who as an outpatient visited a hospital for one month (costing 150 LP), and once for Zaynab, who delivered her ninth child in the Maternity Hospital, staying four days for a cost of 150 LP. During one six-month period between 1972 and 1973 only one member of the family had been to a doctor or a clinic. This was Zaynab's daughter Nancy, who had been taken to a doctor once and a clinic twice for "thinness" (total cost 8 LP). During that same period, they had paid 30 LP for medications for the entire family, so their total medical expenses came to about $118.00. Zaynab and 'Adil were not in debt in 1973, although they had on two previous occasions borrowed sums of 2,000 LP and 3,000 LP which they had repaid.

In some ways Zaynab was conventional and in others she was rather unconventional. All the girls in her family had married Lebanese Shi'ite men, but only one of the seven brothers had married a Lebanese Shi'ite woman. Four of the brothers were unmarried and the two others had married American Catholic and Spanish Catholic women. By 1972 Zaynab had more children than any of her siblings; she had eight and was pregnant with the ninth; two brothers and one sister had no children, one brother and one sister each had one child, and one sister had six.

Zaynab and 'Adil were both supporters of Lebanese nationalism. Even though they supported the Palestinian and other Arab causes, they said that these often conflicted with Lebanese interests. Left alone, the Lebanese could prosper and live peacefully, they felt. But international powers were continually interfering in Lebanese affairs and turning the Lebanese against each other. Both of them did not support the traditional Shi'ite candidates. 'Adil voted for conservative Christian candidates, as did Zaynab's father. Many of 'Adil's political ties were outside his religious sect. If he wanted advice about an electoral candidate, 'Adil said that he would seek out a Christian friend in the municipality or a Maronite woman who lived on the same street and was a member of the Kata'ib Party. He said that he would even use his Christian ties to intervene for him with officials of his own religious sect. He named Fuad Lahhud and Pierre Edde, two Christian national leaders for whom he had voted, as the people he would seek out if he needed mediation on his behalf with the Shi'ite religious officials. Zaynab and Zaynab's family shared 'Adil's outlook in this regard.

But in other ways Zaynab was very conventional. Like perhaps most lower-class women in Lebanon, she was married to a man of her own religious sect, lived with her husband and children, and had a rather sizeable family. She was a housewife, spending most of her time at home with housework. Only occasionally did she leave her neighborhood. Almost all her leisure time was spent visiting, mainly with neighbors. Her political position was mainly that of her family and her husband. Since she did not read newspapers or watch TV and only listened to the radio irregularly, she learned the news from neighbors and relatives. She felt that women should have enough education to be informed and to take care of themselves but should not be involved with politics, which is men's responsibility. She felt women could be assertive and take leading roles in household decisions, but that this should be done cooperatively with their husbands.

But, unlike most lower-class Muslim women, Zaynab said she wanted her children to marry Christians. This came from her positive experience with her brothers' wives. Her best friend was a Chaldean Catholic woman with whom she and her children spent most of their time. This was a rather common attitude in the mixed neighborhoods of Burj Hammud, where proximity was a powerful influence on friendships. But it was not as common in the rural areas of Lebanon, where whole villages may belong to a single religious sect.

Zaynab's natal family was somewhat unusual in having one son with a university degree, another working on a degree, and a third about to enroll in a university—and all three in the United States. Among most lower-class families in Burj Hammud, there might be one child who had received higher education, but it was more common to have a cousin, uncle, or distant relative who was educated. Most Lebanese of all classes have relatives living abroad, many in the United States, South America, West and North Africa, Canada, and Australia. Some families in Camp Trad had on-going communications with relatives abroad. A number of neighborhood youths had worked abroad in Arab countries for periods of time, and many aspired to go to the United States, but very few had the real possibility of migrating to the States, as Zaynab and her family did, since her brother in Michigan was an American citizen.

The fact that her brothers had married foreign Christians also set Zaynab somewhat apart from other Camp Trad residents, although not completely, since many people in the neighborhood could name some relative who had a similar foreign or Christian spouse. Zaynab also differed from many Muslims in preferring that her children not marry relatives. Most Muslims accepted the custom of marrying relatives, but I encountered a few in Camp Trad who did not. On the other hand, I encountered a number of Christians who preferred marriage with relatives even though the Christian churches opposed the practice. Finally, Zaynab differed from most of her lower-class Muslim neighbors in her support of right-wing Christian Lebanese political parties. I did encounter some Muslims and a few Armenians in Burj Hammud who supported these parties, but they were a minority. While these people were a minority, most people did have political ties that cut across sectarian lines. On the whole this pattern appears to be far more common in the mixed urban areas than in rural areas, where social networks may be almost entirely in one's sect. Like a few, but only a few, Muslims in Camp Trad, Zaynab sent two of her children to a Christian school. Perhaps more would have done so except the Christian schools were less numerous and on the whole more expensive than the Muslim schools in the neighborhood.

Many Camp Trad women, Muslim and Christian, shared Zaynab's spirited and joyful outlook. Marital relations varied. Violence, such as wife beating, was rare and considered outrageous in the neighborhood. Most men and women, Muslim and Christian, expected to be married only once. All the households in Camp Trad were monogamous. Large families were common, but families of one to three children were also numerous. Most families educated male and female children to some degree.

In the summer of 1974, I returned briefly to Burj Hammud. Zaynab was still cheerful, although she had aged. Her brother had returned from his tour of boxing matches, and another brother was preparing to leave for the States. Her son who had had polio was no better. She and Umm Raymond were still best friends. Inflation was rampant in Lebanon and had hit Zaynab and 'Adil quite hard. The political situation was tense as Burj Hammud was in the middle of many of the class, religious, and political party battles. I asked how she was faring. She responded, "We're alive."

Summary of Zaynab and 'Adil's Household Expenses for 1972

Food	$2,000
Clothes	475
Education	450
'Adil's car	470
Medical expenses	118
Entertainment and personal expenses	350
	$3,863

Notes

1.   For an analysis of the impact of the governmental system on sectarian relations and sectarian consciousness, see Suad Joseph, "The Politicization of Religious Sects in Burj Hammud, Lebanon."
2.   Field work was carried out for twenty-seven months between 1971 and 1973 under a National Institute of Mental Health grant for doctoral work at Columbia University. I would like to thank Lucie Wood Saunders for reading the first draft and offering helpful comments.
3.   Abu Raymond died just before I began field work. The story was told to me by his wife, Umm Raymond.
4.   In 1972, a Lebanese pound (LP) was worth about 35 cents. A kilo is 2.2 pounds, and 1000 grams equal one kilogram.
5.   SIRLAS, *note 13*.
6.   The 73,000 estimate is based on an asserted 150,000 population figure for Burj Hammud. My own studies indicate that the population of Burj Hammud is 200,000. Given a conservative estimate that 63 percent of Lebanon's population is under twenty-five (UNICEF, p. 54), this means that Burj Hammud's school-age population is likely to be more than 73,000.

References

Gendzier, Irene L. "Lebanon: Mosaic of Hostilities." *Nation* 221, no. 9 (1975): 265–268.

Joseph, Suad. "The Politicization of Religious Sects in Burj Hammud, Lebanon." Ph.D. dissertation, Columbia University, 1975.

Secretariat des Instituts Religieux Libanais pour les Affaires Sociales (SIRLAS). *Note 13: Option 12.* Beirut: SIRLAS, 1971.

United Nations Children's Fund (UNICEF). "Democratic Characteristics of Children and Youth in the Arab Countries: Present Situation and Growth Prospects." In *Children and Youth in National Planning and Development in the Arab States.* Beirut: United Nations, 1970.

22

Aminah al-Sa'id

أمنية السعيد

Modern Egyptian Feminist

A.D. 1914–

Aminah al-Sa'id was born in Cairo in 1914. She graduated from Cairo University in 1935, one of the third group of girls admitted to Egyptian universities. A champion of women's rights since her school days, she has been active in journalism, translating, and writing. She has been editor of *HAWWA*, a large-circulation women's weekly magazine, since its inception in 1954. Author of six books, she has also translated into Arabic such American novels as *Main Street* and *Little Women*. First woman elected to the Egyptian Press Syndicate Executive Board, she is also a member of the executive board of Dar al Hilal Publishing House, one of the oldest publishing firms in the Arab world, and a member of the Supreme Board for Journalism in Egypt. Recently she has represented Egypt at several international conferences.

Photo: Aminah al-Sa'id

The Arab Woman and the Challenge of Society/Aminah al-Sa'id

The Arab woman today faces many challenges. Many obstacles hinder her full emancipation, the emancipation of half the Arab peoples, and prevent her from achieving her freedom at the necessary rate for our time.

Discussing these obstacles, and thus exposing their origins, takes great courage and frankness, a task which is not easy for those of us in Arab society, and in the developing countries generally, to deal with openly, for the areas in which these obstacles to woman's emancipation are found are sensitive areas in our society, partly because of our regret over the lost glory of our ancestors and partly because of our embarrassment at our backwardness in relation to the acceptable standard of living throughout the world. Our pride places us in a difficult situation, for it seems that over the centuries we have become accustomed to taking refuge from facing the painful realities of life by recalling our past historical glories.

In spite of my respect for and my understanding of the causes of this familiar ambiguity felt by all the developing societies, I find myself differing from the general attitude. It is true that, from past experience in trying to deal with the grave challenges of modern life and from sometimes failing in their efforts, the developing countries have become weary of trying. Their weariness prevents their consideration of even greater dangers, which are rapidly approaching us today. I differ from the general trend in that I believe deeply in the value of self-criticism as an aid to positive achievement. Why should we be ashamed to admit our weaknesses? Only when we know what they are can we recognize their dimensions and work to overcome them and thereby utilize all our potentialities toward elevating ourselves to a higher level of civilization.

Like any other Arab, I know that at one time ours was a leading civilization, a civilization which had surpassed others in many fields: science, economics, social science, history. I also know that this past was lost, for reasons often stronger than our own will, and these reasons have contributed toward stripping us of our leadership for a thousand years or more. Periods of imperialism have fallen upon us, one after the other, and have lasted for many centuries, undermining the basic elements of our society and draining us of our natural resources. And the general

[Aminah al-Sa'id, "Al-Mar'ah al-Arabiyah wa-Tahadi al-Mujtama," a lecture delivered in Beirut on December 12, 1966, and published in *Muhadrat al-Nadwah* (Les Conferences du Cenacle) 21, nos. 11–12, 1967. Translated by the Editors.]

evils of imperialism did not really cease until we regained our freedom only a few years ago.

One cannot deny these facts, but I do not believe it is wise to waste time in sorrow and sadness, in lamenting our lost past, for a far more important goal lies before us: that of regaining and reshaping our existence, as a necessary means to the eventual regaining of our self-confidence, our respect, and our pride. I think we may be proud that we are already laboring hard toward this goal; we are progressing along the path of reform and have achieved some of our aims in the past few years. These steps which have already been taken may seem small compared to the achievements of the developed nations, but, in reality, they are respectable indeed, considering the short period of time in which these reforms have been accomplished and the many sacrifices necessary for such achievement.

If we look at women as a group which represents half the Arab nation, we cannot help but admit that this group is the weakest area of our social body. Why? Because women have been subject, more than men, to the pressures of ignorance, poverty, and general backwardness. These pressures in turn reduce the total value of the society and delay or retard new movements in our national life.

I do not think I am exaggerating if I say the general situation of women as a group forms the greatest obstacle to national progress to be found in our country today. I say this, despite the great efforts made in the cause of emancipation of this group and despite what has already been achieved for women in the past ten years in some of the Arab countries (I will not say all of them) where the achievement of rights seems almost complete. Many years and much effort lie ahead of us before we are able to reach women of all classes in all Arab countries and raise all socioeconomic levels to a standard suitable for the twentieth century. It is true that Arab men, too, have a long way to go before they are raised to a higher level, but, with all their problems, they are farther ahead than women. To begin with, the percentage of illiteracy is much lower among men than among women. This is because men in our society have always had a better lot than women. From past times, our society has traditionally favored men and given them opportunities denied women. Further, society did not enslave men with the veil, a custom which has continued to hinder our civilization until very recently and which is still preventing the progress of our sisters in more than one Arab country.

As a result of this obvious difference in the situations of men and women, a strong imbalance between men and women is found in the percentage of trained persons. This imbalance only increases the burden of the progressive Arab governments who are struggling with development. Because of the great diversity of socioeconomic levels throughout the Arab lands, different plans and approaches to reform must be developed which answer the needs of each level. And the needs of the weakest level, that is, women, call for a different approach as well. We should remember, as we plan, that this backwardness of women as a group is not a part of all our traditional history.

Women enjoyed a reasonably good status in our ancient civilizations, under the Pharaohs, the Assyrians, the Babylonians. In these periods, women sat on thrones and exercised positions of importance in religion and politics. Then Islam arose, and in its time Islam appeared as a great social revolution in the history of women's position, not only for us in the Arab nations but also for the whole world.

Just before the rise of Islam, thirteen centuries ago, woman was scarcely a human being; she had no rights, and no respect was accorded her as a person. But this new religion, which arose in the desert, among people who lived with nature, managed to reverse the situation of women at that time. Islam restored to woman her total humanity; it armed her with weapons of independence and freed her from the domination of the male by giving her (a) the right to education, (b) the right to buy and sell property, and (c) the right to hold a job and go into business. She was even drawn into participating in managing affairs of religion and politics.

While the European woman was still living on the margin of life, as a follower of the man, we find her Arab sister, daughter of the empty sands and the primitive desert society, enjoying her existence as a person and exercising the same basic rights as man, with the same obligations as a man to her duties on earth. Islam did not differentiate between men and women except in giving the woman half the man's share of inheritance, in return for the fact that the man was to be responsible for the woman's material needs. At the time this was a gain, but it is now considered a curse. For with the decay of Arab civilization reactionary forces gained ascendancy, and these forces used inheritance as an excuse to lower the entire status of woman to that of half the man or even, in some cases, less than half.

I am not pursuing this point simply to defend Islam. But I do want to emphasize that Islam, as far as codifying laws is concerned, was the first religion to give woman a status as an independent person. And the rights given to women by Islam, 1,300 years ago, did not appear in the western world until many centuries later. Economic independence of women, particularly a fixed right to inheritance, equality with men in inheritance, and equality in earning an independent living: these rights were not found in Europe until the end of the nineteenth century and the beginning of the twentieth century.

Thus Arabs were innovators in the field of woman's rights.

We may be proud of this, but we must not deny the fact that the Arabs stopped at this magnificent beginning and did not develop the situation of woman as time passed. Nor did they make any attempt to conform their spiritual and social values with the changing of the circumstances of life. European women's emancipation began at the point where the Arab women's emancipation ended. We were the predecessors, they the successors. They moved with the times, but we stayed in one place. The result was that the procession of civilization passed us by and has been ahead of us in many areas.

Why, one may ask, did the west move forward while we did not? The dogmas of the west were envisioned only as a set of rules created by man to achieve the common good. Why not? I see no reason why men cannot change their dogmas and their sets of rules when necessity demands such change. Our society did not do this. With the decline of all civilizations which came upon our countries, the reactionary thinkers were encouraged to protect the old social beliefs and dogmas, and they did so by surrounding them with an aura of holiness which prevented the dogmas from being touched or changed in any way, except by a society open enough and strong enough in its own pride and culture to challenge such reaction. And during that period we were not strong enough to overcome these forces. This situation is hardly unique in world history. One of the basic characteristics of a backward society is an inability to adapt to new situations. This in turn creates an imbalance between what is happening in the society and the society's perception of it, and such imbalance influences spiritual values so that in time they diverge from their original meanings. History is full of many examples. During the Dark Ages, Europe committed great mistakes in the name of Christianity—human mistakes which had nothing to do with this great religious belief, based on peace and love, mercy and forgiveness. Galileo, as well as other scientists and philosophers, was condemned to death; the Inquisition fostered horrible deeds, and nothing in these acts expressed anything of the spirit of Christianity. The situation stayed this way generally until European civilization began to mature; then the reaction was slowed, and the Christian church managed to raise the flag of peace and mercy once again.

The Arab world offers a similar case.

Here, too, backwardness and reaction have cast dark shadows across our own spiritual values; it is hardly necessary to say that woman was the principal victim, and until now she has continued to suffer from the effects of reactionary thought, which is still rooted deeply in our collective mind. Even in those countries which have established laws to facilitate the emancipation of women, we find that the implementation of those laws is quite a different matter; in practice, the new ideas of emancipation clashes with the static attitudes of thought so prevalent in our society, attitudes remaining from the inherited traditions which have militated against women in general over the centuries.

The problem may be seen more clearly if we move from the general to the specific. Women, in Arab society, do not fit into a single category. They may be placed in three general groups:

1.   The rural sectors, about 60 percent of the total group
2.   The small-town sectors, about 25 percent
3.   The large-city sectors, about 15 percent

Women of the first group, the rural sector, are in a very backward condition, due to the high illiteracy rate, the low standard of living, and the women's own lack of awareness; all these factors are a result of our own long-standing negligence of the rural peoples. Under the older ruling systems, reforms were instituted only in the capital cities, which formed showcases for the new policies; even these small reforms tended to favor men more than women.

In the United Arab Republic, the state has assumed as its responsibility the emancipation of women. As a leader among the Arab countries in giving women their full political rights, providing assurances in the fields of education and health, child care and family planning, Egypt has stated in its constitution that equality between the sexes should be assured. Yet, even in Egypt, the actual benefits of these laws are very limited for rural women. And if we find such limited success in a country where laws guaranteeing equality are actually on the books, what can we expect of a village or rural area in a country where nothing is even proposed toward the cause of women's emancipation?

Women in the second sector, that of the small towns, have generally been much better off materially than their sisters in the rural areas. But the strict traditions of the east have influenced their social situation a good deal, and, consequently, they have been held back twice as much as women in the other areas of society. In the small town women have adapted by seeming to be satisfied with the trivia rather than the essence of knowledge; they have been content to be isolated and have confined their efforts to the house and family only. The veil has had a greater influence on women in the small towns than in either the rural or big-city areas; first, it has prevented them from participating in any productive work, such as that performed by the farm women. The traditions and ideology of this sector bear the stamp of the petit bourgeoisie in its worst form and they have affected the women of the small towns in a very repressive way.

Curiously, women of this sector have changed rapidly in the past few decades, more even perhaps than in other categories, particularly in the UAR. Somewhat surprisingly, they have proved to be very receptive to the national mood of reform and have assumed their new political rights with enthusiasm. Three out of eight women elected to our National Assembly are from the small-town group, this group which was so isolated and restricted only a few years ago.

The third sector, women living in the major cities, has always been luckier than those in the rural areas and small towns; these women have had more opportunities for education, and sooner; they were pioneers in taking off the veil and taking jobs in various fields outside the home. There is no doubt that the role played by the women of the cities, in taking advantage of the opportunities offered them and in performing well in the jobs assigned to them, greatly influenced the whole national attitude toward women's rights and freedoms.

Literacy rates are much higher in the cities, but we must always bear in mind that people in the cities constitute only a small minority of the whole (about 15 percent) and the lives of "exemplars"—the women who have made the efforts toward new lives, gained educations, assumed jobs—are scarcely free from new problems, a topic we will discuss presently. What needs to be stressed here is that the new model of woman's personality in the Arab world is, even in its best form, not yet clear but rather vague and shadowy and full of contradictions. Why? In the last sixty years, the entire world has been transformed to an astonishing degree, a factor that cannot be ignored in any discussion of women's emancipation and its effect on the woman herself. The world has moved in scarcely more than half a century from the period of horses and carriages to that of spaceships which circle the planets searching for new worlds.

As the world has changed so radically, so has the status of woman changed from that of a follower or marginal person to one who has the status of a full and equal person and citizen. In the western countries, this movement proceeded gradually, and the changes took half a century, passing through several stages; this length of time is perhaps long enough for people to digest the changes. But as for us, in the Arab countries, the change, when it did come, came very late and very suddenly; woman did not begin her emancipation until the period of the Arab revolutions, revolutions which were not only political but also social. The Arab wished to be free of colonialism, but he also wanted to raise his standard of living high enough so that he might be able to appreciate the freedom he was seeking and to maintain that freedom once he had achieved it. If we consider the granting of political rights as a starting point for the stage of woman's emancipation, then we see that the woman in our society has been obligated to develop and change herself in less than twenty years as much as her western sister did in sixty years.

These changes came so fast that they disrupted the norms of our society, and the new values were bound to clash with the old inherited traditions. It is easy to pass laws and present examples of what should be, but the acceptance of those laws and examples takes time, perhaps as much as two or three generations.

Thus, one of the most important challenges facing the Arab woman today is that of trying to equate her inner self, her thoughts and attitudes and feelings, with the contemporary social reality about her. It is not easy to resolve the contradictions, both personal and societal, which are bound to occur between the old inherited traditions and the new currents of thought. Society may move at an astonishing speed, but the mind is not able to keep up with the pace, and this applies especially to matters related to women. In summary we have yet to achieve a balance between the development of the *form* of our new societies and the development of the *content* [personal, general] of those societies.

Local situations, local traditions resist change. This is to be expected. But the conflicts between old and new have a great impact on the individual, and particularly on the woman, whose status is changing so rapidly. We should not be surprised that her personality, the personality of the new Arab woman, is not yet strong and solidified in its new mold.

This lack of firmness in the woman's personality is obviously a result of the transition period through which our society is now passing, from a backward, agricultural-nomadic society to a progressive, industrialized one. But such a lack of firmness also delays woman's own progress in *assuming* the new role which legally has been established for her. This in turn hinders the progress of the entire society, for women's emancipation is not a matter of concern for women only, but for all members of the new society.

Thus we cannot simply design a new person, a new society, by building an outer model. What we must do is change the person, the society, from the inside. For it is difficult for an individual to work to change the life around him until he has been successful in changing himself into a person with a new style of ideas, a new set of mores which he may apply in the fields of work, as well as in personal relations. Such change must come to the whole community before new goals can be achieved.

Thus it must be clear by now that not only should woman be changed and elevated, from inside as well as from outside, but we must work with the same force to change the essence of the man as well. For the man must work together with the woman to be able to coordinate these new values, to be able to face the obvious difficulties, the inevitable clashes which will occur in both the spiritual and the material spheres of life.

Even in the most progressive parts of the Arab world we have scarcely begun this mammoth task: where the woman enjoys all her legal rights, for example, the new rights, when put into practice, are not at all in accord with the old values of our traditional, agricultural, and nomadic society. What happens? Women still submit to the sovereignty of the family, which is still represented by the domination of the male—the father, the uncle, the eldest brother, or the male cousin. Woman's own mentality is still strongly influenced by her sense of duty to the old values; she tries to be independent but manages it inefficiently and in only small and rather limited areas of life. This, too, slows the emergence of an independent womanhood and in turn hinders national progress.

The idea of women's emancipation has always met with resistance in our society, but never so strong as in the last few years. This is because until very recently women's liberation was not really taken seriously. Our reactionaries thought that women's rights were mere hallucinations, dreams which would never become reality, would never be put into practice. But some of the progressive Arab governments' stated positions on the need for equality between the sexes have shocked the reactionaries out of their dream worlds. As a result, they have gathered all their forces to resist the movement before it can become a reality.

However, I am not afraid of this reactionary counterattack. You may be surprised, but I am optimistic about the effects of such attacks. They seem to me the last desperate efforts of the old, backward forces to defend their own existence and to maintain what is left of their own sovereignty. I believe that such efforts will not succeed but will gradually die out.

Resistance will continue, however, through the transition period and until we have been able to change from an agricultural, backward society into a more progressive, industrial society. Gradually, I believe these progressive values will become fixed in our minds and will eventually drive out the old ideas that women are the weaker sex and that the law of nature has prevented society from benefiting from women's over-all abilities by limiting them to a specific range of activities: the bearing and raising of children.

I have outlined the general nature of the challenges facing the Arab woman in the current period of transition. Perhaps the challenges will emerge even more clearly if we trace their effects in specific areas: education, legal rights, participation in politics, and participation in the labor force.

Education

I have placed education first, for I believe that it is the basis of progress. In our Arab nation, education for men goes back to ancient times, and, despite all obstacles, the Arab man has managed to continue this tradition. The University of al-Azhar, the oldest university in the world, founded in the tenth century, continued to operate throughout the centuries, despite pressures of imperialism and backwardness. Al-Azhar remained the source of our education, the source of culture, not only in the Arab world, but in the Islamic world as a whole. Leaders of different nationalities have graduated from al-Azhar and returned to their own countries to raise the banners of social, political, and ideological movements, to open avenues to progress and civilization which did not exist there before.

But the situation with women is different. Education, even its most minor and superficial form, did not really begin for her until very recently. We can pinpoint its appearance in the whole Arab world with the opening of the first secondary school in Cairo in 1925; at that time, the number of girls in all its classes did not exceed forty. These girls were from families who were able to afford the high cost of the school. The idea of free compulsory education still did not exist. In 1922, after the Egyptians first gained their independence, it was suggested, but free compulsory education remained merely an idea until 1932, when the Egyptian government passed a compulsory education law.

Although the law was designed to benefit both boys and girls, it did not succeed in the beginning. First, the number of schools was far below the needs of the nation; hence the classes were limited to one or two years at most. After that period, the students were set free, with no regrets, to return to the lap of illiteracy; during the short period of time, they were hardly able to become literate! As far as girls were concerned, the law was only a law on paper and was not implemented at all. Only after 1952 did the more general public awareness create an atmosphere in which it was recognized that the girl as well as the boy must be prepared for the new life.

The new regime in Egypt after 1952 was the first Arab government to actually implement a law of free compulsory education on a broad level, for both boys and girls equally. More funds were appropriated for schools and the government began to economize by creating "mixed" schools, attended by both boys and girls. This act not only doubled the spread of literacy among the Egyptian youth, but also was a factor in destroying the separatist tradition which until that time had dominated the schools.

All Egyptians benefited from this important reform movement, and, for the compulsory period of education, the number of girls enrolled almost equalled the number of boys. Other Arab countries who were ambitious to raise the standard of education adopted the idea, and with this spread of education the situation of the new generation of Arab girls improved.

Still, illiteracy among women remained high. In some Arab countries, reactionary thought triumphed and, intentionally or unintentionally, the cause of women's education was neglected. Even in countries where compulsory elementary schools have been built, the number of schools falls short of the community's need, and sometimes the intermediate and secondary schools, the next stages in the educational process, are not yet constructed. Added to this problem is an apparent negligence in the establishment of vocational and technical training institutes, which might give women particularly an opportunity to work in addition to acquiring knowledge.

Such negligence and shortages in some Arab countries keep women as a group in a state of backwardness. We can only hope that other governments will take the same serious steps in promoting women's education as equal to that of men, steps already taken by their progressive sister governments. The situation in Egypt now, I believe, is most satisfactory in terms of assuring equality in education for both sexes. Laws have been passed, according to the student's academic ability and level, without any discrimination on the basis of sex. These amendments to the original law were put into final form last year. Thus at last the doors of education have been opened to Egyptian women, from elementary through university levels. I believe it is high time for the Arab countries who are more backward in the field of women's education to put an end to their reactionary ideas on the subject. For these ideas hamper the larger Arab cause, which we envision as enabling women in the Arab countries to progress to the degree to which they can achieve their, and our, hopes for a better life for all our citizens.

We can summarize the problems remaining in the field of education as follows:

1.   Negligence of some Arab countries in implementing compulsory education laws for girls

2.   Favoritism toward boys in these laws

3.   Shortage of schools for girls above the elementary level, a shortage apparent in both private and public schools

Legal Rights of Women

The challenges in the field of legal rights cannot appear clearly without first outlining the rights of women guaranteed by Islam. Islam in its essence, was very generous to woman and did not deny her what man enjoyed in the basic situations of life. The Koran gave women the following legal rights and protections:

1.   Economic independence

2.   Half of the man's share in inheritance; in return, the man to be responsible for maintenance and support of the family

3.   The minimum age of marriage set at the time of puberty, but leaving the interpretation of what is meant by "the time of puberty" to society

4.   Right to education: as much as the woman is capable of and to its highest levels, if she so wishes

5.   Right to work and be involved in trade and commerce, to own property, to sell and buy without the influence or the compulsion of the man

6.   Right to participate in dealing with religious and worldly affairs

7.   Right to choose her own husband; prohibition of forced marriages (without the woman's consent)

These rights, given to women in the early period of Islam, seen from a theoretical point of view, seem to approach what modern women hope to achieve, not only in our country but also in more progressive countries with brighter prospects than ours. But after the early period, Arab civilization declined, and a misunderstanding of the basic religious values led to the appearance of the veil. The veil, at first a novelty, became a very strong tradition and played a role in excluding the Arab woman totally from the world of public affairs. This in turn lowered the general status of woman, reduced her own awareness of the need to exercise her rights, and robbed her of the power and ability to ask for those rights. Thus, gradually, all powers came to rest exclusively in the hand of the man, and he alone became the decision maker, with power over the woman's wealth, education, marriage, and over-all destiny.

The situation began to change with the liberating, revolutionary movements of recent times. Governments recognized the necessity for developing national identities and goals according to the needs of contemporary civilization. In the Arab countries today, where women have regained many of their rights, it is no longer considered acceptable that fathers allow their daughters to attend mixed universities and work with men in different fields and still expect to control or interfere in those daughters' marriages. A more accepted view today, within educated circles, is that women not only should have the right to choose their own husbands, but also should exercise the right of dealing with their own finances and work in the area most suited to their individual qualifications and abilities.

But this view is found only within a rather limited group, comprising a small percentage of the total Arab population. Some Arab countries still deprive their women of their legal rights under Islam and keep them veiled and in ignorance so they are not able to recognize their rights and duties; these women's ability to demand and exercise their rights is thus diminished.

If we look at the new Egyptian constitution, which in my opinion is one of the leading documents in terms of women's emancipation, we find it rich in laws designed to assure equality between men and women *except* in matters relating to personal status. These laws [the *shari'ah*, or canon, laws governing the family, divorce, inheritance, marriage] were established in the time of ignorance and are based on faulty interpretations which are no longer suitable for the needs and the spirit of our present day. Since these old, harsh laws deal with the most important Institution within the nation, that is, the family, the fact that they are still in operation leads to the biggest contradictions to be found in our new life. It is hard for the mind to connect these two situations: the home and family situation, in which the Arab woman's position is very weak, and the public and social situation, in which she has achieved so many victories—victories which have placed her in important cabinet posts, in positions as deputy ministers in the government, as judges in the courts, and as representatives in important economic and political conferences.

I feel reasonably certain that the reform we hope for in this area is not far from being attained, for indeed this is the right time for it to occur. We will not be beginners in developing and revising our religious values, for even the Christian church, headed by the Catholic church, is today occupied with similar reforms. Committees of well-known bishops and progressive laymen are busy today developing religious ideas which are consistent with the requirements of contemporary life. This is an obviously necessary step to eliminate the barriers which today stand between the mother church and the people. Such reforms will demonstrate to Christians all over the world that their spiritual leaders are not isolated from them but exist side by side with them in the constant problems of their daily lives.

The Arab countries suffer from this same malady: the separation of the people from their religious leaders. I earnestly hope that the Arab countries will hasten to ameliorate and change this situation by amending the personal status laws. The responsibility for taking the initiative rests on the shoulders of the progressive revolutionary Arab countries, who are obligated, as part of their duties as leaders (unlike the other Arab countries) to pave the road to reform. And if the changes are rooted in basic needs rather than being merely superficial, then the progressive Arab governments will have returned, to the institution of the family, both its dignity and its stability.

We can then summarize the legal problems of women as follows:
1.   Prevalence of illiteracy and ignorance among women which results in an incapacity to regain their rights
2.   The influence of the logic of the backward, agricultural society in hampering the woman in exercising her rights
3.   The lack of equality between the sexes under the law
4.   The misunderstanding of religious values, which dominates the personal status laws regarding the family

The Field of Politics

Dealing with political matters is one of the rights given to women in Islam. History records that women participated in the *bay'ah* (or pledge of allegiance) at the time of the Prophet. But the forces of reaction prevailed in later years, and this right, like many other rights granted to women, was reduced to the point that women's participation in political life became almost a forbidden activity.

The picture began to change once more in 1953, when the Lebanese woman won her political rights, followed by the Egyptian woman in 1956. According to the temporary Egyptian constitution of that same year, the Egyptian woman, like the Lebanese woman, was given the right to vote and to run for parliament if eligible.

Granting these rights gave women in both countries the strength to begin actively taking part in their countries' affairs. And, for the record, we must point out that women's success in winning many electoral campaigns has influenced the majority of the Egyptian people to support this aspect of our revolutionary development. At first, two women were elected to parliament; this was soon followed by four more, and, after seven years, eight women were sitting in the Egyptian parliament. We hope for more such victories in our political and legislative life.

Although many other Arab countries followed the Lebanese and Egyptian example in granting women political rights, either conditionally or unconditionally, the majority of the people in these other countries did not support the progressive movement. As a result, women did not enter the parliament or legislative councils or, to be more precise, they were unable to win any electoral battles because these campaigns lacked the necessary elements of open competition.

We must not forget that still today there are Arab countries which deny political rights to their men, and in these countries this denial extends doubly to women. Political rights are more important than all other rights, I believe, for human freedoms are derived from political rights in the long run. Unless such rights are given to all peoples, men and women, and such rights are supported, particularly for women, the Arab nations will never be able to stand on their own feet. Since the primary responsibility for such legislation falls first on the man, it is important for the progressive Arab leadership to redouble its efforts to make both men and women aware of the needs, the meanings, and the values of the civilization for which we strive.

We can summarize the challenges that face women in the political field as follows:

1.   Depriving women of their political rights in many Arab countries
2.   Passivity of woman in using these rights when she has been granted them
3.   Lack of awareness of these problems among men, which prevents them from supporting women in political campaigns
4.   The impossibility of woman exercising her political rights totally independently of the wishes of the male in the family
5.   Origin of these obstacles in a faulty understanding of the religion of Islam, which is a remnant of many centuries of customs during the period of stagnation in Arab thought

Careers and Professional Fields: Women and Work

This whole area is related to the participation of women in the labor force. Again, women have participated in the labor force of our countries since ancient times, and for hundreds of years the nomad and the peasant woman has gone out with her husband to his fields and flocks, to help him in his work and to save him from hiring extra hands. But this situation is not found in all sectors of the Arab nation. The social segregation imposed on women of the middle and upper classes by the backward trends of thought resulted in driving women completely away from the general area of work (outside the home). This segregation prevented them from participating in the world of work except in a limited way, such as nursing, teaching, even doctoring occasionally, but only on condition that such work was a financial necessity. Thus, among the middle and upper classes, the idea of women's work was always associated with poverty and need.

The period when women began to take jobs and enter professions, apart from the traditional positions, dates only to 1933, when the first group of women graduated from Cairo University. As more and more women graduated, the avenues toward different areas of work and the professions gradually widened. Women began to be employed in commerce, political economics, and scientific research, as well as in law and engineering.

Even despite these achievements the idea of women working remained linked with poverty and necessity, or at least with a lack of means of financial security. This view did not change until after the 1952 revolution, when the openness of mind which followed this movement of freedom gradually rejected this distorted view. Work for women no longer bore a stigma but was recognized as a national duty, and women who performed this national duty were to be accorded both honor and respect.

Accordingly, all sectors of our society were affected by the new attitude, and the number of women seeking employment rose by 65 percent above what it was before the revolution. This picture repeats itself in many of the progressive Arab countries. Nevertheless, in terms of the total women's group, the percentage of female participation in the labor force is a mere drop in the sea, particularly in many of the sister Arab countries, where few work opportunities are available to women.

Further, we cannot escape admitting the fact that women in the Arab countries are still a sector to be exploited, rather than a force in production. This is partly because the peasant or nomad woman, who still represents the largest sector of our nation, is engaged much of the time in seasonal labor. Such seasonal labor occupies not more than 15 percent of her time and the remainder of her working hours are spent on household tasks, the economic value of which is very little compared to the economic needs of the nation. Housewives form the next-largest group of women, and generally they waste their energies on household tasks alone. Although we have a great respect for their efforts, we must point out that a scientific evaluation of their work places them again in the sector of exploited, rather than productive, forces. In Egypt women who work outside the home for wages comprise only 7 percent of all women! This total is no doubt much lower in other Arab countries, and, even if it is not, such a small group of women is far too weak to push itself forward toward full emancipation.

We can summarize the difficulties of women in the field of work and careers as follows:

1.   Unequal pay in the laboring sector
2.   Difficulties in being promoted to higher positions
3.   Submission of women to the sovereignty of the family, which deprives women of work opportunities which might be found far from home
4.   Lack of facilities, such as child care centers, to make it possible for women to carry out duties in the labor force and care for family and household at the same time
5.   The man's stubborn hold on his traditional domestic sovereignty and his refusal to participate in household chores.

All these problems worry the woman who works and take a lot of her energy. This in turn affects her performance in the labor force and contributes to any doubt which may exist as to the woman's ability to perform such work in the first place.

This has been a general survey of what the Arab woman faces today in terms of social challenges. I meant to be general because of the difficulty in obtaining reliable statistics with which one might discuss more specifically each country and each city. But, from the general view, I think we can see that the task of elevating woman in the Arab world is far too complex to be accomplished easily. In fact, some social shocks may be necessary to open the narrow circle of reactionary thought in our country to a view of wider, more civilized horizons.

How can this be done? First, we must be willing to study our social realities and analyze the basic causes of the Arab woman's backwardness. We must create a program for the Arab woman which fits her needs and our national needs, and we must spread public awareness of these needs so that other groups in the society will participate in implementing the new program, with full understanding of its implications. Laws alone are not sufficient to raise the backward nations or even to raise one section of the nation, such as women. We must also be willing to support the laws with full understanding, willingness, and acceptance of those laws.

Progressive leaders in the Arab countries are no doubt aiming at utilizing all the citizens' abilities and talents in their efforts toward obtaining a suitable standard of civilization for our nation. Woman is a vital factor in these efforts toward economic growth and development, for she constitutes half the nation's labor force.

But we should not forget that economic progress is affected, to a great extent, by the philosophy of life which has been adopted by the society. This philosophy plays its role according to the degree to which it either activates or puts a stop to that economic progress. We must reconsider our own philosophy and separate what is useful from what is harmful. We should try to benefit from the experience of other societies and review the plans, the patterns, and the theories from which their structures evolved. Civilization is a matter for all human society and belongs to everyone; it is not a concept which is limited by geographical boundaries or by sectarian traditions. If it is considered in the latter, narrow sense, then it becomes a danger, a brake on our movement toward civilization, and will only toss us back into the dark ages of backwardness once more.

Civilization, the idea of civilization, assumes that the human being is the goal as well as the means to reach that goal. Civilization is composed of the customs of man, his way of living and thinking, and no standard of civilization can be achieved unless the customs and the way of living and thinking can be related to the new spirit of growth which has been set as our national goal in the Arab world.

As I have said, a backward nation cannot reach this stage of "relating" to the new spirit of growth merely by establishing laws or spreading education or limiting production to high quality. These are all important factors, all linked together. But the governments must not only use the power of law to encourage the growth of civilization; they must also protect the future destiny of those laws. If this is done, many clashes between the passive and active forces in our nation will be avoided. And this is necessary, for such clash and conflict create contradictions which shake the new structure of progress.

Thus, the task of the Arab governments is great.

We consider the governments to be, in some countries, the progressive parts of the societies, for they constitute the force, the group which can foresee new situations and designate the areas of the society which need to be reformed. The government can persuade the local groups, the groups who cling to old beliefs and tradition, of the desirability of change. The governments, then, in the progressive Arab countries are the greatest and most powerful factor which can affect change in our civilization. And the speed of our journey toward that desired goal depends on their efforts.

23

Ghadah al-Samman

غاده السمان

Modern Lebanese Novelist

A.D. 1942–

Ghadah al-Samman was born in 1942 in Damascus, Syria. Her mother, Salms Ruwaiha, was herself a writer and her father is a former rector of the University of Damascus. She took a degree in English literature in 1961, has worked as a civil servant, journalist, and university lecturer. She has published several collections of short stories and has completed a novel. She now lives in Beirut, where she is considered part of a growing number of young writers who are attempting to explore, in their work, the current tensions between tradition and modernism in the Middle East.

Photo: Beirut before the civil war

The Sexual Revolution and the Total Revolution/Ghadah al-Samman

Question 1:
How do you think a sexual revolution could take place in Arab society?

Answer: No sexual revolution can take place without a total human revolution on all levels: economic, ideological, political, and social. The "sexual revolution," in my opinion, is only one part of the revolution of each individual Arab against the forces which have taken from him basic human rights—his economic, political, and moral powers and strengths. That is to say, the sexual revolution, in the last analysis, is only part of the total revolution against a deprivation in human freedoms.

I make a distinction here between "sexual revolution" and "sexual license." I make a distinction between the sexual revolution to achieve a greater humanity and the provocation, the exhibitionism, which springs from the mating instinct. In this latter sense, many flags are raised and slogans coined, which in the long run call for a numbing or drugging of the bodily senses; then the opposite sex becomes a form of opium, to help us pass the time, so that we will forget important rights which are being taken from us on the local political level and also on the international level. Thus, I repeat, it is impossible for me to envision a sexual revolution taking place by itself or existing outside the total revolution of the individual Arab against all that conspires against the realization of his full humanity, all that restricts his freedom and regulates all his relationships, whether with a loaf of bread, books, arms, or his bed.

Question 2:
Which of our current values concerning sex do you find unacceptable?

Answer: Let me start by answering that question indirectly. The day when in more than one Arab country a group of Arab youths began to revolt, I was astonished that the first priority in the new states was to establish laws nationalizing business enterprises. They did this before they thought about establishing new personal status codes, to "nationalize" a citizen's freedom, regardless of sex, and, for example, to abolish the light sentences currently assigned to crimes which are defined as "committed in the defense of honor."

[Ghadah al-Samman, "Al-Thawrah al-Jinsiyah wa-al-Thawrah al-Shamilah," an interview published in Beirut in *Mawaqif* 2, no. 12 (1970): 68–73. Translated by the Editors.]

Thus you can see I believe that revolutions in the Arab countries will remain crippled as long as they continue to compromise with reactionary forces and with inherited fetters. Such fetters operated in an economic context and perhaps they were appropriate for one time, but that time has now passed. The economic situation has changed in the Arab countries, but the inherited values and customs have not changed, and they continue to restrict the total body of revolution almost as though it were caged. The area in which this compromise is demonstrated most clearly is in the area of male-female definitions under law: the importance of freeing all citizens from such definitions and from humiliating traditional laws cannot be underestimated. For instance, an educated woman who supports herself, such as a university professor, is still forced to bring her brother (even though he may be retarded or illiterate or supported by her) to city hall before she can obtain permission to travel. Today, when a woman has achieved some educational or political status, she still finds that her brother (male) is her legal guardian.[1] When such legal definitions persist, it is obviously impossible for men and women to have any sort of constructive human relationships, in bed or out of bed. The relations which do take place become soporific or businesslike, or exploitive for both sexes.

Question 3:
Then what of our society's current moral values regarding sex do you accept?

Answer: Nothing, of course, since the starting point is wrong. And I will continue to reject them as long as each sex has the wrong attitude toward the other and as long as the formal society and the informal one (tradition, the family) expend all their efforts to enforce this wrong attitude. I should stress that I do not plead here only for women's rights, for this is a partial and superficial solution, a sentimental one which does not touch the core of the problem. A revolution for the sake of greater humanity between the sexes is as important to the man as it is to the woman. Their current relationship in our society is a phony one, an inhuman one, which degrades the male as much as it does the female and destroys male creativity as much as female creativity. When I ask for "equality," then, I am asking for the right of the man and the woman equally to have sound and healthy relations.

Thus, as I have said, a sexual revolution is necessary for every citizen; and, to achieve a true revolution, the starting point is not merely a female awakening but a cry of joy which erupts from the depths of every true revolutionary, man or woman. It is a revolution which demands rights for every revolutionary person, not a revolution by a slave to demand to be able to choose its master.

Question 4:
What would you suggest in the way of new moral values?

Answer: Well, to begin with, let us look at Britain, which has now granted the right to a male to marry another male. This, despite the fears which may arise in a society about the consequences of such behavior, does demonstrate something we have totally forgotten over the past centuries: that there is of course sexual degradation as well as nonsexual. When we consider this, we are reminded that sharing a bed is, or should be, the result of two humans coming together on the intellectual and spiritual as well as the physical level, and that this coming together of two human beings no longer has to be simply a reason to hatch children in order to preserve the lineage of humankind. Today this goal may be achieved through artificial insemination and test tubes, without the two human sexes exploiting each other for this purpose alone. So you ask me what do I suggest in the way of new moral values? I suggest the following as a beginning:

1.   Remind the individual Arab that he or she is ill with "ideological venereal disease" as far as sexual relationships are concerned; "sharing" is missing. When both sexes participate in the relationship, equality is imposed. One of the symptoms of this ideological venereal disease is one sex's use of the other as a commodity, and this usage will continue as long as the current situation of slavery exists.
2.   Stop discussing "sexual revolution" on the level of arousal, for this, too, is another way to make sex a business or economic enterprise in which the person and the relationship are transformed into usable commodities.
3.   Correct the individual Arab's mistaken belief that woman, as a species, is inferior and not equal. This kind of thinking has run in the veins of all men (and women) for a long time, accumulated, alas, over the centuries, for ancient religions and philosophies and primitive laws have emphasized the inferiority of women. Even the Greek philosophers are not immune from this shameful error. Pythagoras, for example, differentiates between "the good that has created order, light, and man; and evil that has created chaos, darkness, and woman." According to Hippocrates, "the woman is in the service of the belly." Aristotle says, "The female is a female as a result of a certain defect in her character." In the Dark and Middle ages in Europe, the woman was the property of

the man and considered part of his estate and, if a knight were forced to travel, he had the right to ensure his wife's faithfulness by imprisoning her in a chastity belt.

In Arab society today, we find that the "chastity belt" is still forced on a woman, forced on her mind as much as or more than it is forced on her body. For a woman who allows herself to express freedom in her thinking and speaking will face strong public censure far more than does the prostitute who never bothers to face such a situation.

4.   The individual revolutionary Arab must try to bridge the gap within himself, between his "progressive ideology" and his "reactionary behavior." This attempt would constitute a revolution of the revolutionary against the sexual double standard and would indicate a sincere effort to achieve some correspondence between ideology and practice. Such an effort alone would save the so-called sexual revolution from becoming simply a rhetorical revolution.

What I suggest, however, cannot be achieved within the social conditions which exist today, for the sword of inherited traditions, of backwardness, and of ignorance is unsheathed and ready to attack. The revolution of which I speak can be achieved only through sacrifice and, as has always been the case, by pioneer fighters, commando troops, if you like, to challenge official establishments on the battlefield. And the "intellectual" commandos, the pioneers in the field of thought, are needed, too; only they can save us from tragic incidents which continue to repeat themselves, even under our so-called progressive laws. "Sexual pioneers" then are the solution, and what I mean by a sexual pioneer is the revolutionary who is not satisfied with simply accepting or adopting new ideas or progressive ideologies but acts accordingly, without fear of public censure. The public is not yet ready to accept the revolutionary ideas we are discussing on any level and especially on the level which our society calls "honor." Until this very day, the public views the matter of honor in the same way as Yusuf Wahbi,[3] that great Arab philosopher of sex, who summed up the whole matter in his well-known aphorism, "The honor of the girl is like a single match." And this "fine" slogan still carries more weight in our society than other slogans which mention the honor of the land or the honor of the country.

Question 5:
How do you view the subject of mutual fidelity between a husband and wife?

Answer: What can I say about marital fidelity when marriage today, in my opinion, is a corrupt institution. How can we discuss marital fidelity when this fidelity is in direct opposition to man's fidelity to humanity and to himself? Marriage in my country is, on the whole, a kind of human prostitution, legitimized by two witnesses and a legal document. And marriage as an institution enjoys the protection of the corrupt institutions in other areas of our present society. Thus, in its basic corruption, its lowering of humankind, marriage is slow death to any kind of individual human creativity or innovativeness. Further, it serves to support those other institutions which continue to sap the lifeblood of humanity on a broader level. Thus, when we find marital infidelity in our society, it usually results from one partner being faithful to himself and his own being. The fault lies not in the fact that one of the partners is unfaithful; the fault lies in the institution itself, which betrays and undermines the basic goodness of the human soul.

Question 6:
Do you approve of complete sexual relations before marriage?

Answer: What do you mean by "complete"? Do you mean the act of two bodies becoming attached to one another, like the male and female animal coming together? Do you mean by "complete" the number of centimeters in a woman's body which a man is able to penetrate for a few moments?

To me, a sexual relationship cannot be "complete" unless it is a total relationship of human closeness which begins with the head and involves a mutual drowning in each other's depths. Thus, a complete sexual relationship such as I have described cannot take place either before or after marriage. For it is itself marriage. (And here of course I must apologize to *al-madhun*, the official who performs a marriage ceremony, to the notary public, and even to the documentary stamps, all of which are needed at the moment to make a marriage legal in our society.)

Question 7:
To what extent do you see sexual concepts as related to moral concepts?

Answer: The answer to this question depends, of course, on what we mean by a "moral concept." Do we mean by morals or morality that we opened our eyes on the world and found the morals ready made for us? Or that they are inherited from past generations? That they are like wide garments which do not really fit at all but flap in the wind and slow down the freedom of our movement? Or garments so narrow that they are not wide enough for us to step forward easily? I believe that "moral concepts" emerge or develop in certain times or eras which have their own particular historic and economic circumstances. Thus it is wrong to assign an absolute value to the moral concepts of any period. Let us look at some rather well known, even stereotyped examples: First, an Eskimo husband will offer his guest the privilege of sleeping with his own wife; this is quite in accordance with the morality of Eskimo land. Second, a daughter of the Pharaohs often married her own brother; this was not only accepted but preferred behavior. These two examples help explain the relativity of moral values in different societies and periods but do not necessarily deny that a kind of base line or limit of absolute morality may exist. I would define this as perhaps the essence of what I would call our basic humanity, a code which might emerge from common universal human experiences, such as death, birth, aging, pain, and hunger. The peaceful co-existence of all human beings is marred, I believe, by man's selfishness and weakness and his rather unbalanced attitudes toward what we call moral matters. Killing a lion, for example, is considered a heroic deed; but killing an animal of the species of man is a crime. Why? Because it destroys the peaceful co-existence of one man with another. Now, therefore, until other truths find their way to me, I am trying to take a neutral, realistic position in these matters (as neutral as a human being is able to be), not a position which has been inherited or one which is emotionally derived alone. Thus I view the relating of moral concepts to sexual concepts (in the traditional meaning of morality) as a mistake. The latter is a traditional position, a passive position, the position of the receiver or object of the action, not of the subject or doer of the action.[4] One might add that this is also a restful and safe position, like that of the sheep which simply follows the flock.

In the last analysis, it is a nonrevolutionary, noncreative position and whoever takes such a position might be classified or termed a "tamed" human being. And the fate of tamed human beings and tamed societies is well known; they end in the stables of stronger empires. (The historical name for such socially tamed groups is "colony" although the modern period has given us other terms for the same thing, such as "military base" . . .)

Thus, as much as the moral concepts of a certain society are capable of absorbing the realities, the truths of mankind, then so much will these moral concepts (and with a limited amount of falsification) approach perfection, the absolute . . . But, you will ask, what are the realities and truths of man or mankind? Is the real person the man of religion, the man of the old word, is he the man of Marx, the man of Darwin, the man of Durkheim, or the man of Beckett and Ionesco? Or is he all of them together? Is the whole business of being human a vicious circle or is it a continuing chain, a chain of humanity of which we have seen scarcely two thousand of its links? If so, this is a very short space in terms of the eternal existence of being. I myself do not know. No one, I believe, can tell precisely. For if there had been any human being who knew the answer, the question would never have been asked and no one would have needed to answer it.

Question 8:
To what extent can one measure the progress, advancement, and liberation of a certain society in terms of sexual liberation, and why or why not?

Answer: Progressive toward what? Advancement toward what? Progress and advancement, at least in my understanding of these terms, are not necessarily related to progressing or advancing toward Mars or the moon. Sometimes I think that in the civilizations of the old world or perhaps in some of the so-called primitive societies a superior or higher quality of humanity is to be found which certainly equalled, if it did not surpass utterly, what we find in many of the so-called advanced technological, industrial societies of today (the time of the atom bomb, Hiroshima, and Vietnam)! We must obviously agree on definitions of words like *progress* before we use those terms. I would define progress as any movement toward more discovery of human realities in mankind, and *liberation* as the freedom of individuals and groups from any attempt to rob them of their humanity.

Therefore, if we define sex as a bohemian kind of practice, its only condition a kind of unconscious adolescent freedom (sex without humanity, in other words), then in this sense sexual freedom is not progressive but backward. We must be very careful when we discuss "progressive or advanced" societies, as the terms are used today. I say this, despite the obvious logical fact that the logic of the armed tank always wins over the logic of the camel. I don't believe, however, that on this basis the time of the tank is more progressive (on the human level) than the time of the camel. The reverse may also not be true. To conclude, I would like to pose as an example of advancement something which is almost forgotten in this age of technology. That advancement is called man, or the human being, a phenomenon that testifies to my contention that what seems practical and logical at this moment in time may not necessarily be the truth forever. But what is truth and does it exist? If it exists, are we ever able to approach it, and, if so, how closely? Obviously, these are all questions without satisfactory or complete answers at the moment, but the lack of an exact, absolute answer to these questions does not necessarily mean that they may not need to be asked, and asked again, and it does not necessarily mean that they are futile or wrong questions. To me, the lack of answers to these questions and the vehemence of the position which states that they are meaningless indicate that a terrifying battle is in progress in the world today and has been for many centuries: the battle for the discovery of truth or for the proof of its nonexistence. And this is a match or struggle which cannot be resolved in a mere two thousand rounds of human history.

Thus, until further developments (as the newscaster might say), I would say this about the sexual revolution and the total revolution: to begin the battle, sex should not be allowed to remain in a sacred tower surrounded by taboos which seal our lips. We must first separate sex from the confused and mistaken beliefs and concepts which have surrounded it for such a long period of time. We must free ourselves from these confusions and mistakes. Then we can begin to speak about a sexual revolution.

Notes

1.   This law varies from one Arab country to another. For example, it does not exist in Iraq.
2.   A noted Egyptian actor during the 1940's and 1950's.
3.   This is a metaphor using grammatical Arabic terms:
m'ful: object (accusative)
fa'l: subject (nominative)
The general implication is that man is the doer (the nominative case) and woman the receiver or object of the action (the accusative case).

Susan Schaefer Davis is completing her Ph.D. for the University of Michigan and is now assistant professor of anthropology at Trenton State College in New Jersey. She lived in a Moroccan village from 1965 to 1967 and from 1970 to 1972. Her dissertation focuses on the roles played by women in traditional Moroccan Moslem society, and she has presented several papers on these women's economic roles and local status. Currently she is interested in refining the tools of anthropological analysis so that they are more adequate for describing the social roles of both women and men.

Elaine Upton Hazleton was graduated from the University of Texas with a B.S. in biology and education. She spent two years in Amman with her three children and her husband, who was in Jordan with the Ford Foundation. She taught at the American Community School in Amman. She met Jawazi in 1974 through their husbands' friendship, and their relationship developed as their families became closer and language lessened as a barrier. The Hazleton family now lives in Austin, Texas.

Michael C. Hillmann was born in Maryland, received his B.A. in English literature from Loyola College, Baltimore, and his M.A. and Ph.D. in Near Eastern languages and civilizations from the University of Chicago. He spent six years in Iran, both teaching and doing research, and has published widely in both Persian and English. He presently teaches Persian literature at the University of Texas at Austin.

Suad Joseph was born in a small village outside Beirut, Lebanon, and came to the United States as a child. In working out the confrontation between her family background and the world she experienced outside her home, Suad became very concerned and interested in the idea of culture. She studied at the University of Pittsburgh and received her Ph.D. in anthropology from Columbia University. Intrigued with "culture" and its mystification, she did historical and field research on religion in Lebanon. Her doctoral thesis and many of her articles focus on the politicization of religious sects in Lebanon. She is currently teaching at Hofstra College.

Mohammed Razi was born in Kabul, Afghanistan, and received his B.A. from Kabul University. He was awarded his doctorate degree in education from Indiana University and now is a member of the faculty in the School of Letters, Kabul University.

Lucie Wood Saunders was brought up in a large extended family (matrifocal) household on a farm in eastern Virginia. She received an A.B. from Sweet Briar College with a major in English in 1949; she then shifted to anthropology at Columbia, receiving a Ph.D. in 1959 with the Middle East as her area of specialization. She had research experience as a student in Tobago and in psychiatric hospitals before going to Egypt in September 1961. She and her interpreter-assistant, Mrs. Mehenna, lived in Kafr al-Hana, Egypt, from October 1961 until the following August. Since returning to the United States, she has been teaching anthropology at Lehman College in New York City.

Susan Spectorsky was born in New York City and received her B.A. from Radcliffe College. She spent three years studying Arabic in Cairo, received an M.A. from the University of California at Berkeley, and her Ph.D. in Islamic studies and Arabic from Columbia University. Currently she teaches at Queens College.

Sabra Webber was born in San Francisco in 1945. She graduated from Occidental College in 1966 with a B.A. in English and spent the next two years in the Peace Corps in Tunisia. Following her Peace Corps experience, she remained in Tunisia to complete the collection and publication of approximately one hundred Tunisian lullabies, nursery rhymes, and children's games in a children's book, *Lisagharina* (To our children). Ms. Webber received her M.A. in folklore at the University of California, Berkeley, and is currently pursuing doctoral studies in the Anthropology-Folklore Department of the University of Texas, at Austin.

1

2

3

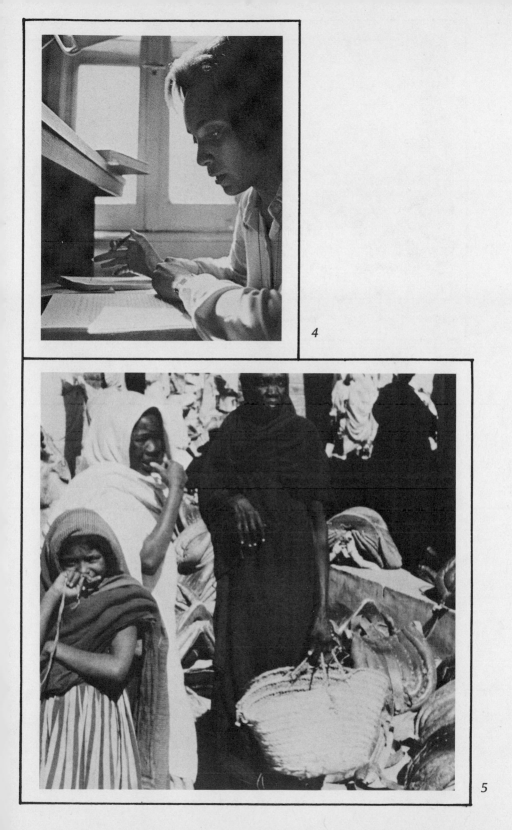

4

5

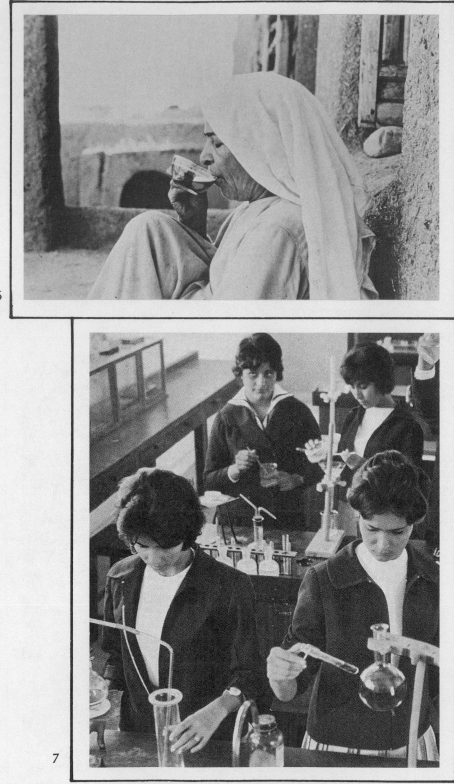

6

7

8

9

10

11

12

13

14

15

16

17

18

19